Haim Goren is an historical geographer in the Department of
Interdisciplinary Studies, Tel-Hai College, Israel.
His main fields of interest are European activity in Ottoman Palestine
and the Near East, the history of the scientific study of
that region, mainly the Holy Land, and pilgrim and traveller literature.

TAURIS HISTORICAL GEOGRAPHY SERIES
Series Editor: Robert Mayhew, University of Bristol

Though long established as a field of inquiry, historical geography has changed dramatically in recent years becoming a driving force in the development of many of the new agendas of contemporary geography. Dialogues with historians of science, art historians and literary scholars have revitalised the history of geographical thought, and a new, vibrant, pluralistic culture of scholarship has emerged. The Tauris Historical Geography series provides an international forum for the publication of scholarly work that encapsulates and furthers these new developments.

Published and forthcoming in the Series:
1. *Zambesi: David Livingstone and Expeditionary Science in Africa* by Lawrence Dritsas
2. *New Spaces of Exploration: Geographies of Discovery in the Twentieth Century* by Simon Naylor and James Ryan (eds)
3. *Scriptural Geography: Portraying the Holy Land* by Edwin Aiken
4. *Bringing Geography to Book: Ellen Semple and the Reception of Geographical Knowledge* by Innes M. Keighren
5. *Enlightenment, Modernity and Science: Geographies of Scientific Culture and Improvement in Georgian England* by Paul A. Elliott
6. *Dead Sea Level: Science, Exploration and Imperial Interests in the Near East* by Haim Goren
7. *Nature Displaced, Nature Displayed: Order and Beauty in Botanical Gardens* by Nuala Johnson

Dead Sea Level

Science, Exploration and Imperial Interests in the Near East

HAIM GOREN

I.B. TAURIS

LONDON · NEW YORK

This book is published with the assistance of The James Amzalak Fund for Research in Historical Geography, which supports the series of Israel Studies in Historical Geography, edited by Yehoshua Ben-Arieh and Ruth Kark, The Hebrew University of Jerusalem, Israel.

Published in 2011 by I.B.Tauris & Co. Ltd
6 Salem Road, London W2 4BU
175 Fifth Avenue, New York NY 10010
www.ibtauris.com

Distributed in the United States and Canada Exclusively by Palgrave Macmillan
175 Fifth Avenue, New York NY 10010

Tauris Historical Geography: 6

ISBN: 978 1 84885 496 3

A full CIP record for this book is available from the British Library
A full CIP record is available from the Library of Congress

Library of Congress Catalog Card Number: available
Typeset in ITC Stone Serif by Keter Publishing House, Jerusalem
Printed and bound in Great Britain by CPI Antony Rowe, Chippenham
From camera-ready copy edited and supplied by the author

FSC
www.fsc.org
MIX
Paper from
responsible sources
FSC® C013604

Contents

Illustrations

Preface and Acknowledgements

The whole idea at first seemed impossible. It was a project that began with seemingly fanciful ideas, out of the blue, the 'wishful thinking' of a wild imagination. As I continued searching, digging deeper and deeper into the material – and it did take a long time, about six years – I found that some of the main issues which I had planned to investigate had already been examined, even thoroughly, by others. It rather reminded me of two of my ultimate 'heroes', leading figures in nineteenth-century Palestine research – the Swiss physician Titus Tobler (1806–77) and the American scholar and clergyman Edward Robinson (1794–1863). Tobler, who had returned home from his first voyage to the East in 1835, frustrated by the lack of scientific information available concerning the Holy Land, began to collect material for a well-planned research excursion in which he would attempt to rectify what he considered an unacceptable lacuna. He aspired to achieve 'the victory of the truth' by issuing 'the most possible embracing description of Jerusalem and its vicinity'. In 1841 or 1842, well advanced in his preparations, Tobler received Robinson's newly published book, *Biblical Researches*, which was a record of Robinson's extensive travels in the Holy Land in 1838, accompanied by his student and translator, the Presbyterian missionary Eli Smith (1801–57) from Beirut. At first Tobler felt that the rug had been pulled out from under him, that this had entirely upset his plans, and that Robinson had left nothing to be studied. But after much reconsideration he decided to go on, as 'there is still a lot to do, exactly about the topography and history of the consecrated places in Judea, as Jerusalem and Bethlehem...'[1]

I shared the same feeling at various points of this research. It all started when I decided that it was time to find out exactly who were the 'two Englishmen' who, according to every possible source, had been the first to publish the fact that the level of the Dead Sea was lower than that of the Mediterranean.[2] Having identified them, it was not difficult to discover the strange fact that the first two individuals who had sailed on the Dead Sea with the intention of studying it scientifically, had come from Ireland, and that both had purchased a boat in Beirut, taken it by sea to one of the Palestinian ports and conveyed it eastward overland, one to the Sea of Galilee, the second directly to the Dead Sea. These two projects happened within less than one and a half years of one another. I found it difficult to accept that all this had been purely coincidental.

But then came the first blow to my own study: Three people, not one, had already been interested in these early 'sailors', conducting cogent research and publishing a number of articles and books. The first was Con Costello (1929–2006), an Irish officer who served with the UN in Israel and Syria in the early 1970s, and who became highly interested in his countrymen's connections with and exploits in the Holy Land. In addition to several articles, all of them in difficult-to-reach Irish periodicals, he published a book in 1974 entitled *Ireland and the Holy Land*.[3] After deciding to go on with my study nonetheless, I found his book and papers to be highly important resources.

Erik Olaf Eriksen followed in his footsteps, but he was interested solely in the study of the Dead Sea. He conducted thorough research and discovered many primary sources concerning some of the 'great heroes of the drama'. The drama, of course, was the revolutionary discovery of the relative level of the lake.[4]

The third was the American scholar Barbara Kreiger who, in 1988, published her book narrating the story of the Dead Sea during the modern period. She devoted a number of long passages to the history of its exploration, also mentioning the intensive scientific research done there.[5]

Turning to my other trajectory, that of Francis Rawdon Chesney and the story of his Euphrates Expedition, I employed the works of Eliahu Elath (1903–90), the well-known Israeli diplomat – his dissertation, of course, and also his book about Britain's routes to India.[6] This presented me with a solid foundation on which to establish my argument connecting this expedition and some of its participants to the study of the Jordan Rift Valley and the Dead Sea. Only at a later stage of my work did I discover that the almost fantastic story of the expedition had aroused the interest of the American John S. Guest who, in 1992, published a detailed and comprehensive book, making use of almost all the existing archival sources.[7] Interestingly, Guest does not mention Elath's work, probably because he could not read Hebrew.

In any case, at almost every juncture, I had to stop and reconsider: Should I go on? Would I accomplish anything which had not already been accomplished? Could I establish my case concerning the strong connections between the three 'bases': the beginning of the study of the Dead Sea, a kind of 'Irish connection' to the lake and its study, and British imperial motivations, interests and actions in the Near East, during two decennia: the 1830s and the 1840s?

The present book, I believe, will affirm my positive answer to these questions.

Six years of work is a long time. During this period, while conducting my research and later writing this book, I was more than simply fortunate to receive the assistance, cooperation and encouragement of many colleagues, friends and organizations. The list is quite long, but my gratitude to every one of them is tremendous. I do hope that I have not forgotten or neglected anybody.

I was fortunate enough to receive a grant from the Israel Science Foundation at a crucial stage of the research, and my deepest gratitude goes to the foundation and its extremely professional staff. Further financial and technical help was provided by the Research Authority of Tel-Hai College, my academic home. The same authority also helped me finance the preparations for publication. I am very grateful to the James Amzalak Fund for Research in Historical Geography, which supports the Israel Studies in Historical Geography series edited by Yehoshua Ben-Arieh and Ruth Kark of the Hebrew University of Jerusalem.

In England I was helped by Andrew S. Cook of the India Office Library and Records in the British Library; Peter Barber, curator of its map collection; Francis Herbert and the staff of the RGS/IBG Archive; Yoland Hodson, Mike Heffernan, Andrew Lambert, Peter Collier, Rose Mitchell in the British National Archives/PRO; Adrian Webb, former curator of the Hydrographic Office of the Navy Archive, then in Taunton; and Henry Blosse-Lynch of Longcross House, Headley (Berkshire).

In Ireland, a country which I got to know and cherish during these years, I received much help – and found many friends. I would mention here Jean and Gordon Harris-Davies; Anngret and David Simms (David, himself related to the Brownes and the Moores, also for first leading me along the paths of Irish gentry genealogy and sources); Anne Buttimer; Linde Lunney from the *Dictionary of Irish Biography*; the staff of Marsh's Library; Art Ó Súilleabháin, director of the Mayo Education Center, who for the first time introduced me to Moore Hall and the Mayo vicinity; William Nolan of the Department of Geography in UCD; Christopher Woods; John Bartlett of Trinity College who studies our region; Bernard Meehan and staff, TCD Archives; the Old Books reading room staff, TCD; the National Library of Ireland, Reading Room; the National Library of Ireland, Manuscripts Collection: Noel Kissane and Timothy Collins; Birgid Clesham, The Westport Estate Papers. In Northern Ireland I received much help from Steve Royle and Edwin Aiken from Queen's University, Belfast.

Among the many people who helped me on the German leg of my research, I would like to mention Michael Reuter, former head of the information desk of the University Library in Göttingen, who made that my base in Germany throughout these years. I used my periods as guest-scholar at the Simon-Dubnow-Institute in Leipzig to add material concerning the German dimension, and also consulted Olaf Hillert of the Stadtarchiv Leipzig.

Last, but not least, are my Israeli friends and colleagues, Guy Beyner, Rehav 'Buni' Rubin, Revital Bookman, Hila Tal, Yossi Vardi who was of great help in the study of the Dead Sea research, Shoshana Klein and Ayelet Rubin of the Laor Map Collection, as well as Shlomo Goldberg of the National Library of Israel in Jerusalem, Shaul Katz, the late Jacob Wahrmann, and my two teachers, tutors, colleagues and friends, Yehoshua Ben-Arieh and Ruth Kark. Barbara Doron, my language editor for many years, did magnificent work and was an important source of encouragement throughout the whole project. Lynn Pitelis provided me with the most valuable assistance in the technical aspects. There is no proper way to express my special gratitude to Tamar Cohen for a highly professional copyediting and proofreading, to Yohai Goell, who never misses a thing, and to the team of the Pre-Press Department at Keter Publishing House, Jerusalem, in particular Miri Revivo and Tal Zeidani.

It was a unique and encouraging experience to work with the highly professional team of I.B.Tauris: David Stonestreet, Jayne Ansell, Cécile Rault and Alan Mauro. Their continuous encouragement and cooperation has been a great help during the long and sometimes frustrating process of the book's preparation.

Introduction

The study presented in this book has set as its main goal the presentation of a number of geographical projects – whether expressly so or only in the broadest sense – conducted during the 1830s and 1840s, mainly by representatives of the expanding British Empire, in different parts of what was then called 'The Near East'. At the focal point of this discussion is an outstanding 'test case' taking place at the intersection of religious conviction and scientific investigation: the story of how the exact level of the Dead Sea was determined. This will help illuminate the role that geographical exploration (mainly in the sense of data-gathering) and scholarship, including cartography, have played in two parallel, interrelated processes: the scientific study of the Near East in general, and Palestine – the Holy Land – in particular; and the historical and geo-political processes in these regions, in one of the most important and influential periods in their history.

The British Empire, already well established and functioning, but still constantly safeguarding its vital interests, plays a major role in this study. Almost needless to say, one of the vital issues for the Empire's economic and strategic – political as well as military – survival, had always been the connection with the Indian subcontinent, the so-called 'jewel in the crown'. The traditional route around the Cape of Good Hope, which dated to the beginning of the sixteenth century, was losing its advantages. Britain realized that it had to find different solutions which would be safer, cheaper and, primarily, quicker than the long sail. This was one of the major issues motivating the intensification of British involvement in the countries bordering the Mediterranean immediately to the east, and those stretching between the Mediterranean, the Persian (today Arabian) Gulf and India.

This geo-political fact led Britain – as well as other European powers – into involvement in three regions of highly important historical, cultural and religious significance: Mesopotamia, Egypt and the Holy Land. One should also bear in mind that Egypt had just been 'rediscovered' by the French. Such so-called 'geo-religious', 'geo-traditional' or 'geo-cultural' connections are among the leading factors in this research, forming one of the main threads weaving together its various parts.

Being what some might call an old-fashioned historical geographer, a positivist of the former generation (and, as a matter of fact, a guardian of a tradition that began with nineteenth-century German geography), I attach great importance to a detailed reconstruction of processes and events, as well as to a comprehensive study of the personalities involved, their backgrounds and deeds. My salient argument is that the conventional approach that maintains that all of the large organized surveys undertaken during the period under discussion in the Near East can be examined and explained almost solely by citing geo-political interests of European powers, is only part of the picture. Conversely, I argue that the study of the Dead Sea, so loaded with biblical reminiscences, also owes its development to other, non-pietistic considerations, and cannot be perceived as an isolated process or case.

The complex picture presented in this study thus crystallizes at the intersection of three spheres: (1) the purely scientific disclosure of the topography of the Jordan Rift Valley and mainly the Dead Sea, first and foremost the establishment of its level in accordance with advancements and developments in geographical technology; (2) European, primarily British, geo-political interests, policy and involvement in the Near East, in particular the search for a better route to India; and (3) the geo-religiously motivated goal of deciphering the geological mysteries described in the Scriptures. The dramatic unfolding of each of these dramas and the sometimes surprising junctions between them were driven by the deeds of specific actors and the network of connections between them.

While conducting my research, I was constantly made aware of the important role played by private individuals and organizations (today we might call them NGOs) in the various projects and processes surrounding both the scientific study of the Jordan Rift Valley, with the Dead Sea at its center, and the initiatives and projects concerned with finding better, easier, safer and quicker routes to India. The central role of such personalities differs greatly from the conventional wisdom that most developments should be attributed to the games of the great powers and their dominant leaders, whether they be emperors, kings, chancellors or ministers. This was eloquently expressed by a great authority on the nineteenth century, Stanley Lane-Poole (1854–1931), orientalist, archaeologist and author of numerous books, in his preface to Chesney's biography, edited by him and written by Chesney's second wife and one of their daughters, published in 1885:

> The adventurous exploring spirit which is so dear to those among us who have not yet been corrupted by too much philosophy or too much money-making, and which is characteristic in a pre-eminent degree of our nation, brought us India and America and Australia, to make no longer catalogue, and converted the Islands of Great Britain into the British Empire. Whatever economists may tell us of the wisdom or folly of this expansion, one fact is beyond dispute: the stout hearts that led the first voyages of discovery, made the first settlements, and confronted barbarism with the confidence born of courage and determination, have ever been the heroes of the English people.[8]

In this somewhat naive, but very enthusiastic description, Lane-Poole attempts to characterize Chesney's unique spirit and thereby to explain his almost incredible story of endurance, persistence, devotion and adventurism. But the description could be applicable to a larger group of people, many of whom were, in one way or another, the heroes of the events and processes described in this book. First and foremost, they have all shared this British 'adventurous exploring spirit'. The fact is that this spirit has not been limited to the people traveling and working under the Union Jack. But, as will be demonstrated in the following pages, it was the citizens of this growing and expanding Empire who took a leading part in the process of establishing the world geo-political map during the eighteenth and nineteenth centuries, and of course during the two decennia dealt with in this book.

Modern study has devoted much attention to the link between science and imperialism in general, and particularly to geography, including cartography as a central theme. Much has been written on the role of science, scientific organizations and institutions, and of 'colonial scientists' in the expansion of the British Empire, mainly during the nineteenth century. Matthew Edney chose to entitle his 1997 study, *Mapping an Empire: The Geographical Construction of British India*, while his preface included such statements as 'The Great Trigonometric Survey of India shows the workings of British policy.' The book's first chapter opens with the following sentence: 'Imperialism and mapmaking intersect in the most basic manner.'[9]

The nature of British imperialism and the establishment of India as part of the Empire are matters beyond the scope of this book. But one should never forget that, whereas policy for the British Isles as well as in the Indian sub-continent was determined in the capitals, its implementation had to rely on 'the men in the field'. Even Edney's abovementioned book discusses at length the role played by the 'surveyors' in the achievement of this 'geographical construction' of India through detailed, modern measurement and mapping. It was the work of geodetic pioneers, such as James Rennell (1742–1830) and George Everest (1790–1866), which enabled the fulfillment of this tremendous endeavor. The same might be said when examining the Cassinis and their role in the narrative of the French Ordnance Survey, as demonstrated by Anne Godlewska.[10] It was thanks to such intersections between burgeoning vital interests and the presence of well-trained, highly capable and passionate individuals in the right place at the right time, that such projects could be realized.

It was only natural that geographers should be the vanguard of imperialistic expansion, as they, more than anyone else, were able to study and illuminate the hitherto unknown territories being added to the Empire. Gary Dunbar aptly expressed this in the title of his paper about the French intervention in Mexico: 'The Compass Follows the Flag.'[11] Modern study has also focused much attention on the role of the ordnance survey, as well as on that of Royal Geographical Society, in these imperialistic processes.[12]

Palestine, the Holy Land, Eretz Israel, forms the core of this study. This very particular space will be considered, of course, as part of a larger area, and its historical development and processes studied accordingly. However, there is no way nor is there any intention of ignoring its special and unique cultural-religious status. An enduring element in the historical development of Palestine has been its religious significance. Christian-inspired interest in and study of the Holy Land led to centuries of European biblical scholarship, resulting in the accumulation of a wealth of publications. The area of biblical Palestine constituted a space where historical knowledge and development were inspired and guided by its sacredness, where geo-religious perceptions stimulated research. Therefore, it should be borne in mind that we are dealing with a region that is small in area but that, for decades, was already relatively well-known to the scientific-cultural world.

But, as Yehoshua Ben-Arieh pointed out in the 1970s, its sacredness cannot be accepted as the only reason for European scientific interest in the country itself, and of course, does not explain the interest in its bordering lands, which do not share this tradition. Other personal motivations, such as sheer adventurism, combined with geo-political and imperialistic considerations, found their way into the motivations behind research projects conducted in the Holy Land and its neighboring countries.[13]

Its period of 'rediscovery' had already reached a certain basic culmination in the 1830s. Until then the country had been the subject of a diverse body of research, comprising regional and thematic studies, with relatively intensive attention to geography and cartography. The majority of mapmaking efforts took the form of map compilations, with very few existing measurements and little precise geographic data.

Most research devoted to the varied expressions of European-Christian activity has stressed the influence of religious tradition and motivations during the years in question, and, in fact, has accepted it as a basic assumption. Palestine in its biblical borders, 'from Dan to Beer Sheba', constituted a 'sacred space' and its investigation was inspired and guided by this fact. Christian involvement in the Holy Land, which intensified throughout the nineteenth century, found expression in many different fields; of these, this study concentrates mostly (though never solely) on scientific study, its background, its development and its results. There is no doubt that geo-religious perceptions at least partially inspired the research of some regions, such as the Dead Sea and the Jordan Rift Valley; certain sites, such as Jerusalem, Bethlehem and Nazareth; or defined subjects, such as biblical wildlife or the inhabitants of Palestine as reminiscent of the ancient inhabitants and guardians of their traditions, customs and life styles.

One of the widely studied topics has been the participation of military personnel in gathering different kinds of geographical data, a process which probably reached its peak in the eighteenth- and nineteenth-century ordnance surveys and military-organized research expeditions. This is rather self-evident, if we take into account the necessity of accurate measuring maps and other geographical descriptions for any government and for any modern army. In his detailed history of the Admiralty Hydrographic Office, Archibald Day simply and bluntly pointed out that 'surveys were undertaken in the interests of defense and trade as well as science.'[14] The Near East was no exception to this process. As shown in detail by Anne Godlewska, it was the surveyors of the French army under Napoleon I Bonaparte (1769–1821) who took the first trigonometrically based measurements in the region, encompassing parts of Palestine. Colonel Pierre Jacotin (1765–1827), military engineer-geographer, who at some point took command of the geographers-engineers in Cairo and, during the 1799 campaign in Palestine, was responsible for the publication of the maps, including six sheets covering areas within the territory of Palestine. The measurements that he and his team managed to take in the course of the brief campaign were quite incomplete and they certainly did not produce survey maps worthy of the name, at least concerning Palestine. It would seem appropriate here to quote the evaluation of Carel Willem Meredith van de Velde (1818–98), one of the leading cartographers of nineteenth-century Palestine, who wrote that '*Jacotin's* map is engraved with such an amount of topographical detail, and on so large a scale, as to impart the belief that all this is a correct copy of nature, whilst it is for the greatest part the mere fancy-work of the draftsman.'[15]

Such mapping projects, based on systematic, on-site measurements of Palestine, reached their peak during the nineteenth century with the 'Survey of Western Palestine', conducted between 1871 and 1877 by a team headed by officers from the Royal Engineering Corps for the Palestine Exploration Fund (PEF), established in 1865, but, as shown recently, receiving all the necessary support from the War Office.[16]

According to these considerations and research questions, the book is divided into two main parts. The first chapters deal with the wider regional processes, going into detail when investigating the interests of European forces as well as local rulers. Naturally this section concentrates on the British involvement, and on the highly important Euphrates Expedition. The second part deals with the history of the scientific revelation and study of the Jordan Rift Valley, including the Dead Sea, and highlights the significant participants, people and organizations therein. A recurring theme is the continuous connections between participants in the two processes, between the 'heroes' of the two parts of this book. My main argument is that this 'local' scientific process should be considered as connected to, even as a central part of, the larger processes in the Near East during the fourth and fifth decennia of the nineteenth century, and of Britain's leading role in them. The discussion of the central role played by Irish actors in both parts of this drama is essential for the establishment and evaluation of the role of personal connections.

Part 1

Britain, Europe and the Near East, 1830–50

1 Palestine and the Near East, 1830–50: Historical and Geo-Political Background

Nineteenth-century European interest in the Near East began with the French conquest of Egypt and its subsequent march into Palestine, which came to an end only after the fruitless siege of Acre in 1799. Whatever were Napoleon's real motivations, as can be surmised from the many contemporary accounts as well as from later accounts and studies, it is clear that one of his prime incentives was his constant desire to strike a blow at his principal enemy, the British Empire.[1] What is equally clear is that the central role played by the British in the French defeat and retreat became a basic element in the development of the British Empire's own policy, at least during the first half of the nineteenth century, until the Crimean War.

Following the failure of the French campaign and the uninterrupted rule of Paşa Ahmed el-Djezzar (1720?–1804), Palestine continued to be governed by the Paşas, who ruled from Acre and generally maintained the Ottoman policy which regarded the area as a province of minor importance and limited interest for Constantinople. This relatively uneventful situation came to an end in the early 1830s.

Mehemet Ali Paşa (c.1769–1849), the Egyptian ruler, conquered Syria from the Ottomans in 1832, and only strong European political intervention would keep him from continuing into Asia Minor.[2] There is no intention here to reconstruct the entire story and its development, nor are the actual reasons for his military campaign relevant at this point. As in all campaigns after 1775, Acre proved to be the key to the whole country. After taking Gaza, Jaffa and Haifa, Ibrahim Paşa (1789–1848), Mehemet Ali's son and an outstanding military commander,

Fig. 1: J. Arrowsmith, Turkey in Asia, London 1832. Showing squares
('95 by 75 miles') for Chesney's planned detailed maps

reached the walls of Acre on 27 November 1831 with an army of '17000 infantry, 3000 cavalry, and about 1000 artillery'. Although subsequent dispatches from British consuls provided varying numbers, it seems that Ibrahim had 25,000 well-disciplined troops at his disposal, and about 15,000 irregulars.[3] A number of attacks, including heavy bombardments in December (10,000 shots and 2,000 shells 'thrown into the town' on 9 December), could not subdue Abdullah Paşa, who defended Acre with 8,000 men.[4] The Egyptians added to the '68 shifting – and field guns, including 12 mortars and 2 howitzers' brought by land, '16 field guns and 12 mortars' belonging to the Egyptian fleet of 7 frigates, 6 corvettes, 3 brigs, 7 ships of the line and 17 transport vessels, under the command of the Kapudân Paşa Osman-Nureddin-Bey.[5] The ships participated in the bombardment of Acre, and 'suffered considerable damage from the artillery of Abdullah Paşa'. After a long siege, the Egyptians succeeded in conquering the city only on 27 May 1832.[6]

The numbers given in this source concerning the somewhat surprising size of the Egyptian war fleet coincide with other reports by European observers, which add some interesting data, such as the number of cannon on the different ships, the biggest two ships of the line having 134 cannons. The fleet also included two British-made steam boats. The entire navy had been organized with the help of European officers.[7]

The Egyptian army could now begin contesting the Ottoman Empire's imperial forces, which had gathered in Syria. A series of battles – Homs (9 July), Beylan (30 July), and mainly Konieh, on the other side of the Taurus (21 December)[8] – paved the way for an Egyptian conquest of the Empire's capital, and brought the Russian fleet into the Bosporus for what they claimed was its defense against Mehemet Ali.

Henry John Temple, third Viscount Palmerston (1784–1865), the energetic British politician who for more than a generation led Britain and its imperial policy, was appointed for the first time at the end of 1830 to the office of Foreign Secretary under a Whig administration. This was the beginning of a long service, as both foreign secretary and prime minister, temporarily interrupted only by governmental changes in London and ending with his death in 1865.[9] He was the decisive and leading figure behind British efforts to maintain the independence and integrity of the Ottoman Empire, effectively using British naval supremacy as often as possible to maintain political interests. 'More

5

Fig. 2: Ibrahim Paşa by Estcourt

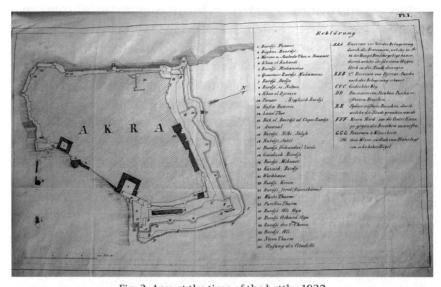

Fig. 3: Acre at the time of the battle, 1832

than anything else', wrote Andrew Lambert, 'some maritime operations and battles were incidents [which] demonstrate a rare combination of confidence and experience that distinguished the Royal Navy from all its rivals.' These actions, exploiting the confidence, experience and arrogance of some leading commanders, helped the British maintain their naval superiority during the first half of the nineteenth century.[10] Regarding Syria and Palestine, Palmerston's policy can be epitomized as aiming to maintain Ottoman sovereignty over both countries while securing and assuring Britain's predominance in Constantinople and defending its empire from French and Russian encroachments as well as from the ambitions of Mehemet Ali. Some British scholars have stressed the fact that Palmerston's hostility to the latter derived from Ali's threats to the Persian Gulf, the Red Sea and the Euphrates, three areas which were considered crucial for the security of the Empire.[11] In any case, it is clear that, in the words of Lambert, 'armed diplomacy would be the key to the success of British Diplomacy' in the Near East as well.[12]

'The fact that this British policy was, for an exceptionally long period of years, under the control or subject to the influence of one strong and single-minded individual [...]', wrote John Marlowe, 'ensured an unusual consistency, amounting sometimes to obstinacy.' Consequently, Britain was also highly consistent in its objections to all plans to combine the Mediterranean with the Red Sea, as this was expected to contradict British as well as Ottoman interests and to provide a significant advantage to France and to Mehemet Ali.[13]

As for the 1832 crisis, probably also due to 'insufficient naval power in the Mediterranean', Britain showed little involvement, as long as its imperial interests were not directly threatened. Only blunt Russian involvement aroused more active British intervention, this time diplomatic.[14] Yet despite all this activity, even contemporary observers in the mid-1830s continued to criticize Britain's Near Eastern policy for being inactive – responding to rather than anticipating events.[15]

Palmerston's policy during the various stages of the crisis has been a matter of some debate. It is quite clear that, although he had all the information, he neither reacted nor sent instructions, even after the Egyptians entered Aleppo in mid-July 1832. Scholars have found it difficult even to find any evidence that would enable them to ascertain whether Palmerston had any idea as to which side Britain should support. Meir Vereté claimed that Palmerston was, from the beginning, unsympathetic to the Paşa.[16] Only after his suspicion that Russia would exploit the situation to undermine the Sultan's authority, belittle British influence and 'bully the Porte' had proven correct, did he make up his mind to adopt a policy of safeguarding the independence and integrity of the Ottoman Empire. The details concerning the situation had been convincingly forwarded to him by the highly experienced British ambassador in Constantinople, Stratford Canning, first Viscount Stratford de Redcliffe (1786–1880), a key figure in British–Ottoman relations during the first half of the nineteenth century.[17] The son of a London-based Irish merchant, he had been repeatedly dispatched to the region until 1832, and continued his involvement even after his return to London. Canning had served in the Ottoman capital in various positions from 1808, when he participated in Robert Adair's (1763–1855) mission, aimed at restoring relations between Britain and the Ottoman Empire.[18] This was his first serious diplomatic endeavor as well as his introduction to Constantinople. Canning, 24 years old, remained in Constantinople following Adair's departure in 1810, as minister-plenipotentiary in charge of a key embassy, and stayed there until 1812. After serving in Switzerland and Washington, he returned to Constantinople as ambassador in 1825–8, the difficult years of the Greek Revolt. Following the unforeseen results of the Battle of Navarino, he had to flee from the Ottoman capital, later resigning and returning to London. Palmerston succeeded George Hamilton Gordon, fourth Earl of Aberdeen (1784–1840), at the Foreign Office in November 1830, and was dissatisfied with Ambassador Robert Gordon (1791–1847), Aberdeen's brother.[19] In autumn 1831 he asked Canning to return to Constantinople, where he coordinated the negotiations that ended the Greek Revolt and led to its independence. His third and fourth terms, 1842–5 and 1848–52, respectively, were spent mainly trying to enforce the promised Ottoman reforms, especially those securing equal rights for non-Muslims. During this period, he also played an important role in the construction of the Protestant Christ Church in Jerusalem. He was appointed again, for the fifth time, in 1853, and played a central role in the developments that led to the outbreak of the Crimean War.[20]

At the end of 1832, Stratford Canning was involved in another issue, a dispute between Palmerston and Princess Dorothea von Lieven (1785–1857), the highly influential wife of the Russian ambassador, who had served in London since 1812. The princess had become a political figure in her own right, participating in every major European diplomatic event. Relations with Palmerston were already in bad shape and von Lieven tried to further discredit him regarding his intention to nominate Stratford Canning as British ambassador in St. Petersburg. Canning was sent to Spain, but in 1834 the Tsar decided to withdraw both Lievens from London.[21]

After solving the 1832-3 crisis, even if only temporarily, Palmerston tried to enforce a program of liberal reform on the Ottoman Empire in which he would impose western standards of improvement. He planned to use British advisors to put both the administration and the army and navy in order.[22] Seven years later, the humiliated sultan, Mahmud II (1785-1839, reigned from 1808), sought revenge against the Egyptian army, only to be defeated at Nisibis. The Sultan's sudden death six days later was followed by the desertion of the Ottoman fleet to Alexandria, and the coronation of a 16-year-old successor, Abdülmecid I (1823-61, reigned from 1839).[23]

Fig. 4: David Wilkie, Sultan Abdülmecid

A short discussion of European geo-policy is unavoidable at this point. The main actors were Britain, France and Russia, along with the Austro-Hungarian Empire and gradually joined by developing Prussia. Russian and French interests and actions in the Levant will be dealt with later. But undoubtedly the central actor in Near Eastern policy became Great Britain, led by Palmerston. The latter was anxious to maintain British interests in the Near East, which was regarded as lying 'within Britain's informal empire'.[24] These interests lay mainly in safeguarding the routes to India (the late 1830s being years of great debate over an easier route to India, following the successful results of Chesney's Euphrates Expedition, as will be discussed later) and controlling the Mediterranean. As always, deeply suspicious concerning Russian plans in Asia, Palmerston ordered his fleet to disconnect all sea routes between Egypt and Syria.

One of the most important lessons Britain had learned from Napoleon's expedition was that it was vulnerable to indirect attacks through its vital imperial interests. The French offensive demonstrated that this could be achieved by threatening India through directions other than the sea route around the Cape of Good Hope. Consequently, a land attack by Russia, through Persia, Afghanistan or Turkey, the countries of the mainland routes to India, could, under certain circumstances, be possible. Thus, Mesopotamia and the Persian Gulf began to play an important role in British strategic calculations and Palmerston estimated that this area was crucial for the defense of India. The 1830s and 1840s witnessed a long list of political campaigns between the British and Russians in Persia and Afghanistan.

London began to serve as the center of intensive political negotiations in an attempt to alleviate the Egyptian–Ottoman crisis. Mehemet Ali's refusal to accept the ultimatum of the European forces and withdraw to Egypt led to European intervention. Beirut was bombed mainly by the British fleet on 11 September 1840, and conquered a month later with the help of British and Austrian marines. Acre fell following a heavy naval bombardment, which, using explosive bombs for the first time in Palestine, hit the main Egyptian explosives storage and destroyed a large part of the city. Gaza, the last Egyptian stronghold, was evacuated on 18 February 1841. This campaign, which will be discussed in detail, was summarized by Andrew Lambert:

The campaign demonstrated that in the mid-nineteenth century Britain was a unique global power. Her maritime strategic posture, built on a combination of economic primacy, fiscal strength, naval forces, and global basing enabled her to project power across the world in a way that no other power, or combination of powers, could contemplate.[25]

The Ottomans returned to Palestine for the final three quarters of a century of their regime. But the nine years of Egyptian rule had become a crucial turning point in the history of Palestine, as well as in the ongoing struggle between the leading European forces for influence, presence and control in western Asia. The origins of the next significant international crisis in the region, the Crimean War of 1853–6, could clearly be perceived at the end of the 1840s. Ignited by a local – religious – event in Palestine, this war was, once again, actually a struggle between the European powers for geo-political, economic, military and diplomatic interests.

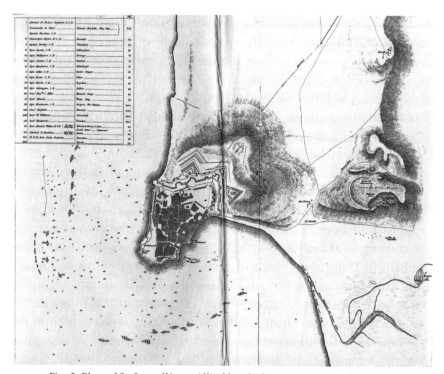

Fig. 5: Plan of St. Jean d'Acre. Allied battleships in position, 3.11.1840

It would appear that most British efforts in the East, in the Near East as well as in Central Asia, were deeply affected by real or imagined fears of Russian southward expansion, whether military or merely political and commercial. The possibility, discussed at length, was that Russia would reach India through Persia but that, like Napoleon, it might also advance southeast into Egypt. Ever since the French occupation, Egypt had been regarded as having major strategic value for the Empire, as an area whose occupation 'by any independent power would be a fatal circumstance for the interests of this country [i.e., Britain, HG]'.[26] Following Napoleon's campaign, the British government realized that such a move could cause serious problems for their imperial lines of communication and commerce, as well as for strategic and military interests. In fact, British agents were feverishly crossing the eastern countries in an attempt to fight their Russian and French rivals, and trying 'to preserve the tranquility of India which they [Russia and France] seek to disturb in order to pave the way for ulterior projects'. Britain blamed both forces for doing everything they could 'to encroach upon the independence and the integrity of the Porte'.[27]

There is no doubt that this posed a nightmare, not only for British political and military officials, but for leading merchants and their companies as well. The Russian Empress Catherine II the Great (1729–96, reigned from 1762), her son Tsar Paul I (1754–1801, reigned from 1796), and his son, Tsar Alexander I (Pavlovich, 1777–1825, reigned from 1801), had all shared the same view concerning their country's interests in western Asia and India; they wished to maintain a Russian foothold in the Caucasus and favorable relations with Persia that would enable the Russian empire to apply pressure on the eastern Ottoman provinces. But, whereas Catherine's policy was more aggressive, Paul preferred to promote Russia's interests by gaining allies and thus achieving political and commercial advantages. He therefore implemented a policy of conciliation vis-à-vis Persia, Russia's long-standing rival in the Caucasus.[28] Despite his mediating and conciliatory policy in dealing with Asia, Paul 'appears to have followed an uncommonly aggressive course in the incorporation of Georgia into the Russian Empire and in the attempt to conquer India', writes Muriel Atkin, who claims that the Tsar's real intentions have thus far been misinterpreted.[29] In December 1800 he annexed Georgia, extending his empire into western Asia. Following this, his plans to conquer India, which the British perceived as 'conclusive proof of the man's madness', seemed to have some realistic basis. Atkin challenges the accepted theory viewing this as madness and claims that 'Paul's decision to attack India was based on a widely shared strategic assumption.' Consequently, an invasion force of about 23,000 soldiers set out for India at the end of February 1801. Encountering tremendous difficulties, they did not reach the subcontinent and returned home after hearing about Paul's death.[30]

These Russian efforts were part of a more grandiose scheme of a joint French–Russian offensive, which Napoleon was purported to have offered to both tsars, Paul and Alexander, although later historical research claims that the earlier plan was a forgery. This scheme, as it exists in the sources, seems almost imaginary, but Napoleon had already proven his ability to initiate, and then actualize, the impossible. In the later plan, from 1807–8, which is considered by historians to be genuine, Napoleon suggested to Alexander that Russian troops advance through the Caucasus while the French approach through the Ottoman Empire. A large force of Cossacks did actually set out on its way.[31]

In 1799, the British in India succeeded in defeating their longtime enemy, Sultan Fateh Ali Tipu of Mysore (1750–99), also known as 'the tiger of Mysore', who had been strongly supported by France, to the extent that he had been discussed as a possible ally for Napoleon in conquering Egypt.[32] It is no wonder that in London they were incredibly suspicious and highly sensitive to any plan, real or even imaginary, concerning a European power's attempt to conquer India or any part of it. The same could be said for Egypt, from which the French troops had been recalled due to strong British military intervention.

Following their penetration into the Caucasus, the Russians continued advancing their plans for a gradual annexation of Persian territories. The first quarter of the nineteenth century saw an increase in British missions to the Persian court – both by government officials and representatives of the East India Company – as the perception grew that Persia was an essential element in the defense of India. The envoys would make every effort to advance British interests, but even more significantly, to reduce and combat French and Russian influence. Only following the French decline in 1809, did the disillusioned Shah sign an agreement with Britain, which was followed by definitive treaties in 1812 and 1814.[33] Notwithstanding growing British–Russian antagonism over Persia's continuing loss of territories to Russia, the British failed

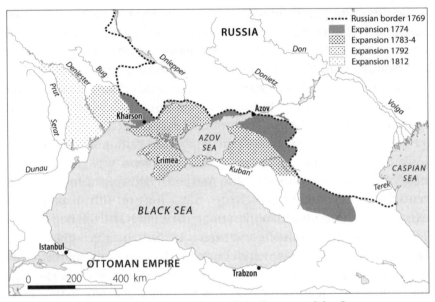

Fig. 6: Russian expansion to the south in the areas of the Caucasus
and the Black Sea, 1774–1812

to help Persia when they were needed. The Persian princes, who felt
deserted by Great Britain, now sought the help of their northern allies.
Throughout the 1820s, Persia would continue to be an area of intensive
struggle between the European forces. In the 1821 war between Persia
and the Ottoman Empire, the army of Muhammed Ali Mîrza (1789–
1820, a dowlat shah of the Persian Afshar dynasty) was trained and
well-disciplined by French officers.[34] In 1826, after Russia's total failure
in a Persian-initiated war, the former sent Prince Alexander Sergeyevich
Menshikov (1789–1869) – later famous as the uncompromising envoy to
Constantinople whose demands led to the Crimean War – to Teheran,
to settle a boundary dispute. This sparked another war between Russia
and Persia which ended after two years, with the latter's defeat and the
relinquishing of many of its northern territories. The British government
offered to help the Shah in Persia's payment to the Russians, whose
sum was stipulated in the British-brokered agreement. In Markham's
words: 'To save themselves from possible future embarrassment, the
government of England virtually broke their solemn agreement,
deserted an old ally in the moment of her deepest misfortune, and very
naturally forfeited their former influence at the Court of Teheran.'[35]

14

Recalling army marches led by Alexander the Great (356–23 BC, to the East from 326), Trajan (53–117, reigned from 98, in 106 constructed a fleet in the mountains near Nisibis [Nissib] which he floated down the Euphrates) and Julian (332–63, initiated the same project in 362–3), the possibility of a Russian campaign into India had actually been considered. Russia had annexed Georgia in 1801 and Armenia in 1828, had captured Adrianople in 1829 and, before signing a peace treaty, had advanced as far as Erzurum. All these provided Britain with legitimate reasons for suspicion.[36] Russia's aggression toward Turkey and Persia and its territorial expansion in Asia in the direction of the India-bound transportation routes, had a tremendous effect on British policy. As early as the Treaty of Adrianople and, more significantly, following the 1833 Treaty of Hünkâr Iskelesi, in which the Sultan agreed to close the Dardanelles on Russia's demand, London began to identify Moscow as the greatest source of danger to the security of the British Empire and the stability of its reign in India. British representatives repeatedly raised the issue of the vulnerability to Russian aggression of various countries in the East.[37]

Britain's disastrous involvement in Afghanistan, which came to be known as the First Afghan War, had its roots in the early 1830s. British military involvement began in 1838, ending with the disastrous retreat of winter 1841–2. The whole episode was, of course, part of the general struggle between western interests in Asia, along with the deep suspicion held by each of the western powers regarding the policies and actions of the others. This is an incredible story of incompetence and flawed, even devastating, decision-making. It is no wonder that these events, including the inexplicable stubbornness of India Governor-General Lord Auckland (George Eden, first Earl of Auckland, 1784–1849) and his 'politicals', i.e., political consultants, led by William Hay Macnaghten (1793–1841), in response to every recommendation of their military commanders, are devoted a detailed description in William Jackson's *The Pomp of Yesterday*. The events might just as easily have found a respectable place in Barbara Tuchman's *The March of Folly*.[38] The whole idea behind this disastrous project was to promote Afghanistan as a buffer between India and Russia, in line with Palmerston's policy. The vivid but frightening possibility of a clash between 'the Sepoy and the Cossack' in Central Asia led Palmerston to the conclusion that the British should ensure that this took place as far as possible from India.[39]

The fact that 'in no region [...] was Great Britain more jealous of intrusion than in the Persian Gulf' is accepted in most of the later studies devoted to the Empire in Asia. Some of the tremendous difficulties faced by Chesney and his Euphrates Expedition of 1834–6 have been attributed to Russian antagonism and to the activity of Russian agents. Although this point awaits further research and clarification, which would require extensive work in Russian archives, the presence and intensive activity of 'Russian agents' can nonetheless be found in most documents and studies concerning the expedition.[40]

Other major players in the region were the British trade companies, which were well established, well connected and determined to do everything in their power to realize their interests. The earliest such company was the British Levant Company, chartered by Queen Elizabeth I (1537–1603, reigned from 1558) in 1581, following the Capitulations treaties. It was re-established in 1606, from which time it functioned continuously for over two centuries until its ultimate dissolution in 1825.[41] In addition to developing its trade, the company was constantly concerned with fighting to keep its monopolies, mainly against merchants from other European countries, against the Ottomans, who every now and again threatened to confiscate company factories and buildings, and against Mediterranean pirates. From its inception, it had also been expected to finance the salaries and expenses of ambassadors and consuls in the Levant, a fact that added another burden to its budget and endangered its existence. From the beginning of the seventeenth century, its representatives in Constantinople served as British ambassadors to the Ottoman court. The Company also had to fight the relative disinterest displayed by official England in developing eastern trade via the land route.[42] The Company also sent chaplains to their bigger factories, as, for example, Henry Maundrell (bap. 1665, d. 1701), who studied and taught at Oxford and, from 1695, served as chaplain to the Aleppo factory of the Levant Company until he died of fever. He is known for his informative and extremely popular *Journey from Aleppo to Jerusalem at Easter 1697*.[43]

At the end of the eighteenth century, the company consisted of 800 'Turkey merchants', paying wages 'to ambassadors, secretaries, chaplains, consuls, and physicians at Constantinople, Smyrna, Aleppo, Alexandria, Algiers, Patras, &c'. The disintegration of the Company began in 1803, when the government in London took over the appointment and payment of the ambassador in Turkey and his secretaries.[44]

By contrast, the East India Company was in its prime at the beginning of the nineteenth century and was more than happy to infringe upon the monopolies of the Levant Company, directly contributing to its disintegration.[45] Established in 1600, The East India Company very early developed into a 'massively armed colonial empire' of its own, using commercial as well as military means to build its own administration, navy (civilian and military), army and political and commercial networks. The British government tried to assert more control over the company with the East India Act of 1773, which mainly limited the independence of the company's colonial administration and its ability to make major political and military decisions. The 'civil disturbances' in India were growing more extensive, and in 1833, with the Government of India Act, the company was subordinated to the Crown, which assumed direct control of the sub-continent. In 1858, Queen Victoria (1819–1901, reigned from 1837) was proclaimed Empress of India.[46]

England's first political treaty with the ruler of Omân, the strongest emirate in the Arab Peninsula, dates to 12 August 1798. That treaty was certainly connected to the alarm caused by Napoleon's invasion of Egypt, which also directly led to the establishment of a British agency in Baghdad. A second treaty, from 1800, arranged for a British resident at Máskat.[47] Later activities included two joint sea-and-land military expeditions against the el-Juwâsimi (el-Kuwâsimi), the ruthless pirates operating in the Persian Gulf, expeditions which continued into the Arabian Sea. The first was in 1810 and the second in 1819, just after Ibrahim Paşa had captured the Wahhâbi's capital and put an end to their rebellion against the Ottomans, which had begun at the beginning of the century.[48] From the early 1820s, it became necessary for Britain to maintain a regular naval base in the Gulf, and the island of Kharak was taken in 1838 in a minor, but very efficient, naval operation. Following this, Aden was conquered in January 1839.[49] Both of these relatively extreme British moves were taken because of the Empire's global and regional interests, but also, and no less so, because of the Egyptian moves in the Arabian Peninsula, which brought the Egyptian army closer to its southern and eastern shores.

17

It was only natural for the company to take special interest in surveying, mapping and, especially, charting the seas which were crucial to its connections with the British Isles, as well as with other trade centers in Europe. Victor Fontanier (1796–1857), French diplomat and traveler of the Orient, could not hide his excitement about all 'the charts of the Red Sea, the Persian Gulf, the elaborate surveys of the coast of India, those of the gulf and the coasts of Arabia, part of Africa, Ceylon, the Maldives and Laccadives, and many parts of the straits', which he viewed in Bombay. '[I]t is especially during the last twenty years that the surveys of the Persian Gulf, the shores of the Red Sea, the examination of Socotra and of the southern coast of Arabia, ha[ve] been carried into execution.'[50]

Mesopotamia, 'the land of the two rivers', was also an area of dispute whose importance for nineteenth-century British interests had slowly been revealed. 'Many of the most important events in the world's history have taken place on the shores of the 1400 miles long river Euphrates, or on its sister stream Tigris', wrote one nineteenth-century English historian, but this sentiment, in one version or another, appears in each of the many studies devoted to the area, with its rich and very long history. And he added: 'Here the fate of nations was often decided in battles, fought by armies which had been collected from every part of the known world.'[51] Commerce between East and West had always been navigated in part through the Persian Gulf and the two rivers, which were also the scene of some important military expeditions, such as those of Alexander, Trajan and Julian. Centuries before that, in 401 BC, the area had been the scene of the march of the Ten Thousand from Mesopotamia all the way to Anatolia and the shores of the Black Sea, and then back into Greece, the account of which is given in the *Anabasis*, written by their elected commander Xenophon (435–355 BC).[52] The conflict between British and Russian commercial interests in eastern and central Asia over control of the old and new trade routes, began during the last quarter of the eighteenth century and continued into the nineteenth century.[53]

One important step taken by the East India Company was the appointment of a representative in Baghdad and in Bussora (Basra), respectively. In October 1831, the Paşa of Baghdad issued a warrant 'in favor of Captain Robert Taylor, the Political Agent at Bussora'. In 1808, when Taylor had been a lieutenant and assistant resident in Bushire, his

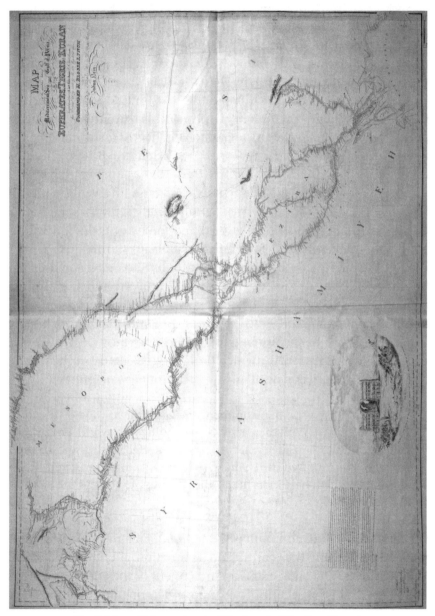

Fig. 7: Map of Mesopotamia, 'The Land of the Two Rivers'

wife and son had been taken captive by pirates, later to be ransomed. Ten years later he was assistant political agent in Turkish Arabia. In 1826 he was the Resident in Basra, and in the early thirties, already a major, he was Resident in Baghdad.[54]

David Urquhart (1805–77), a Scottish-born diplomat and prolific writer, was fluent in Turkish and modern Greek. He had been injured while intervening on behalf the nationalist side in the Greek War of Independence, and had been appointed to Stratford Canning's 1831 mission to settle matters between Greece and Turkey. This is where his pro-Ottoman approach began, an approach directed mainly against the Russian threat and which earned him the description as Britain's 'leading Russophobe'.[55] In the 1830s, during the battles against the Egyptians, he was one of the most active advocates of British intervention against Mehemet Ali. In addition, he was a prolific representative of a highly influential group of Russophobian writers which persuaded the British public and even affected governmental policies during the 1830s.[56] His anti-Russian views brought him into conflict with some of the leading politicians in London, and in 1837 resulted in his recall from his position as secretary of the embassy in Constantinople. Upon his return to London, he continued to attack the government from his seat in parliament and in his various publications.[57] His most prolific writing dates from the 1850s, during which time he wrote almost exclusively in opposition to Russia and dealt mostly with commercial interests:

> Turkey and Russia stand in commercial legislation, as the north and south poles. [...] With her activity pervading the world England had no time to consider what might be effected with the empire through which flowed the Danube, and the Nile, the Tigris, and the Euphrates; which held in its hands the Isthmus of Suez and the Strait of the Dardanelles; [...].[58]

His book about Lebanon, published in 1860, includes much valuable material concerning the country and its situation, about its inhabitants and their lives. The book is also an indictment of the European powers and their part in the decline of Lebanon and its ongoing civil wars. The country, he claimed, had now regained its international significance, 'affording to Russia a pivot on the south for the upturning of the Ottoman Empire, and to France in Algeria on the east of the Mediterranean, so as to envelope Egypt, and furnish a basis for military and naval operations against India'.[59] The constant references to Napoleon's campaigns in the East is evidence of the tremendous general effect these had for at least half a century after they ended.[60]

French interests and involvement in the region had always been guided by a combination of considerations, perhaps best described by Marlowe:

> French commercial and strategic interests in the Levant have always been powerfully sustained and, it may be, exaggerated by religious sentiments imponderables which, from the landing of St. Louis' [Louis IX, 1214–70, HG] crusaders at Damietta in the thirteenth century to the landing of French paratroops at Port Said in the twentieth [1956, HG], have exercised an always potent, a sometimes irrational, an occasionally obsessive, and an ultimately disastrous, influence of French international policies.[61]

This combination of motives may be demonstrated, for example, through the personality and history of Victor Fontanier, who in 1821 reached Constantinople and in 1833 began traveling through Asia Minor. Five years later he was nominated as French Vice Consul to Bussora, '(e)ntrusted with the charge of watching over the political and commercial interests of France in a large portion of Asia'. He planned to prepare himself by first visiting London in order to examine 'the plans of communication with India', and then to go to Bussora via Bombay. From Bussora he traveled in Iraq and Arabia and returned to France after spending much time in India. In 1846, after being decorated with the *Légion d'honneur*, he became consul in Singapore.[62] Fontanier met Chesney for the first time in Trabzon, upon his return from his first tour. He had direct and intensive contact with Chesney's expedition, mainly during its last stage in Bussora, as he tried to impede the *Euphrates'* sailing to Baghdad. 'I was struck with the novelty of his [Chesney's] plan, and the evident facility of its execution', Fontanier would later write. In Bussora he was able to use the home of Taylor, who had moved to Baghdad, with all its colonial conveniences.[63] His writings are a good reflection of French interests and involvement and an indication of how the French observed Russian, but mainly British, activity. He tried to put events and processes, as far as French interests were concerned, into their 'right' perspectives.

A number of other French consuls will appear throughout this book as well. Baudin, for example, served as Consular Agent in Damascus in the 1830s. His general employment, according to a French officer who met him there, 'is in matters of commercial nature'; he used to accompany French officers who were sent by the government to purchase stallions. He married and resided in Damascus, where he was 'obliging, zealous, and invaluable to Europeans'. Edmund Guys, consul in Beirut, was mentioned in connection with Moore and Beek's boat; his brother, H. Guis, was consul in Tripoli.[64]

Another issue which strongly affected British policy throughout the 1830s was undoubtedly the development of steam vessels. This major technological innovation was influential in many respects and had far reaching geo-political effects on the maritime powers. More than any other country, Britain's foreign and imperial policies changed significantly with the introduction of new sailing methods which were not subject to the unpredictability of winds and currents. One primary effect obviously concerned the connection with India.

A salient expression of this concern was the extensive body of literature dealing with steam-powered transport, beginning in the 1830s. It seems that anyone who had any connection to this technological advance – politicians, railroad engineers, maritime representatives and many others – felt obliged to contribute his views to the developing discussion. The shelves of the British Library, as well as other libraries holding collections of nineteenth-century literature, reveal the importance of the issue and the vast attention it received, and there is certainly no way to cover the topic here. However, some examples are worthy of mention. These include essays dedicated to the technological innovation itself and the promise it held for world commerce and communications.[65] As we will see later, Chesney was one of those who directed such long, detailed, strongly fact-based memoranda at leading politicians, in Britain as well as in India.[66] Others discussed the ongoing question of potential steam communication with India, using various data, documents and arguments to advocate their preferred route – the Red Sea or the Euphrates. Melville Grindlay, who, as a 'Captain, East India Army Agent and London Agent to the Steam Committees of Calcutta and Madras', claimed to be a leading authority and was convinced of the superiority of the Red Sea route. Though admiring Chesney and his efforts, he demanded that a similar delegation be sent to Egypt.[67] He reconsidered a different route, including the one following the Rhine, the Danube, the Black Sea and the Euphrates, reaching Trabzon and from there via the Black Sea or the northeastern Mediterranean harbors. 'The value of these suggestions depends upon the *certain and permanent* practicability of the passage of the Euphrates', wrote Grindlay, but, 'unfortunately this is not established to a sufficient extent.' Consequently, there was only one possible route.[68] A contemporary publication by the Dublin-born physicist and astronomer Dionysius Lardner (1793–1859), a clergyman and graduate of Trinity College who excelled in the study and development of steam engines, examined both routes thoroughly, adding many calculations of times, costs and distances and reaching the clear conclusion that 'the route by Egypt and the Red Sea should be that which ought to be, and which can be, immediately and permanently established [...] this, however, is no reason why the project of opening the Euphrates should be abandoned.'[69]

2 European Military Agents in the Early 1830s: 'The Early Spies'

European intelligence perceptions changed dramatically during the Napoleonic Wars. As early as 1777, the French ambassador in Constantinople arranged an espionage mission to Egypt and Syria in order to evaluate the possibilities of their occupation by France. The mission was carried out by François Baron de Tott (1733–93), an army officer of Hungarian origin with an impressive résumé in military data-gathering, 'secret diplomacy' and military consulting.[1] The early years of the nineteenth century led to the development of global geographical intelligence, as the European powers began to understand that wars could be fought in regions of the world outside of their own continent. There is no doubt, nor is it coincidental, that the Near East re-entered the Powers' sphere of strategic considerations in this period. All participants considered their lack of sufficient geographical and military data to be a significant problem; they began sending competent representatives – geographically trained army officers – to collect this information. The events of the early 1830s – the French colonization of Algeria and the occupation of Palestine and Syria by Mehemet Ali, in addition to the dangers from the north and the rebellion in India – all strengthened Britain's realization that it would have to devote attention to a quick solution to the problem of communication links between their country and the most important colony in the Empire.

The art of data-gathering in the East for military and political aims, by trained and capable personnel, was certainly not an innovation of the nineteenth century. In the preceding period there had been numerous projects involving such military personnel, who were sent to the eastern Mediterranean by their governments or their representatives in order to collect information, either as a specific mission or as a by-product of another project. One early example is the 1770s Russian maritime involvement in the battles between the Ottomans and the local ruler in Palestine, Daher el-'Umar (1689–1775). The Russian reports and maps of these have recently been found and studied by Mitia Frumin.[2] The role of Napoleon's agents, scholars and cartographers in mapping and information-gathering for military use has also been intensively studied.[3]

Francis Beaufort's (1774–1857) pioneering naval expedition in Asia Minor, probably one of the earliest organized and targeted data-gathering sea journeys in the eastern Mediterranean, also marked the beginning of a brilliant career, which would be connected in many ways to the study of the region. A native of County Meath, Ireland, Beaufort joined the East India Company at the age of 15 and then transferred to the Royal Navy, where he spent twenty years in active service. In 1810 he was sent to measure the southern coast of Asia Minor (Karamania), a mission that ended two years later when he was badly wounded and obliged to return home. In 1829 he was appointed head of the Hydrographic Office of the Navy, where, over the next 25 years, he would become the most outstanding figure in this position throughout the entire nineteenth century. Beaufort also served as cartographic advisor and issued maps and atlases for the 'Society for the Diffusion of Useful Knowledge', founded in London in 1826 and aimed at publishing inexpensive scientific material for the general public.[4]

Under his untiring leadership and activity, 'everywhere Hydrography took a new form and existence', and the office achieved supreme international status, according to Dawson's *Memoirs of Hydrography*. 'The master mind of Beaufort [...] did more for the advancement of maritime geography than was affected by all the surveyors of European Countries united.'[5] Naturally, he was one of the founders and an active member of the Royal Geographical Society (RGS). Being a great advocate of British naval supremacy during the period of *Pax Britannica*, he encouraged 'the freedom of the seas to all using British naval supremacy as the instrument, and which also included the availability of Admiralty charts to mariners of all nations'. He actively nurtured a correspondence with his surveying commanders and many others. He eagerly sent suggestions and instructions, above and beyond his implementation of numerous naval and coastal surveys.[6] Although he never set foot in Syria/Palestine or participated in its surveys, his name and central position appear many times throughout this book in connection with the surveys, reports and publications of many others. In this respect, his strong ties with the RGS were of vital importance, as a distinguished member of the Society through whom much material reached the Society and its journal.

A careful examination of the list of projects initiated and supported by Beaufort and a consideration of the list of captains he dispatched all over the world reveal that the eastern Mediterranean shores were in fact almost the only location that had not yet undergone any organized maritime survey. There is one exception: the measuring of the coast of Anatolia, which was included in Beaufort's measuring of Karamania.[7]

The nature of British intelligence, which involved the gathering of military as well as non-military information, is quite understandable when one considers the nature of the cartographical and military data-gathering training at the various British military academies (The Royal Military Academy, Woolwich; The Royal Military College, founded in 1813, first located at Great Marlow and then at Sandhurst) and at the East India Company (The East India Company's College, Haileybury, founded in 1809; and the Military Seminar, Addiscombe).[8] As part of their military education and practice, the officers-in-training were expected to collect and present any available information on any foreign country. The cartography had to be performed scientifically, so it was important to instill in the officers an academic, investigative approach. In an interesting example of this process, a young Lieutenant Symonds, before being called to join the forces in Syria, served in Bermuda, from where he sent a collection of limestone specimens to the London Geological Society.[9]

As early as the second half of the seventeenth century, the chief royal engineer had been assigned the task of collecting and producing maps and charts of 'British defense property' wherever it might have been. In the same year, 1683, the British established the 'drawing room', where all cartographic material was coordinated. Consequently, wherever the British army arrived, all available cartographic (including topographic and statistical) material which might be of use was collected. In 1803, the depot of military knowledge became the 'Quarter Master General [QMS] Department'.[10]

As mentioned above, Beaufort, physically limited by his injury in Ayas (Bay of Iskanderun) in June 1812,[11] stayed in his London office, developing his expansive network of connections all over the world. Participants in scientific delegations would request existing cartographic material concerning their target regions and solicit ideas and instructions. Given the large numbers of individuals and groups that solicited his advice, it was only natural for him to seek a way to establish organized instruction tools for surveyors. Consequently, the instructions were summarized in the *Manual of Scientific Enquiry for the use of Officers in Her Majesty's Navy, and Travellers in General*. This manual, based on the surveying tradition of Alexander Dalrymple (1737–1808, first Hydrographer of the Admiralty 1795–1808), Beaufort and others and published regularly from 1849 by the Admiralty,[12] asserted:

> [...] it would be the honour and advantage of the Navy, and conduce the general interests of Science, if new facilities and encouragement were given to the collection of information upon scientific subjects by the officers [...] of Her Majesty's Navy, when upon foreign service [...].

The question of 'observation in the field', namely, of what and how to observe, of the culture of exploration, had been a main issue with British (as well as other) travelers of various professional backgrounds, mainly scientists and officers. The *Manual of Scientific Enquiry*, published for the first time in 1849 by authority of the Lords Commissioners of the Admiralty, was the standard guidebook for any British traveler, explorer, collector and mainly, of course, for officers. Originally edited by John Frederick William Herschel (1792–1871), the leading astronomer, it included contributions of 'some of our most eminent men of science' in various fields: astronomy, botany, geography and hydrography, geology, mineralogy, magnetism, meteorology, statistics, tides and zoology.[13] In addition to technical innovations such as the prismatic compass, the proper outfit for travelers or the use of a notebook, the instructions in geography, originally written by traveler and antiquarian William Richard Hamilton (1777–1859), included data-gathering concerning the form of the country, mountain ranges, rivers, springs, lakes, coastlines, oceans, population, languages, government, buildings, agriculture, trade and commerce. All British officers, of course, were meant to follow these detailed instructions. The first *Hints to Travellers* of the RGS, a manual for observation in the field published some years later, in 1854, has been recently discussed by Felix Driver.[14]

Naturally the Near East was no exception in all of this, although its study had only barely been initiated by Beaufort. On the contrary, objects of great scientific interest and value for the western cultural heritage were scattered throughout the region. These items were also of tremendous economic value. Consequently their discovery, study and purchase, legal or illegal, came to play an important role in western scientific activity in the Levant as they began to fill European collections and museums.[15]

Perhaps the best example of the personal missions which will be examined in this chapter is the journey of artillery officer William Martin Leake (1777–1860), who reached Turkey for the first time in June 1799 as a member of a British military mission led by General George Frederick Koehler (1758–1800). The aim of this mission was 'to give the Sultan technical assistance in driving Bonaparte out of Egypt'. Following Napoleon's occupation of Egypt, the British government decided to send a military mission, 'including artillery, stores, and 100 personnel', to help the Ottomans expel the French. Koehler had been allowed to consult the Ottomans on the Dardanelles but was not permitted to join the campaign in Syria. He arrived in Jaffa only in July 1800, visited Jerusalem in October and then died of the plague, his wife following him fifteen days later. Both were buried in Jaffa.[16]

Between 1802 and 1811, Leake was intensively involved in various reconnaissance missions in the Near East:

Membership of the British military mission to the Ottoman Empire allowed him to travel in Anatolia (18 January–9 February 1800), Cyprus (11 February–7 March 1800), the Holy Land (September 1800–February 1801), Egypt (February 1801–March 1802), and Syria (April–June 1802), [...]. On his way home he spent time in Athens (30 June–9 July and August 1802) and on excursions into central Greece (9 July–7 August 1802) and the eastern Peloponnesus (September 1802). Most of the materials collected on these journeys, however, were lost when the *Mentor*, on which Leake was travelling to Malta with a consignment of Lord Elgin's marbles, foundered off the coast of Kithera on 16 September 1802.[17]

Leake's first employer was the abovementioned William Richard Hamilton, private secretary to the well-known Thomas Bruce, seventh Earl of Elgin and eleventh Earl of Kincardine (1766–1841), and then British Ambassador to the Sublime Porte. Hamilton, who served as secretary to Lord Elgin from 1799 and traveled in the East, was responsible for the recovery of the Rosetta Stone (from the French) as well as for the shipment of Elgin's Grecian marbles and the recovery of those lost at sea. Permission to retain these priceless objects had been granted to him by the Sultan in gratitude for Britain's help in facilitating the withdrawal of French troops from Egypt, ending in October 1801.[18] As for Leake, he spent the following years, 1804–10, mostly in Greece, in what can only be described as espionage and other secret missions.

The French, in the meantime, were busy sending their own special personnel to the region. 'M. Caillet [sic]', wrote the French poet Alphonse de Lamartine (1791/2–1869) in 1835, following his meeting with Camille-Antoine Callier in Syria in 1832 or 1833,[19] 'has spent three years in exploring the Isle of Cyprus, Karamania, and the different districts of Syria, with the zeal and intrepidity which characterize the well-educated officers of the French army.' Callier (1804–89) had studied in the École Polytechnique (1823) and the School of Engineers-Geographers.[20] In 1830, along with a colleague, P.J. Stamaty, he was appointed to accompany Joseph-François Michaud (1767–1839), a well-known poet and historian of the Crusader period and a member of the French Academy, on a tour of the scenes of events described in the latter's monumental *History of the Crusades*, published between 1808 and 1822. Michaud left Paris on May 1830 and returned on August 1838.[21] Lucie Bonato, who studied Callier's travels and achievements, found the latter's objectives described in a document written by him:

> [...] the execution of this enterprise promised historical information of great interest, and the Minister of War considered it as convenient to equally use it for the benefit of the geography [...] While supporting M. Michaud in his research after the crusaders' itineraries in different periods, the topography of the sites where the crusaders' most remarkable actions have occurred, they took charge to shed new lights on the geography of Minor Central Asia, Syria and the Arabian Petree; regions that are far from being known for their historical

celebrity merits, and mainly as could be reclaimed one day by events France couldn't be stranger to. Instructions were consequentially given to Amm. Stamaty & Callier, by the director of the War Depot – they embraced all that has any pertinence to the physical description and the history of the country they were about to cross around.[22]

Actually, both officers left Michaud and his companion Jean Joseph François Poujoulat (1808–80) after reaching Smyrna, proof that this companionship was only a cover for a mission of the War Office.[23] Being more than anything else a geographer by nature, Callier had been commissioned by the War Office to conduct as precise a study as he could of 'la géographie physique et descriptive de l'Asie mineure', the topography of its various countries and regions. He traveled in the Orient for four and half years, from May 1830 to November 1834.[24] In the Ottoman capital, he and Stamaty met with the French ambassador, General Armand Charles Guilleminot (1774–1840), who asked them to study the route of the Euphrates in order to verify a possible and preferable connection with India. Writing about this to their superiors in the Dépôt de la Guerre, the officers added that an English firm was also interested in the matter, and that it was important for France to anticipate England in the competition for this highly important route.[25] Consequently, the voyage included Greece and Asia Minor, going through Antalia to Mesopotamia, back to Aleppo (where Stamaty died)[26] and on to Syria. The 1832 Ottoman–Egyptian war forced Callier to go to Cyprus for three months, after which he returned to Syria and traveled through Lebanon, Palestine, Arabia Petraea and Egypt. Dissatisfied with his findings in Palestine, he returned to Jaffa and traveled through the Samaria Mountains to Tiberias and Beirut.[27] In 1833, while traveling – to the extent that this was possible under the problematic security conditions – along the depression of the Jordan toward the Dead Sea, and along the Arabah Valley to the head of the Gulf of Akaba, he tried to test the theory that in ancient times the Jordan River connected the Dead Sea with the Red Sea. All that he could establish, was 'l'existence d'un bassin fort étendu appartenant en propre à la mer Morte', and the urgent need for a 'connaissance de tout le Ghor et de la partie inexplorée de la vallée d'èl-Araba'.[28] According to a map of his routes which can be found in the Map Room of the RGS, he reached only the northwestern shore of the Dead Sea and then returned to Jerusalem and continued south through Hebron – an indication that he did not pay much attention to the lake itself.[29]

This had been one of his most daring routes. His most unusual travels in the Negev Desert and to the northern shore of the Gulf of Akaba aroused great interest due to the fact that almost no other European had preceded him there. His report was translated into German and was added by the RGS to a map by the leading cartographer, Heinrich Berghaus (1797–1884), from Berlin, which then showed the whole Negev Desert and the pioneering routes taken by both de Bertou and Robinson and Smith in 1838. A letter and the map were published in the London journal of the RGS, further proof of international interest.[30] There is no doubt, that besides Seetzen, Callier was the first to report about the ruined Nabatean cities. Callier was also interested in antiquities, transcribing and later publishing inscriptions he had found.[31]

Contemporary geographical periodicals, not only French ones, showed some interest in his travels. The German weekly *Das Ausland* reported about him, publicizing mainly translations and summaries of the French reports.[32] A map of his, 'of Meridional Syria and Palestine' on a scale of 1:500,000, which was constructed in 1835 and published in 1840, includes some improvements on former ones.[33]

Callier's responsibilities did not include touring and reconnoitering the Egyptian lands, where the French officers who had been serving, since 1820, in Mehemet Ali's army, infantry and navy were an ongoing source of information.[34] As will be shown later, Britain did not have such a privilege, and would have to send its own agent to Egypt.

After returning to France, Callier pursued a military and diplomatic career. He served as aide-de-camp to Marshal Nicolas Jean de Dieu Soult, Duke of Dalmatia (1769–1851, Marshal of France from 1804, minister of war in 1830–4, prime minister in 1832–4, 1839–40, 1840–7) in 1839. During the 1840s he was sent repeatedly to Cairo; in 1841 to Algeria; in 1842–4 he fought in Oran and Morocco; in 1846 conducted a mission to Prussia; traveled in 1849 to Rome; from 1850 was military attaché in Austria; and so on. In 1836 he received the *Grande médaille d'or* of the Parisian Geographical Society, of which he became secretary in 1839. He died as a general at the age of 85.[35]

Carl Ritter (1779–1859), the leading geographer from Berlin who had been extremely active in the study of the Holy Land, met him in 1845 in Paris. Given permission to check Callier's documents, he nonetheless complained that the works had not been of a special use for science 'until today', although he had personally used them repeatedly in his *Comparative Geography*. In addition, the RGS wrote in 1837 that they had been expecting to profit by Callier's observations, 'but they seem not to have yet been made public'.[36]

Although a large amount of his material has never been published, Callier still earned a place of note in the history of French military scientific study. His map, published in 1840 by the Ministry of War, includes corrections of many of the errors of his predecessors. He left extensive collections of rocks, plants and insects from the Orient, as well as many plans of cities and copies of inscriptions.[37] A special committee of four *savants* was appointed to evaluate Callier's material in a report which was signed by Baron Antoine Isaac Sylvestre de Sacy (1758–1838), the leading orientalist who had turned Paris into the main center of Oriental Studies.[38] In their view there were three sorts of documents of interest to the Academy: topographical maps and routes; itineraries including distances; and the large number of booklets with astronomical observations using a small sextant which were aimed at fixing the exact positions of many spots on his way.[39] De Sacy was also somewhat critical and demanding:

[The Academy] has acknowledged [...] that, hitherto, the topographic plans reported by M. Callier, and his observations on the course of the rivers and the direction of the mountains, in several parts of Minor Asia and Syria, were true discoveries assured improvements to the geography of these regions; however, should these observations and documents lack the precision needed in order to coordinate them with the already known ones, they would lose a great deal of their importance and credit.[40]

Callier continued to be involved in the study of the Jordan Depression in the following years, collaborating on the work of his successor, Jules de Bertou. Having told de Bertou about the importance of solving the lacunae in the study of the Dead Sea, the Jordan Depression and the Arabah Valley, he naturally joined Bertou in many his papers and discussions.[41]

Francis Raudon Chesney (1789–1871) is one of the most prominent figures in the history of Britain's efforts to improve its connections with the most important colony in the Empire, in the struggle for the 'sea routes to India'.[42] He devoted his life to promoting 'the northern route', i.e., 'the direct route' which included a land-bridge from the northeastern Mediterranean to the Euphrates and then sailing down the river. He consistently claimed that it was better, quicker, easier and safer than the other route, which included a land-bridge in Egypt between the Mediterranean and the Red Sea, either at the city and small harbor of Suez or at Cossair. He himself told his story in detail, as did other participants of the famous 'Euphrates Expedition'.[43] The expedition has been studied[44] and even described in novels.[45]

This should be of no surprise, as the story of the stubborn, red-headed, hot-blooded Irish artillery officer, 'descended [...] from a sturdy race of Ulster farmers, a man of Scottish origin and Scottish perseverance',[46] surpasses the imagination. Not intending to write another Chesney study or novel, a few comments will suffice here concerning his background and his first reconnaissance voyage in the East, and, in the following chapter, about the expedition.

Even before the age of fourteen, his father sent him to the Royal Military Academy at Woolwich for military training, where undoubtedly, in addition to his military duties, he developed the inclination to study everything worth studying in all possible fields. His education there 'was directed almost entirely to mathematics, with the exception of the limited knowledge of the classics requisite for Woolwich'. His fearless behavior had already been demonstrated when he saved the lives of some fishermen during a strong storm in Guernsey.[47] Storms were apparently the source of important climaxes in his own life story.

Israeli diplomat Eliahu Elath, envoy in London in the 1950s, devoted his dissertation to the problem of the routes to India and developments between 1834 and 1872. Naturally, Chesney plays a central part in this study. Elath devoted seven pages to Chesney's early travels in the East, those which made him the strongest advocate of the northern route for forty years.[48] The sources also include Chesney's *Narrative*, the biography written by 'his [second] wife and daughter', some of his letters kept mainly in the National Archives (former PRO), and the summary of John S. Guest's book.[49] Additional information may also be obtained from the book written by George Robinson, the American traveler whom Chesney met in Beirut and who, subsequently, traveled with him through Lebanon and Syria. Robinson's book supplies us with

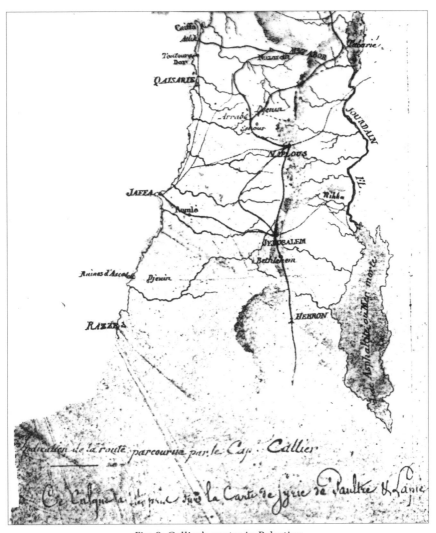

Fig. 8: Callier's routes in Palestine

Fig. 9: Camille Callier, Map of Palestine, 1840

much interesting information concerning everyday life and reality in the Near East.

Born in Ballyveagh, County Down (Northern Ireland) to a coastguard officer who had fought with the Loyalists in the American Revolution, Chesney's military career had been anything but impressive. He in fact did not see battle, although from 1815 on he held the rank of captain. Most of his time was spent in various coastal positions on the Channel Islands. The only striking narratives of these years are his long but characteristically stubborn efforts to gain the hand of a woman from Guernsey, in which his main rival was the artist David Wilkie (1785–1841), who – strangely enough – later spent time in the Holy Land and tried to calculate the level of the Dead Sea.[50] Chesney married another woman who died in childbirth, and in 1828 received a final refusal from the first. All these led him to seek his fortune overseas.

Accompanied by his two dogs and carrying a strong recommendation from Admiral Sir William Sidney Smith (1805–81), the British hero of the 1799 Battle of Acre who was credited with expelling the French troops from Egypt, Chesney left England in June 1829, as 'a military observer and to organize covertly a Turkish rocket corps that would defend mountain passes too precipitous for guns' by using a new sort of rocket. Unluckily for him, the fight between the Ottomans and the Russians, which he was so eager to join, ended before he arrived in the Balkans. Following a series of defeats, the Sultan had been forced to sign the Treaty of Adrianople, which, rather than making peace, heightened Russia's aggressiveness toward the Ottoman Empire.[51] Like many other British officers, Chesney waited for the renewal of the fighting, hoping to help the Ottomans against the 'arch-enemy'. In the meanwhile, he toured the Balkan battlefields and sent his report ('Journey over the seat of War, including the Balkans, the Fortresses on the Danube, and the different positions of the Turkish and Russian Forces') to Robert Gordon, British Ambassador to the Sublime Porte (1828–31) and brother of Aberdeen (foreign secretary and later also Secretary of the Colonies and prime minister, 1852–5).[52] Chesney admitted that he had gladly taken upon himself to reconnoiter the Balkan battlefields, 'in the hope that if I succeed in doing anything useful, it might be the means of recommending me to the notice of the Government; and that obtain the professional distinction, which the hopeless state of promotion, had denied in my own Corps'.[53] One should bear in mind that, almost at the same time, the French envoy to Constantinople was giving Callier and Stamaty parallel instructions concerning the Euphrates route.[54]

In the same document, written upon completion of three years of travel in the East, Chesney added with his usual 'modesty', that 'it seems also desirable that my own preliminary examination of the River Euphrates should not be withheld from those who may be interested in knowing what a single man may be able to accomplish in the way of field and water surveying and exploration.'[55] Chesney is referring to the results of this first expedition, performed at the request of Gordon, who liked the reports from the Balkans and asked Chesney, who had remained in the Ottoman capital for six months and had had many discussions with him, to accept a mission in order to establish 'the state of Turkey'.[56]

Chesney was strongly determined to achieve his aims. As he proved over and over again on all his travels and in the ongoing battles for his various causes in London, he could not take no for an answer; he did not understand the word 'impossible'; he did not show much patience or understanding for any sort of difficulties. 'Whatever is to be attained by superior intelligence', wrote George Robinson, his traveling companion, 'indefatigable perseverance, and undaunted courage, may be expected at his hands.' The latter gladly accepted Chesney's invitation to join him in the excursion, as he was 'well aware that under the guidance of so amiable and intelligent a traveller, I could find pleasure and instruction'.[57]

Realizing the fragility of the situation in the whole region, Gordon, who first, of course, invited Chesney for dinner in order to get a personal impression of the officer who had submitted the reports, acted both on his own initiative and as a messenger of two other diplomats. Guest has established the most important role of the first of these, Thomas Love Peacock (1785–1866), a poet and life-long close friend of the poet Percy Bysshe Shelley (1792–1822). Peacock was also a scholar of Greek and Roman cultures and from 1818 served as 'Assistant to the Examiner of Indian Correspondence at the East India House'. In Chesney's narrative he appears as the principal Examiner and, accordingly, is the subject of a long discussion in the first chapter of the book.[58] Edward Law, first Earl of Ellenborough (1790–1871, from 1828 President of the India Board and from 1846 First Lord of the Admiralty), asked Peacock in mid-1829 to prepare a report concerning the urgently-needed steam communication with India via the Red Sea. In his memorandum, Peacock was the first to suggest the possible northern route through the Euphrates, also pointing out the rapid Russian advance in steam navigation and the hazards of having their boats sail on the Euphrates and Tigris within a short time.[59] Thus began his long and intensive involvement with the 'direct route' through Mesopotamia, making him the most important advocate of the expedition.

Ellenborough and Peacock were jointly suspicious concerning Russia's actual goals regarding India.[60] According to Elath, these were the main reasons for the instructions handed to Chesney by Barker, British consul-general in Egypt. John Barker (1771–1849) belonged to the group of British diplomats who had actually stayed in the East throughout their careers. He was a source of contacts and information for every European involved with the area, from the beginning of the nineteenth century and until his death.[61] He was born in Smyrna and educated in England, serving from 1797 in Istanbul as private secretary to British Ambassador

Fig. 10: Francis Rawdon Chesney, 1841 and 1863

John Spencer Smith (1769–1845, brother of the naval officer), and from 1799 as proconsul in Aleppo and interim agent for the Levant Company and the East India Company.[62] In 1803 he became full consul for the Levant Company,[63] receiving some fame for introducing vaccinations into Syria.

In March 1807, anticipating a war between England and the Ottomans, Barker had been forced to leave Aleppo, finding refuge with the Emir Bashîr Shihab II (1767–1850, 'Besheer' in Barker's book), the Druze prince in Lebanon. Until his ceremonial return to Aleppo in June 1809, he stayed in the Harissa Monastery, situated a 'one hour ride' from Junieh.[64] Today, the Lady of Harissa, a monument to the Virgin Mary located on a hill 600 meters high and inaugurated in 1908, can be reached by cable car from Junieh. The Harissa area holds many churches and monasteries. A letter from Barker to the Franciscan Custos in Jerusalem testifies that his refuge had been in the St. Anthony of Padua Franciscan Monastery,[65] built in 1628 on land given to the Franciscans by the Druze Emir Fakhreddine II (1572–1635, governed from 1590) of the same Shihab family.

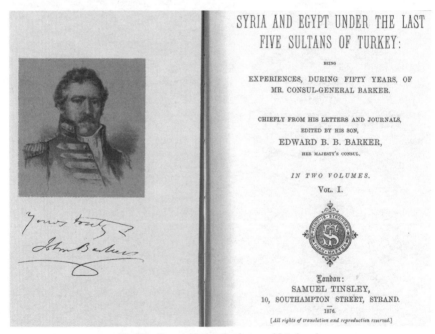

Fig. 11: Consul John Barker and his book

Barker continued conveying information between Britain and India and gained repute for transmitting the news of the suspension of the Peace of Amiens and the landing of Napoleon at Cannes in record time, consequently preventing the surrender of Pondicherry to the French during the long French–British war in India, which had begun in 1793. Following the elimination of his post of consul-general for the Levant Company in Aleppo, in autumn 1825 he was appointed British consul in Alexandria. He served there until May 1833, when he retired to his splendid villa and garden at Souedeeyah in Syria, where he died in October 1849.[66] His son, William Burckhardt Barker (1810/11–56), was named after his godfather, the famous Swiss traveler for the British 'Association for Promoting the Discovery of the Interior Parts of Africa', Johann Ludwig Burckhardt (1784–1817), who had been residing with his father when he was born.[67] A trained orientalist and knowledgeable in many languages, Barker the younger continued traveling in the region, gaining some important information. His voyage to the sources of the Orontes, for example, could have supplied Chesney with much information, had it reached the latter before the beginning of his long expedition, during which he landed at the opening of that river while trying, unsuccessfully, to sail it to Antioch. Undoubtedly, young Barker met with the participants of Chesney's expedition. From August 1835 he stayed with his father at his palace near Antioch, 'and during part of the succeeding winter played chess almost every evening with Ibrahim Pasha'. William Francis Ainsworth (1807–96), veteran of the Euphrates Expedition, later edited his more extensive publication, a historical survey of Cilicia and its governors. Barker died of cholera in the Crimea.[68]

There is hardly any doubt that, in former centuries, Aleppo had been the key to much of the overland commerce between Asia and Europe. The British Factory, established there as early as 1583, and the British Levant Company were the main bearers of this trade. During its most prosperous period, there were as many as eighty British firms in Aleppo; in 1795 only four remained. The very existence of this British colony enabled numerous travelers to take these routes and describe them.[69] There is proof of earlier trade between Aleppo and cities along the Euphrates by ship as well.[70]

A 'memo regarding Capt. Chesney', kept in the NA (PRO), depicts Chesney's intensive timetable, but more than that, enumerates his reports sent from different stations on his way to Gordon and also some to Stratford Canning:[71]

10 April 1830 – on events of the Russian war

17 May, from Syria – the general state of Greece

26 August, from Damietta – the social and military state of Egypt, its government, politics and resources

2 September, from Jaffa – first report on steaming by the Red Sea, and the isthmus of Suez

21 September – state of defenses of [?]

December, from Damascus – the Paşaliks of Syria

3 June 1831, from [?] – memoir on the navigation and survey of the Euphrates and Red Sea, comparative advantages, maps

12 March, from Aleppo – plan of operations to subjugate the Paşa of Egypt by a direct Turkish attack on Cairo

May, from Constantinople – [no text original]

25 July, from Busheir – memoir on political state and resources of the Paşalik of Baghdad

In August and September 1832, from the frigate which took him home, Chesney sent Stratford Canning two long memoirs concerning 'the designs of Russia in Persia' including a detailed report on its military, political and topographical state, and on the general state of Turkey and the designs of the Egyptian ruler. He continued in London, adding to his reports a 'Manuscript Map to illustrate the general position of Persia and Atlantic Turkey, with respect to India, and showing the 6 different Lines by which Russia may reach the Indies', submitted first to Palmerston and then to the President of the India Board (5 January 1833), 'a paper of remarks on the different lines by which rapid [...] communication may be established between England and India' and 'a paper on the way of opening the line of the Euphrates for a mail communication as well as the important auxiliary of the Steam Flotilla' (2 July).

The main questions which Chesney was expected to answer concerned 'the relative advantages of the Egyptian and Syrian routes to India'.[72] In Alexandria he had an audience with Mehemet Ali and became acquainted with some residing or visiting Europeans. The German-born traveling missionary Joseph Wolff (1795–1862, 'Wolfe' in Chesney's report) had converted from Judaism to Catholicism in 1812 and six years later joined the Anglican Church. He had been sent to the

East by the 'London Society for Promoting Christianity amongst the Jews' and was on the last stage of his tour, which began in 1827 and also included Yemen.[73] Other people mentioned are Consul-General Barker, Gliddon, Sardinian Imperial Consul to Alexandria Carlo Rossetti (the son) and Thomas Galloway.[74] Regarding Gliddon, there is no hint as to whether he means the father, John G. Gliddon, an English merchant who became US consul in Alexandria, or his more famous son, George Robins Gliddon (1809–57), American vice-consul in Egypt until 1842, later establishing a reputation as the first writer on ancient Egypt in the United States.[75]

Chesney traveled from April to September 1830, starting by ascending the Nile to Cairo, crossing to Suez ('a miserable place of abode, hemmed in between the arid desert and a boisterous sea'), with a boat to el Tûr on the eastern shore of the Sinai Peninsula and inland to visit the St Catherine Monastery and to climb Mount Sinai. Returning to el Tûr, he sailed again to Cossair, another potential Red Sea harbor for connecting with the route to India. Returning to the Nile in Kenneh, he continued north to Damietta, checking possible overland routes connecting the Gulf of Suez with the Mediterranean, directly or via the Nile.[76]

His companion through all these travels was a count, Frederick Chorinsky, 'a man of considerable literary attainments, agreeable social qualities, and an easy-going disposition'.[77] One of Chesney's interesting reports to Gordon, written from several Persian cities and sent on 31 July 1831, deals with 'the Pole', as Chesney found it difficult to decide whether he was a Pole or a Russian agent. Chesney testifies that the Count was making his way across Arabia to Máskat, spoke about having Russian credits, talked openly about the Russian advance to India and spoke about his uncle Prince Radzivil, probably Ludwig Nikolaus Radzivil (1773–1830) or his son Leo (1808–82), who started out as a Polish officer but joined the Russians and also had a career as a diplomat. Together, Chesney and Chorinsky paid an interesting visit to the Persian ruler Abbâs Mirza (1789–1833).[78]

Chesney's interesting reports include an outstandingly important finding. He was the first to point out the crucial mistake made by Napoleon's surveyors, who had ruled out the possibility of a canal between Suez and the Mediterranean, calculating a ten-meter difference in the levels of the two seas. In his letter to Gordon, dated Jaffa, 2 September 1830, which includes his report concerning the pros and cons of the Egyptian route and reaching a positive decision about its reasonability and feasibility, Chesney added:

> Any of these routes, however, which may be adopted, will probably only pave the way to the realization of the grand idea, so long indulged in England and other parts of Europe, of connecting the Mediterranean with the Red Sea. A little time will probably remove the ill-founded apprehension of increasing the height of the former by the influx of the latter; [...]
>
> As to the executive part, there is but one opinion. There are no serious natural difficulties; [...] and in a country where labour can be had without limit, and at a rate infinitely below that of any other part of the world, the expense would be a moderate one for a single nation, and scarcely worth dividing between the great kingdoms of Europe [...].[79]

Chesney proved that a canal was feasible, and his reports had an important influence on the later plans and realization of the Suez Canal. Needless to say, he always had in mind the pharaonic canal which connected the Nile and Suez, so well described by Herodotus (484–25 BC), Strabo (64/3 BC–24 AD) and others, descriptions repeated by nineteenth-century travelers and other interested figures.[80] As early as 1504, the idea of connecting the Mediterranean and the Gulf of Suez emerged again, first by the Venetians, then by the Ottomans, but mainly by various French entrepreneurs from the seventeenth century. Most of the time, these ideas and plans were associated with a French occupation of Egypt.[81]

On 17 May, Chesney sent Gordon a report concerning 'the general state of Greece, and the proposed boundaries of that Kingdom', to be followed, after two weeks, by a 'military report [...], on the state of the Army, Fortresses, Fleet, and designs of the Pasha of Egypt', and soon afterwards, 'on the social and military state of Egypt, its Government, Politics, and resources; also the ambitious projects of the Pasha' and 'on steaming by the Red-Sea, the Istmus [sic] of Suez, Lake Manzaleh etc.'. It is almost unnecessary to mention that he added a memo concerning the Sultan's army which could be activated in Syria.[82]

While traveling in Egypt, he was handed 'a series of queries drawn up by the late Mr. Peacock, [...] as to the relative advantages of the Egyptian

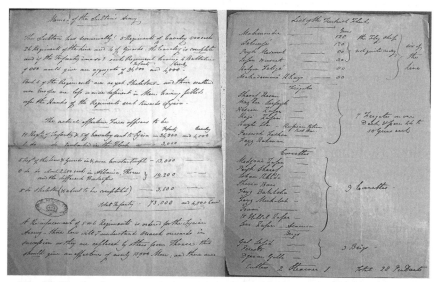

Fig. 12: Chesney's reports: Memo of the Sultan's Army; List of the Turkish Fleet

Fig. 13: Chesney rafting on the Euphrates

and Syrian routes to India'.[83] This led to the second part of Chesney's travels, which caused much interest while laying the groundwork for his future Euphrates Expedition and for his fame as the major advocate of the Northern Route. His reports from this stage of his travels included his 'Journey through the Arabian Desert from Damascus to El-Karim', his 'Descent of the River Euphrates on a Raft and by Boat', his 'Ascent and Descent of the River Karūn' and then his 'Journey through Persia and Asia Minor'. These almost legendary travels, accomplished alone, lasted from 11 December 1830 until his return to London on 26 September 1832.[84] The lithograph showing 'Capt. Chesney's Raft [named *Kelek*, HG], in 1830, descending the Euphrates towards Hadisah',[85] should serve as a fitting monument for the officer who was described as somebody who 'seemed to think that "nothing was impossible"'[86] and who proved this at every step in his 'Euphrates career'. During this adventurous voyage, Chesney planned his great expedition – many times erroneously, as would later be discovered – with its landing sites, overland route, as well as the choice of the city of Bir (today Birecik, Bírehjík) as its point of departure. More than one hundred and thirty years earlier, in April 1699, Henry Maundrell, chaplain of the British Factory in Aleppo, had traveled from there to the 'Euphrates, Beer and Mesopotamia'.[87] Ainsworth, geologist of the Euphrates Expedition, 'felt a certain degree of pleasure [...] in being able to test the accuracy of Maundrell in the description given in his travels [...]'.[88]

In Baghdad, Chesney met and was greatly impressed by Captain Robert Taylor, who would have a great influence on Chesney, his travels and chosen routes, and play an important part in the eventual history of the expedition. Two of his daughters married two of the expedition's participants.[89]

The military nature of Chesney's mission is easily demonstrated through many of the reports, as is their extraordinarily all-encompassing character; Chesney proved to be interested in almost everything he could see and report. But it was the situation in the Near East, the prospects of an impending war between the Egyptians and the Turks, the possibilities of a Russian advance southward and the better, easier, quicker and safer routes for connection with India using steam boats (including the problem of supplying them with sufficient coal), which were of supreme interest for the British government and its representatives in the East.[90] One cannot ignore the numerous documents, such as 'Memo of the

Sultan's Army', in which Chesney tried to establish the possible strength of the Ottoman army which would face Ibrahim Paşa's Egyptian forces.[91]

His movements were noticed and reported by the French consuls, who diligently reported on every *voyageur anglais*. Baudin, consular agent to Damascus, reported on the visits of Chesney and Gliddon, the English merchant residing in Alexandria, in 1830. Edmund Guys, consul in Beirut, reported in the same year about a certain Scott, a *capitaine de l'armée anglaise*, as well as about Sevoin from the East India Company. Naturally, everything was connected to the discussion concerning the routes to India and the use of steamships. For the French, this appeared to be the basic factor leading Britain to appoint a resident consul-general in Damascus.[92]

In a report, dated Pera, 13 June 1832, Chesney described 'three directions along which the Sultan may march' when sending his army to face Ibrahim Paşa who would be advancing into Syria: through the desert, east of the mountains; along the sea; and 'along the plain-valley extending from the Orontes to Baalbek, skirting the Anti-Libanus all the way to Lake Tiberias, *or rather the Dead Sea itself*' [my emphasis, HG].[93] Checking all possibilities, he added that the situation on the ground was so favorable to Ibrahim, that 'I quite expect a failure of a[n Ottoman] land Expedition'. Then he considered that Mehemet Ali would easily take Baghdad and Asia Minor as well. In July, following the Ottoman defeat near Homs, he sent another letter, writing about 'the most *lively* espionage at work' [my emphasis, HG], a mission of a certain British officer, Captain Kelly, to the Ottomans, and the ongoing French and Russian involvement through their political policies and their agents in the field. He also mentioned the possibility of Russian maritime action, which actually did take place some months later, after the final Ottoman defeat in Konieh.[94]

There is one part of Chesney's reconnaissance which has so far been relatively neglected by scholars, as it was virtually skipped over in his own *Narrative*. These are his travels between Jaffa and Damascus from 2 September to 11 December 1830.[95] In the single page of his diary dedicated to this leg of his journey, he expressed his special interest in Acre, in its crusader heritage, in its defenses against Napoleon and in the death of Major Oldfield, who, according to his text, might have been an acquaintance. Thomas Oldfield (1756–99) of the Royal Marines died fighting side by side with Djezzar's troops defending Acre against the French:

> At daybreak of 7 April a party of the defenders with Oldfield leading the centre of their three columns sallied out from the walls to attack and destroy a mine which was being dug by the French to weaken their defences. Oldfield's column advanced to the entrance of the mine and according to General Berthier [...] attacked like heroes. Oldfield was one of the first to be cut down. Both sides tried to recover his body, a French grenadier succeeding [...] only to discover that he was still alive. Oldfield died shortly afterwards, and was buried with full military honours by the French...[96]

After sending the abovementioned report from Jaffa, Chesney proceeded, accompanied by his friend Chorinsky, to look for possibilities of implementing his plan – about which he had already written to Ambassador Gordon – to establish 'the most direct line to India by the Euphrates' and to build two boats in Iskanderun to be transported to Bir on the Euphrates.[97] Gordon actually discouraged him from this idea and suggested that he take the desert road to Baghdad. Chesney followed the ambassador's advice with regard to the destination, but as for the route, he chose to travel along the Euphrates.

After examining the harbor of Jaffa, he proceeded to 'Jerusalem, the Dead Sea, Hebron, the Jordan, [...] Mounts Tabor and Carmel, the fortress of Acre, the towns of Nazareth, Tiberias, Sidon, the remains of Tyre, and on to Beïrút'.[98] His *Narrative* does not include any further details about the country, except for a long story about a life-threatening situation he found himself in while traveling in Lebanon.[99] After meeting with Consul-General John William Perry Farren (?–1864) in Damascus, he decided to spend some time going through 'the countries east of the Jordan', again in order to find out whether they offered a better alternative for approaching the Euphrates. He was assisted by two people: Baudin, acting French consul in Damascus, and George Robinson, whom he met in Beirut and who agreed to accompany him on his travels.[100]

Their course led them through virtually unfrequented routes and places, some of them only ruins, in the Syrian Desert. Most of their time was spent copying inscriptions and taking measurements. Chesney had to see every place, every ruin, with his own eyes. Starting in Damascus,

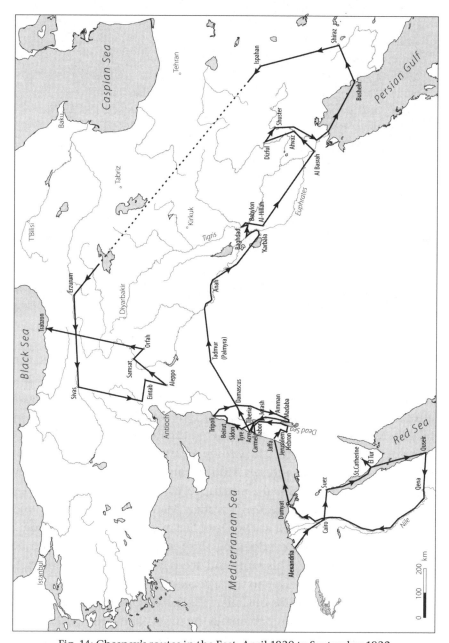

Fig. 14: Chesney's routes in the East, April 1830 to September 1832

Fig 15: Memorial of Major Oldfield and Colonel Walker, Acre

they first traveled in the Hauran, traversed the Ledja and examined the Roman ruins in Shohba, Kenath, Soueida and many deserted villages, before reaching Bosra. Chesney and Robinson continued south, and after finding an 'Arab chief', a Bedouin of the Anizah tribe who agreed to take them through to Petra, they entered the Bashan and visited Der'aa (Edre'i). Chesney was able to take some measurements during the night in spite of their escort's refusals. Continuing south to the Gilead, they visited Djerash and reached Amman, to whose ruins they devoted a rather long description. Passing through Madaba, Hesban, Petra and Mount Nebo, they arrived at the Dead Sea and parted ways at Gadara (Omkēs), a Roman city overlooking the Sea of Galilee.[101] It would be quite natural to compare his route and deeds to those of his compatriot, George Henry Moore, less than three years later.[102]

After studying the ruins of Gadara, Robinson continued directly on to Damascus while Chesney ascended the mountain to the banks of the Hieromax (Yarmuch), and crossed the Jordan to Tiberias 'where I found an American Jew, a Mr. Samson, who, on hearing that I was without money, kindly supplied me with immediate wants'. He made his way through the Galilee to Acre and continued via Safed (an interesting site, he noted, where he spent the night) to the Huleh Valley, then through the Upper Jordan and Banias, and on to Damascus.[103]

Strikingly, Chesney failed to supply any detailed account concerning his exploits in the Holy Land. This visit was described in his biography, written and issued by his daughter and wife and based on his diary, which revealed that he reached the shores of the Dead Sea only once and for a short time. His intention to go there again on a planned tour to Djerash was thwarted due to unfavorable security conditions.[104]

Still a captain, Chesney was hoping to be promoted in appreciation of three years of reconnaissance, espionage, reports and strategic estimations, a desire he expressed quite explicitly in a letter sent to Stratford Canning. 'I trust', he wrote, 'neither your Excellency nor Lord Palmerston, will think me very unreasonable in believing, that the Euphrates in all its bearing on India, is quite as much important to the British Empire [...].'[105]

Chesney's work and persistence in promoting his idea received their acknowledgement in 1834, when he was elected a fellow of the Royal Society,[106] but his biggest achievement was the establishment of the House of Commons's 'Select Committee on Steam Navigation to India', which conducted its first meeting on 9 June 1834, just over one and a half years after his return to London. 'Mr. Blake of Gallway and Mr. Martin of Sligo', whose families will be later mentioned in connection with George Henry Moore, were members of the Committee.[107] The London authorities, who traditionally considered the Suez route unworthy, found it easy to adopt Chesney's enthusiasm. Elath's descriptions and analysis of the decision-making process and of the Committee's meetings are most comprehensive and convincing on this issue.[108] These two years, 1832–4, were critical for the consolidation of Palmerston's policy toward the Ottoman Empire and its dominions, and Britain's policy in the Near East in general. Chesney, extremely active and very persuasive, acquired several influential advocates for his plan. Meanwhile, the newspapers were regularly warning about Russian influence and plots and public opinion was mobilized for the cause. Consequently the committee was announced, to be chaired by Charles Grant (1778–1866, from 1835 Baron Glenelg), who replaced Ellenborough as President of the Board of Control, and from April 1835 was also Secretary of State for the Colonies. In contrast to Ellenborough, who distrusted Chesney, Grant emerged as one of his strongest supporters.[109]

Chesney's testimony before the committee, which lasted for four meetings and was the longest the committee would hear, proved his thorough mastery of the issue; he was well acquainted with the facts, with local and regional conditions and people, and with the advantages and disadvantages of both proposed routes.[110] The committee's decision, published on 14 July (in about five weeks, with impressive rapidity), was very clear, and was a total triumph for Chesney:

> [...] we certainly give the preference to that [route] of the Persian Gulf; as being the easiest, the most certain throughout the year, the most in the line of all our Asiatic interests, and the most economical.[111]
> [...] there appears to be difficulties on the line of the Euphrates, [...] but that those difficulties do not appear to be by any means such as cannot be surmounted, [...] and that this route, besides having the prospect of being less expensive, presents so many other advantages, physical, commercial, and political, that it is eminently desirable that it should be brought to the test of a decisive experiment.[112]

Chesney's enthusiasm struck a chord with traditional British official dislike of the Egyptian land route. The recommendation was adopted unanimously in the House of Commons and was issued an impressive budget of £20,000. The 'Euphrates Expedition', which had begun as a dream, evolved into a plan and was now a reality.

While Chesney was busy laying his plans in London, another British officer, who seven years later would play an important role in measuring Palestine, Charles Rochfort Scott, 'Captain, H.P., Royal Staff Corps', was traveling in Egypt and Candia. He was apparently a private traveler, not officially representing any governmental authority. Following his travels in 1834, in 1837 he issued his most informative two-volume book, whose subtitle clearly depicts his aims: to bring 'details of the Military Power and Resources of those countries, and observations on the government, policy, and commercial system of Mehemet Ali'. In his preface he indicates his aim 'to describe the country as it really *is*', while being rather critical of Mehemet Ali's tyrannical regime and its consequences.[113] His descriptions and reports are of great value for students of Egypt, in particular those interested in its military and governmental aspects in the mid-1830s, and are worth comparing with the parallel and contemporary reports of the Duke of Ragusa. Inter alia, Rochfort Scott supplies detailed descriptions and evaluations concerning the Egyptian army, its size, organization and training, the harbor of Alexandria, and the Egyptian navy in 1834. His claim that 'the Viceroy, when residing in Alexandria, usually passes much time in the Naval Arsenal', corresponds with other information concerning Mehemet Ali's maritime policy.[114] Naturally, he devotes a full chapter to the discussion of the routes to India, including descriptions of the old canal, the city of Suez and its anchorage, the problems of sailing the Red Sea and the difficulties of sailing the Euphrates. He compares both routes from different points of view, and generally prefers the Egyptian option.[115]

When, in 1831, Mehemet Ali commenced hostilities against the Ottoman Sultan Mahmud II, Russia found itself in a very unusual situation. On the one hand, the Ottoman Empire was a major Russian enemy. On the other hand, the possibility of having the energetic and powerful Mehemet Ali on the Ottoman throne instead of the relatively weak and already defeated Sultan, was extremely unpleasant and provoked anxiety for Russia. Finally, Tsar Nikolai I (1796–1855, reigned from 1825) decided to back the Ottomans in order to secure the achievements of the Treaty of Adrianople, which had ended the recent war in the Balkans in a Russian victory.

In December 1832 the Tsar dispatched his general, Nikolay Nikolayevich Muravyev (1794–1866), already famous for his 1818–20 mission to Central Asia and later a member of the State Council, to convey to the Sultan promises of Russian assistance. From Istanbul the general proceeded on to Alexandria to convince Mehemet Ali to enter into negotiations with the Sultan. Although General Muravyev was warmly received in Alexandria, this visit did not lead to the withdrawal of the Egyptian Army from Asia Minor.[116] Left with no other choice, the Sultan finally agreed to the Russian proposition, and in February 1833 the Russian Navy Squadron of the Black Sea under Rear-Admiral Michail Petrovich Lazarev (1788–1851) arrived in the Bosporus with several thousand landing-troops in order to prevent a further advance of the Egyptian army. General Muravyev took command of this detachment.[117] Consequently, Russia and Turkey became allies. Syria was added to

Mehemet Ali's dominions, but both sides prepared for the resumption of the hostilities.

Subsequently the Russian general staff undertook major efforts to reconnoiter this potential war theater. Among the Russian expeditionary force were several general staff officers. During the stay of the Russian expeditionary force in Turkey, they mapped the Straits, established a triangular network in Asia Minor and conducted many reconnaissance missions, whose findings were processed and systematized after the detachment's return to Russia. However, not all of the officers returned with the main body of the expeditionary force; two of them stayed and received personal missions.

Colonel Alexander Duhamel (1801–80) was the son of a Russian officer of French origin. He began his service in 1820 in H.I.M. Quarter-Master Suite. During his career, Duhamel took part in the triangulation survey of the St. Petersburg area (1820–3) and in an expedition to the Caspian and Aral Seas (1826). In 1826 he was sent, along with two other general staff officers, to Istanbul under diplomatic cover to collect information regarding the upcoming theater of war. Duhamel participated in the Russian–Turkish War of 1828–9 and in the suppression of the Polish Uprising of 1831. He then accompanied General Muravyev to Istanbul. From there he was dispatched to meet with Ibrahim Paşa who was in command of the Egyptian army in Asia Minor. Duhamel purposely chose the land route in order to test the Turkish road infrastructure. After the end of the Russian expedition to the Bosporus he was appointed Russian General Consul to Egypt. He established good relations with Mehemet Ali and, until his call back to Russia in 1837, he managed to collect very comprehensive information regarding the Egyptian army. He succeeded, for example, in attaining plans of the fortress of Acre, which had been renovated and fortified by the Egyptians, from a European engineer who was in charge of its renovation.[118] Between 1837 and 1841 Duhamel fulfilled the position of Russian ambassador in Persia, and after returning to Russia he left the diplomatic service and formally rejoined the general staff.[119]

Lieutenant-Colonel Petr Lvov (1802–after 1840?) joined H.I.M. Quarter-Master Suite in 1820 and within three years received his first officer's rank. Between 1824 and 1826 he participated in the survey of Bessarabia, at the time a border area between the Russian and Ottoman Empires, and in 1828–9 participated in the Russian–Turkish War. In

March 1830 he fulfilled his first mission, a reconnaissance journey from Istanbul, Angora, Sivas and Erzurum to Tiflis (Tbilisi).

While the Russians were preparing to return home from the Straits, Lvov had been dispatched, in July 1833, to Asiatic Turkey with a special reconnaissance mission. He traveled through Asia Minor, Syria, Lebanon and Palestine, returning to St Petersburg after almost a full year. He compiled detailed descriptions of eight different routes, taking notes on distances, travel times, topography, major stops, suitability for troop transportation and more. These descriptions were accompanied by elaborate watercolor-sketch road maps. Based on his observations, Lvov provided a general geographical overview of the region and added recommendations on a preferred course of military action. He most probably also visited Turkish Kurdistan; however, there and in Asia Minor his achievements were surpassed by excellent works and maps prepared by a younger colleague from the general staff. Russian preparations for intervention were soon abandoned due to rapid political changes, and Lvov's report lost its actuality. The materials found their way into the Russian State Archive of Military History, which holds two of Lvov's reports: 'Eastern Anatolia and part of Turkish Kurdistan' (partially published in Russian in 1991) and 'Syria'. Both contain military and geographical descriptions, including brief reports on physical geography, hydrology, climate, natural landscape, population, trade, industry, etc.[120]

It is not surprising that Lvov crossed paths with participants of Chesney's expedition, and he mentions mainly Chesney and his deputy, Lynch. Lvov wrote that members of the British expedition, mainly Captain Lynch, whom he met in Antioch, provided him with much information and their plans:

[...] The space between Antakia and the mouth could be considered as the most important part of the Orontes stream, because of huge amount of water, which flows from a big Antakia lake, extraordinarily enlarges the stream and gives it a constant depth. Here the English traveller Captain Chesney (appointed now as a Chief of experimental steamboat navigation on the Euphrates) considered the possibility of connecting the Orontes with the Euphrates by a channel, passing from Antakia to Aleppo and then to Blis. This idea is completely senseless and couldn't be accomplished. For such a channel it is necessary to dig through two considerable mountain ridges, which

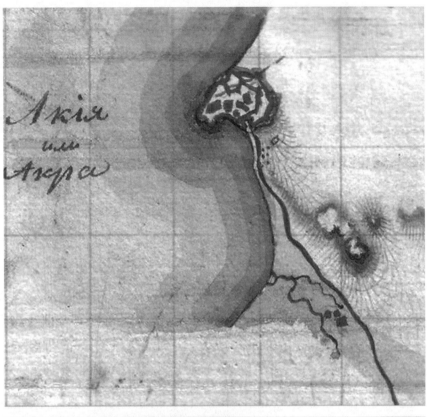

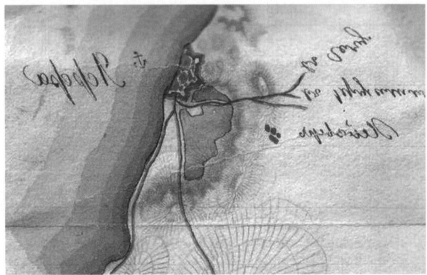

Fig. 16: Lvov, maps of Acre and Jaffa

start not far from Kilisa; and in addition, most probably, Antakia lake waters will change their direction and expenses needed for turning the Orontes into a navigable river will be too high. As for a railroad between the Mediterranean and Euphrates, this is quite possible, and in case of success with a steamboat connection with India, it could draw special attention.[121]

This note regarding the railroad is especially interesting because the first Russian railroad, aimed to ferry the royal family between St Petersburg and their country residences at Tsarskoe Selo, had only just been opened in September 1837.

In 1838 Lvov retired from the general staff and moved from St Petersburg to Vitebsk where he reportedly was assigned in 1840. His later fate is unknown.

3   The Euphrates Expedition, 1834-7

It is with Feelings of the deepest Regret that I do myself the Honour of informing you that the Tigris Steamer was totally lost during a Hurricane of indescribable violence, which, after the short struggle of Eight Minutes, sent a fine Vessel to the Bottom in Five Fathoms Water, and deprived His Majesty of Fifteen valuable Men, with Five Natives in Addition.[1]

'An enterprise which must eventually promote the advantage and the credit of this country', those were the words of King William IV (1765-1837), himself a naval officer, in his letter to Chesney after hearing the tragic news concerning the sinking of the *Tigris* in a hurricane on the Euphrates on 21 May 1836, with the loss of twenty of the thirty-seven aboard.[2] Sir John Cam Hobhouse, second Baronet Broughton (1786-1869), had been a close friend of Byron and a companion on his travels, and they had stayed in the Ottoman Empire for more than a year (1809-10). From April 1835 he became president of the Board of Control for India ('The India Board', 1835-41, 1846-52), and was an enthusiastic supporter of Palmerston on the question of the Russian threat in Central Asia. He had undertaken the very unpleasant mission of conveying the bad news to the elderly king:

[...] that Y. My's [Your Majesty's, HG] loyal servants who have thus perished risk their death with that dauntless composure which characterises the British seaman and soldiers and your Majesty, will also observe, that Colonel Chesney and the survivors, still bearing up with true courageous resignation against this great calamity, still purpose to continue their exertions, and do not despair of final success.[3]

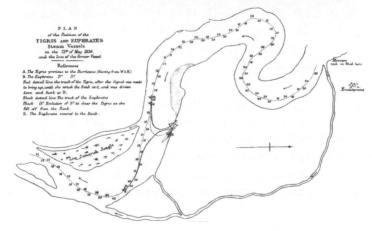

Fig. 17: The loss of the *Tigris*

William, who had succeeded his brother on the throne in mid-1830, had been well acquainted with Chesney and the expedition, supporting it after receiving the officer for an interview in April 1833. It is no wonder that on the day after receiving the tragic news, he asked that another letter be sent:

> [...] conveying to Col. Chesney and the officers and men under his command the assurance of his entire satisfaction at their conduct, and of his sense of their exemplary zeal, preserving, exertion and fortitude, manifested under very trying circumstances. [...] Col. Chesney [...] and those under his orders [...] maintained the high Character of the British native, and established it where it had not been previously known, and where it was most essential to the future results of this important enterprise in which they have been employed, that a favourable impression should be made at the outset.[4]

A further sentence in the same document, 'the importance of the expedition for British presence and name in so far unrecognized parts of the globe', presents a typical imperial point of view. The twenty men had lost their lives so that the British name would be established in the Mesopotamian plains. Intensive correspondence was devoted to their loss; even a poem, published in 1840, commemorated the tragic event and its casualties.[5]

In June 1831 Chesney had sent his report from the Shatt el-Arab to Gordon. In order to avoid a plague that had broken out in Iraq, he hurried back north through Tabriz. February and March of 1832 were spent in Aleppo, during which time he studied the harbors on the northeastern Mediterranean coast (Iskanderun, Latakia, the ancient harbor of Seleucia), and in April he reached the Ottoman capital, where he met Gordon's replacement, Stratford Canning. He returned to London in September and immediately began advocating his scheme.[6] Being already 'a celebrity', as Guest terms it, Chesney had the ear of the government, the press and the public; the theme of steam navigation to India became a source of intensive discussion. At first, all existing data and findings favored the 'rival', Egyptian, route. It was only Chesney's strong determination and persuasive powers which gradually began to convince more and more influential persons.[7]

The expedition was of tremendous importance for British interests in the East and the government in London invested in it considerable means, in money, organization, equipment and political initiatives and procedures. John Ponsonby (c.1770–1855), Ambassador to the Sublime Porte, had been recruited for assistance in the matter; he was probably the only one capable of obtaining the *firman*, or decree, from the Ottomans, which would allow the two British steamboats to navigate the Euphrates and order governors and officials to cooperate and help the British. This had been issued on 29 December 1834 by the Paşa of Baghdad and was translated and signed by Robert Taylor.[8] Although there were also opposition voices, the editor of the *JRGS* must have represented the majority view when he wrote:

> Without presuming to offer any opinion of what may appear to us to be the probabilities or improbabilities of the substantial success of the enterprise, it is impossible not to sympathize with the zeal and confidence which animate the adventurous party engaged in it; and an expedition by which science must gain, whatever may be otherwise the results, is entitled to the especial good wishes of a literary and scientific journal.[9]

Although the advantages of the route through Suez would be established quite quickly, mainly in comparison with the tremendous difficulties encountered by the expedition and the significant delay in its planned schedule, the British and Indian governments would continue pursuing the project. 'It will even serve for an example of extraordinary daring, and a proof of the perseverance and foresight of the British government', praised the French agent Fontanier, Resident in Bussora, who followed the expedition through all its stages and, at least according to British sources, 'excited the hostility of riverain Arab tribes against the expedition'.[10]

Another topic that arises from the reams of paperwork inspired by the expedition is the pioneering use of steamboats and the idea of transferring them, dismantled, by sea and land, to a distant place where they could be reassembled and launched. The whole project became tremendously complex, both logistically and technically, not to mention the financial aspect. 'John Laird Shipbuilders', the leading British company from Birkenhead, was naturally very interested in the prospects of the rapidly developing technology. The Scot, John Laird (1805–74), from Birkenhead had been the builder of many of the early iron steamers. In that same year, 1834, his brother and partner, Macgregor Laird (1808–61), established a company and received governmental assistance for his exploration (surveying and evaluating commercial prospects) of the Niger and one of its tributaries. From the early years of steamboat technology, both also established a close connection with Peacock.[11]

Chesney was, without a doubt, the central protagonist in a long, complicated and often almost fantastic execution of his plan:

> Again and again obstacles, physical, diplomatic, personal, threatened the collapse of the enterprise; and through all dangers and difficulties the leader, now 45 years old, preserved the coolness, courage, and determination which alone can justify a man in holding, as he did, that nothing was impossible to a strong will.[12]

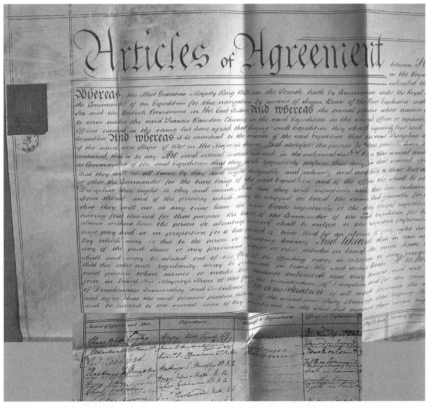

Fig. 18: Articles of Agreement between leader, Col. Francis Chesney, and officers and members of expedition with notes by J.B.B. Estcourt on fate of members, detail

Through all these obstacles he led his group, consisting of 53 men at base, with some others joining later. The fact that many of the problems the expedition encountered in the beginning could have been foreseen and thus at least partially avoided[13] does not change the heroic narrative of a group of stubborn officers, soldiers and civilians, fighting their way through and overcoming endless setbacks caused by natural and human factors.[14] All studies concerning the expedition devote long descriptions to the obstacles, difficulties and delays it encountered (for example, the arrival of the last boiler of the *Tigris* in Port William 329 days after the landing at the mouth of the Orontes, instead of the planned 13 days). The archival sources, ranging from the participants' accounts to numerous reports and documents, unintentionally recount a saga of men fighting impossible natural obstacles, unendurable diseases, unforeseen political difficulties and despair.

The loss of the *Tigris* in the twelve-minute hurricane which caused ten-foot high waves and claimed the lives of twenty expedition participants, was surely a kind of tragic climax in the heroic expedition, and naturally it had a deep effect on the British public.[15] Although it has not yet reached the movie screens, the narrative of this almost unbelievable effort and adventure has been the subject of some recent studies and even novels. Chesney's first summary of the expedition was published only in 1859,[16] although earlier drafts found in the archives testify that he was in fact working on the written material and the maps from as early as 1838. Francis Beaufort, John Washington (1800–63), as Secretary of the RGS, and cartographer John Arrowsmith (1790–1873), 'the Cartographer of the Queen', were involved in the process.[17]

Eliahu Elath in the 1950s, John S. Guest in the early 1990s and, to some extent, Ursula Naumann in the 2000s, all went to the trouble of going from one British archive to another, first the British Library and the Public Record Office and then some smaller ones, in order to try to reconstruct the narrative, its background and repercussions.[18] Needless to say, the vast body of literature about the expedition also recounts the incredible story of its deeds and adventures, from the moment it left Britain and up until its dismantlement. Consequently, there is no intention in this study to repeat the narrative in detail or even to reconstruct it in general terms. Rather, we are concerned with the various, sometimes hidden, links between the Euphrates Expedition and the study of the Jordan Rift Valley. Therefore, it is important to

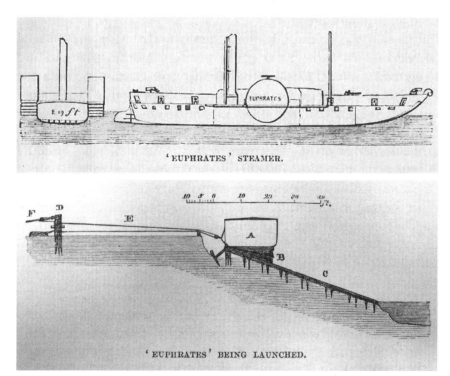

'EUPHRATES' STEAMER.

'EUPHRATES' BEING LAUNCHED.

Fig. 19: The Euphrates Expedition: 'Euphrates' Steamer; The Launch on wheels;
The Steamers Passing Tapsacus

point out some central facts, processes and events which will be of use later in the discussion.

Chesney was apparently quite disappointed with the attitude he encountered upon his return to London. Although famous and respected, he could not help but divulge his dissatisfaction. Accordingly, in a letter to Hobhouse recommending the decoration of Major James Bucknall Bucknall-Estcourt (1802–55) and Lieutenant Richard Francis Cleaveland RN, 'a skilled navigator and a tower of strength for the expedition' loaned from the navy to command the larger vessel, he felt the need to convince Hobhouse that it should be called 'a Naval Operation' whose 'operations were also Military'.[19]

In contrast to the British military and political world, the scientific milieu appreciated the expedition, its tremendous efforts and its innumerable scientific achievements. In 1838 the RGS decided to decorate Chesney with its 'Royal Premium' medal for 1837:

> [...] for his various travels in the East preparatory to the plan of the Euphrates Expedition; for the energy and perseverance shown by him in its general conduct & during its progress; and for the valuable material, both in comparative, mathematical & physical geography, resulting from the labours of that expedition, [...].[20]

Though of a geo-political nature and objective, the participants had conducted a tremendous amount of research in various fields, as described, for example, by Ainsworth:

> I made [...] many determinations of ancient sites, alone or in company of others, the details of which have not yet been given to the public. I crossed and re-crossed the plain of Babylonia [...] in order to determine satisfactorily the positioning of ancient sites, the course of its different canals of communication or of irrigation, [...]. The positioning of the mounds of Babylon determined in these explorations, [...] have since been adopted as correct [...]. Arrived at Bushire on the Persian Gulf, I made a personal exploration of the renowned passes of the Persian Apennines, visited the ruins of Persepolis [...].[21]

In addition to its strategic goal of facilitating the route to India, the expedition had some subsidiary ones, namely 'warning Russia away from Ottoman and Persian Territory, opening the country to Western commerce, gathering scientific and political data, and locating the sites of ancient cities'.[22] It seems that these were better achieved than the primary aim. Consequently, although there were many questions raised as to the success in attaining its political and economic goals, there was no doubt concerning the scientific significance and achievements of the expedition.

The outstanding cartographic achievements most likely surpassed all prior expectations. Chesney kept in constant touch with Beaufort and enlisted him as a consultant for the expedition. Their scientific work was universally praised, primarily, of course, by the officials of the RGS, who reported regularly at the meetings and published much of the written material as well as many of the maps. 'In spite of climate, delays, and difficulties that would have deterred any', declared Washington, these 'resolute officers and men' collected the needed materials for a correct map of Northern Syria, established a line and levels from the Mediterranean to the Euphrates, explored and surveyed greater parts of Mesopotamia, and surveyed the 1,200-mile-long Euphrates from Bírehjík to the Persian Gulf, followed by a line measured from Iskanderun to Bussora.[23] Some of the officers were also trained in magnetic measurements, which they performed regularly. The thirties and forties, and even later years, saw the building of the 'Magnetic Empire' led mainly by General Sir Edward Sabine (1788–1883) of the Royal Artillery.[24] Among those who participated in establishing the world's magnetic map was James Fitzjames RN (?–1848), 'destined to be one of the finest sailors of his generation', a born leader who excelled in the expedition as its best draughtsman. In 1840, already a lieutenant, he served in the naval expedition to Syria. In 1845 he sailed on the *Erebus* as second-in-command to Sir John Franklin (1786–1847), losing his life in the Arctic along with the entire crew of the two-ship expedition. There, too, Fitzjames's most important task was his magnetic measuring.[25]

But in the best geographical tradition of Humboldtian science, first and foremost in importance was, of course, the survey and its fruits – mainly maps, but also the papers and books which followed. The letters, reports, diaries and books are full of descriptions of surveying and measuring projects, positioning, leveling, collecting and registering of barometrical and other climatologic data, and more.[26] We have much evidence of natural history collections led by the expedition's naturalist, William Ainsworth, including 'considerable entomological

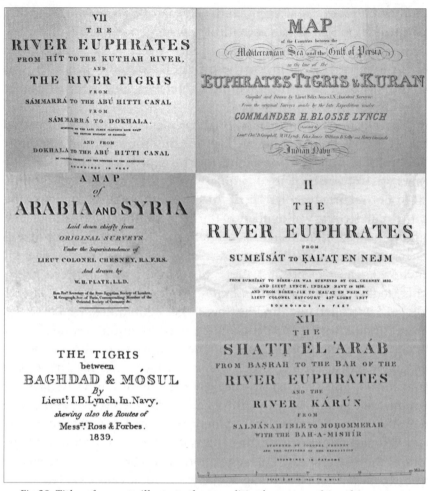

Fig 20: Titles of maps to illustrate the expedition's cartographic achievements

and botanical collections', specimens of which are now housed in collections all over Europe. Lieutenant Edward Philips Chalewood RN (1814–?) testified in his personal biography, printed in 1869 'for family circulation', that he collected snakes and raised them, and also told a story about a collection of centipedes.[27]

There is no doubt that the expedition also raised a tremendously high level of interest among European residents in the East. The American missionary John D. Paxton (1784–1868), for example, wrote about the attempt to establish regular communications between Damascus and the Euphrates, and later described the expedition and some of its participants whom he met in Beirut.[28]

Major-General James Bucknall Bucknall-Estcourt, Adjutant-General of Her Majesty's Forces in the Crimea, died on June 23, 1855, in camp before Sebastopol, of cholera, in his 53rd year. Educated in Harrow, he entered the army as an ensign. As a captain (later major) in the 43rd Light Infantry Brigade, he served between 1835 and 1837 in Chesney's Euphrates Expedition, where he was in charge of the survey and magnetic experiments.

After having been engaged in the Anglo-American boundary question, Estcourt was appointed to the staff of Lord Raglan (FitzRoy James Somerset, first Baron, 1788–1855) as Adjutant-General of the British forces, and participated in some of the Crimean battles until his sudden death from cholera, with his commander following twenty days later from dysentery. His papers are kept in the Gloucestershire Record Office, Gloucestershire County Council. In addition to family papers, these include vast material concerning the expedition, such as the full and exact texts of the agreement between Chesney and the officers and members of the expedition 'with notes by J.B.B. Estcourt on fate of members' (see fig. 18), Estcourt's letters to his family concerning the organization and progress of the expedition, extracts from his diary, a 53–page-long journal of his explorations along the Orontes River to Antioch and Damascus, to Diarbakir in 1835, from Baghdad to Beirut through the desert and to Malta following the dismantlement of the expedition in 1837. This archive also holds copies of journals by Caroline B. Estcourt, possibly prepared for publication.[29] Illustrating the memoirs is a reduced map from Chesney's survey of the Euphrates, drawn by J. & C. Walter and dated 1838.[30] The letters, which have already been used by Guest and Naumann to reconstruct the narrative of the expedition, remain an untapped resource for valuable data concerning the region's natural, cultural and scientific attributes.

In a letter to his father, probably from 1835, Estcourt urges him and the family to come for a long tour 'of visiting Baghdad, Babylon, Palmyra, Damascus, and Jerusalem', as 'the whole distance from India to this is as safe as any part of England'. His brother, Reverend William John Bucknall-Estcourt, 'accompanied the expedition during its earlier stages'.[31] 'I travel as a Bedouin', he wrote in another letter, a fact

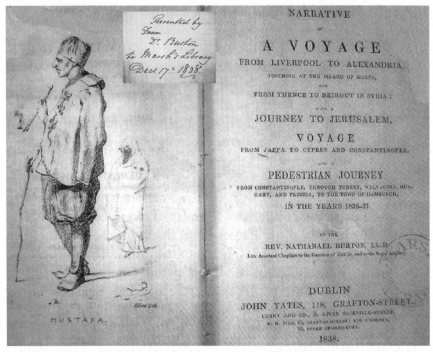

Fig. 21: Nathanael Burton, book and dedication

corroborated by Nathanael Burton (c.1794(?)–1897), Chaplain of the Garrison in Dublin, who traveled in the Near East and crossed paths with the expedition in Beirut during the first days of 1837 and

> [met with] some of the officers of the Euphrates expedition [...]; one of them, who has been in the navy, is dressed in a half Bedouin, half Turkish costume, yet all will not conceal the good-humoured laughing face [...]; he is on his way to England, and does not speak highly of the expedition.[32]

When Chesney decided in summer 1836 to go to India, Estcourt replaced him in command of the *Euphrates*. The decision to break off the expedition was made in January 1837, and Estcourt took his party across the desert from Baghdad to Damascus by camel. After suffering repeated attacks by Bedouins, they arrived in Damascus (where they resided with Consul Farren) on 14 February, continued to Beirut on 25 February and sailed to England via Malta, where 'we have arrived, thank God! Safe, sound and in glorious health'. They had to stay in quarantine, but on

3 March, Estcourt could report that they had departed for England and announce the 'final breaking of the expedition'.[33]

This itinerary shows that George Henry Moore must have met him in one of the abovementioned cities or in both. Moore and Beek, who were in Damascus on 1 February, left Beirut on 15 March on their way to the Dead Sea after a sojourn of some weeks. As will be discussed later, Moore was expecting a letter from Estcourt, a fact that hints at an earlier acquaintance, but there is no information as to the nature of the news Moore expected to receive. There is, however, at least one thing that would have been of common interest to Estcourt and Moore: the Lynches and their participation in the Euphrates Expedition, and more – the impressive role of Irish and Irish-connected people in the expedition.[34] Estcourt might have been the first to tell Moore about the loss of the *Tigris*, in which Lieutenant Robert Blosse Lynch, the younger brother, lost his life. The elder brother, Captain Henry Blosse Lynch, who was the commander of the *Tigris*, survived.[35]

There were many parallels between the two families, the Moores of Moore-Hall and the Lynches of Partry House, Parish Ballyovey, Balinrobe, County Mayo. According to the 'Genealogy of the Lynch Family', the founder arrived from Linz, Austria, in 1172, and his son was the first Lynch to settle in Galway. From that period on, the family history was strongly connected with this city, as, for example, '84 members of the Lynch family had been Mayors of Galway'. Arthur Lynch, third son of Sir Robert Lynch, of Currendullagh Castle, County Galway, settled in Mayo after having been granted the land in 1678, and in 1683 married Kathleen Blake of the Blake family of Lehinch, County Mayo. Sir Henry Lynch, fifth Bart of Castle Carra (?–1762), married Mary Moore. His son, Sir Robert Blosse Lynch, sixth Bart, in 1749 married the heiress of Tobias Blosse of Suffolk, who was a rich merchant in Persia, and assumed Blosse as an additional surname.

'The rise of the Lynch-Blosse family', wrote Patrick Melvin, 'shows how large land acquisitions were gained in their progress from early commercial fortune through municipal and public office.' The family estate, 1500 acres of land and the Partry House (origin: Partraigh, a tribe living there in ancient times), as everybody called it, 'A plain 2 storey 5 bay Georgian house with a central Wyatt window above a porch. Eaved roof',[36] had been acquired in 1667 and was called Cloonlagheen at the time. During the sixteenth, seventeenth and eighteenth centuries,

Fig. 22: Partry House, Mayo, 2005

various marriages took place between the Lynches and other noble Mayo families. Joseph Lynch (1744–85) was confirmed Protestant in 1766. Following his father and grandfather, he also married a daughter of the Blakes of Ballinafad. His son, Henry Blosse Lynch (1778–1823), a major who served under the Irish-born Arthur Wellesley, first Duke of Wellington (1769–1852) in the Peninsular War, married Elizabeth Finnis from Kent, having eleven sons. The Lynches of Partry had a coat of arms, as well as a motto (*Semper constant et fidelis*).[37]

The Moores and the Lynches were two of five noble families living around Lough Carra in the eighteenth and nineteenth centuries. They maintained close connections, and Mrs Elizabeth Lynch paid frequent visits to her friend, Louisa Moore. The Lynches had eleven children, with the boys usually enlisting in the army, infantry or navy in India. The combination of military and colonial service was one of the best ways for these people to find employment and subsequently establish a career, two goals which were difficult to achieve in Britain proper. Near the Lynch manor house, some hundred meters north of the house and in a beautiful secluded spot surrounded by ancient trees, in 1823 they established the last resting place for members of the family, 'at a point where Lough Mask and Lough Carra and the Connemara Mountains are in full view'. Out of eleven, only six of the children were still living in 1854, at which time the family erected a pyramidal monument in the family cemetery, a 'column of four sides, on each face and base of which are carved particulars as to those members of the family whose remains lie near'.[38] Many of the sons of Major Henry Blosse and Elizabeth Lynch chose 'the East as a career'; they were perfect examples of quite a few generations of British, mainly Irish and Scots:[39]

1. John Finnis (1805–55), Barrister of Law.
2. Robert Blosse (1806–36), Captain in the Bengal Army, had been highly distinguished in the first Burmese War. About to return to his regiment from a leave at home, he voluntarily joined his brother in the Euphrates Expedition, and lost his life in the sinking of the *Tigris*, aged 30.
3. Henry Blosse (1807–73), the third son, volunteered for the Indian Navy at the age of 16, serving in the survey of the Persian Gulf.[40] He displayed a special gift for eastern languages, and acquired outstanding knowledge of Arabic, Persian and Hindustani. Promoted to lieutenant in 1829, he served until 1832 as the formal interpreter to the Gulf squadron, whose ships measured and mapped the Arabian coasts and the Gulf, and to the Commodore of the Navy. He spent some time traveling in Arabia, and developed the position of the director of communications with Arab tribes and their 'shaykhs', his main occupation being endless negotiations with them. In that year he took a leave from the navy, and made his way home through the Red Sea to Ethiopia, and up the Nile to Egypt.

His abilities and experience made him the perfect candidate for Chesney, who chose him in 1834 as his second-in-command. Lynch was in charge of many delicate negotiations with various Arab tribal leaders, as well as with the often hostile governmental representatives. He was in charge of the landing of the British delegation at the Gulf of Antioch, the assembling of the two steamers, brought from England in parts, and their launch on the Euphrates. He then commanded the *Tigris* until its sinking, from which he managed to escape alive, although losing his brother. His relations with Chesney were always tense, including some major disagreements; Chesney once even wrote that 'preparations were already made to supersede him'.[41] In a letter to Hobhouse from early 1838, Lynch wrote that he had received a prospectus from Chesney, which 'contains many points in which I think him mistaken', and he hoped that 'Chesney will not command any more Euphrates Expeditions even if he is successful in getting one up which I fear is doubtful.'[42]

After the loss of the *Tigris* and the drowning of his brother, Lynch returned home in August and September 1836, revisiting Mosul and Trabzon on the way. It is impossible to determine whether he again met with Moore, who was, during these months, traveling in Syria. Chesney left the expedition in 1837, and Lynch was recommended by Hobhouse to be the commander of a continuation project, a steam flotilla that would patrol the two rivers. He commanded the never-before-accomplished ascent of the Tigris to Baghdad in order to establish this as a packet- and commercial line.[43] By 1839 he had finished surveying the river Tigris, reaching the highest point that had ever been reached by Europeans. The *Euphrates* continued serving in India, taking part in the effortless 1838 capture of Karachi.[44]

The Board of Directors of the East India Company sent three dismantled steamers around the Cape of Good Hope under the command of Lieutenant William Michael Lynch. The *Nimrúd*, the *Nitocris* and the *Assyria* were assembled and launched in the harbor of Bussora, and joined the *Euphrates* in Baghdad; now, four steamers flying the Union Jack, under the command of Commander H.B. Lynch, were sailing in the Gulf and on the Mesopotamian rivers. At first the whole flotilla navigated and surveyed the rivers, but then the authority was given to Lynch to maintain two steamers, and the others were removed to India.[45]

Simultaneously with his trigonometric survey of Mesopotamia in 1841, he was busy with his brother Thomas Kerr in a family enterprise, establishing a postal service between Baghdad and Damascus, together with establishing further commercial ties. After being on sick leave at home, Lynch returned at the end of 1841. Now a commander, he decided to continue with the surveys, but his disappointing conclusion was quite simple: The Euphrates 'is not well adapted for the purposes of steam navigation'.[46]

From 1842 he was again employed in India, both as a naval commander and in civil duties. He was an active member of the Bombay Geographical Society and founded the Indian Navy Club.

He was sent on very delicate diplomatic missions to Arab tribes, but sometimes his deeds were quite 'misinterpreted'. His service, from 1851, in the battles in Burma earned him the C.B.[47] Upon his return home he inherited the Mayo estate in 1855 and retired from the navy in the following year. He was sent by Palmerston to head the Paris negotiations with the Persian ambassador following the Persian War of 1856-7, which ended in the Treaty of Paris of 4 March 1857. The Great Rebellion in India in 1857 and the difficulties in sending reinforcements again indicated the need for a quicker route to the jewel of the Empire. Much was done to carry out a plan for a railway to the Euphrates; Lynch was also asked his opinion.[48]

In August 1838 he married Caroline Anne Taylor (1817-84), daughter of Colonel Robert Taylor, HM's Minister in Baghdad. The Persian Shah conferred upon him the Highest Order of the Lion and the Sun.

H.B. Lynch made a comprehensive contribution to the survey and study of the countries in which he traveled and worked, publishing in the *JRGS*[49] as well as in the journal of Bombay's Geographic Society and maintaining close ties with both organizations. Many maps also bear his name.[50] 'An accurate and daring observer from the school of Ormsby, Wellsted, and Wyburd', said Henry Cresswell Rawlinson (1810-95) in his 1873 Presidential Address to the RGS, 'but even more gifted than they as a scholar and linguist, and in having those rare qualities of geniality, tact, and temper, which command respect of the wildest, and win the confidence of less barbarous Orientals.'[51]

4. Edward Patrick (1809-84) served in India beginning in 1827. Belonging to a detachment of British officers and NCOs sent to Persia in 1833 as part of British policy to ensure Persia as a buffer against Russia and to support Abbâs Mirza, he fought with distinction and was also decorated by the Shah, receiving the Order of the Lion and Sun. Later, in the early 1840s, he fought in Afghanistan. He attained the rank of lieutenant-general.[52] A manuscript of his from this period, sent to the RGS, does not seem to have been printed. Leaving Ireland in February 1834, he decided that as 'the hunting season [was] over I determined in carrying out a long cherished wish to visit Turkey and Persia en route to join my regiment in India'.[53] There is no doubt that he had been encouraged by his brother's letters. He returned home in 1872 and published his 'narrative of our doings in Persia in 1834 & 5'; upon his death, he was buried in Partry.[54]

5. William Michael (1811–40), a lieutenant in the Indian Navy, died in 1840 at Diarbekir (other sources say in Argana, Armenia) on his way home for sick leave, while serving in the second Euphrates expedition.[55]

6. George Quested (1814–48), MD, served with the Euphrates Expedition, then returned home to lend a hand during the Irish famine; later he himself succumbed to typhus fever.

7. Brownlow (1817–54), reverend, Rector of Ballyhane.

8. Thomas Kerr (1818–91), a student at Trinity College, Dublin, joined his brothers on the second expedition and with them initiated and managed the Baghdad–Damascus postal service.[56] In 1840 the Lynch brothers formed a commercial house in Baghdad as well as another company aimed at financing trading steamers, called in London 'Lynch Bros., Ltd.', and in Baghdad 'Stephen Lynch and Company Ltd.', run by Thomas and their older brother John Finnis, barrister at law, who was probably the London representative. In the 1860s, it was 'The Euphrates and Tigris Steam Navigation Company', and he was its 'Chairman and Managing Director'. Thomas continued living in the East and traveling throughout Persia and Mesopotamia. After returning to England, he served as Persian consul-general in London and was made a Knight of the Persian Order of the Lion and Sun.[57] During the 1880s he published several books, in which he described the history of the navigation efforts, the political background and his family's role in the region from the 1830s.[58] Like his older brother, he married a daughter of Colonel Taylor, Harriet. Upon his death in 1891, he was buried in the family cemetery.

Fig. 23: Thomas Kerr Lynch: Silvercups, 1873

In addition to much material in his personal archive (marked HBL in the list of archives in this book), Major Henry Charles Blosse-Lynch (b. 1933) of Longcross House, Headley (Berkshire), who sold Partry in 1991, is presently the owner of various artifacts, including two magnificently decorated silver cups (see fig. 23), bearing the inscription:

> Presented to Thomas Kerr Lynch Esqr. by the Shareholders of the Euphrates & Tigris Steam Navigation Co. In acknowledgment of their sense of his long faithful and most successful exertions in the Management of an Enterprize which has been alike Beneficial to the Interest of its Promoters and to the Community on those rivers who were through its Agency first made Acquainted with the Inestimable Advantages of Steam Communication. 1873.

9. Stephen (1819–96), one of the founders of the Baghdad branch of Lynch Bros., Ltd. in 1841. At the age of twenty he also took a trip to the East, as indicated by John Acton, his neighbor from Castlebar, who spotted his name written in graffiti on a column in the Roman ruins at Baalbek. Acton, a surgeon in the navy, participated in the British expeditionary force of 1840, and while being stationed in Jaffa traveled in Palestine and recorded his impressions in a long letter, published in his hometown.[59]
10. Frederick (1821–34).
11. Arthur Noel Hill (1822–70), colonel in the Madras Army, distinguished in the Burmese War and in the Indian Mutiny.

Five of the Lynch brothers served in various units of the Indian Army and six of them participated in the Euphrates expeditions and/or the company later founded by the family. These significant numbers testify to the opportunities open to the Irish to engage in a military career, although these careers involved service outside the British Isles. The numbers also testify to the effect of family connections and to the commercial opportunities available in the East for entrepreneurs who were familiar with local cultures, languages and customs.

Of all the expedition's participants, Lieutenant Hastings FitzEdward Murphy (1798–1836), the second-oldest participant, brought with him the best and most professional experience in surveying.[60] Born in

County Kerry, Ireland, and educated at the Royal Military Academy in Woolwich, he participated from 1827 in the Ordnance Survey of Ireland, established in 1824 under Thomas Frederick Colby (1784–1852) RE, later major general, known as 'Colby Bar' for his use of 'compensation bars' in the surveying led by officers of the Royal Engineers. Within twenty years this produced a map of the entire island on a scale of six inches to one mile.[61] Appointed the Euphrates Expedition astronomer, Murphy was its leading mathematician, making much use of all of his acquired skills, including those in magnetic measures. He died in Bussora because, according to the French representative, Fontanier, like all newcomers, he despised precautions and came out of the sea at noon with his head exposed to the sun, consequently falling ill with a fatal fever.[62]

The expedition's medical officer, Charles Frederick Staunton of the Royal Artillery, was another one of its Irish participants, having studied at Trinity College and receiving his MD from the University of Dublin.[63]

William Francis Ainsworth, geographer, geologist, explorer and prolific writer, was probably the last participant of the expedition to die, and his RGS obituary mentions the fact that he was also 'the last of the 460 Fellows whose names appeared on the first list of the newly established [society] in 1830'.[64] After studying the cholera epidemic, he was appointed in 1833 surgeon at various Irish hospitals, including those in Westport, Ballinrobe, Claremont and Newport. This invites the interesting probability that he would have met George Henry Moore and the Lynches. His two degrees, from the Royal College of Surgeons in Edinburgh and from the École des Mines in Paris, made him an ideal candidate for Chesney, who was looking for people of double qualifications in order to reduce the number of participants and 'diminish the expenditure'.[65] It seems that from the beginning of the expedition, Ainsworth was occupied with making research forays. He constructed geological sections across northern Syria and the Taurus Mountains, discovered several deposits of commercially important minerals in Mesopotamia and Anatolia and explored a substantial part of southeast Persia:

> Attached as I was to the Surveying Party, and carrying out my zeal for geological and antiquarian research several excursions apart from the proceedings of the Expedition proper, I came in contact with places and scenes of which no mention is made in the official record.

I also explored the Upper Euphrates in company with Captain Lynch, upon which occasion we further surveyed portions of Mesopotamia, including the previously undescribed sites of Haran [...] and were enabled [...] to recognize the fatherland of Abraham [...].

I was deputed on the breaking of the expedition to explore certain portions of the mountainous regions of Kurdistan in the search for coal [...].[66]

From the very start, Ainsworth exhibited impressive mastery of both historical and contemporary sources on the region, including Wilbrand of Oldenburg (1212), Pierre Bélon (1547), Maundrell (1697), Richard Pococke (1738), Fredric Hasselquist (1751), Burckhardt (1810), as well as Beaufort and Callier.[67] He continued to perform numerous excursions. While returning from the expedition, he traveled through Persia, Kurdistan and Asia Minor. He later returned to the region, sent by the RGS and the Society for Promoting Christian Knowledge, to Mosul and Kurdistan. In both of these journeys he was accompanied by Christian Anthony Rassam (1808–72), a Chaldean-born resident of Mosul who joined the British Church Missionary Society (CMS) in Cairo and became its Arabic translator in Malta in 1832. He served as the principal interpreter for the expedition from 1835 to 1837.[68] Rassam maintained constant contact with the RGS, which at least partially financed his travels, though the second of these two missions was much less successful than the first. The stated reason for this excursion was to contact the survivors of the Nestorian Church and to purchase or transcribe ancient manuscripts, while 'the ulterior motive was to map and explore remote areas which were politically sensitive and possibly contained mineral deposits'. Ainsworth was arrested as he observed the battle of Nisib in 1839; the British ambassador secured his release, but his maps and plans were confiscated. Their irrelevance to the Nestorian Church exposed the real motives behind the expedition. He returned to Constantinople in late 1840, after borrowing much money on the credit of the RGS and leaving the latter with a bill nearly four times the size of the agreed-upon sum.[69] His impressive list of publications includes his narrative of the Euphrates Expedition, two later travels and a geographical commentary on an English translation of Xenophon's *Anabasis*.[70] In 1844 he published his *Travels in the Track of the Ten Thousand*, in which he summarized his *Anabasis* studies, claiming that out of the total distance of 3465 miles covered by the Greeks, there were less than 300 which he did not cover himself.[71]

John Bell had not been an original member of the expedition, but he was recruited in Malta, where he had been working as a school teacher, in order to head, together with Rassam, a team of 'twelve Arabic-speaking interpreters'. Being described as 'quite a young man, of adventurous disposition', he served mainly as Ainsworth's companion, until May 1836 when he was left behind at Beles. In 1843 he joined Harris's expedition to Ethiopia, thus meeting two other 'heroes' of our story, Roth and Beke, and becoming the bodyguard of the Ethiopian king.[72]

Henry Blosse Lynch's career, as described above, earns him a place of honor among the group of British officers, mainly from different units of the Indian army, who possessed a tremendous gift for oriental languages and an affinity for oriental habits and lifestyle. Their services were required, mainly from the 1830s, in order to establish British contacts with peoples, tribes and leaders of the entire region lying between the Persian Gulf and the Arabian Peninsula in the south, and Kurdistan, Armenia, Persia and Eastern Anatolia in the north.

James Raymond Wellsted (1805–42) could be described, at least professionally, as an almost twin brother of Lynch.[73] He began his career in 1828 as secretary to Captain (later Admiral Sir) Charles Malcolm (1782–1851), Superintendent of the Bombay Marine (1827–37), renamed the Indian Army in 1830 due to Malcolm's reforms. Wellsted joined Malcolm's brother, General Sir John Malcolm (1769–1833, Fellow of the Royal Society from 1824 for his *History of Persia* and *Memoir of Central India*), from 1827 the Governor of Bombay, who 'was one of the first to understand the "Great Game" by which Britain strove to keep Russia away from India'.[74] Wellsted's first experience with naval surveying, as well as with the inhabitants of the Arabian Peninsula, was in 1830, when he was appointed second lieutenant on the *Palinarus*, an East India Company ship under Captain Robert Moresby (1794–1863, some sources claim 1854), engaged in making 'the first systematic measurement' of the northern parts of the Red Sea. In January 1833 he reached and described Akaba and the island of Jezirat Pharoun.[75] Wellsted was mentioned in a testimony before an 1834 special parliamentary committee for the study of steam navigation to India as the person who proved the possibility of going to India by steamship through the Red Sea via Akaba, which was only a three-day trip from the Mediterranean.[76]

Returning in 1833, the ship, this time under Captain Stafford Bettesworth Haines (1802–60), was sent to explore and map the southern coast of Arabia. Later, in 1839, Haines commanded the troops who seized Aden, becoming its political agent and administering it until 1854. Wellsted left the ship on Socotra, explored the island for two months and sent his report to the RGS.[77] He continued his wanderings in different parts of Arabia, starting in Omân and Muskat (1835–7). The Government of Bombay, 'desirous of obtaining some insight into the real extent of power possessed by the Imám of Maskat', appointed him and equipped him for the journey. One of the widespread stories about his travels and achievements among the Arab tribes tells about his 1837 arrival at the Benu-bu-Ali tribe, which had fought gallantly against two British military expeditions. Wellsted succeeded in turning them into allies. The RGS conveyed its anticipation that some of the Indian Navy would follow Wellsted's example and also penetrate the inland provinces, while the Royal Society, for its part, accepted him as a member.[78]

In a delirium caused by high fever, Wellsted discharged both barrels of his gun into his mouth, but was only slightly wounded. He returned to service but, being wounded and physically and mentally ill, he died in 1842, aged 37. In addition to several papers published mainly in the *JRGS* and translated into different languages, his most important works were the two volumes published in London in 1837 in which he summarized his travels and research in Oman, the Sinai Peninsula and the shores of the Red Sea. Lieutenant Wellsted, wrote the reviewer for the journal:

> has been for upwards of ten years attached to the survey now carrying on the shores of Arabia, [...]; yet, not content with the daily routine of the survey, he has invariably profited by every opportunity of endeavouring to penetrate into the interior – of gleaning information respecting the natural history and statistics of the country, of the manners and customs of the various Arab tribes that people its coasts, and occasionally has been very successful in exploring remains possessing much antiquarian interest.[79]

Henry Alexander Ormsby (1811–?) joined the Bombay Marine in 1823, but resigned from the service and for three years traveled among the

Arab tribes. He adopted Arab clothing and habits, and by the time he reappeared in Bussora in 1830, he could pass as an Arab.[80] Taylor asked him to complete the survey of the upper Tigris, which had been begun by the Bombay engineer William Bowater (?–1830), joined by Taylor's brother James, who had already obtained from Daud Paşa (Georgian by birth and from 1817 Governor of Baghdad) a concession to run steamboats on both Mesopotamian rivers, as well as an interpreter, William S.A. Elliot (1807–c.1837). In August 1830 Bowater and Taylor were slain during a robbery.[81] Naturally, Ormsby was a respected fellow of the RGS, as well as of the Royal Society. On his survey he was helped by Elliot and by his good friend Wellsted, who also wrote an account of his travels.[82]

Describing Elliot's biography, which reads like a fantasy, Guest chose to present him as a dominant example of the 'varied cast of characters, good or bad but almost all of them recognizable as products of early nineteenth century'.[83] Born in India, educated in England, captured by the Russians while serving as a surgeon in the Ottoman Navy during the 1828–9 war, tortured and sent to Siberia, he returned to Turkey and decided to become a traveler. Ainsworth wrote of him that 'he had received a good education, and had been a medical student, but having come to the East, his passion for wandering became so great as to lead him to sacrifice everything, even his religion, in order to gratify it.'[84]

Consequently Elliot perfected his Arabic, converted to Islam and 'assumed the role of a dervish', becoming known as Dervish Ali. He met Taylor in Baghdad while traveling to India, and was sent as an interpreter on both Bowater's and Ormsby's missions. Continuing to India, he was placed in a 'lunatic asylum' but was released and returned to Baghdad. Taylor sent him to Anatolia on a mission to survey Xenophon's route, and then he joined the Euphrates Expedition in Fort William, where they were assembling the boats. He survived the sinking of the *Tigris* by chance, not being on board at the time of the storm. Naturally, adds Ainsworth, 'his habits were exceedingly flighty, and he could not be depended upon for a moment', but 'notwithstanding his peculiarities, [he was] of great use to the Expedition'.[85] He then chose to leave the group, returned to Syria and in 1837 perished in the desert.[86]

Captain James Felix Jones (1813/14–78), 'the well known Indian Surveyor', began his naval career as a midshipman on the *Pelinarus* under Moresby, surveying the upper parts of the Red Sea along with Wellsted;

this was the best possible cartographical training. Jones later wrote that it 'was carried on by a system of triangulation down either shore. The work was verified by frequent bases, by almost daily azimuths, by latitude, by the sun and stars observed on shore, by artificial horizons, and by chronometric differences'.[87] Jones was later employed in surveying the Maldive Islands, Ceylon, various areas in India and the coasts of Arabia. In May 1840 he joined Lieutenant C.D. Campbell in his Mesopotamian survey, and, leaving the ship at Beles, was sent in September 1841 across the Syrian Desert to Beirut to obtain supplies from the British forces which had just landed there. Educated in the British surveying tradition, he also connected the Euphrates and Mediterranean by chronometric measurement. He remained in Baghdad (a valuable map of which he published in 1853), commanding the *Nictoris* and proving the easy navigability of the Tigris to the Iraqi capital. Actually, he continued where Lynch had left off, sailing, traveling and surveying in Mesopotamia until 1853. He returned to the region as Political Agent for Persia in 1855, serving during the Indian Mutiny, until his retirement to London in 1862.[88]

3.1 BRITISH INTERESTS AND ACTIVITIES IN SYRIA AND PALESTINE

'I believe it is little known in England what treatment has been given to the British flag in the Levant, during the last four years', wrote Richard Robert Madden (1798–1886), an Irish physician, traveler and historian, in a letter from Smyrna dated January 1825:

> [...] it has been torn down in Cyprus [...], the consul's house has been plundered in Rhodes; in Sidon the flag has been trampled under foot; in Tyre the agent has been imprisoned, and the interpreter flogged; in Acre the drogueman [sic] is still in dungeon; in Beirut the consul has been insulted with impunity, and is no longer in relation with Abdallah Pacha...[89]

The situation changed dramatically from the late 1820s onward and mainly during the 1830s. Responsible for this, more than anybody else, was Palmerston, who, during that period, established the definition of British interests and imperial policy in the region extending between India and the Mediterranean, Arabia and Russia.

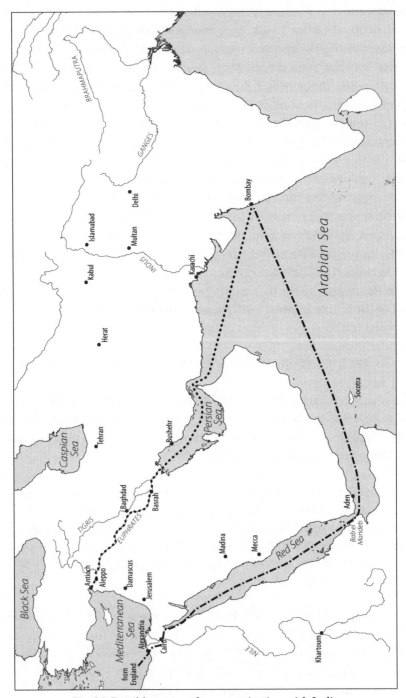

Fig. 24: Possible routes of communication with India

'Palmerston's foreign policy relied on playing off rival powers against one another to secure Britain's freedom of action.'; 'Turkey's survival was a British and European interest.'; these were Palmerston's principles which directed Britain's Middle Eastern policy.[90] The official British policy concerning the fate of the Ottoman Empire directly affected all British interests and actions in Syria and Palestine, as well as in their neighboring countries. The different possibilities of an 'Egyptian route' to India played a major role in these considerations. Chesney's correction to Napoleon's surveyors' mistaken judgment that there was a difference in level between the Red Sea at high tide and the Mediterranean (estimating that the latter was thirty feet higher) was a breakthrough. Thus, the 1830s saw the renewal of the possibility of digging a canal between the two. Britain had originally objected to the canal, not only due to the fear of a French-owned and -run project, but also because they did not want to strengthen the position of the Egyptian ruler vis-à-vis the Sultan.[91]

The British were busy gathering data in the countries bordering the Mediterranean to the east. Although this book does not deal with espionage during the 1839–41 wars, it is worth mentioning at least one high-ranking British intelligence agent – Palmerston's own expert spy in the belligerent countries. A Polish general, a certain 'Chrysanowski', had made a most favorable impression on him. This probably refers to Adalbert Chryzanowski (1788–1861), who had fought in the Russian Army against the Ottomans in 1829–30 and then, through Palmerston's mediation, was recommended to the Ottomans as an expert, described as 'a remarkably intelligent well informed little fellow'. Hüsrev Paşa (1756?–1855), the pro-Russian grand vizier of the young Sultan Abdülmecid and the arch-enemy of Mehemet Ali in the Sublime Porte, requested that Chryzanowski convert if he wanted to serve with them. The vizier probably had in mind Sulaymân Paşa 'al-Fransawi' (1788–1860), originally the French Colonel Joseph Sève from Lyon, who after 1814 sought employment in Egypt, converted to Islam and was the main figure behind the organization of the Egyptian army along French lines, ranking as *médecin-major*. 'To this officer', wrote a British observer, 'is due the credit of having, with infinite pains, patience, and perseverance, despite of jealousies, backbitings, and prejudices, and with but slight assistance from his subordinates, brought the Egyptian army to its present state of discipline...'[92]

Not wanting to convert to Islam, Chryzanowski fled, alarmed at being betrayed by the Ottomans and given up to the Russians, but the British brought him back and guaranteed him protection, and his reports and advice would be of great value to Palmerston regarding the plans for the 1840 campaign. The allied force participating in the 1840 campaign was much smaller than the number of troops commanded by Ibrahim Paşa and Sulaymân Paşa, but Chryzanowski's analysis and estimations of the actual strength of the Egyptian army and the value of its commanders ('Both Ibrahim and Soliman Pacha are only Generals third class whose reputation had mainly been promoted by French newspapers. I hear also that the latter [Soliman] is ready to sell himself, and here the question is asked whether he is worth this sail.'), which were later proved to be highly accurate, convinced the British that they could enter the campaign and win it.[93]

Following Consul Gordon, who sent Chesney as a military expert, all subsequent British representatives were equally active in data-gathering and sending long reports to London. The many studies which have made use of these accounts demonstrate how efficient all of these diplomatic representatives were in their reports.[94] But, whereas Chesney had been a military person, and his interests were focused accordingly, the consuls' reports dealt with every possible topic. The British network of consuls general in the eastern Mediterranean cities was appointed mainly through the first half of the 1830s, with the increase in British commercial, political and military interests in the area. These professional diplomats replaced the old consular agents, who usually belonged to well-established local Christian families. The new representatives were responsible for an articulate and accurate stream of information concerning the 1831–3 campaigns.[95] One such example was the decision to appoint Farren consul-general in Syria, whose seat was to be in Damascus. His nomination was reported by the French consul in Beirut on 15 December 1830, but his arrival was postponed for six months, until the beginning of the first Egyptian–Ottoman crisis. The strong opposition of the local population in Damascus followed by threats to assassinate him if he arrived in the Syrian capital, forced Farren to temporarily remain in Beirut. It should have been possible for him to move there following the Egyptian conquest of Syria, but he settled in the city only in January 1834.[96]

London. Published Oct. 1st 1856 by Day & Son, Gate Street, Lincolns Inn Fields

Fig. 25: David Roberts, Mehemet Ali receiving Col. Campbell, 1839, at his residence
in the naval arsenal in Alexandria

Colonel Patrick Campbell (1779–1857), royal artillery officer and
Consul General to Egypt (1833–40), was already an experienced diplomat,
having served from 1825 in the British legation in Colombia.[97] In 1836
he presented the consuls in Damascus, Aleppo and Beirut with a long
list of questions concerning their countries. He was answered by Niven
Moore (1795–1889), acting consul in Beirut from 1835 to 1853, already
a veteran of service in the Levant, whose appointment in the summer
of 1835 was a step in Palmerston's reorganization of the service.[98] Farren
in Damascus, and Nathaniel W. Werry, vice-consul in Aleppo, also sent
their statements. These long reports, as well as another one from Moore
dated 28 February 1838, and a 'Statistical and Commercial Report of
the Northern Part of Ibrahim Paşa's Dominions by William Burckhardt
Barker', also dated 1838, were added as an appendix to a much longer
document. It is possible to identify a direct thread leading from these
reports to the British–Ottoman commercial treaty, signed at Balta Liman
on 16 August 1838.[99]

John Bowring (1792–1872), one of the preeminent British statesmen
of his time, an accomplished linguist who was fluent in twenty languages

87

and competent in eighty more, was already well known for his two-volume report on British–French commercial relations, published in 1835-6. In 1840, following a tour of the region on Palmerston's instructions and with war imminent, he addressed his 'Report on the Commercial Statistics of Syria'[100] to Palmerston and presented it to both houses of Parliament. This appears to be one of the most detailed and conclusive reports concerning the region, not only for its time, but also for many years to come. In addition to Bowring's report, in the same volume of the *Reports of the Commissioners* in the British Library are included various contemporary additional accounts concerning the military delegation and 'Correspondence relating the affairs in Syria'.[101]

The possibilities, along with the advantages and disadvantages, of steam navigation to India were discussed at length in the reports. These included 'the opinions of a gentleman long resident in Syria and intimately acquainted with Oriental politics', possibly old Consul Barker, who recommended first getting over the impediments demonstrated by Chesney and placing Syria 'under a good & permanent government'.[102] It must be stressed here that British strategy was about access, not control. Britain was above all interested in the harbors and the roads leading to and from them.

Palmerston probably had no illusions as to the real interests of the other powers. It was obvious that France would do everything it could to counterpoise British naval hegemony in the Mediterranean. It had begun implementing its North-African imperial ambitions in 1830, intentionally neglecting Egypt and concentrating on the building of its empire in the Maghreb, in order to secure its eastern flank. Supporting Mehemet Ali could have been one good way to achieve both goals. Palmerston, whose view was bolstered as the crisis in the eastern Mediterranean countries deepened and intensified, accepted the view that Syria was now the military key to all the lands of Asiatic Turkey, and advocated a policy of intervention. But he also estimated that the French would do anything to help the Egyptian ruler, as long as it did not involve entering a war, which would be too hazardous for them.[103]

Following a visit to Jerusalem in the autumn of 1836, Farren recommended that the Foreign Office appoint a vice-consul to the city. This suggestion sparked a period of dispatches and considerations, involving the foreign ministers in London, as well as Farren and Consuls

Campbell in Cairo and Moore in Beirut. According to Meir Vereté, this was the process that led to Palmerston's decision to open the Jerusalem consulate.[104] Jerusalem was probably the last consulate to be opened, with the final decision made at the end of 1838 and William Tunner Young arriving at the beginning of the following year.[105] Syria and Palestine were not of special importance by British calculations, with the exception of their being situated on some strategic and commercial routes. But, following the Egyptian conquest, Palmerston was convinced that a new independent state under Mehemet Ali was liable to become an ally of Russia against both Turkey and Persia. This would, of course, pose a considerable threat to vital British interests. In 1836 the British were aware of Russian interference, sometimes in collaboration with the Egyptians, with the Euphrates Expedition, with their attempts to establish a consul in Aleppo, and mainly through what they perceived as an active increase in the Russian presence, pilgrimages to and activity in the Holy Land. As a matter of fact, the British had opened a number of consulates in Asiatic Turkey only in reaction to the establishment of Russian ones there.[106] In this relatively early paper, Vereté convincingly makes his pioneering argument that the reasons for establishing the Jerusalem consulate had nothing to do with the 'Restoration of the Jews' nor was it connected to the political pressure of the 'Evangelical crusader in politics', Anthony Ashley Cooper, seventh Earl of Shaftesbury (1801–85), as is conventionally accepted in early as well as later studies:

> The decision [...] derives from what Farren wrote on the matter [...]; from the serious Anglo-Russian rivalry of the time; and from what appears as the Foreign Secretary's systematic policy of having a wide network of Consulates in the Sultan's dominions, more particularly where the Czar established his own or where his agents were suspected of having become unduly active.[107]

Why had Young been chosen as the first representative to Jerusalem? Vereté's answer is surprisingly simple. His appointment had nothing to do with any former experience or proven personal abilities, but simply because Campbell, Farren and Moore, as well as missionary John Nicolayson (1803–56) in Jerusalem, had gotten to know him on a twelve-month visit he conducted to the Levant beginning in late 1835, where he had developed some commercial ideas with them.[108]

British documents reveal the steady concern of the leadership in London, led by Palmerston and beginning in 1837, regarding an Egyptian advance not only northward into Asia Minor, but also eastward toward Baghdad and the Persian Gulf. Such a move, the likes of which had been accomplished by the Egyptian army in Arabia, would put the two important routes between Europe and Asia – the Red Sea and the Persian Gulf – within reach of the Egyptian ruler 'who might conceivably join hands with Russia in the valleys of the Tigris-Euphrates'. In a sense, the Egyptian threat to the Persian Gulf was resolved with the British–Ottoman conquest of Acre in early November 1840, described later in this chapter.[109]

The struggle between advocates of the northern and southern routes continued throughout the 1840s and 50s. One of the earliest plans connected with this struggle dates to 1834. A British railroad engineer by the name of Thomas Galloway arrived in Cairo in 1833 and submitted a memorandum to Mehemet Ali proposing two alternatives for the transport of British freight and post: carriages operating on the route from Cairo to Suez, or the construction of a railroad. Galloway thought that freight could be transported by boat from Alexandria to Cairo's Nile port of Boulak. The ruler answered on 8 June 1834, opting for the second alternative and demonstrating his enthusiasm for the project; he also granted Galloway the title Bey. Certain of the benefit to Britain and not suspecting any British hesitation in the matter, Mehemet Ali did not wait for a formal reaction and sent Galloway to England to order the necessary equipment. But London, deeply involved with Chesney's Euphrates project, refused to grant the necessary funding due to regional considerations (the negative attitude of the Sultan, the sensitive situation in the Near East). Galloway himself died unexpectedly and the political struggles in the Orient brought commerce to a halt. The French immediately reacted by raising the canal option.[110]

The idea of a railroad was revived in the mid-1840s by John Alexander Galloway, who wanted to finance it through a portage tax that would be levied by Mehemet Ali. Although this project proved unfeasible, Galloway continued to argue against the canal project. Above all it was clear, as emerges from a report from 1845, that had Egypt been a British colony, Britain would have financed the digging of the canal, but it would not do such a thing for another country that was perceived as being controlled by France.[111]

This highly interesting report, published in a German journal of architecture, includes an addition by the editor describing another plan, this time by Major Sir William Cornwallis Harris (bap. 1807–48), Engineer of the Bombay Army and well known for his previous travels and political-economic missions. In June 1845 he joined the advocates of the Egyptian railway, with a more feasible idea. He offered the East India Company to build a railway between Cairo and Suez which would enable the transportation of merchant ships of up to 800 tons. He wrote that it would require locomotives with steam engines three times more powerful than the ones used, as well as a wider track gauge. Naturally the sails of the ships would have to be dismantled. Since the distance could be covered in a mere six hours, one track would suffice.[112] Though he did not have Harris's calculation in hand, the editor of the journal went into very detailed calculations in order to demonstrate the practicability of the idea. In his view, under certain circumstances and with an exact approach to weights, sizes and costs, it was certainly applicable and even made much sense economically.[113]

The grave of the British brigadier-general, Edward Thomas Michell (1786–1841), marked by a large tombstone, is located in the old, very neglected and almost inaccessible Protestant cemetery in Jaffa. A graduate of the Royal Military Academy in Woolwich in 1802, Michell enjoyed a significant career in the Royal Artillery, fighting mainly in the Iberian Peninsula. In 1840 he had been dispatched to Syria as commander of the land forces – Royal Artillery, Sappers and Miners, as well as Royal Engineers – sent with Admiral Robert Stopford's (1768–1847) fleet to assist the Ottomans in driving the Egyptian army under Ibrahim Paşa out of Syria and Palestine.[114] The British joined the Turkish forces under German General August Giacomo Jochmus (1808–81) in their advance.[115]

Jochmus was a quintessential nineteenth-century mercenary. Born in Hamburg, Germany, he joined the Greek Rebellion in 1827 and his career advanced rapidly, such that in 1832 he was appointed to the general staff of Otto I (1815–67), the Bavarian prince who in 1832 was crowned as the first king of independent Greece.[116] Leaving Greece in July 1835, he saw combat until the end of 1838 in the Iberian Peninsula. As early as December 1838 he was sent by Palmerston to Constantinople as a coordinator for the coming war against the Egyptians, and in July 1840 he was once again appointed head of the Joint General Staff. After the battles, he stayed on at the Ottoman Ministry of War until 1848 when, aged 40 and highly decorated, he could retire and return to Germany.[117]

Michell was present at the battle of Mejdel, 15 January 1841, after which the Egyptians retreated from Palestine. Nine days later he died of fever and was buried by his sappers in the left flank of the Sir Sidney Smith bastion of Jaffa. John Acton, an Irish naval surgeon who participated in the military expedition, counted 'one general and two colonels victims to Syria in five months'. As an eyewitness, he stressed a fact usually missing from the other descriptions, namely, that the biggest problem the armies had to contend with, often without much success, was 'the fearful plague', which claimed numerous casualties among the Europeans. Their continuous efforts to fight it were usually unsuccessful, and 'we must only trust to the mercy of that God'.[118]

Fig. 26: General Michell's Tomb, Protestant cemetery, Jaffa

One of the colonels was William Walker of the Royal Marines, who is commemorated in Acre alongside Major Olfield.[119]

European military intervention in the Near East in the modern era undoubtedly began with the French invasion and the concurrent British military activity on various fronts, including in Palestine. Many sources and studies emphasize, for example, the active participation of officers and sailors from British ships, including their commander, Sydney Smith, in the defense of Acre against Napoleon. The presence of the British flotilla forced the French to concentrate their attacks only on one tower, the northeastern one, which was out of the British range of fire:

> [...] Napoleon, pointing to Acre, said to Murat, 'The fate of the East depends upon yonder pretty town.' Constantinople and the Indies, a new empire in the East, and a change in the face of the whole world! Eight times he led his veteran soldiers to the assault; eleven times he stood the desperate sallies of the Mameluke sabers. British soldiers [...] came to the aid of the besieged; the muzzles of British and French bayonets touched each other [...].[120]

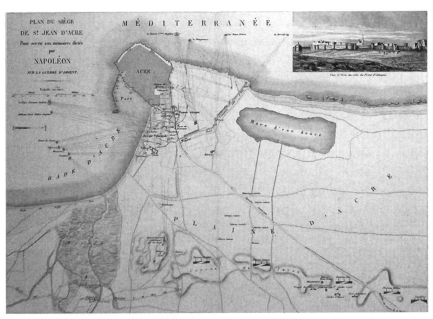

Fig. 27: Plan of the siege of Acre, for use in Napoleon's dictated itinerary of the war in the East

Modern scholars follow this view, claiming, for example, that 'the battle for Acre was the battle for Syria and command of the Silk Road.'[121] Both sides faced difficult and cruel fighting; both showed tremendous stubbornness and persistence.

Sydney Smith became a key figure in the campaigns and afterwards. On his ship, *Tigre*, he brought his old friend, the French Royalist, Artillery Colonel Louis-Edmond Antoine le Picard de Phélippeaux (1767–99), who in early 1798 had helped him to escape from a French prison. Phélippeaux and six more 'volunteering' French officers, comrades of Sydney Smith, had been dispatched to Acre where they were of great assistance to Djezzar Paşa in fortifying the city and later in defending it. One of the most important projects was the erection of 'a second advanced work on the left face opposite the palace of the Pacha', built according to Phélippeaux's instructions and supervision before he died on 2 May of fever caused by exposure and fatigue.[122]

After Napoleon's defeat in Acre, Sydney Smith was the one to order his fleet to lift the blockade on Alexandria, enabling him to take two ships, five generals and all the money left in the army treasury, and sail to France.[123] The British military intervention continued until the French army evacuated Egypt. After rejecting the safe-passage terms of the el-Arish Convention of January 1800 – a brilliant move by Sydney Smith which was supported by Lord Elgin and Henry Dundas, first Viscount Melville (1742–1811, from 1793 secretary of state for war) – the British government found itself again obliged to dispatch troops to Egypt. The 15,000 soldiers under the aged and highly experienced General Sir Ralph Abercromby (1734–1801), commander of Britain's troops in the Mediterranean, landed near Alexandria in order to find a way to abrogate the French military presence in Egypt. During the furious battles, Abercomby was severely wounded and evacuated, consequently dying and being buried in Malta. It was only after these battles and the help of many Ottoman and 6,000 Indian troops under the command of General David Baird (1757–1829) that the French laid down their weapons and left, on exactly the same terms as those of the el-Arish Convention.[124] British forces remained in Egypt until March 1803. The two-year occupation was spent in discussions between the British military and politicians, as to whether to support the Ottomans and retain them as rulers of Egypt, or – and this was the position of the commanders of the occupation force – to leave the country under the leadership of the Mameluk beys.[125]

Due to continuing French efforts in the East, and the British belief that the 'French threat to India via the Middle East had not faded with their defeat in Egypt', Britain in 1807 had conducted two unsuccessful military operations – a naval maneuver against Constantinople and a land operation into Egypt. The British force took Alexandria, but could not advance because of Mehemet Ali's resistance. The Treaty of Tilsit, signed by Napoleon and the Tsar, changed the geo-political situation entirely, including in the East. Turkey, now completely exposed to Russia, was eager to receive British assistance, and the occupation force returned home.[126] There would be no direct European military intervention in the East for the next thirty years, although the European powers did take part in the Greek War of Independence against the Ottomans and the Egyptians in 1821; and they succeeded in solving the crisis of 1831–2 through intensive diplomatic activity. All these events paved the way for the strong intervention of the early 1840s in favor of the Sultan and against Mehemet Ali.[127]

The narrative of European military intervention in Lebanon and Palestine in 1840, with its internal, regional and international background and justifications, as well as its course and results, would have to wait many years to receive a detailed scientific reconstruction. It was treated by some of the dominant participants in their recollections, but accounts of it were usually relatively short in studies of European policy and activity in the region during the nineteenth century.[128] The awaited narrative reconstruction came only in 2000: in a paper by Andrew Lambert recounting the intervention from the British point of view; a study by Caesar E. Farah, based on intensive use of documentary material, but with a slight anti-European bent probably adopting Edward Said's arguments; and the highly valuable work of Muhammed H. Kutluoğlu, which makes particular use of Ottoman sources and documents.[129]

The origins of the European campaign of 1840 may be identified already in the Greek Revolt and in the European intervention surrounding it, which reached its climax at the Battle of Navarino (20 October 1827).[130] Then came the campaigns of the early 1830s, but there is probably no doubt that the chain of events following the 1838 Druze Revolt ultimately convinced Palmerston that he must intervene. These included Ibrahim Paşa's bitter campaign to quell the Druze rebellion, the battle of Nissib of 24 June 1839, the sudden death of the Sultan five days later and the elevation of young Abdülmecid, followed by the appointment of Hüsrev Paşa as grand vizier and the desertion of his enemy, the kapudân paşa, to Egypt. Kultluoğlu demonstrated that much of the crisis and its development can be ascribed to the deep and uncompromising enmity of Hüsrev for Mehemet Ali as well as for some high-ranking Ottoman officials.[131] The Eastern Question had to be solved, and this had to be done according to British interests, in order to deny any advantages to France or Russia.

It must be noted that de facto British military intervention had begun some years earlier. British military men were continuing Chesney's tradition, and, as similarly demonstrated above in the case of the Persian Gulf and Arabian Peninsula countries, they were actively gathering information wherever they could concerning military possibilities. This had also been done by various participants of the Euphrates Expedition, mainly Lynch, Estcourt, Ainsworth and Chesney himself, who endlessly traversed the countries south and north of their route between Antioch and Bir. Farren, the effective and dependable consul-general for Syria, induced Palmerston to send his 'major spy', Richard Wood (1806–1900), to prepare the groundwork for a revolt in Syria against the Egyptians. Wood, a Catholic brother-in-law of Consul Moore in Beirut, was believed to have entrée with the Maronites. Together with Ambassador Ponsonby he was also actively involved in the Druze Revolt, of course with Palmerston's active support. Wood failed in his efforts to convince the Druze leader, Emir Bashîr Shihab II, to abandon his loyalty to the Egyptians, and therefore, with the help of Commodore (later Admiral Sir) Charles Napier (1786–1860), commander of HMS *Powerful* (84 guns), he carried out the Sultan's *firman* and on 8 October deposed the Emir and appointed a replacement.[132] Following the occupation of Beirut, Wood was appointed as vice-consul, and later stationed as consul in Tunis. Farah emphasized the important role played by local rebellions in Lebanon, first in Deyr al-Qamar and in other Maronite centers (May 1840), which the Egyptians had suppressed, and afterwards in Beirut, led by the Maronite and Orthodox patriarchs and actively supported by both English and French consuls. Interestingly enough, the French consul followed instructions from his government to support the Maronite insurrections.[133]

As early as December 1838, anticipating a military campaign, Palmerston sent the young General Jochmus to Constantinople to meet with Ponsonby and draw up 'a plan of a campaign for the probable war in Syria'. He summoned the London convention 'For the Pacification of the Levant' in July 1840. Mehemet Ali's refusal to comply with its conditions provided the British PM with the *casus belli* he was probably seeking and he could send his troops to 'get rid of Mehmet Ali. [...] Kick him out neck and crop and his army too'. Since the British viewed Syria as the key to the Levant, and Lebanon as the key to Syria, there was no hesitation on their part. Although stressing the role of the locals – Maronites and Druze – in expelling the Egyptians, Farah could not deny that much of the campaign had been initiated and supported by the work of British agents.[134]

In the meantime, Palmerston, estimating that the French would not fight for Mehemet Ali, had to encourage the Ottomans not to surrender to the latter's demands. He could then mobilize his fleet, the Mediterranean Squadron, under the seventy-two-year-old, experienced and cautious Admiral Sir Robert Stopford.[135] Serving as Commander-in-Chief in the Mediterranean since 1837 with his flag ship *Princess Charlotte* and 'filling the fleet with his sons and nephews', Stopford, already sixty years in service, was instructed, in August 1840, to demand, and if necessary to enforce, the restoration of the Turkish ships that had been delivered to Mehemet Ali upon the desertion of the Ottoman admiral, with the objective of removing Ali's forces from Syria. By moving rapidly, he believed he could avert the danger of war with France, which naturally actively supported the Egyptian ruler. Palmerston discovered that Stopford, unaware of the wider political implications, favored Mehemet Ali, and 'both as a Tory and as an elderly and cautious officer, he was unsuited to command in this complicated situation, which was little short of war'. Palmerston found the solution by working directly with Stopford's second-in-command, Commodore Napier, a personal and political ally who dismissed the admiral as 'a superannuated twaddler'.[136]

Napier's patron was Henry Dundas, Treasurer of the Navy. The Commodore has been described everywhere as a big man, very unconventional in his dress and behavior and with a distaste for superiors, who had already demonstrated his abilities in the 1810 Peninsula War and in the early 1830s as Commander-in-Chief of the

Portuguese Navy. With this direct channel to Palmerston, Napier could promote his initiatives without the permission of his military superior, as pointed out by Andrew Lambert:

> His commander-in-chief, Admiral Sir Robert Stopford, was an elderly Tory, entirely out of sympathy with the Whig government and its policy, when he understood it. Palmerston and his close friend Lord Minto, the first Lord of the Admiralty, selected Napier to inject a little vigour into Stopford. This was a stroke of genius, for in the following year Palmerston would have need of a covert means of making war.[137]

The naval force under Stopford's command was impressive in size and power. It included thirty-three ships of the Royal Navy, the biggest of 104 guns, eight Austrian and two Ottoman ships.[138] The attached land forces numbered 5,300 Ottomans commanded by Jochmus, 1,500 British and 200 Austrian soldiers.[139] The naval commanders were aware of the fact that winter was arriving, and the assault had to be finished before November. In fact, on 2 December the *Zebra*, with 16 guns, was wrecked in a gale off Mount Carmel.[140]

Adopting the policy of cutting off the Egyptian forces from their supply source, Haifa was taken on 18 September, Tyre on the 24th and Sidon on the 25th. The Egyptians were defeated everywhere while allied troops landed at Junieh and forced the evacuation of Beirut.[141] In all of these battles, Napier also assumed command ashore, replacing Colonel (from October 1840 Major-General) Sir Charles Felix Smith (1786–1858), later commander of the Sultan's army in Syria and of all allied land forces, who fell ill and after recovering was severely wounded during the capture of Acre.[142] Napier 'had always reckoned soldier's work was simple and proceeded, not without a good deal of posturing, to prove his point'. His unconventional tactics, including first storming Sidon, contributed significantly to the relatively easy British victory. On 10 October, Ibrahim's forces, led by Sulaymân Paşa, were forced to retreat from the Bekaa, the inner part of Lebanon. Stopford received orders to attack Acre, which he did successfully on 3 November 1840, not without an incident involving the disobedient Napier:

> On 2 November the fleet attacked. The plan was for the southern watergate to be breached by naval gunfire, allowing Turkish marines to storm the fortress. Napier requested command of this operation,

Fig. 28: Ships positioned facing Acre from the west, 3 November 1840

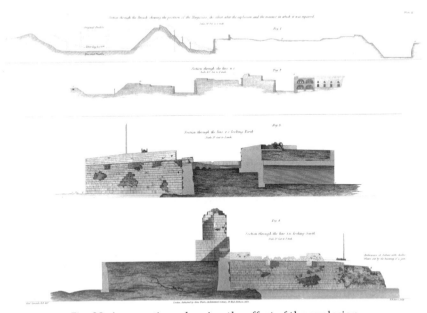

Fig. 29: Acre, sections showing the effect of the explosion

but instead had to be content with leading the diversionary attack on the west face of the fort, as his flagship drew too much water. On the day of battle Napier, displaying his usual initiative, led his squadron in from the north, rather than the south as ordered. He anchored expecting his followers to pass on his disengaged side and continue the line; instead, relying on Stopford's order they all anchored astern, as if they had run in from the south. Stopford was able to rectify their lack of thought by ordering in the reserve ship, but the confusion caused a good deal of ill feeling. The attack was a great success, a shell detonated the main Egyptian magazine, killing over a thousand men. The Egyptians evacuated the city before the allies could land.[143]

In a summary of his long discussion of Napier's biography, Lambert writes:

> Misunderstood and maligned in an age that valued form above function, Napier, more than any other naval figure of the era, represented the spirit that made the Royal Navy the greatest fighting service in the world. He was professional, brave, intelligent, and above all thoroughly at home in any sea or river. [...] He was invariably abreast or ahead of the latest technology, realized that men and not ships win wars, and cared enough for his country to ignore orders and break rules to advance its cause.[144]

Though it had also been described as a 'small, undermanned peace-time fleet', 'the fire of the British fleet was outstanding, both for its rapidity and its precision'.[145] Notwithstanding, the city was taken quickly and easily primarily due to this explosion. The allies were thus able to overcome the fortified city, whose walls had been considerably strengthened following the consultation and work of another European fortification expert, the Polish lieutenant-colonel, Auguste Schultz, known as 'Joussef Aga, Chef de Génie au service du vice-roi d'Egypte'. Schultz, who was wounded in the explosion, had been working on the fortifications as early as 1833, and commanded the gunnery from the besieged city to the British ships.[146]

Confronting his impossible military situation, Mehemet Ali accepted the terms of the British commanders, who were eager to finish the war. He pulled what was left of his forces back into Egypt and was granted the Sultan's pardon. The fleet returned to Istanbul and the Ottomans returned to Syria and Palestine. Wood, who had been the great winner, continued to play a leading role in Lebanon's internal politics, actually appointing the new leaders of the country. Palmerston promoted him to the position of consul and assigned him to Damascus.[147]

The bombardment of Acre had been used as a large-scale experimental field for 'testing the merits of a new system of gunnery' introduced into the British navy by Thomas Hastings (1790–1870) on board the *Excellence* at Portsmouth.[148] It had been such a success, wrote Colonel Ralph Carr Alderson (1793–1849), that its impression was still vivid three years after the bombing. In summary, Alderson drew up some recommendations for placing and using naval batteries in case of a sea-and-land battle against a fortified city.[149]

There was another interesting connection between one aspect of the Syrian campaign and the Euphrates Expedition, namely, the introduction of steam into 'the naval arena of the Royal Navy'. The campaign, described as amphibious in nature, though still using mainly sailing battleships, also made much use of paddle steamers as supporting boats for a variety of needs. On 3 November 1840, Napier and others also suggested these be used for towing the heavy ships into position, but here nature intervened and a shift in the winds made it possible to sail, take up positions and begin the bombardment without delay.[150]

Edward Philips Charlewood, Gunnery Lieutenant on HMS *Benbow*, testified that he had been the first to pull a trigger in the Syrian campaign. He was later credited for his part in the (unsuccessful) attack upon Tortosa on 26 September. Almost exactly three years earlier, along with his companions on the Euphrates Expedition, he had been sitting on the beach in Beirut, waiting for the steamboat that would take them back home.[151] Charlewood had also been one of Chesney's supporters in the expedition, writing very warm words about him in his autobiography. He achieved the rank of admiral, and his son married Emerilda, Chesney's daughter.

The next trigonometric mapping after Jacotin, which was meant to include all of Palestine but was also uncompleted, was initiated and conducted by British army officers, who had been part of this military campaign.

3.2 BRITISH MILITARY SCIENTIFIC ENTERPRISES IN PALESTINE
FOLLOWING THE 1840 CAMPAIGN

More than forty years separate the first trigonometric measurement of Palestine, conducted by Jacotin and his team in 1799, and the second such project. The latter was carried out in 1841 by a number of British officers and also included parts of Syria and Lebanon, though the measurement of Palestine proper was conducted mainly by a young officer of the Royal Engineers, Lieutenant John Frederick Anthony Symonds (?–1852).[152] He belonged to the group of Royal Sappers and Miners, Royal Engineers and additional officers who were trained in surveying and who had accompanied the troops dispatched to Syria in the summer of 1840. Yolande Jones described the course of events in her pioneering 1973 paper[153] as follows: the first to land were the Royal Engineers – Lieutenant Edward Aldrich and Major Ralph Carr Alderson, the latter taking the command – joined by Lieutenants Charles Francis Skyring and Symonds as heads of the groups of field surveyors. They were later joined by some staff officers, Majors Frederick Holt Robe (1801–72), Richard Wilbraham and Charles Rochfort Scott. Among these, only Scott could apparently claim an acquaintance with the East, as indicated in his two-volume book published in 1837.[154] The surveyors erected their own central camp, where Alderson received and signed all of the sketches. The camp is described vividly by John Acton, who was appointed the expedition's 'Medical Attendant':

> Our camp lies on the sea shore, or nearly so, commanding a view of more than 150 miles in expanse of the Mediterranean, opposite to us lies St. Jean D'Acre, in beautiful view, and within two miles the town of Caiffa, whence we procure all necessaries in abundance. An old building in the side of the mountain had been fitted up by the men, each of whom is a first rate tradesman, into a spacious mess room, which we have carpeted and lighted by a brilliant lamp, with a balcony which commands a view which you travel far to see.[155]

They began measuring and mapping the fortifications of several coastal towns and villages. Nineteen sheets of the original maps are presently kept in the British National Archives in Kew,[156] but these do not include the entirety of what they produced.

Maps Prepared by the British Officers[157]

No.	Description of Map	Size in mm
a.	Plan of the South East Front of St. Jean D'Acre showing the state to which its defenses were reduced by the explosion that took place, during and subsequent to the attack on the fortress in November 1840 C. Rochfort Scott	228 × 270
b.	Reconnaissance of Gaza of the village of Harrat It Te Fear and Sejaeah By Lt. Aldrich R. Eng. Scale 200 yard to an inch June 1841. Camp Mt. Carmel (signed) Aldrich, 11.5.1841, Colonel Alderson	450 × 560
c.	Plan of Jaffa 10.6.1841 Taken from a sketch by Major Robe, Assistant Quarter Master General (signed) Skyring, June 1841, Alderson 10.6.1841	420 × 255
d.	Plan of the Town and Environs of Jerusalem Scale 400 ft. to an inch (signed) Skyring, June 1841, Alderson 10.6.1841	550 × 440
e.	Plan of the Defenses of the Town of Kaiffa Scale 60 yards to an inch (signed) Skyring 10.6.1841, Alderson 10.6.1841	425 × 257
f.	Acre Scale 200 ft. to an inch (signed) Skyring, May 1841, Alderson 10.6.1841	530 × 448
g.	Plan of the Town and Defenses of Sidon Scale 200 ft. to an inch Surveyed in the month of March, 1841 by Lieut. Aldrich and Symonds, Royal Engineers (signed) Symonds 9.6.1841, Alderson, 10.6.1841	545 × 460
h.	Sketch of Beyroot and its Vicinity Scale 400 ft to an inch (signed) Skyring, 5.6.1841, Alderson, 10.6.1841	550 ×460
b.	WO 78/1000 (3) Banias or Panias. The Ancient Caeserea Philippi Sketched by Major Fred[k] Robe, 87th R. I. Fusiliers, 7th August, 1841 1:2,880	910 × 620

d.	WO 78/1000 (10) Diagram of a triangulation of a part of Syria By Lieut. J.F.A. Symonds, Royal Engineers, 1841 1:126720 half an inch to a mile Copied for the Quarter Master General's Department, 28th June 1842 F. H. Robe, Bt. Major, 87th Roy. Irish Fusiliers	1325 × 720
f.	WO 78/1000 (25) Sketch of the Roads leading across the Lebanon from Tripoli to Baalbec, Scale one inch to a Mile, Sketched and drawn by Rochfort Scott, 1841	720 × 695
g.	WO 78/1000 (26) Plan of the Environs of Beyrout, Scale 3 inches to a mile	510 × 420
h.	WO 78/1000 (27) Plan of the Environs of Balbec (Heliopolis) 1841 Scale 6 inches to a mile Sketched and drawn by Rochfort Scott	510 × 410
i.	WO 78/1000 (28) Antioch Sketch by Rochfort Scott	523 × 418
j.	WO 78/1000 (29) Plan of Tortosa (Tarsous) the ancient Orthosia attacked by H. B. M.'s ships, Benbow, Carysfort & Zebra, 25th September, 1840. Scale 18 inches to a mile. Rochfort Scott	635 × 400
k.	WO 78/1000 (30) Plan of Djebail, the ancient Biblus attacked by H. B. M.'s ships, Carysfort Dido & Cyclopes, 12th September, 1840 Scale 18 inches to a mile Rochfort Scott	620 × 408
l.	WO 78/100 (31) Plan of Beyrout, the ancient Berytus Scale 12 inches to a mile Rochfort Scott	412 × 625
m.	WO 78/1000 (32) Plan of the Ruined Temple and Turkish Fortress of Balbec Rochfort Scott	645 × 417
n.	WO 78/1000 (33) Map of the country between Beyrout and the Valley of the Bekaa comprising the Districts of Kesrouan, ElKata, ElMettin, Suliema, Zahle and Bellad-Balbec. Sketched and Drawn by Major C. Rochfort Scott hp.R^f Staff Corps. Scale 1 inch to a mile	1240 × 770

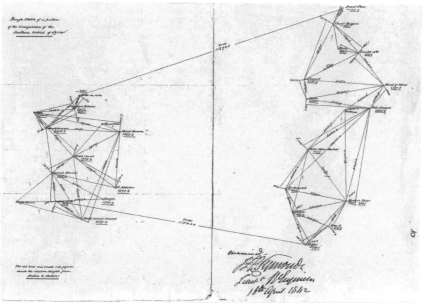

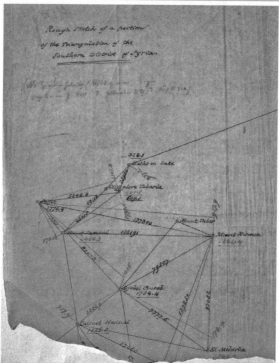

Fig. 30: Symonds, Rough sketch of a portion of the triangulation
of the Southern District of Syria

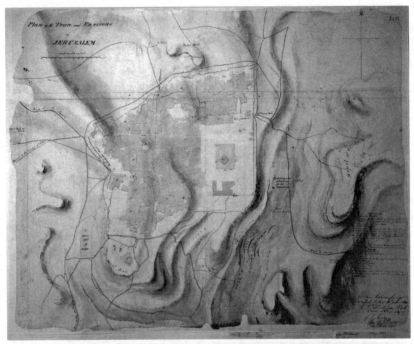

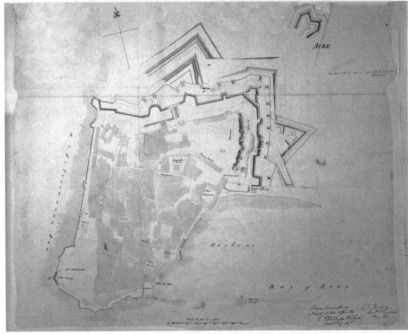

Fig. 31: Surveys of the British Officers 1841: Plan of the Town and
Environs of Jerusalem; Acre

Subsequent to their visit to Jerusalem in winter 1841, the crew performed and drafted one of the first measuring-maps of the city, on a scale of 1:4,800, whose significance has already been demonstrated by Yehoshua Ben-Arieh in his 1973 paper concerning the first modern maps of Jerusalem.[158] This map was used by later cartographers of the city, as well as by scholars. Church of England clergyman George Williams (1814–78) served for more than two and a half years as chaplain of the church of the first Protestant Bishopric in Jerusalem. He was the first to reveal this map to the public, devoting a long appendix to it in his 1849 book, *Memoir on the Map of Jerusalem*.[159] 'The principal advantage derived to the world from the operations of the British fleet on the coast of Syria', he wrote, '[...] was the opportunity afforded to the Royal Engineers of making an accurate Survey of the country.' Their work, he added, was 'of inestimable importance to Sacred Literature'. Although the fruits of these labors have so far seen the light of day only in fragments, they have already been used to provide answers to many important questions concerning the geography and topography of the Holy Land, and 'to stimulate the desire for the whole survey, the value of which it is impossible to calculate'.[160]

The idea of a general triangulation of the country was raised by Symonds in a letter to his father, Admiral Sir William Symonds (1782–1856, from 1832 'Surveyor of the Navy'). Having a reputation as 'a very difficult man to deal with', and though only authorized 'to control the programme of shipbuilding and the dockyards', Symonds the elder also used the title surveyor 'to impose his own designs on the navy, despite widespread objections'.[161] The survey was realized thanks to Palmerston's intervention, who showed much interest in the project. The officers began surveying in May 1841 but never completed the task, as at the end of that year they were assigned to other missions in the Empire.

A letter from Alderson to the RGS, forwarded to Humboldt in Berlin, teaches us that on the way from his position in Spain to his mission in Syria he was supplied in Malta with a small 5" theodolite, and with it some Schmalkalder compasses. These instruments would serve in taking the measurements of the coastal cities. Only later did a 7" theodolite, accompanied by an artificial horizon, chronometer and barometer, arrive from London, which would be used for the triangulation.[162]

Probably the best description of what Symonds actually did while triangulating in Palestine is to be found in his own letter, delivered on

21 February 1842 to Washington, then still secretary of the RGS. Because of its importance, the whole letter is worthy of citation:[163]

Colonel Alderson has this day forwarded to me some queries relative to the levels of the Dead Sea, sent to him through you by Baron Humboldt which he requests me to answer, and I lose no time in doing so, at the same time taking advantage of this opportunity to offer my services in giving all the information I possess relating to the parts of Syria I have visited, to the Society of which I believe you are secretary.

Finding all the maps of Syria so very incorrect, Lord Palmerston acceded to the proposal of having it properly surveyed, and other officers, besides myself, were employed on that duty. The District portioned out to me was all the country south of a line from Cape Bianco to Djessin Jachoub [Jacob's Bridge, HG] via Saffet. I was furnished with an excellent seven inch Theodolite, and after revising with it, the triangulation of the Northern District, (which I had commenced with a five inch instrument) I went south and measured a base from the Martyre's Tower near Ramleh, on the plain of Jaffa, on which I founded my Δ for the southern portion of my district, and finding the instrument sufficiently nicely divided in its vertical arc, to enable me to ascertain the relative levels of my several points with great accuracy. I determined to work towards the head of the Dead Sea with my Δn, taking at every station a very accurate series of vertical angles etc., the mean of which I worked on, making all the necessary allowances for refraction, and curvature; but owing to the want of another instrument, and competent person to take simultaneous observations I could not ascertain what the former was, and had to assume it at 1/12 of the subtended < from the earths center, which I consider to be very near to what it actually is. I completed the levels in this manner by two different times from Jaffa to Nebi Samuel (the highest point of the Jerusalem Range), the one cheeking the other, and found the difference but trifling. From thence I started on the same plan to the Dead Sea, and with nearly as good success the two levels differing from 11 to 12 ft. [...] to the unfavorable nature of the ground about Jerusalem and the cliffs overhanging the plain of Jericho. I could not carry the two lines of levels independently of each other to the required spot, which might have been done in spite of the natural difficulties, but having only stupid, lazy, Arab, and often only Bedouin aide, I found it impracticable. Owing to the above mentioned impediments, this labour occupied me between

June, and ten weeks, traversing a distance of not more than 47 miles. This distance in the direct line (as the crow flies) from Jaffa to the Dead Sea, but round by Nebi Samuel, Jerusalem etc. will be nearly 52 miles. I shall not now trouble you with any further details, [...] that what has been said, will sufficiently explain the questions required to the answers, and have only to add that after having completed a careful revision of my work, which I am at present employed about, I shall, with the sanction of the Lord of Aberdeen give you all the information that lays in my power.

Hamilton, in his Anniversary Address, stresses the point that Symonds was helped only by locals and faced tremendous difficulties, mainly in the mountains around Jerusalem. 'Had he had better assistance', said Hamilton, he could have performed a better measurement, as normally required – two parallel lines of level, despite the natural difficulties.[164]

One of the officers, Major Charles Rochfort Scott, was responsible for collecting the material from the officers and compiling a map of Palestine. A few years later he managed to issue it, in three sheets, on a scale of 1:253,440. It was published under the supervision of the cartographer and publisher John Arrowsmith exclusively for the Foreign Office, and was not distributed to the public.[165]

A closer look at the various maps drawn by these officers reveals that military-aimed projects did not suffice the surveyors, although all of them were army officers. In addition to data gathered for military purposes, they 'sinned' in sketching maps which could have only scientific value. Short as they had been in means, manpower and time, some of them could not avoid the temptation of dealing with the historical-religious significance of what they had encountered.

This is quite understandable, taking into account the nature of their cartographical as well as their intelligence-gathering training in the various British military academies, as mentioned above. Accordingly, the maps reflect not only the enthusiasm and capability of the officers and their teams in their works, but also the various aims and interests they had while measuring 'Syria and the Holy Land'. This group of military professionals, all of them non-academics, reached the region for a very obvious mission, namely, to use their instruments and skills to produce maps for military use. They received no clear instructions, neither from the military nor from the political authorities. The local commanders decided on their own to begin with a mission of a military nature, the mapping of the coastal defense villages and fortifications. They produced a map of Jerusalem on their own initiative, although the city had no military significance during that period. For their next idea – the triangulation of the whole country – they required help from the authorities. However, while performing this task, they continued producing additional, smaller sketches, which were of no interest to the army but of huge importance to the geographic knowledge of the region. Some of their other private initiatives, such as Robe's map of the sources of the Jordan – the first measuring map of that little accessible area – emerged as a source of crucial importance for later Holy Land cartography.[166]

The European scientific world, including the wide circle of scholars connected with Palestine research, awaited the disclosure of the results of the project. Edward Robinson commented in 1843 that 'some of these gentlemen are members of the Royal Geographical Society of London; and when the English government shall have made the use it chooses of the results of their labours, it is understood that they will be given to the world.'[167] That same year, the officers' measurements concerning the coastal cities were used widely by Alderson, who added many descriptions in his own publication, which might have also been accessible to non-military people.[168] The publication in 1845 of a relief map of 'Palestine or the Holy Land' constructed by the Board of Ordnance and dedicated to the Queen, prior to the publication of the two-dimensional maps, also gave further hope of publication for the public.[169] Portions of the survey, as well as some of its results, did begin to appear on the 'civilian' market. But the scholars continued to wait – and to express their expectations and hopes for further publication of the material. Carl Ritter wrote in the second volume of his *Comparative Geography of Palestine and the Sinaitic Peninsula*, published in 1851:

> The publication of the Admiralty survey of Syria would revolutionize the existing state of knowledge, and would make it necessary to reconstruct the maps of Palestine *de novo*. It is to be hoped that that event will take place, and that the world will be enabled to enjoy the valuable results of that expedition which owes so much to the liberality of the English Government.[170]

Until his death in 1859, Ritter continued to hope, in vain, that 'the event would take place'.

However, this fact did not prevent many scholars from making great use of the only partially published British survey. The sketch-map of the sources of the Jordan was published by Ritter and by Robinson in their periodicals. This small sketch was used as almost the only source for maps of that region until the publication of the Survey of Western Palestine (SWP).[171] Maps of Acre and Jaffa were published in 1843 by Alderson in his detailed *Notes on Acre and some Coast Defences of Syria*, a highly illuminating and important, yet neglected, source.[172] One of the sketches in Alderson's publication depicts Symonds' triangulations, which were discussed as the first hypsometric measurement of the Jordan Valley and the Dead Sea, reaching a relatively accurate result for the latter, but a very erroneous measurement for the Sea of Galilee, as will be discussed later. It was no big surprise to find this original sketch also in the collections of August Heinrich Petermann (1822-78), the great advocate of explorative geography, in Perthes's geographical institute and publishing house in Gotha.[173]

The cartographer Johann Samuel Heinrich Kiepert (1818-99), Ritter's student and successor, had since 1840 been deeply involved in Holy Land cartography, working closely with Robinson.[174] In 1842 he issued an updated map of Palestine, 'based on the new sources'; the similarity in some details is the best proof of the fact that he had Robe's sketch, still unpublished, before him.[175] It was Carel Willem Meredith van de Velde (1818-98), a Dutch naval officer who began his scientific career in the Dutch East Indies in charge of the Royal Hydrographic Office at Batavia in 1839-41, mainly mapping the island of Java and training in practical surveying and constructing maps, who wrote that he used 'the small sketch from the *Bibliotheca sacra*' for the compilation of his map of Palestine.[176] Karl Friedrich Zimmermann (1815-1903), another cartographer, from Berlin, made much use of the sketch for the compilation of a map of the Galilee published in 1861, based mainly on routes and field studies conducted between 1845 and 1848 by Ernst Gustav Schultz (1811-51), the first Prussian consul in Jerusalem.[177]

Charles Franz Zimpel (1801-80), a German man of science and railroad engineer who turned to religion in the 1850s, was one of the strongest Christian advocates of the 'Restoration of the Jews'.[178] In 1853 he published a book, attempting to identify anew the sacred sites, mainly those connected with Christ's suffering. His map of the city is 'based on the plan of the English naval lieutenants Aldrich and Symonds, [and] the historian Josephus Flavius and A. C. Emmerich', to which he added corrections he made 'on the spot'. This is a unique combination even for 'Palestine Literature', which has almost always been affected by geo-religious considerations. Even in this context, the combination of the British naval officers, the historian Josephus Flavius (38–c. 100), and the ecstatic 'nun from Dülmen', Anna Catharina Emmerich (1774–1824), whose book served as a geographical guide for Palestine pilgrims, is very exceptional.[179]

Many of the later Palestine cartographers acknowledged the contribution of the British officers to their works. The best proof is probably the extensive use of their material and maps by van de Velde. He visited Palestine in the early 1850s and again in the early 1860s, since, in his words, 'the study of the Holy Scriptures has made me deeply feel the want of a correct and sufficiently detailed map of the land to which they preeminently call our attention'.[180] In the opening comments to the memoirs accompanying his map of Palestine, he stated that:

> [...] it laid beyond my power to set off for Syria with the necessary instruments, and, with the aid of competent assistants, to make what may be termed a complete triangular survey; nor was I aware of any individual who, thrown on his own resources, had ever accomplished such a work.[181]

Van de Velde had intended to perform a trigonometric survey of the country and to construct a map of the Holy Land, but realized that it was an impossible task for a single man. He became acquainted with the works of the British officers and made the best use of these in all his maps, basing his own triangles on Symonds's triangulation. At first he regretted the fact that he was not able to obtain their material when going to Syria because he expected it to be the best possible 'base to work upon'. But on his return to London in 1852, he was 'kindly allowed by the authorities access to these documents at the Board of Ordnance', for which he was 'equally obliged to the authorities of the War-Department'. He adds that this turned out to be an advantage, 'as it had given to my own survey a perfect independent character, and its agreement with the survey of the British Engineers was now a source of much satisfaction'. He had in his possession the three sheets of the officers' 'Map of Syria' and Symonds's original triangulation, and he made a point of mentioning this in the title of his map.[182]

The map of Jerusalem was also studied by Titus Tobler, the leading Swiss scholar of Holy Land studies.[183] 'Their work lasted not less than six months,' wrote the time-conscious, frugal and efficient scholar, 'and the result is known to me, not only through Williams' edition, which is certainly not faithful and reliable on all points, but also through the copy which Mr. C. W. M. van de Velde took at the Board of Ordnance in London'. Tobler, as always strongly critical, wrote cynically:

> (w)hen informed that so great a number of engineers unitis viribus have employed so much time in constructing a ground-plan, one cannot help feeling favourably predisposed towards it, and naturally inclined to the belief that no errors, or at least no important errors, could have found their way into it.

Although Tobler added a detailed discussion of four pages full of inaccuracies which he found in the map, he still approved of van de Velde's use of it for his map of Jerusalem.[184]

British ships continued traversing the eastern Mediterranean. In the best tradition, they also continued supplying the Hydrographic Office of the Navy with large quantities of data, including charts, local surveys and written reports concerning coastal settlements, harbors, naval obstacles, climatologic conditions and any other topics of maritime interest.

George Biddlecomb (1807–78) was master of HMS *Talbot* (28 guns), 'a small, old-fashioned sloop armed mostly with outdated short-range carronades' under Captain (later Rear-Admiral Sir) Henry John Codrington (1808–77). Thirteen years earlier Codrington had been severely wounded in the Battle of Navarino, serving as signal midshipman under his father, Admiral Edward Codrington (1770–1851) on his flagship *Asia*, 'the pride of the Bombay yard, [...], a 84-gun [...] launched in 1824'. He was now commanding the *Talbot*, which had also participated in that battle.[185] Biddlecomb, who developed an impressive measuring and charting career, had special connections with Beaufort, supplying him with numerous reports, measurements and charts. The

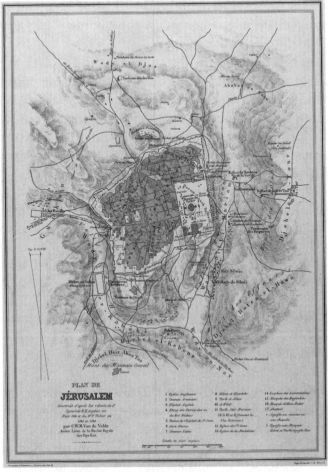

Fig. 32: Van de Velde, Map of Jerusalem, after the British
Officers and Tobler, 1858

latter even offered him membership in his hydrographic team. Four
of Biddlecomb's reports, dated April 1840 to June 1841, are kept in the
HON archive. These personal relations led to comments such as 'I did
not forward this to the Secretary of the Admiralty thinking it might
be mislaid.'[186] Acre and its bay were thoroughly surveyed, but the most
important document is a long report, correcting all the mistakes made
by Captain Edwin Smith RN in his 1840 map of the bay. This report also
holds Biddlecomb's highly valuable sketch entitled 'Sea faces of the
Fortress of St. Jean de Acre showing the position of the Allied Squadron
at the Bombardment Nov 3rd 1840'.[187] James Thomas Russell, Master

of HMS Steam Vessel *Cyclops*, in his report for 1842, includes detailed descriptions of Tyre and its harbor, of the coast by 'The Ladder of the Tyrians' and Cape Blanco and of the Bay of Acre with all its anchoring possibilities.[188]

Major Edward Delaval Hungerford Elers Napier (1808-70), Charles Napier's adopted son, had been accepted as an expert on the Levant since his visit to Turkey with his stepfather's HMS *Powerful* in the late 1830s. With a rank of lieutenant-colonel, he was sent in 1840 as a mediator to the Druze and Maronite leaders in Lebanon, aiming to confirm their allegiance to the Sultan. With a unit of 1,500 irregular cavalry, he chased Ibrahim Paşa's army, acted as military commissioner at the Ottoman headquarters and, after the end of the war, in 1841, succeeded in gaining the release of Ottoman troops detained by Mehemet Ali.[189] The RGS, of which he was a member, received an interesting and, in some details illuminating, account from him of two excursions he had conducted in Lebanon and northern Palestine, mainly through the central mountainous area.[190] While traveling in the country 'from the vicinity of Damascus to the Dead Sea', he had been struck by the inaccuracy of the depiction of the mountain ranges in the existing maps, primarily in the one supplied to him by 'Wilde', probably referring to William Robert Wills Wilde (1815-76) from Dublin, who had traveled along the eastern coast of the Mediterranean in 1837-8 as surgeon to a consumptive Glasgow merchant.[191] Consequently, he performed his own observations and sent them to John Washington. But, as 'this is however very insufficient to remedy the evil' and, hoping for support from the Society, Napier offered to take a survey of the mountain ranges. Another important objective would be a survey of the Depression, in order to address the question of the old route of the Jordan and the possibility of a canal which had existed between the Dead and the Red Seas. Napier even asked his acquaintance George Thomas Staunton (1781-1859), diplomat, sinologist and MP, inter alia founder of the Royal Asiatic Society (1823), to raise the subject with his educator John Barrow (1764-1848), Second Secretary of the Admiralty for forty years, co-founder of the RGS and its third president, and the greatest promoter of exploration, mainly of Arctic voyages of discovery.[192] In 1847 Napier published his detailed two-volume *Reminiscences*, an important eyewitness description of the events of 1840-1.[193]

Part 2

The Dead Sea and the Jordan Rift Valley: Myth and Research

4   The Dead Sea and the Jordan Rift Valley: Geological Mysteries, Biblical Memories and Scientific Explanations

The unique geological, historical, political and theological significance of the Jordan Rift Valley, 5650 square kilometers stretching from the sources of the Jordan to the Gulf of Akaba and including, at least in the past, three lakes, has made it the subject of ongoing interest and study, mainly since the advent of the modern scientific study of the region in the nineteenth century. The multi-disciplinary nature of the study of this 'geographically, geologically and environmentally unique entity', conducted by travelers and explorers, geographers and cartographers, geologists, theologians and natural historians, has supplied a wealth of information and produced various, often contradictory, theories. Undoubtedly, the focal points were the physical-geographical and geological phenomena, their history, significance and consequences. Many years of intensive research were required to determine the geological structure of the valley and reconstruct the history of its formation, not to mention to reach a consensus concerning the process itself.[1]

'As my principal object was to call attention to the extraordinary nature of the Dead Sea, to account for its probable formation, and to show how it may be made the means of communication with our East Indian possessions...'; these were the introductory words of Captain William Allen (1792–1864) to his two-volume book entitled *The Dead Sea, a New Route to India*.[2] Allen, whose career included service in the Mediterranean as well as the West Indies, participated in two ill-fated expeditions up the Niger, in 1832–4 and 1841–3, respectively. From 1844 onwards he became a fellow at the RGS, where he often lectured and presented his ideas. Accompanied by his nephew, he set sail from Plymouth in November 1849 and arrived in Beirut exactly a year later, after adventurous travels in Malta, Greece, Turkey and the Aegean Islands. Their tour of the Dead Sea commenced in December 1850. Allen was very well informed about prior studies and descriptions of the area, recent as well as ancient, and did not fail to mention 'Messrs. Moore and Beck [sic] in 1837' as the first to notice 'the peculiar phenomenon of the depression'.[3] Regarding the result of his tour, in 1853 he presented to Palmerston a 'Plan for a Ship Canal to India by the Dead Sea'.[4] His abovementioned book on the subject, published in 1855, advocated the construction of a canal from the Mediterranean to the Red Sea through the Jordan Rift Valley and the Dead Sea, comparing it to the proposed Suez Canal and rivaling the French program.[5]

Allen realized that in order to establish any plan for a canal, he had to ascertain the geological history of the region, already a subject of heated debate among scientists, who never failed to raise the religious and historical connection as well. Consequently, he devoted long discussions to various geological and topographical features such as the slope of the Arabah Valley, in which he used the works of Burckhardt, Irby and Mangles, de Bertou, Schubert and Robinson.[6] In papers published in the *JRGS,* he discussed the watershed in the Arabah, pointing out an anomaly: 'appearances of sudden and violent drainage on the sides of the basin of the Dead Sea' (which cause major problems to this very day).[7] All these studies led him to one solid conclusion:

> Communications being thus established by canals sufficiently broad and deep, the rushing in of the two seas would restore the *now* Dead Sea to its ancient level, and convert it into the active channel of intercourse between Europe and Asia; the whole bulky commerce of which might then pass through this canal instead of taking the circuitous route of the Cape of Good Hope, shortening the time of the voyage between England and India to the time in which it is performed by the overland route.[8]

The Dead Sea and the entire Jordan Valley aroused ongoing political, scientific, as well as theological interest. Alexander von Humboldt (1769–1859), undoubtedly the leading geographical authority of his

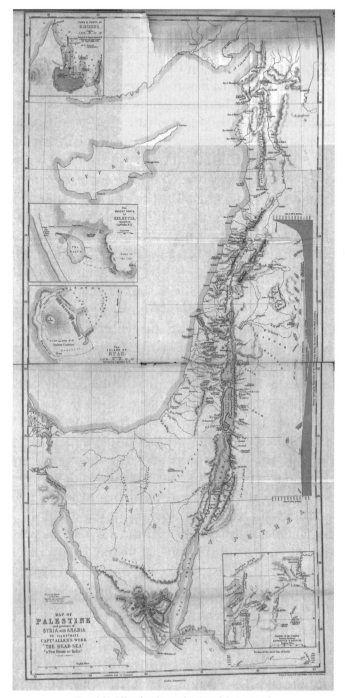

Fig. 33: Allen's plan of a Dead Sea canal

time, made extensive use of the new data, which will be described later, in his discussion of the physical geography of the terrestrial portion of the cosmos, as the best example of an area lower than 'the general level of existing seas'. Writing in the first half of the 1840s, and being perfectly informed on all the new results presented by Moore and Beek, de Bertou, Russegger, Schubert and Symonds, he wrote, that 'the isolated basin of the Jordan and the Dead Sea (the Asphalt Sea) show the best similarity with the isolated basin of the Caspian Sea; their relative levels had only very recently drawn on them the attention of the travelers'.[9] Carl Ritter, a colleague and partner in the development of geography as a modern and comparative scientific field, in 1850 published his own lecture dealing with the Jordan and with the idea of sailing on the Dead Sea. In this lecture he collected, organized and summoned, in his usual systematic scientific manner, all available information concerning these topics. In one of his opening sentences, he wrote that he had been guided by the idea, 'that there is no other spatial desert on our globe that has been of [such] value for thinking people through several examinations in connection with the entire appearance'.[10] While establishing the uniqueness of the rift of the Jordan, Ritter perceived it, along with the Dead Sea, as a barrier that existed throughout history, separating Palestine and the desert tribes, and repeated that Palestine had been an 'unapproachable land of fable'.[11]

Reverend James Edmund Boggis, who in 1932 descended the River Jordan in a canoe, studied the writings of pilgrims from the fourth century onwards, and their impressions of the Jordan and its lakes. One interesting comment he makes is that 'it is somewhat surprising to find that the Sea of Galilee and its sacred sites attracted them much less than the lower part of the river and the mysterious Dead Sea'.[12]

Biblical memories had a lasting effect on almost everyone who decided to make the long, dangerous and difficult journey from Jerusalem down to Jericho, then on to the baptismal site, through the embouchure of the Jordan into the Dead Sea and along its northwestern shore, up the canyon of Wadi Kedron to Mar (St) Saba, the Greek-Orthodox monastery, and back to Jerusalem. This had never been a simple task, not in the Byzantine period and not in the nineteenth century. All who undertook it – pilgrim, traveler, artist and scientist, military, clergy and layman – were deeply affected. The dark, mysterious, gloomy mood inspired by the lake and its desolate mountainous surroundings, the sense of danger inspired by desolation and the extreme climate, along with the legends connected with the lake, the biblical memories it evoked, the palpable connection with the Creator's deeds and with the effectiveness of His wrath; all these had an immense impact on every visitor. As one scholar pointed out:

> [...] the Biblical traditions transfer to us the memory of two late catastrophes, which, since the human race arrived at the surface of the globe, agitated the inhabited world on these periods: the one is the flood, the other the destruction of the cities of the valley of Siddim and the formation of the Asphalt lake.[13]

What were the reactions of the visitors?

Painter William Holman Hunt (1827–1910), co-founder of the Pre-Raphaelite Brotherhood (1848), explored the East in 1854–5. He spent seventeen days near Sodom, on the coast of the Dead Sea, drawing his famous *Scapegoat*, in which he tried to depict the unique setting in which this goat, according to the Bible, was sent out into the desert bearing the sins of the People of Israel.[14] He was not the only one to be affected by the unique aura of the area:

> It was indeed a scene of unmitigated desolation [...]. The glare of the light was blinding the eye, and the atmosphere difficult of respiration. No bird fanned with its wing the attenuated air through which the sun poured its scorching rays upon the mysterious element on which we floated, and which, alone, of all the works of his Maker, contains no living thing within it.[15]

This text was written by William Francis Lynch (1801–65), the initiator and commander of the 1848 'United States' Expedition to the River Jordan and the Dead Sea'. Another visitor wrote, three years later:

> Solemn ride along this briny strand! [...] The burning and vanishing ground, with its doomed cities, comes up vividly before the mind. What a tract of country! What a terrible witness to the righteous vengeance of God's justice![16]

These very typical impressions and feelings were expressed, not by a devout pilgrim in the Middle Ages, but by one of the leading cartographers of Palestine in the middle of the nineteenth century, van de Velde. As a pious Protestant, he harnessed his talents and experience for the study of the Holy Land, exploring and measuring it twice, first in 1851–2 and again in 1861–2. He also stressed the fact that his recollections of the lake were quite different from Lynch's:

> In vain my eyes sought for the terrific representations which some writers, and especially the American travelers of 1848, have given of the Dead Sea. I expected a scene of unequalled horror, instead of which I found a lake, calm and glassy, blue and transparent, with an unclouded heaven, with a smooth beach, and surrounded by mountains whose blue tints were of rare beauty.[17]

Van de Velde published a large volume of paintings, a two-volume description of his voyage and, most importantly, a map of the country at a scale of one half inch to a mile, the most accurate until the great 'Survey of Western Palestine' performed by the English Palestine Exploration Fund during the 1870s.[18]

The River Jordan, 'more famous than the Mississippi or the Amazon, though infinitely smaller than either' in the words of a contemporary writer, and its 'two lakes' (the third, northernmost, Huleh Lake, was usually ignored), had been the arena of many important and significant events described in the Old and New Testaments.[19] The traditional site of the Baptism in the Jordan is represented as a short distance from the river's embouchure to the Dead Sea. The stories in the book of Genesis concerning Abraham and Lot, the cities of the plain and especially the destruction of Sodom and Gomorrah as divine punishment, attracted special attention to these areas. Naturally, every observer looked for the remains of the destroyed cities. In any given travelogue, one can find all sorts of perceptions, theories, 'imagined' sites and long, detailed discussions. To take one example, when reaching the lake in 1696, Maundrell tried in vain to locate at least some remains, but was reassured by the Franciscans in Jerusalem that they had seen some when the water level had been lower. If this is not complete fiction, they must have been referring to the Rujum el-bahr, an elevation at the end of a rampart protruding from the northern shore. This 'island' had occasionally been noted by travelers and scientists and has been used in modern research as one of the best indications of the changes in the water level.[20]

The reality of its being such an important sacred space naturally also had its effect on research. All the central questions explorers sought to answer in their study of the Dead Sea derived from its scriptural descriptions and from the peculiar characteristics and features attached to it. It was common practice to look for the lost cities and for geographical evidence of the catastrophe that God had created in his wrath. 'Recent explorations of the sea and the surrounding region tend, I believe,' later wrote Josias Leslie Porter (1823–89), an Irish Presbyterian Church missionary stationed in Damascus for ten years beginning in December 1849, 'to throw some light on one of the most remarkable events of physical geography and of Biblical history.'[21]

Many of the geographical, geological and environmental phenomena known today, which exemplify the uniqueness of the Dead Sea, were still waiting to be established as late as the fourth decade of the nineteenth century. One of the lake's first *curiositates* to be studied, long before the 1830s and the Egyptian period in Palestine, were the chemicals contained in its water which enabled everything to float upon it. This first example of a scientific approach dates to the first half of the eighteenth century and was already included in some earlier as well as modern research, the latter including Cippora Klein's dissertation, which cites an impressive variety of sources, and Aharon Horowitz's book.[22]

Holy Land explorers differed from those who set out to study other countries, mainly in this one aspect, namely, in the geo-pious influence of their subject on their research. Clearly no one could ignore the uniqueness of Palestine, the 'Holy Land', with all its implications.[23] Geo-pious (or, more accurately, geo-religious) beliefs were a motivating force, influencing and even encouraging scientific study, and affecting the fields, means and methods of study of one of the most 'stirring geopious areas' in Palestine, the River Jordan and its lakes, 'places where the divine manifest, [...] to the eyes of believing women and men, and which were cherished or revered as concrete, tangible, spatially defined testimonies to the reality of the divine [...]'.[24]

The participants who undertook this scientific adventure usually did their best to perform their studies according to the highest scientific standards of their time, but they could not be oblivious to the religious connection, which strongly influenced their choice of topics and objects of investigation. The French Romantic writer, traveler and diplomat, François René de Chateaubriand (1768–1848), who, 'under the banner of the cross' as a modern crusader, visited Palestine in 1806 and started a genre of romantic Palestine-literature, tried to solve the obvious contradiction. In agreement with Johann David Michaelis (1717–91) and Anton Friedrich Büsching (1724–93), two outstanding eighteenth-century scholars from Göttingen in central Germany, the leading university with the strongest connections to and inter-relations with British academia, Chateaubriand claimed that physics might be admitted in explaining the catastrophe of the guilty cities, without offending religion.[25]

As has been said, one of the major issues in the study of the Dead Sea, derived from its scriptural descriptions and from its strange and interesting peculiarities, was the search for the lost cities and for existing signs of the catastrophe that God had created in his wrath. That event might also explain the fact that the Jordan and some more minor tributaries flow into the Dead Sea without any visible outlet but without seeming to affect the water level. Did the Jordan ever continue on into the Red Sea? If the answer was positive, then the change must have been due to the same catastrophe. And what was the situation in the present? Was there a subterraneous connection between the Dead Sea and the Red Sea? Or perhaps between the Dead Sea and the Mediterranean?

Many of the facts that are known today which explain the geographical and chemical uniqueness of the Dead Sea, were still waiting to be established. No one had realized, or written down, at least, that the level of the surface of the Dead Sea is much lower than 'sea level', that it is actually the lowest point on earth not covered with water:

> Who thought it is possible that all the stream valley [of the Jordan], in a stretching of 30 geographical miles with two lakes is that deep, and that the level of the water of the Dead Sea can actually lie more than 1,300 feet under the level of the neighbouring Mediterranean?[26]

What they did have, and which they tried to verify and understand, were facts – sometimes romantic speculations – based on the writings of early historians and geographers, and on the plethora of pilgrims' descriptions.

One of these mysterious facts had to do with the buoyancy of the Dead Sea, which is linked to the salty environment of both the lake – known in Hebrew as *Yam Hamelach* ('the salt sea') – and its surroundings. The biblical story of Lot's wife seems to fit in with the 'salty' terrain and Mt Sodom bordering the lake. Yet another common belief was that no living creature existed within its waters, and that birds attempting to fly over it would be suffocated by the vapors and plunge to their death. Many wondered how so much water could flow into the lake with no obvious outlet and without causing the water level to rise. Others looked for the reasons for the existence of masses of asphalt, which also gave the sea the name 'Lake Asphaltis'. Josephus and Strabo had claimed that with the destruction of Sodom, the whole valley became the Lake Asphaltis.[27] The various names appear on different maps of the lake, such as the one of southern Palestine on a scale of 1:343,000, published in 1532 by the German scholar Jacob Ziegler (c.1470–1539), in which 'the Dead Sea is too long, much too narrow and has the form of a rainbow open to the W[est]'.[28]

More than just defining the nature of the research done by travelers who reached the area, I would argue that the special characteristics of the Dead Sea in fact determined the very nature of those scientists who chose to direct their studies particularly at the region. Almost every researcher of Palestine included the Jordan Depression in his itinerary; but those who chose the Dead Sea as their main object of study were motivated by a common, powerful religious belief, by a geo-religious approach to the area as place and past, which naturally influenced their study. It would appear that they all shared a strong impulse to decipher these secrets in order to prove and verify the narratives and descriptions found in the scriptures.

As early as 1722, the English chaplain and scientist Thomas Shaw (1694–1751) rejected the theory of the existence of an invisible underground outlet for the water of the Dead Sea:

... I computed it [the Jordan, HG] to be about thirty yards broad; but the depth I could not measure, except at the brink, where I found it to be three. If then we take this, during the whole year, for the *mean* depth of the stream (which, I am to observe further, runs about two miles an hour,) the *Jordan* will every day discharge into the *Dead-sea*, about 6,090,000 tons of water. So great a quantity of water being daily received, without any visible increase in the usual limits of the *Dead-sea*, has made some authors conjecture, that it must be absorbed by the burning sands; others, that there are some subterraneous cavities to receive it; others, that there is a communication betwixt it and the *Sirbonic* lake; not considering that the *Dead-sea* alone will lose every day, near one third more in vapor, than what all this amounts to.[29]

Thus far, a very logical, learned observation; Shaw even draws comparisons with other lakes with no outlet. As for the 'scientific' explanation of the phenomenon:

> For all and every one of these, by receiving as much water from their respective rivers, as they lose in vapor, will preserve, as near as can be expected, their usual limits and dimensions: the Almighty providence having given *to them*, no less than to the elements, a *law which shall not be broken*, (Ps. cxlviii. 6.) *Which hath said* (Job xxxviii. 11.) *to the sea, Hitherto shalt thou come and no further; and here shall thy proud waves be staid*.[30]

Johannes Heyman (1667–1737), professor of oriental languages in Leiden, traveled in the East in 1700–9. Johan Ägidius van Egmond van der Nyenburg, Dutch ambassador in Naples, visited the area in 1720–3. They combined their accounts into a single volume, published in Dutch (1757) and in English (1759), wherein it is impossible to establish which parts were authored by which of the two travelers.[31] While visiting the lake, one of them tried, among other things, to prove the accepted view that birds could not fly over it. In an experiment which would probably have not been acceptable today, they 'plucked out some feathers from each wing' of a pair of sparrows brought with them, so 'that they could not fly long', and set them free; in a short time they naturally fell to the sea, but both got safely ashore – the best proof that there was no such 'noxious effluvia'. They also wrote about 'the extraordinary quantity of salt in it' as the source of its buoyancy.[32]

Büsching, the eighteenth-century German theologian and geographer from Göttingen, gained much fame through his geographical volumes describing different parts of the world. His series also included a detailed description of the Holy Land, which was necessary, according to him, for biblical commentary and interpretation. The importance he attributed to the Dead Sea led him to publish a separate print in 1766, including all of the extant information he could collect until that date.[33]

Alexander Marcet (1770–1822), an exiled Swiss chemist and physician living in London, received 'a phial of it', which was brought to England at the request of Joseph Banks (1743–1820), traveler, naturalist, botanist, patron of the sciences and leading figure in many scientific societies; the results of his analysis were published in 1807.[34] This was no coincidence, as Banks's nephew, William John Banks (1786–1855), an experienced traveler, collector and antiquarian, had been a central participant in a group of young British men, mainly officers, who traveled in Palestine and the surrounding countries in 1816–18. The story of their travels was published in 1823 by the two naval Captains among them, Charles Leonard Irby (1789–1845) and James Mangles (1786–1867). The fourth participant was Thomas Legh (1793–1857). In their book, they gave some important descriptions of the Dead Sea and its environs, added a pioneering sketch of the southern part of the lake and bringing to light the results of Marcet's analysis.[35]

Other travelers, not necessarily explorers or men of science, also tried to establish the lethality of the water. Barbara Kreiger, in her *Living Waters*, accepts as anecdotal evidence Chateaubriand's account about hearing sounds from the water while camping by the lake and being told by his Bedouin companions that it was caused by small fish.[36] An important early scientific experiment trying to identify microscopic signs of life in water samples taken from the Jordan and from the bottom and body of the Dead Sea, was conducted in Berlin in 1846. Christian Gottfried Ehrenberg (1795–1876), a leading natural historian who started his career with eighteen months of research and specimen-collecting on the shores of the Red Sea (1823–4), and a highly distinguished member of the Academy of Science in Berlin, presented his results at the Academy meeting.[37]

The French Count Jules de Bertou, one of the main participants in the leveling of the Dead Sea, testified about another 'experiment' executed in Beirut in 1838. Not mentioning names, he described a traveler who had lately brought some water from the Dead Sea. De Bertou decided to see 'what effect would be provided by it on fish from the Mediterranean'. The first fish put into water from the Dead Sea was immediately affected by convulsions; after two minutes, almost dead, it was again put into water from the Mediterranean but died in some seconds. A second fish of greater size ('17 centimetres in lengths and 7 centimetres in breadth') and very lively, was put into the water of the Dead Sea and died within three minutes after very strong convulsions. Upon examination, the stomachs of the fish did not present any visible alteration, and de Bertou raised the probability that this poison, so subtle, acted on the nervous system.[38]

In accordance with Ehrenberg's request, samples were collected by the orientalist Karl Richard Lepsius (1810–84) during his travels in the East in 1842–6.[39] Building upon the findings of former expeditions, both American and English, which reported the existence of various living creatures on the shores and surface of the lake, it was found that the Dead Sea water did indeed contain many living maritime creatures. He found 17 species from the Polygastrica family in the Jordan waters, seven in the Dead Sea and four in both. From the Phytolitharia family, nine species were found in the Jordan, three in the Dead Sea and two in both. Two additional species were found in the Dead Sea, bringing the total to thirty species.[40]

Arie Nissenbaum devoted his PhD thesis and a number of subsequent papers to the history of chemical analyses of the Dead Sea and the Jordan waters.[41] According to him, the first ever chemical analysis of sea water was performed in 1772 by 'the father of modern chemistry', Antoine-Laurent Lavoisier (1743–94), with the second known analysis being performed six years later, again by Lavoisier and two collaborators and using water from the Dead Sea.[42] Lavoisier and his pioneering laboratory were undoubtedly the best candidates for such an historical role. But after some years Nissenbaum had to correct himself, and in 1986 he conceded that the first examination of the specific weight of the water of the Dead Sea had already been conducted in 1739. Charles Perry (?–1780), an English traveler and medical writer who traversed the Middle East between 1739 and 1742, collected specimens while traveling in Palestine, and in February 1741 presented the results of a chemical analysis of Dead Sea water, publishing them a year later.[43]

Nissenbaum also failed to mention the learned English traveler and clergyman, later bishop in Ireland, Richard Pococke (1704–65), who visited the Dead Sea in 1738, during his 1737–40 travels in the Near East. Pococke wrote a detailed and well-organized description of the Dead Sea, according to Barbara Tuchman: 'missing nothing, studying everything for what it could reveal of the famous past' and, with a measure of skepticism, writing 'by far the most learned work of the eighteenth century dealing with Palestine'.[44] After bathing in the lake to test a statement of Pliny ('the Elder', 23–79) about its water's specific gravity, he brought home a bottle of Dead Sea water to analyze it, and found that it contained only some salt and alum.[45]

'By 1830,' continues Nissenbaum, 'the number of analyses performed on Dead Sea water was second only to the number of sea water analyses,'[46] further evidence of the importance accorded to this lake and its study during the period dealt with in this book. Among these analyses was one published in France in 1778 (the above-mentioned analysis of Lavoisier), and another in 1809 in Germany, both analyzing water which had already been collected in 1767.[47] One of the more advanced early-nineteenth-century analyses was conducted in 1819 by the French chemist Joseph Louis Gay-Lussac (1778–1850), the sample being collected and delivered in 'un vase de fer-blanc fermé hermétiquement' by the French painter, writer and traveler Louis Nicolas Phillipe Auguste, Comte de Forbin (1777–1841), who had come to acquire antiquities for the Louvre in 1817–18. The publication was of course in Gay-Lussac's and François Jean Dominique Arago's (1786–1853) periodical. Forbin also added a short *essai* of the water of the Jordan.[48] A detailed study, also based on analyses of previously collected water samples, is included in a dissertation published in Tübingen in 1827. Joseph Friedrich Weishaar, who performed the study under the leading chemist Christian Gottlob Gmelin (1792–1860), received the water sample through Jakob Leutzen, who traveled in Egypt and Palestine in 1822.[49]

Madden, the Irish physician, reached the Dead Sea in 1824, disguised as a Bedouin, and took home a bottle of the water to have it analyzed. In his publication, issued in 1833, he compared the results of his analysis to an earlier one provided by Chateaubriand, using information from the French geographer Conrad Malte Brun (1775–1826), founder of the influential periodical of explorative geography, *Les Annales des Voyages*. In order to prove his conviction that no living creature could be found, Madden also tried fishing in the lake for two hours, catching only bitumen.[50] Finally, samples collected by Lynch's 1848 expedition were analyzed and published in his report of 29 February 1849.[51]

Geology and mineralogy were naturally also subjects of much interest, and there are continuous examples of travelers collecting specimens from the shores and the vicinity during this period. The American ABCFM missionary Isaac Bird (1793–1876), a Connecticut-born Yale graduate, served in the East from 1822 to 1835 (first in Malta and Beirut, and from November 1823 in Smyrna).[52] Before leaving for the East, he promised his instructor at Yale, F. Hall, who was also the editor of a scientific journal, to send him 'any such interesting specimens of mineralogy as might fall in my way in the country', and he kept his promise. Many of the specimens were collected at the Dead Sea: 'a vial of Dead sea water', 'animal relic of a convoluted form, from the Dead Sea', and more of the same.[53]

One of the most outstanding and surprising facts concerning the early study of the Dead Sea is the striking ignorance of its relative level. Some travelers did mention that the Jordan Valley was one of the lowest regions in Palestine; as did Burckhardt when citing the fact that the melons at Tiberias were ripe four weeks before those of Acre.[54] But it appears that nobody knew, or at least no one wrote as much, that the surface of the Dead Sea was much lower than 'sea level'. The process which first led to this discovery has not yet been studied systematically. There are some relatively early studies which mention it, but most are partial, erroneous and misleading. Modern studies, from as early as the 1880s, bring more detailed and explicit information,[55] but the comprehensive process of discovery has only been recently reconstructed.[56] The reasons for this lacuna lie in the inaccessibility of many sources, the lack of mastery of languages and the fact that many were simply copying from one another. In 1937, the Israeli geographer Abraham J. Brawer published a short essay, commemorating the centenary of Moore and Beek's ('two British explorers') revelations. He mentions Schubert's group, in addition to Russegger, Bertou, Symonds and 'Lynd [sic]'.[57] This case study represents a typical and important part of the history of the 'scientific rediscovery' of the Holy Land, connecting the contemporary physical geography with biblical traditions, as, in the words of van de Velde, the Depression 'may be called the great hypsometrical question of Palestine'.[58]

Modern Israeli research has made some efforts to establish the process for determining the Dead Sea level, first establishing the fact that it is lower than regular sea level and then determining its exact altitude. A pioneering, even outstanding, but very short, publication was issued by Yossi Vardi in 1990.[59] The same volume also includes a short and partial review of the study of the Dead Sea by Nathan Schur.[60] Both could of course have had at their disposal some material from Barbara Kreiger's detailed study, published two years earlier.[61] The following pages present the whole, detailed narrative, adding to and correcting this previous research.

The narrative of this research should also naturally include a review of the question of who was the first to discover – and publish – this groundbreaking piece of information. One obvious (though ultimately mistaken!) candidate for this historical role would be the French Marshal Auguste Frédéric Louis Viesse de Marmont, Duc de Ragusa (1774–1852), Napoleon's aide-de-camp, who toured the area in 1834–5 and provided military consultation to Mehemet Ali. It was his second visit to Egypt. Napoleon's acquaintance and friend, he had joined the latter on his expeditions to Italy and Egypt, became Inspector-General of Artillery (1804), Grand Officer of the Légion d'honneur, occupied Dubrovnik (Ragusa) and served for five years as its governor. He took part in many campaigns after 1809, served as governor of northern Spain, was gravely wounded, returned to service before recovering and participated in all battles until 1814. He became infamous and mistrusted for his secret agreement with the allies, in which he had surrendered 20,000 men, and spent his last twenty-two years, from 1830 onwards, in exile in Vienna.[62]

The sixty-year-old duke's 'grand tour' lasted eleven months, taking him through Hungary, Transylvania, central Russia, Crimea, Sea of Azov, Constantinople, parts of Asia Minor, Syria, Palestine and Egypt. He traveled as a private citizen with an Austrian passport, and was highly interested in everything he encountered. In Egypt he was received with great honor by the Paşa, although the local French community expressed hostility.[63] His four volumes of reminiscences and impressions, in which he predicted the decline and fall of the Ottoman Empire, aroused great interest, and parts of it were immediately translated into English. He wrote that 'England is, of all powers, the most able to exercise an influence in the regeneration of Turkey', and 'if she will therefore exert her energies in such a cause, Turkey can still be saved from the grasp of Russia'.[64] The English edition also contained a long treatise by the editor, considering the 'Observations on the Political Relations of England with Turkey and Russia'.[65]

The duke's written impressions of Palestine and its environs begin in Syria on 26 August 1834 – towards the end of his second volume – with his 'painful disappointment at his [Mehemet Ali's] unpopularity'.[66] He enumerates the European officers whom he encountered in the Egyptian army in Syria, and gives a detailed description of the 'war of

1832'.[67] The third volume, containing his travels in Palestine and Egypt (from Damascus through the Pont de Jacob, Tiberias, Tabor, Nazareth, Jezreel Valley, Jenin and Nablus to Jerusalem and Jaffa, then sailing to Acre and visiting Mount Carmel, and back by sea to Alexandria), was apparently not deemed important enough to be accorded an early English translation.[68] The Jordan, he claims, 'est très-peu large, mais il a une grande profondeur: on peut le comparer à la Seine au dessus de la ville de Troyes'.[69] In Nazareth he verified the exact whereabouts of Kléber and Napoleon's battle of the Tabor, and in Jerusalem he was mostly shocked by the internal Christian hostility: 'Grande humiliation et grand scandale pour la chrétienté'.[70] He reached the city just after Ibrahim Paşa had managed to subdue the powerful so-called Peasants Rebellion, and he certainly put great effort into trying to establish the reasons for the troubles the Egyptian army was facing.[71]

Leaving Jerusalem on 22 September 1834, it took him six hours to cover the distance to the northern shore of 'lac Asphaltite', returning to Jerusalem on the following day after an overnight stay in Jericho.[72] His short comments concerning the lake are of no importance, although he had been deeply impressed by the region's 'extrême aridité' and he thought it to be the opening of a crater. He also accepted the theory that before the 'catastrophe', the Jordan had flowed into the Red Sea. But in Jerusalem he climbed the Mount of Ascension in order to observe and determine the elevation of the Judean Mountains. After ascertaining boiling temperatures of water, he established the level of the Mount of Olives at 747 meters. Hans Fischer claims that these were actually the first hypsometric measurements conducted in Palestine.[73] Despite the duke's own admission that he 'did not do any operation in order to decide the respective heights of the Dead Sea and the Mediterranean', he wrote that

after some signs, and the difference of temperatures in corresponding hours, I can suppose that the Dead Sea is five hundred metres under the Mount of Ascension, and through consequence more than two hundred metres *above* [my emphasis, HG] the Mediterranean.[74]

The duke was not a scientist, nor did he have any measurement devices with him. But he could certainly ascertain a difference in the level of the Dead Sea from that of the Mediterranean. He simply reached the wrong conclusions.

Until the fourth decade of the nineteenth century, the altitude measurements conducted in the Holy Land and its neighboring regions were coincidental, sporadic and usually far from accurate.

Heinrich Berghaus (1797–1884) was founder and director of the Kunstschule für Geographische und Kartographische Studien in Potsdam, co-founder of the geographical society in Berlin, a close friend of Humboldt and Ritter and their house cartographer. The Holy Land was never a principal region in his works, as his attention was concentrated mainly on physical geography. Nevertheless, the few works he did devote to the Near East were of great significance for the development of its professional cartography in both methodology and practice, mainly in its approach and in the execution of the compilation. He made use of all of the available material – maps, measurements, as well as written and oral descriptions – in order to compile a map which would fulfill the evolving demands of modern cartography. Complementing Ritter's works and adopting his methods and perceptions, Berghaus used his superb cartographic ability to fully exploit a variety of types of sources. For example, he recounts how he needed to synthesize the reports of eight travelers in order to establish the distance between Jaffa and Jerusalem. Ritter would conclude about his contemporary and student that 'his work opened a new era in the cartography of Palestine and Syria'.[75]

Berghaus was involved in the compilation of two maps of the Holy Land. The first, containing two parts with different scales (1:450,000 for most of the country, 1:800,000 for Arabia Petraea) and published in 1835 as part of Berghaus's *Atlas von Asien*, was dedicated to Jacotin and Burckhardt. The second, later map, entitled 'Palestine after old and new dependable sources', was published nine years later in collaboration with his colleague J. Friedrich von Stülpnagel (1786–1895), who worked for the geographic publishing house of Justus Perthes in Gotha.[76]

While compiling the detailed maps of the area for his 1835 atlas, Berghaus wrote two memoirs, in which he described and evaluated all his sources.[77] Both Ritter and van de Velde, as well as the British RE Charles William Wilson (1836–1905), a leading scholar in the measuring of Jerusalem and in the PEF, agreed that 'it was the first serious attempt to classify and portray in a careful and systematic manner the results obtained by the earlier travellers of the present century'. Berghaus's memoirs should serve as a model, Ritter added, as 'will they at all times remain a monument of indefatigable zeal and extraordinary discernment'.[78]

Actually these memoirs are the best description of the cartographic study of the region until that year, as they deal specifically with *Ortsbestimmungen*. Some of the travelers and explorers to whom he refers, such as Edward Wilhelm Peter Simon Rüppell (1794–1884), also did some leveling. Rüppell's significant measurements were performed in the Sinai Peninsula, and were aimed at answering the question 'how high is Mount Sinai?'[79] Born in Frankfurt, he had accompanied his father on his travels and was interested mainly in natural sciences and mineralogy, later integrating commercial activity into his travel and research. He reached Egypt for the first time in 1817, where he met with the British 'artist, traveler, diplomat, Egyptologist' and collector of antiquities, Henry Salt (1780–1847), and Burckhardt, who, shortly before dying, strongly recommended that he concentrate on a scientific study of the East and that he thoroughly prepare himself for this mission.[80]

In Genoa, Rüppel met with the astronomer Franz Xaver von Zach (1754–1832), who began teaching him the basics of astronomical observation. After studying in some Italian universities, he returned to Frankfurt and was accepted as a member of the recently established Senckenbergische Naturforschende Gesellschaft, which became his life-long academic center.[81]

His next long voyage began in early 1822, in the company of a surgeon, Michael Hey, who had been appointed and financed by the Frankfurt society. After receiving letters of recommendation from Mehemet Ali, they set out in April for the Sinai. One of the important results of this expedition was the first modern description of Akaba and its environs, including an accurate determination of its geographical position and a refutation of the conventional opinion about the existence of a peninsula at the head of the gulf separating two small half islands, Eilat and Akaba.[82] Returning to Cairo, they continued south and spent the next three years in Upper Egypt and in the regions of present-day Sudan, collecting and purchasing (Rüppell had no financial limitations) specimens and sending them to Frankfurt, where they came to comprise a significant part of the museum's collections.

In 1826 he returned to complete his studies of Sinai and Arabia Petraea, making topographical sketches and measurements, and studying the fauna of the Red Sea. After that he returned home, spent some time organizing and publishing his findings, and, in late 1830, sailed to the region again. This time he continued his hypsometric measurement, reaching astonishing accuracy for the height of Jebel Mussa (Mt Moses) in central Sinai. On 7 May 1831 he measured 7,035 Parisian feet, the equivalent of 2,286.375 meters, whereas current maps show 2,285 meters. Rüppell generally reached unprecedented accuracy in his measurements.[83]

Within fifteen years, Edward Rüppell had completed four exceptionally important explorations of the Sinai and parts of northeastern Africa and the Red Sea. His impressive scientific achievements have already been highly acknowledged, but his contribution to the scientific exploration of the Near East has yet to be the subject of a comprehensive contemporary study.

Following Rüppell's travels, the hypsometric study of the Holy Land still awaited a breakthrough. This would come in the second half of the 1830s, and would be propelled by the rising interest in the Dead Sea and the need to address its mysteries in a scientific way.

5 Early Explorers

The earliest significant steps in the geographical, primarily cartographical, exploration of the Jordan Rift and the Dead Sea region, were taken during the first three decades of the nineteenth century. As in many other areas of Syria, Palestine and Jordan, here, too, Ulrich Jasper Seetzen (1767–1811) was the modern era's pioneer European explorer. In our context, he was indeed the first European since the Crusader period to actually encircle the Dead Sea. Seetzen's almost legendary story has been told in a number of studies, and his findings and acquisitions still form an important part of the oriental collections in Gotha, the seat of his scientific guide and mentor, the astronomer Franz Xaver von Zach, as well as his financier, Emil-Leopold August (1772–1822), Prince of Saxony-Gotha and Altenburg. All of his letters were published by von Zach, founder and director of the Seeberg Observatory near Gotha, in the latter's pioneering journal *Monatliche Correspondenz zur Beförderung der Erd- und Himmels-Kunde.*[1]

Seetzen reached the Dead Sea for the first time in April 1806, during his 1803–7 sojourn in Syria (where he was learning to pass himself off as a Muslim). During this trip he circled the southern end of the lake on his way from Kerak to Jerusalem.[2] Between 15 and 20 December he traveled to the western shore of the lake, accompanied by a Catholic resident of Bethlehem.[3] He supplied a long and detailed description of the oasis of Ein Gedi and its unique flora and fauna, predicting that 'through a careful cultivation it is still now quite easy, to turn Ein Gedi into a charming settlement, which would be separated from the world from one side by the sea and from the other by a barren desert'.[4] He continued northward through Jericho and returned to Jerusalem. In his last and longest voyage to the same area, which lasted a full month, from 5 January to 5 February 1807, he encircled the entire Dead Sea. It should be noted that for many years following, no other European traveler dared follow in Seetzen's footsteps and walk along the shores of the lake.[5]

The traveler John Carne (1789–1844), who visited the East in 1821, erroneously wrote that 'the only traveller who has made the circuit of the shores of this sea, was a Mr. Hyde, an Englishman, about twenty years since'. John Hyde (?–1825) of Manchester had embarked on his travels in 1818 – more than a decade after Seetzen. He traveled through Egypt, Palestine, Syria and Mesopotamia to India, where he died in the city of Murshidabad (eastern India).[6] Carne's error is understandable given that Seetzen's travels were published only in the 1850s.

Seetzen's unprecedented contribution to the 'rediscovery' of the region has been established by many nineteenth-century as well as contemporary scholars, who have pointed out, in addition to his discoveries, the innovativeness of his method:

> He was the first to study the Land of the Bible with the Bible in his hand, but especially the until then unstudied regions of the upper Jordan, the other side of the Jordan and the Dead Sea and Phoenicia, and there to locate many sites, that are mentioned in the oldest books of the Holy Scriptures, but had totally disappeared from the eyes of the world.[7]

His detailed itinerary included numerous comments concerning the wide variety of natural and human phenomena he encountered. He offered logical explanations for some of the 'mysterious' and 'curious' features related to the Dead Sea and described the flora and fauna in and around it. Although there is no mention of any difference of level from the Mediterranean, he did discuss changes in the level of the Dead Sea itself, which he discerned by the various objects, mainly wood, cast out by the sea upon its shores.[8] Seetzen discussed the absence of any sort of life in the sea. He refuted the Swedish natural historian, Fredric Hasselquist (1722–52), who had been sent by his teacher Carl Linné (1707–78) to collect specimens of fauna in the country: 'I spent much more time by the sea than the Swede,' wrote Seetzen, 'and could not find even one mussel, and the snails are land-snails.'[9] He also refuted the stories about the unusual air which killed any creature flying above it; the possibility of drowning; and the masses of asphalt seen floating on its surface.[10]

Seetzen sketched a map of the entire Jordan Valley from the sources of the river to the southern end of the Dead Sea, based on observations

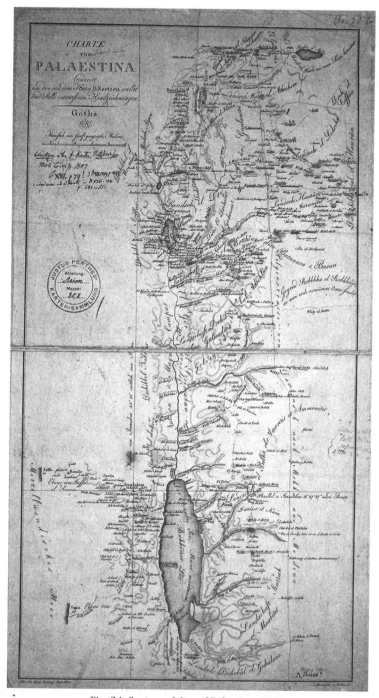

Fig. 34: Seetzen, Map of Palestine, 1810

(but not measurements) in the field; this was probably the first map of its kind since the sixth-century Madaba mosaic map.[11] The story of its compilation was told in Seetzen's diaries and published, along with the map, in 1810 by the astronomer Bernhard August, Freiherr von Lindenau (1779–1854), von Zach's colleague and successor as editor of his journal.[12] In the accompanying text to the map, Seetzen testified:

> In order to make my diaries more understandable, I decided to sketch a map of the countries surrounding the sources of the Jordan and its eastern side and the Dead Sea; but I lacked my diaries, which I forwarded with my packages to Egypt. Consequently I had to suffice myself there by producing a map of the Dead Sea. [...] My unexpectedly long stay in Cairo led me to think about again looking for work which I had to postpone in Jerusalem due to a lack of means [...] My map would teach its viewer to know totally new landscapes, and shed much light on a large part of Palestine.[13]

In fact, while staying in Cairo from mid-1807 to 1809, Seetzen had drafted three sheets based mainly on his field sketches and diaries. All of these were 'the result of my own remarks, or carefully made inquiries' and therefore include almost only areas which he actually visited. His travels around the Dead Sea produced a relatively detailed and accurate description, as he would write: 'I had the pleasure to observe from here the exact outline of the Gôr el Mesráa peninsula and so, to add it with great faithfulness to my map.'[14] Consequently Seetzen's map is the first to show the shape of the Lisân. His excursions were not without challenges. One time his watch, which was crucial for distance calculation, was stolen by Bedouins and when he succeeded much later in getting it back, it was no longer functioning.[15]

The publication of Seetzen's map was delayed, as Lindenau had been looking for more material in order to try 'to issue something more complete'. This evidently yielded nothing, as even the best maps until then – those compiled by the French cartographer Jean-Baptiste Bourguignon d'Anville (1697–1782) in the mid-eighteenth century and which were considerably more accurate than any other maps to date – still had very limited sources at its disposal, for the Jordan Rift Valley in particular.[16] Ultimately Lindenau reduced Seetzen's 'three folio-sheets' into one, and then published it, seeing, as did Seetzen, its tremendous value for 'friends of geography'. About twenty years later Berghaus tried

Fig. 35: D'Anville, Map of Palestine, 1767

unsuccessfully to locate Seetzen's original sketches, which were crucial for his own map. An original copy of Seetzen's published map exists in Petermann's collection.

Johann Ludwig Burckhardt, who followed in Seetzen's footsteps in many respects and whose contribution to the early rediscovery of many parts of the region is of tremendous importance, actually did not visit the Dead Sea. As described in his travels east of the Jordan, he remained in the mountainous area, stayed in Kerak and continued south to gain fame as the first traveler in the new era to describe Petra. 'Not having had an opportunity of descending to the borders of the Dead Sea,' he wrote, 'I shall subjoin here a few notes which I collected from the people of Kerak.' But he added, 'I have since been informed that M. Seetzen, the most indefatigable traveler that ever visited Syria, has made the complete tour of the Dead Sea.'[17]

5.1 COSTIGAN, THE FIRST VICTIM, AND THE SAILING ON THE DEAD SEA

One of the most affecting stories connected with the enterprising devotion of travellers, is that which describes the fate of the unfortunate Costigan. The memory of a man is deserving of profound respect, when he has been found possessed of the peculiar energy which leads him to peril even life to accomplish an object believed to be good and great. Had this enthusiastic Irish wanderer in the Holy Land, employed his earnest spirit in some more practical undertaking, his name might have been ranked among the most honourable in the annals of humanity. But even as it was, he ought not to be forgotten.[18]

All who are acquainted with this story will certainly agree with the above words of clergyman and author Henry Stebbing (1799–1883), who, it seems, never visited the Holy Land.[19] The relatively well-known story of the first attempt to conduct research in and around the lake and to treat it as an object of study in its own right is attributed to the ill-fated voyage of Christopher Costigan (or Costigin, 1810–35), a young student of theology from Maynooth College, Ireland.[20]

Costigan's biographical details and the story of his expedition have been studied and published by Con Costello and Erik Olaf Eriksen, and it is not necessary to repeat them here in full. Like other members of his family, he studied at Clongowes Wood (1819–26), a Jesuit lay college associated with the Roman Catholic seminary at Maynooth. Some sources claim he also 'gained considerable experience by travelling in eastern lands'.[21] A certain Costigan (also sometimes called Costigin) is mentioned in some letters – actually detective reports, located in the TCD archive – as being connected with the 1798 rebellion.[22] A John Costigan of Drogheda, a member of the family, perhaps a brother, was in touch with Admiral Beaufort, as revealed in a letter dated July 1834, mailed to Beaufort's private address and mentioning the Admiral's close friend, Maria Edgeworth (1768–1849), a famous English novelist from an Irish landowning family, who spent most of her life and performed most of her work in Ireland. Being 'the most commercially successful novelist of her age', Edgeworth also had a wide circle of friends, including the poet and novelist Sir Walter Scott (1771–1832) as her most important reader.[23]

It is worth exploring how Costigan's narrative came to light and how the memory of 'the first victim' has evolved during the century and a half following his death. Costigan planned to sail the length of the Jordan into the Dead Sea in an attempt to explore its shores, measure its depth, explain its buoyancy and understand other curious phenomena. In the summer of 1835, probably during a longer journey in the East, he transported a small boat from Acre to Tiberias and launched it on the Sea of Galilee. He subsequently succeeded in sailing on the Dead Sea for eight days (probably starting on 25 August), but only barely survived the difficulties he had to face. He died on 7 September in Jerusalem, where he was buried in the Franciscan cemetery on Mount Zion, leaving behind not a single document about his explorations or any results of his scientific endeavors.[24]

His travel companion, Lieutenant J. Webber Smith, probably from a Sligo County family whose sons served with the Royal Engineers,[25] did not accompany Costigan to the Dead Sea. In 1837, following a publication about the Mt Athos monasteries and his journey from Constantinople to Salonika, Smith's request to the RGS for financing of his travels in Central Asia was declined. About a dozen years later, he transmitted for publication an interesting map 'of the Interior of the Hedjaz, from Surveys by the Officers of Mahommed Ali's Troops' to cartographer James Wyld (1812–87), 'Geographer of the King'. The informative map was of great military importance as well, as it contained data as to the 'Strength of the Principal Tribes of the Hedjaz and Jemen'.[26] With these scraps of information end the biographical details we could find about Webber Smith.

Costigan's narrative became known to contemporary travelers and to later generations mainly through the American lawyer, John Lloyd Stephens (1805–52), who, while visiting Palestine in 1836, traced the ill-fated researcher's steps. He found Costigan's boat in Jericho, interviewed his Maltese servant – the only witness to the voyage – and in his popular book told a major part of Costigan's story including a map in which he tried to give a day-by-day reconstruction of Costigan's water route.[27] Another description was provided by the daughter of John Nicolayson, a Schleswig-Holstein-born Protestant missionary employed in Jerusalem by The London Society for Promoting Christianity Amongst the Jews. Nicolayson, who had transported the ailing Costigan from Jericho to Jerusalem, told the story to his daughter, who, several years later, presented it at a meeting of the Jerusalem Literary Society, held on 12 February 1850.[28]

The role of the Maltese in the port cities on the eastern Mediterranean through the first half of the nineteenth century still awaits a thorough study. The observant Dublin priest Nathanael Burton, who traveled in 1836-7 in the Middle East and claimed that he had returned on foot from Syria to Dublin, devoted some descriptions to the Maltese, indicating that 'the superabundant population of Malta is scattered over the Levant in the various characters of artificers, tailors, &c. – there is no part of Syria or Egypt where you may not meet them'.[29] The American missionary John D. Paxton was accompanied for over two years by Angelo, a servant and a cook, 'who had been our factotum in all our travels'. Angelo became strongly attached to the reverend's children, and the missionary could not hide his disappointment when the Maltese chose to stay in the East instead of accompanying them back home.[30] George Robinson had been surprised to find, in Beirut in 1837, 'an excellent inn, [...] the only establishment entitled to that name throughout the whole of Syria', managed by the Maltese Giuseppe.[31] This 'Maltese connection' is another thread, tying together many travelers to the East during that period. Chesney, too, recruited a number of Maltese for his expedition, as interpreters and laborers. Ainsworth in his narrative of the expedition did not hide his deep disappointment with them, as, 'with the exception of two or three, [...], turned out very useless fellows'.[32] William Allen devoted a full chapter in his book to Malta – and especially to the Maltese, 'natives, good and bad'. 'Away from Malta, however,' he stated, 'so many black sheep are found, that the race is brought disrepute; and especially at Alexandria, Smyrna, and Constantinople they are notorious for their cleverness....'[33]

Stephens, who was suffering from laryngitis due to his enthusiastic involvement in an election campaign, headed across the Atlantic to convalesce in Europe.[34] In a short time, this sojourn evolved into a voyage to the East, including Greece, Turkey and Russia. The winter of 1835/6 was spent in Paris as he missed the last ship back home. Spending his time in libraries, he became acquainted with the highly popular travel account of Constantin François Chasseboeuf, Comte de Volney (1757–1820), philosopher, orientalist, politician and member of the Institut de France, who had traveled in the East from late 1782 to 1785,[35] as well as the beautiful lithography in the book of Léon Emmanuel Simon Joseph, Comte de Laborde (1807–69), later curator of the Department of Antiquities at the Louvre, who had visited Petra in 1828 along with the young French engineer and Orient-traveler, Louis Maurice Adolphe Linant de Bellefonds (1799–1883), later bey and paşa, Director of Public Works under Mehemet Ali and the person who first presented the idea of the Suez Canal to the French vice-consul in Alexandria, Ferdinand-Marie de Lesseps (1805–94).[36] It was Barthélemy Prosper Enfantin (1796–1864), a devout disciple of Claude Henri de Rouvroy, Comte de Saint-Simon (1760–1825), and responsible for implementing the latter's ideas of cutting canals for the improvement of the material state of mankind, who planted the idea of digging the Suez Canal in Linant's mind. In 1833 he arrived in Egypt with a small entourage, including an engineer. In Cairo they met two countrymen, Sulaymân Paşa ('al-Fransawi', the reader recalls) and Linant, at the time Mehemet Ali's main irrigation advisor. Enfantin left Egypt after some work and an audience with the Paşa in 1836, but the idea of the Canal already captured the imagination of the French living in Egypt.[37]

Stephens reached Alexandria in December 1835, had an audience with the viceroy and traveled in Upper Egypt. These experiences were sufficient to create in him a 'metamorphosis, and he turned into Abd-el-Aziz, in costume and in name', propelling him into a relentless quest for adventure and for experiencing the unknown.[38] In Cairo he met with Linant, who proved to be a highly valuable source of information. Subsequently, Stephens took his voyage through Sinai to Akaba and Petra, fulfilling his ultimate dream.[39] Continuing on to Jerusalem, he saw the Dead Sea for the first time:

> Lying between the barren mountains of Arabia and Judea, presenting to us from that height no more than a small, calm and a silvery surface, was that mysterious sea which rolled its dark waters over the guilty cities of Sodom and Gomorrah; over whose surface, according to the superstition of the Arabs, no bird can fly, and in whose waters no fish can swim; constantly receiving in its greedy bosom the whole body of the Jordan, but, unlike all other waters, sending forth no tribute to the ocean.[40]

He took his comprehensive tour of the lake and its vicinity only in March 1836, heading off from Jerusalem, as usual toward the small, wretched and anything but impressive village of Jericho, which included some mud-and-straw huts and one old square stone tower.[41] In Jericho, by chance, he saw Costigan's boat:

[...] I had looked round and selected another [hut] for my lodging-place, chiefly from the circumstance of its having a small boat set up on its side before it, so as to form a front wall.

That boat told a melancholy story. It was the only one that had ever floated on the Dead Sea.[42]

Stephens added that he had heard about the boat from Reverend Nicolayson in Jerusalem, who, about eight months earlier, had tried to help nurse Costigan back to health. Only the lack of a suitable companion prevented Stephens from adopting the idea himself and using the boat for sailing on the lake.[43]

Making up his mind to reconstruct the 'melancholy story' in detail, he went to Beirut, where he located Costigan's companion and servant and heard his narrative. In his book, Stephens recounted the first half of Costigan's story, from purchasing the boat, sailing with it to Acre, transporting it by camel to Tiberias and launching it in the Sea of Galilee, to the failure to sail on the Jordan, its transfer to Jericho and its launching on the Dead Sea, and the eight days of sailing thereon. His description leaves off with the ailing Costigan under the care of an old Arab woman in Jericho.[44]

Stephens returned home and published his book, which became highly popular and brought him a considerable sum of money, enabling him to take his second well-known voyage, to the Yucatan Peninsula in Mexico. There he became responsible for the rediscovery of Maya civilization and, on 17 November 1839, for the advent of a new science – American archaeology.[45]

The second and last part of Costigan's story has reached us from an entirely different source. It was first partly published in 1911, in the PEF quarterly, by Ernest William Gurney Masterman (1867–1943), then resident physician and director of the Anglican Hospital in Jerusalem. Arriving in Jerusalem in 1892, he served there and in Safed until the beginning of the First World War.[46] Being also an amateur scientist and archaeologist, he was appointed honorary secretary of the Palestine office of the PEF, and gained fame for his marking of the level of the Dead Sea on a rock south of Ein Feshcha, starting in 1900 and twice annually for thirteen subsequent years.[47] The idea for such a project was first raised by Charles Wilson, who, reacting to a letter of Lord John Edward Gray Hill (1840–1914) concerning the changes in the level, added the hope for continuous observations of it during different parts of the year. Gray Hill, a lawyer, and his wife, Caroline Emily (1843–1924), a painter and photographer, acquired a tract of land in 1889 on Mount Scopus and built a home with a panoramic view of the Dead Sea.[48] Masterman's close friend, the Irish archaeologist Robert A.S. Macalister (1870–1950), famous for his excavations of Gezer, was the one to acquaint him with the idea.[49] Macalister was the first to acknowledge the importance of the first two volumes of the protocols of the Jerusalem Literary Society. Looking into them, he decided that they held much material which should be rescued from oblivion. Consequently he initiated the publication of many of these protocols, partial or complete, in the *PEFQS* volumes between 1908 and 1911.[50] The two descriptions concerning the 'Sailors on the Dead Sea' included in the first collection were transferred to his friend Masterman, who was busy performing the measurements of the lake level, and the latter published them.

'Some years ago,' wrote Masterman in the opening lines of his paper, 'I came across some notes in the *Proceedings of the Jerusalem Literary and Scientific Society* bearing on Costigan and Molyneux.'[51] After a preliminary and partial publication in the American periodical *The Biblical World*, he decided, together with Macalister, that the texts were worthy of more comprehensive publication.[52]

The idea of founding a literary society in Jerusalem had been raised around 1846 by the British consul, James Finn (1806–72, consul in 1845–63).[53] The first meeting of the newly established Jerusalem Literary Society took place in his home on 20 November 1849, and it quickly gained supporters and members from the resident Europeans in the city, as well as from visiting scholars. According to Finn, who was acting president, the aim of the society was to learn and study any interesting theme, literary and scientific, of any period within the Holy Land. The papers presented at the meetings were those of members as well as of visiting scholars.[54] They were all copied, usually by Finn himself and in his handwriting, into the protocol books. The first two volumes include meetings until 1854. At the twelfth meeting, which took place on 12 February 1850, Miss Nicolayson presented her 'Notes of the First Exploring Expedition to the Dead Sea'.[55]

John (Johannes, Hans) Nicolayson, born in Schleswig-Holstein, reached Jerusalem for the first time in January 1826 as a missionary of The London Society for Promoting Christianity Amongst the Jews (also known as the London Jews' Society, or LJS), in order to preach to the German-speaking Jewish population in the city. He came to help the resident missionary physician, the Irishman George Edward Dalton (D'Alton, ?–1827). Dalton, his wife and infant left Ireland in June 1824, first to Alexandria and then to Beirut, where he studied Arabic, and subsequently to Tyre. They reached Jerusalem late in 1825, becoming the first missionaries to settle in the city. But Dalton died in January 1827 of fatigue, fever and medical malpractice, three weeks after Nicolayson joined him.[56] Nicolayson, who continued on for some months in Jerusalem, married Dalton's widow and then moved north and concentrated his activity in and around Beirut. He returned to Jerusalem in summer 1831 and, following the Egyptian conquest, was able to rent a house on the outskirts of the Jewish quarter. This made him the first permanent resident Protestant missionary in Jerusalem and a key figure in all Protestant activity in the city over the course of the twenty-three years following, until his death in 1856.[57]

Nicolayson and his daughter joined the literary society on 14 December 1849, and his wife followed two weeks later. It was the daughter who attended most of the meetings[58] and she was the one to present the paper at the twelfth meeting, written from her father's memories, either from a diary or simply from his recollections almost fifteen years after the events took place.[59] Masterman pointed out that there were some considerable differences between Nicolayson's and Stephens's versions, and that he preferred the latter which had been written closer to the events.[60]

It is to the Israeli historian and pioneer of Land of Israel Studies, Ze'ev Vilnay (1900–88), whom we owe the rediscovery of the few existing remains from the travels of Costigan and his successor, Molyneux (see chapter 9). An Irish Catholic, Costigan was buried on the day of his death, 7 September 1835, in the Franciscan cemetery on Mount Zion. The inscription on his gravestone testifies that it was erected by his mother, as his father had died some years earlier. We have testimony, from 1911 and again from 1932, of the stone being identified, though not in its original place. Later, the Irish Franciscan Father Eugene Hoade (1904–72) tried in vain to locate it, probably in the 1940s. Vilnay had also attempted to locate it in 1935, intending to put 'a bunch of flowers' on the grave to celebrate the centenary of the event, though he was unsuccessful. He did succeed in finding it after

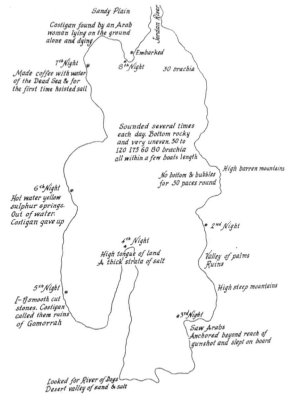

Fig. 36: Costigan: Tombstone; Route by JL Stephens

the 1967 war, following which the tombstone was cleaned and placed near the cemetery wall.[61]

Costello has already pointed out the somewhat strange fact that Reverend Porter failed to mention Costigan in his many publications concerning Syria and the Holy Land, including his writings on the study of the Dead Sea.[62] This might be explained by their different denominations, Porter being a Protestant missionary from Northern Ireland. Surprisingly, he was also not mentioned by Nathanael Burton, who stayed at the Franciscan Casa Nova in Jerusalem at the beginning of 1837!

But Costigan's memory was nonetheless kept alive. William Francis Lynch, who followed in his footsteps thirteen years later, was the first to immortalize Costigan's presence on the map of Palestine, terming the northern point of the Lisân 'Point Costigan'. To this day, although the name is not formal, Costigan, as well as the other ill-fated Dead-Sea sailor, Molyneux, are strongly embedded on all maps of the region, as well as in collective memory:

> It was indeed a scene of unmitigated desolation. [...]. While in full view of the peninsula, I named its northern extremity 'Point Costigan', and its southern one 'Point Molyneux', as a tribute to the memories of the two gallant Englishmen who lost their lives in attempting to explore this sea.[63]

On Wednesday, 26 April 1848, around noontime, while sailing in the shallow water of the southern part of the Dead Sea, Lynch decided to honor the memory of his two predecessors by sailing on it and investigating its secrets. Was it the dark, mysterious, gloomy mood inspired by the lake and its desolate mountainous surroundings that caused him to commemorate the two sailors? Or was it the biblical memories it evoked and the close connection that was felt to the deeds of the Creator? Or was it just a carefully considered, almost scientific decision? Perhaps a combination of all three factors?

Various travelers who visited the grave and mentioned 'poor Costigan' in their writings, supplemented their narratives using Stephens's book. William Wilde, guided in Jerusalem by the son of the late missionary-physician, George Dalton, showed great interest in the story of the 'ill-fated Costigan, the first circumnavigator of the Dead Sea', but added that he found himself 'unable to add any thing of consequence' to what was written by Stephens. He did have one amendment to make, having been informed by Webber Smith that the boat was not purchased in Beirut and carried across the Jordan, but that it was built in Tiberias, launched on the Sea of Galilee and floated to the Dead Sea.[64] Here one must certainly prefer Stephens's version, which is confirmed by Nicolayson. Webber Smith's version, as given by Wilde, also contains an internal geographical contradiction.

Another long text, later transcribed by Costello, appeared in John Carne's book, describing his travels in Greece, Turkey, Syria and Egypt. Carne did not mention Costigan in his first itineraries published in the 1820s, but added him to his later book published in the late 1830s. Carne's description, not mentioning him by name but surely referring to Costigan, waxes poetic and is full of factual mistakes, but it forms the beginning of a narrative:

> But he had a mightier enemy than the Arab, the desert, or the pestilential air of its waters – it was Azrael, the angel of death. [...] When they bore him slowly away [from Jericho] to Jerusalem, and he cast his eyes for the last time on the dark waters, whose hope had perished, and with it every hope of home, of all he loved – did not the iron enter his soul?[65]

Carne's visit took place almost three years after Costigan's death and only a year after Moore's adventure; still, there is not one word about the latter. His description, so erroneous on many points, can serve as evidence of the fact that collective memory had already begun to combine the two stories.

Henry Stebbing, writing that 'the memory of a man deserving a profound respect, when he has been found possessed of that peculiar energy which leads him to peril even life to accomplish an object believed to be good and great', followed Stephens's description, which was more accurate than Carne's on this point. Both praise the old woman from Jericho (one must wonder if herein lay a hidden reference to another woman of Jericho, who helped the spies of biblical fame[66]), who tried to ease Costigan's last days and who, according to them, had been 'blessed with his dying breath'.[67] John Gadsby (c.1809–93), a printer and publisher who traveled throughout the East during the late

1840s and early 1850s, visited the Dead Sea in March 1847. He devoted six lines to Costigan, which included that 'his remains were interred in the Armenian [sic] cemetery on Mount Zion', and that his diary was lost 'through the carelessness of his servant'.[68]

Undoubtedly, Masterman and Vilnai were the ones to restore the narrative in today's collective memory. In the 1930s, Reverend Boggis, himself successfully canoeing down the Jordan to the Dead Sea, devoted a long chapter to his predecessor.[69] Eriksen also tried to establish the exact reason for Costigan's death, which was followed by the death of two other Dead Sea explorers, Molyneux and Lieutenant John B. Dale (?–1848), Lynch's second-in-command. In a paper published in 1986, Eriksen claims that the death was 'a case of heat stroke'.[70] There is no doubt of the facts: Costigan, who chose the hottest month of the year, was already exhausted by the time he reached the Dead Sea. His eight days of sailing proved constant torture. Eriksen wrote about 'voluntary dehydration', worsened by drinking coffee made of the hypertonic water of the lake. The death was also brought about by the ineffectiveness of Nicolayson's rescue efforts, so that by the time he was brought to Jerusalem, there was no hope of survival.

Andrew Jampoler, a veteran US Navy pilot, in 2005 published the most comprehensive study concerning his countryman, Lynch, and his 1848 expedition.[71] Jampoler's preparations included a tour of Israel and Jordan, to the extent that this was possible within the political and security situation. During this tour his interest was aroused about the cause of death of the three victims. He found a valuable partner in the late Prof. Michael Friedlaender (1942–2004), a nephrologist at Hadassah University Hospital in Jerusalem. From a long letter sent on 12 October 2003, Friedlaender makes it quite clear that Costigan did not stand a chance of surviving after drinking the water, as, 'ingestion or aspiration of small amounts of [Dead Sea] water is sufficient to cause extreme hypercalcamia and hypermagnesemia which have a high fatality rate', i.e., the high magnesium and calcium levels are very toxic, even before taking into account the problem of the concentration of NaCl, that 'has serious physiological consequences and is eventually fatal'. His death had been inevitable.[72]

'Only on the last years had boats with sails and foreign flags shown themselves again on the blue water, surprising the residents, in order to measure the shores and to establish the unknown depth of the Sea of Galilee,' declared Ritter in 1850, mentioning the fact that these were people of 'seafaring nations' – Ireland, England and the United States.[73] Costigan had been the first to actualize the idea in the new era, though as yet none of the studies about him have managed to locate the origin of his idea to sail on the lake. His 'friend and companion', Webber Smith, told William Wilde that he first conceived of the idea on the voyage in Beirut.[74]

It would have been virtually impossible for Costigan to have read the itinerary of van Egmond, the Dutch consul in Naples who testified in the early 1720s that he had heard about an English nobleman who spared neither effort nor expense when trying to satisfy his curiosity. He carried a boat by camel to the Dead Sea, with which he wished to sail and explore it. But, adds van Egmont, 'I cannot prove that his Lordship's observations have ever seen the light'.[75]

Had Costigan read the extremely popular travel description of Chateaubriand, the French novelist who, following his voyage of 1806, wrote that 'on ferait certainement des découvertes curieuses sur ce lac' if a vessel were transported from Jaffa and launched in its waters?[76] One clue to Costigan's intentions comes from the inscription that his mother put on his tombstone: It simply read *Loca sancta lustraturus* – 'exploring the holy places'.[77] Whatever the case may be, the idea must have been somewhere 'in the air'. John Carne, as an example, arrived in 1821 at the Dead Sea in Arab garb, after being refused the required permission by the governor of Jerusalem. In contrast to the conventional route through Jericho, his group went first to Mar Saba monastery, and then advanced by night to the lake. After reaching it he wrote that 'it has never been navigated since the cities were engulfed, and it is strange that no traveller should have thought of launching a boat to explore it'.[78]

One interesting point here is Costigan's preference for the shorter Acre–Tiberias route for transporting the boat, though this necessitated sailing from the Sea of Galilee to the Dead Sea. The road from Jaffa via Jerusalem to Jericho was of course much longer, and the Jerusalem mountains much higher and certainly more difficult to pass, but it would bring you directly to the Dead Sea. The fact that Costigan, and later Molyneux and Lynch, chose to launch their boats in the Sea of Galilee, derived probably from their aim to study the upper lake and the Jordan, but also from the assumption that this route would prove easier than the southern one, chosen, as would be demonstrated, by Moore and Beek.

According to the title of the book containing his letters, the American missionary Reverend John D. Paxton from Kentucky resided in Palestine and Syria in the years 1836–8.[79] In the beginning of the 1830s, he took part in the heated debate between abolitionists, of whom he was one, and advocates of slavery, in which both used the Bible as a source for their claims.[80] Later he went on a grand tour through Europe to the East and, after visiting Turkey, arrived in Beirut in mid-June 1836. He stayed mostly in the Lebanese capital and then spent a time in the mountains, until spring 1838. Although he showed his commitment to helping the resident missionaries and even married there, he decided not to stay in the region; after a visit to Egypt, he departed on 15 July 1838 for New York.[81] During his time in the East he traveled widely in Palestine as well as in Lebanon and Egypt. His detailed reports are of prime importance to anyone interested in the study of the country during this period.

Accompanied by the American missionary John Francis Lanneau (1817–55) of South Carolina, Paxton visited the Dead Sea in October 1836. His impressions, described in a letter that would appear in his book, were quite positive. He wrote that 'still the bank, the water, and the bottom, so far as I saw and tried it, had much less of the terrible, fearful, and unnatural, than I had expected'. And, moreover, '[i]nstead of the dark, gloomy, and turbid spread of water, that from my childhood I had imagined, it struck me as a very pleasant lake.'[82]

Even from this first visit, Paxton showed great interest in the study of the Dead Sea. He pointed out what he determined as a 'singular fact', namely, that there was actually so little known about this lake 'which for ages has excited more intensive interest than any other in the world', and that so far, there were only very few who had seriously attempted to explore it. 'There has not, as far as I know, been but one boat on the waters of the Dead Sea for ages,' he wrote, referring, of course, to Costigan, who had preceded him by a little more than a year.[83]

One of the last letters in the book, dated Jaffa, 21 May 1838, described his last visit to Jerusalem. Here, he returns to a discussion of the Dead Sea. It was already known that the lake was lower than the Mediterranean, and Paxton now argued that on his first visit he noted the great difference in the descent on either side of Jerusalem, to the

Dead Sea and to the Mediterranean, respectively. In Jerusalem he met with Robinson, Smith and de Bertou, who told him of the watershed in the Arabah, and Lindsay and Dr. Wilson, who confirmed his data. This led him to a discussion of the possibility that the Jordan flowed into the Red Sea, and of the prospect of constructing a water connection between the Red and Dead Seas, which would 'even raise the level of the waters of Lake Tiberias'.[84]

This also brought him to a relatively long discussion of Costigan's excursion. He, of course, did not know of Stephens and his book, and learned about the boat being in Jericho only after returning to Jerusalem. 'Last year an intelligent Irishman took a boat across from Acre to the Lake of Tiberias,' began his description of Costigan and his death:

> I did not know it was there, or I should have ascertained its fitness for another voyage. Were some one, acquainted with navigating a small vessel, and capable of taking soundings and making a proper survey of the lake, to spend a month or two in doing it, and to publish a full account, with a correct map of the sea and the coast, he would confer a very great favour on the Christian world. It would be so easy of execution, and of so universal interest when done, that I wonder that none of those men who long for public fame have not before now thought of it.[85]

The points raised here by Paxton uncannily resemble the objectives expressed by Moore and Beek, including those mentioned in Moore's letter to his mother after failing in his mission.[86] The similarities are much too striking to be coincidental. Although I have no proof, I would suggest that Paxton met Moore and Beek prior to their voyage and that he was 'the missing link' between Costigan and Moore. Moreover, Paxton was accompanied on his travels by a certain B., in addition to Angelo, the Maltese servant and cook. Was it Beek? Of course, there is no proof of this, but the possibility exists. Whatever the case may be, Paxton was in Beirut in September 1836, he went by sea to Jaffa and he spent the first half of October in Jerusalem and its environs. Returning through the Galilee, he was in the Lebanese capital by 23 October and remained there for more than a year. Moore and Beek left Damascus on 1 February 1837, and continued from Beirut to the Dead Sea on 15 March. No doubt, they did meet in the Lebanese capital!

5.2 'IT APPEARS TO BE CONSIDERABLY LOWER THAN THE OCEAN':
MOORE AND BEEK

The year 1837 saw a genuine advance in the study of the Dead Sea, when two teams, almost simultaneously and without knowledge of one another, determined and announced that the level of the lake was actually lower than that of the Mediterranean.

The first to publish this was the *Journal of the Royal Geographical Society*. The earliest hint had arrived at the beginning of 1837, inside a report on developments in geography over the previous year: '[...] we hear that a spirited young Irishman, Mr. George Moore, instead of loitering in fashionable pilgrimage along the beaten paths of Palestine, has actually devoted the past year to a minute geographic examination of the Dead Sea and its shores.'[87] This item of gossip was published at the end of that same year in the 1837 volume of the *JRGS* along with its confirmation in fact as the journal reported the findings of two researchers, George Henry Moore and William G. Beek. There is no way of knowing who informed the editor initially about Moore, and why there was no mention of his partner in the earlier instance. Conversely, the letter that reached the RGS on 19 October 1837 and was subsequently published was signed exclusively by Beek. Dated Marseille, 22 August, the letter makes no mention of Moore by name, referring only to 'my companion' and 'a friend'. It seems that Beek had decided to take all the credit for himself:

> It was my intention to have given some information regarding the Dead Sea, having taken a boat and all that was necessary to complete a survey of that lake. I remained with a friend on the shores 20 days during which time we repeatedly crossed it, and I have surveyed about a fifth, [...]. My observations were made with Capt. Kater's repeating circle.[88]

The letter was published immediately, with only slight editorial corrections, in the 1837 volume of the *JRGS*:[89]

> In the month of March, 1837, Mr. G. H. Moore and Mr. W. G. Beek, having made the necessary preparations and produced a good boat, left *Beïrut* in a small coasting vessel for Jaffa, their intention being to make a trigonometrical survey of the Dead Sea, to ascertain its depth,

and to procure collections of all that could be of use to science. From Jaffa they conveyed their boat, stores, &c., to the Dead Sea, passing through Jerusalem and descending on Jericho; a work of great labour, considering that they had no assistance from the authorities, but rather the contrary. After surveying a great portion of the shores, these gentlemen were obliged to abandon their work, the guards and guides declaring they would not proceed. The width of the sea has been established beyond a doubt; soundings have also been taken showing great depth, in some parts upwards of 300 fathoms. The length of this sea is much less than is generally supposed. *There appears also to be another remarkable feature in the level of the sea, as from several observations about the temperature of boiling water, it appears to be considerably lower than the ocean* [my emphasis, HG].

'The reader's attention ought to be called particularly to the fact that it is to this expedition that we owe the direct discovery of the depression of the Dead Sea.'[90] This remark, made by Carl Ritter in his *Comparative Geography of Palestine and the Sinaitic Peninsula*, characterizes the importance that even leading twentieth-century scholars attributed to the one-page letter. Following Ritter, contemporary scholarship on the history of Dead Sea research reiterates the role of 'the two Englishmen' as the creators of 'the drama of the scientific community's awareness of the depression of the Dead Sea'.[91]

And yet, Moore and Beek themselves have remained relatively anonymous in this whole story. Much has been written about the history of the study of the Dead Sea; some important artifacts, such as Costigan's gravestone or Molyneux's boat, have been found; many of the explorers and scientists involved have been the subject of longer biographies which have made them known to the interested public – but nothing, in fact, has been written about 'the two Englishmen'. Even the exact details of their measurements, the exact temperatures at which the water boiled, were published only in de Bertou's report.[92]

George Henry Moore (1810–70) of Moore Hall on the shore of Lough Carra, County Mayo in western Ireland, had been touring the East without any scientific pretenses.[93] But his two extant diaries – the only two to have escaped his own destruction in later years – reveal intensive scientific activity in Syria and in and around the Dead Sea.[94]

Moore spent the winter of 1836/7 wandering among the villages in the Hauran, describing their antiquities and transcribing inscriptions. In

(456)

V.—*On the Dead Sea and some Positions in Syria.*

In the month of March, 1837, Mr. G. II. Moore and Mr. W. G. Beek, having made the necessary preparations and procured a good boat, left *Beirut* in a small coasting vessel for Jaffa, their intention being to make a trigonometrical survey of the Dead Sea, to ascertain its depth, and to procure collections of all that could be of use to science. From Jaffa they conveyed their boat, stores, &c., to the Dead Sea, passing through Jerusalem and descending on Jericho ; a work of great labour, considering that they had no assistance from the authorities, but rather the con-trary. After surveying a great portion of the shores, these gen-tlemen were obliged to abandon their work, the guards and guides declaring they would not proceed. The width of the sea has been established beyond a doubt; soundings also have been taken showing great depth, in some parts upwards of 300 fathoms. The length of this sea is much less than is generally supposed. There appears also to be another remarkable feature in the level of the sea, as from several observations upon the temperature of boiling water, it appears to be considerably lower than the ocean. Mr. Moore has been down to Egypt to procure a firman from the Pasha to enable him to continue the survey, and has returned to Syria, but nothing is yet known of his success. Mr. Beek has been obliged to return to Europe on account of the influence of the climate on his health; but as soon as these two gentlemen meet in England, or when Mr. Moore has completed the work, should he be fortunate enough to succeed, an account of the whole will be laid before the public. In the mean time we are happy in being enabled to give a few results of observations for latitude made by these gentlemen on a former journey; that of Petra is, we believe, the first observation on record for that place :

Convent on Mount Sinai	.	.	26° 33½′	N.
Akaba Fort	.	.	29 32	
Petra	.	.	30 19	
Hebron	.	.	31 31½	
Jerusalem	.	.	31 45½	
Jeraish	.	.	32 16½	
Jaffa	.	.	32 4½	

From some rough observations, Jeraish was found to be 2000 feet, and Jerusalem 2600 feet above the level of the Mediter-ranean.

Fig. 37: Moore and Beek's letter: publication and original

Baalbek he met William G. Beek, an Englishman about whom we know almost nothing, though one source claims that he had been a lieutenant of the English navy.[95] They journeyed together to Beirut, Beek planning to cross the desert to Baghdad and Moore intending to sail home. But in the Lebanese capital they changed their plans, purchased a small boat, recruited two boatmen, collected all the necessary supplies and loaded them onto a local coastal vessel. Moore, the one with monetary means, withdrew £100, of which 'the greater part [...] was expended in paying servants & other bills'.[96] In a coastal vessel they transported the boat and the equipment by sea to Jaffa and by land through Jerusalem, to be launched in the Dead Sea. There they began measuring, collecting specimens, sailing and establishing depths, among other activities. Security conditions and the refusal of their local guards and servants to proceed to the eastern and southern shores, forced them to leave, and the only direct scientific result was the short letter published in the *JRGS*.[97]

The similarity between Moore and Beek's surprising decision, as well as their objectives and methods, and those of Costigan, can hardly be coincidental. There must have been someone in Beirut who planted the idea of sailing in the minds of the young travelers. The central location of Beirut and Damascus is pointed out in all contemporary travel accounts. The European consuls resided in these cities; Robinson described Beirut as 'a place of some trade' and this port of Damascus as 'one of the few places in Syria, where a bill of exchange can be discounted, without great loss and much trouble'.[98] It was not only the exchange of money, but of ideas, that took place regularly in the Lebanese and Syrian capitals. This situation, I argue, offers a plausible explanation for many as yet unexplained and surprising decisions made by European travelers in the region and it played a very important role in the specific developments described here. I argue here, that it was most certainly through Paxton that the idea to descend to the Dead Sea had been adopted by Moore and Beek, and they did all they could to accomplish their aims.

It is not difficult to trace Moore's life story. A detailed biography was written by one of his two sons, Colonel Maurice George Moore (1854–1939), a renowned soldier, legislator and diplomat.[99] Moreover, the fact that his older son, George Augustus (1852-1933), became a famous novelist and art critic, led to the existence of many detailed descriptions of the father, included in his son's books and biographies.[100]

George Henry was the eldest of three sons of George Moore 'the second' (1770–1840), a philosopher, historian and political theorist who 'lived a calm uneventful life in his library', and Louisa Browne (c.1780–1861), a granddaughter of the first Earl of Altamont, 'a strong-minded, dictatorial woman of great business capacity'.[101] His youth, as well as other parts of his life, were spent at the Georgian house that was built by his grandfather on the shore of Lough Carra.[102] His grandfather, George Moore 'the first' (Jorge Moro, 1729–99), a native of Ashbrook, County Mayo, made his fortune heading one of the wine and brandy trading houses in Alicante, Spain, as well as manufacturing iodine, a valuable commodity at the time, which his fleet extracted from seaweed brought from Galway. After selling his property in Spain in 1784 he returned to Mayo in 1790, having to sign an 'Act for the Relief of His Majesty's Subjects of this Kingdom professing the Popish Religion'. In 1792–6 he erected the 'big house' overlooking the eastern shores of Lough Carra, called 'Moore Hall'. In 1798, his son, John Moore (1767–99) was appointed president of the 'Republic of Connaught' during a rebellion against the English. This lasted one week, until the rebellion was suppressed and he was arrested in Castlebar and brought to court (at the full expense of the family), dying the next year. Recognized also today as the first Irish president, he was reburied in 1961 in Mayo.[103]

The large square late-eighteenth-century Georgian house with a basement and three floors had been designed by the eminent Waterford architect John Roberts (1712–96). The stones were brought from a quarry three miles away, carried across the frozen lake. The basement, which could be entered either by steps from the ground floor or through a back entrance and a tunnel leading to the servants' quarters, housed the kitchen and other service-rooms.[104] The ground floor contained the dining room and reading room, smaller chambers for the doctor and the priest, and a school room. The first floor included the library, a 'summer room' which opened to a balcony, and bedrooms; and the top floor included a billiard room, nursery and more bedrooms. The solemn ornamented façade, overlooking the slope to the lake, included a wide entrance door ensconced by pillars, and seven large windows on each of the two upper floors. The family motto, carved on the upper floor, read *Fortis cadere cedere non potest* ('He who proceeds with courage should not fail'). The house was occupied by the Moores until 1910 and then intermittently, until January 1923, when it was burned and destroyed during the Irish Civil War.

The estate amounted to 12,330 acres of land.[105] Planned as a manor, it had all the outbuildings needed for self-sufficiency. The servants' area behind the house included several buildings: residence, smithy (the only building still existing today), barns, granary, laundry, sawmill, byres and stables. The big garden, north-east of the main building, was surrounded by a wall and included some fruit trees (apples, pears, peaches, cherries), vegetable plots, a greenhouse and the racing stables with the coach house.

The family had a vast network of connections – through marriage, social status and economic and political interests – with the other Mayo

Fig. 38: George Henry Moore and Moore Hall

Catholic noble families, mainly the Brownes, Marquesses of Sligo and Lords Altamont, who lived in the Westport House. Howe Peter Browne (1788–1845) was second Marquess of Sligo from 1809 and his son, George (1820–96), was third Marquess from 1845. John Thomas Browne, born 1824, succeeded his brother as fourth Marquess from 1896 until his death in 1903. The Westport Estate papers provide evidence that John Thomas Browne, Royal Navy, and James Browne, Ninth Lancers, served in India during the late 1840s.[106] James's first letter, from on board ship, is dated 11 March 1844. After visiting Gibraltar and Malta he landed in Alexandria, sailed with a steam boat to Cairo and, on 22 April, seven weeks after leaving England, reached Calcutta and joined his unit. His brother, John Thomas, sent a letter from on board his ship in the island of Paros on 8 July 1844, after hearing about the death of their sister; this was followed by a letter from Smyrna. The Captain of his ship, HMS *Beard*, was Robert Graves. A trained surveyor and probably recommended by Graves, in 1845 Browne was offered and subsequently refused a salary of assistant surveyor, for which he was praised by Beaufort. In 1851, Graves offered Dr. Browne an appointment as Beaufort's surveyor for the Cape of Good Hope.[107]

Like almost every youngster of these Anglo-Irish noble Catholic families (and demonstrating that 'Irish-Britishness' was not restricted to Protestants),[108] George Henry Moore ('the third') began his studies in England at the age of seven (Oscott College, Birmingham, for eight years), and in 1828 entered Christ College, Cambridge, but never graduated. He displayed an early gift for prose and poetry, in 1825–7 contributing poems to his college's paper and to the *Dublin and London Magazine*.[109] Despite his being a man of extraordinary talents, to whom writing came all too easily, he seemed to prefer to perfect his skills in billiards, as well as in hounds, horses and racing. For four years he passed the time in Moore Hall, having to accept his mother's authority and total control and her insistence 'on calling the tune'. Though 'they loved each other fiercely', they 'fought as fiercely as they loved'.[110] In 1830 he was again sent to study, this time law, in London, where he continued his involvement in racing and faced the risk of running into debt, as his yearly allowance of £400 could never be sufficient for these purposes. Actually Moore was always in debt – overstretching his yearly allowance – a fact that made him even more dependent on his mother, his only source of income.[111] His close relationship with his mother, probably a subject warranting psychoanalysis, is evident in the long, detailed letters exchanged between them.

The mother did everything she could to find an 'amiable Catholic girl' for him, but to her despair in 1832 he fell in love with a married Anglican woman, whom all referred to as 'the lady from Cheltenham'. This evoked strong opposition from his mother, who sent someone to spy on him, and even threatened to suspend his allowance. The next months were spent in a kind of cat-and-mouse game between Cheltenham and Bath (the residence of his aunt, his mother's sister), where he preferred to stay:

> My dearest mother,
>
> The tone of your last letters including the one which you wrote to my aunt has wounded me and surprised me. I declare to heaven I have done every thing I could to pleasure you. I have committed no extravagance, I have kept away from every thing that could lead me into it; and I have got to learn in what *one* way I have been 'undutiful' to you since my return. [...] Do tell me what else I am to do and I will endeavour to please you. As for my aunt it is in vain to attempt it. If you have not found Augustus [his brother, HG] quite so bad as her description and her continual attacks upon him warrant, recollect you should take her philippic upon me also with a few grains of allowance.[112]

Louisa Moore made no effort to hide the scandal. As she wrote in a letter to the second Marquess of Sligo (Howe Peter Browne, often known simply as 'Sligo'), the family's close friend in the Westport House, 'others wrote it and everybody knows it'. She continued to be very concerned about her son, as 'he will be like the shipwreck's sailor clinging to the only plank that he can hope to be saved by'.[113] It seems that both were playing with the idea that Moore would accompany Sligo in 1834 on his two-year appointment as Governor-General of Jamaica, his family (as other Mayo merchant families) having long-established connections in the island. Appalled at the treatment of the slaves, Sligo led the first stages of the Emancipation Act and became known in the island as 'Emancipator of the Slaves'.[114]

The mother–son crisis was solved only after Moore returned in 1833 from a five-month stay in Brussels and an excursion to Italy to plan his longer travels abroad. In a letter to his mother, he complains that

'George Jackson and Martin Kirwan, both of whom are at present here [in Cheltenham]', did not seem likely to be able to accompany him, and 'I should hardly like a solitary wandering journey'.[115]

The 'grand tour' began in mid-1834, when he went, along with Charles J. Kirwan of Dalgan Park, Galway, a Cambridge student,[116] neighbor and friend, to Russia and to the Caucasus. According to several diary entries, they reached Russia in June. Typical of Moore, the first entry in his diary described their visit to the stud farm at Krinavaia, which belonged to the Count of Orloff, probably the prominent officer and statesman Alexey Fyodorovich (1787–1862), in the early 1830s the commander of the Russian military and naval forces in the Black Sea and the person behind the treaty of Hünkâr Iskelesi, which declared peace and friendship between the Russian and the Ottoman Empires.[117] Orloff held 1,500 horses of the best and fastest breeds.[118] Through Georgia (Tiflis at the end of November) they reached Tabriz and Teheran (17 March 1835). One of the only surviving letters, found in the National Library in Dublin and dated 2 January, mentions the problem he faced when trying to have money transferred to him in Persia. As England did not have any representative there, it was suggested by the banker Hugh Hammersley (1774–1840), partner at Hammersley & Co., Bankers, Pall Mall, who wrote the letter, to get in touch with the Foreign Office because they were planning a diplomatic mission to Persia.[119] There is almost no evidence of Moore's whereabouts during the next twenty months, though from his diary we know that in May 1835 he was staying in Syria, and then visited Constantinople, Athens and the Greek Islands (Scio, Rhodes, Cyprus in September 1835).[120] He also visited Egypt. Another document indicates that in September 1836 he visited the Dead Sea area, and on 3 October he stayed in Jerusalem.[121] There is no hint as to how and when he parted ways with Kirwan. The latter apparently served later as surgeon in India. The title of a book he published in 1859 describes him as 'Charles J. Kirwan, Esq., L. R. C. S. I., Formerly Demonstrator of Anatomy, &c. &c. &c. Assistant Surgeon, H. M. 13th (Prince Albert's) Infantry'.[122]

Whereas, in his later years, Moore kept his drawings from the East and even allowed one of them to hang in one of the bedrooms in his mansion, he destroyed every written document that passed through his hands, especially those which revealed his continual agony caused by the separation from the woman he loved. It also seems probable – at least this was the accepted rumor, and most biographies subsequent to that of his son George, accept it as a fact – that she followed him with her husband to the East, and that they traveled together for about a year; it is quite clear that he met with them in Athens and the Greek islands. She might even be one of the figures mentioned in his Dead Sea diary. This was, as George Moore, the novelist, wrote in the preface to his father's biography, '[a] very wrong thing to do if we consider the question from an ethical point of view, but if we look at it from a literary, how felicitous, how Byronic!' She returned to England, leaving behind the heartbroken George Henry Moore, feeling desperately betrayed, in the East.[123]

Moore destroyed the longer letters from his voyage – an unforgivable act that has been discussed at length in some places. Novelist Maria Edgeworth was a friend of Moore's mother and a frequent visitor to Moore Hall. One of the 'entertainments' provided for her 'was the reading aloud by Mrs. Moore of George Henry Moore's latest communications from the East'. The novelist praised Moore's reports, observing that 'it was indeed [...] uncommon to find both judgment and imagination in one so young...'. She also became aware of the scientific value of his works in the Hauran and around the Dead Sea, and forwarded his report to the RGS as well as to the Hydrograph of the Admiralty.[124] Married to Edgeworth's sister, Beaufort was well acquainted with both women. In one of her letters, Maria Edgeworth hints at praise by Beaufort 'of Mr. George Moore and the Dead Sea'.[125]

Following his return, Moore was introduced to Mrs Edgeworth, who, along with his mother, urged him to seek the fame which he hoped to gain from the expedition by writing, claiming that 'the man who could write such letters could write anything he pleased and become famous'. But Moore was bitterly disillusioned, and his father's advancing illness added to his negative mood, as 'fame teased him not'. Instead, once again it seemed that stables and racing grounds were the only places where he could find any sort of amusement. The two women did not ease their pressure and the discussion continued for years. It ended only on one afternoon, when the letters and diaries were brought out again – and Moore began throwing them, one by one, into the fire.[126]

Only two notebooks, both diaries, were saved hidden in a box labeled 'rubbish of all kinds'.[127] These diaries contain information concerning his travels. On 5 April 1837, while visiting the canyon of the Arnon River (Wadi Mujib) that flows into the Dead Sea from the east, Moore mentioned that he 'passed it near 7 months ago', meaning the beginning of September 1836.[128] This put him into a nostalgic mood:

> Since then how many troublous thoughts have rushed from my heart into the bitter wave of memory that lake into which a thousand streams run daily yet none come forth, into which every drop however fresh it enter, is in a moment as bitter and salt as the water that received it.[129]

On 3 October 1836 he was in Jerusalem, and received a document signed by the Franciscan purveyor verifying the fact that he had performed a sacred pilgrimage.[130] One of the diaries that escaped destruction begins on 5 December 1836, and describes Moore's travels from Damascus to the ruins of Bussora and Djerash (Jarash) in the Hauran, east of the Jordan. The entries in Moore's biography, where this diary is widely cited, end in Djerash on 16 January 1837.[131]

The next paragraph in the biography deals with the journey itself to the Dead Sea. There is a gap of two months, in which Moore returned to Baalbek, reached Beirut, fetched a boat, arranged his supplies and measuring equipment and looked for a ship that would take them to Jaffa. The Dead Sea research lasted four months: the expedition was carried out from 15 March to 28 April (from Beirut to Jaffa, Jerusalem, the Dead Sea and back to Jerusalem), and the next two and a half months, between 1 May and 16 July, were spent, in vain, trying to get a *firman* to organize its continuation (from Jerusalem to Jaffa, on to Alexandria and back to Jaffa).[132] Questions as to which boat he used, how he could fetch it and from whom, whether it was a used boat or a new one, remain unanswered.

On 15 March 1837 Moore was 'busy in preparations all day'. With these words he began his Dead Sea expedition diary, which naturally will be discussed at length. It ends on 14 July. Here again we find a gap of four months in the available information. The next document in Moore's narrative is a letter sent to his mother, dated London, 13 November 1837:

> My dearest Mother, You will be astonished at receiving a letter from me at this address, and the surprise will not altogether be an agreeable one, when you learn that I have failed in an enterprise in which I had hoped to gain some little credit, which I pursued through so much toil, danger and mortification, and on which so much money has been expended.[133]

Does this letter provide us with the answer to the great mystery concerning Moore's unexpected decision 'to produce science'? Did he hope that becoming an explorer would be his route to fame? I could not ignore his astonishing resemblance to another English historian and explorer of Africa, William Winwood Reade (1838–75), who is described by Felix Driver. An 'aspiring novelist and the heir of an estate',

> from what can be gathered of his experiences as a young man, it appears that Reade's journeys were as much an escape as a quest [...]. As historians, we do not have to choose between these different motivations for travel: at different times, each helped to shape Reade's vision of himself as an explorer in the making.[134]

But the similarities end there. While Reade continued his travels and writing until his sudden death, George Henry Moore returned to England, his mother covering his debts and expenses (£100 in Beirut, £30 in Malta for the sail home, and £20 when arriving in London), and immediately resumed his former habits. His younger brother, Augustus, showed himself to be a gifted mathematician, as discovered by the family quite early and indicated by the intensive correspondence between the mother in Moore Hall and Professor William Rowan Hamilton (1805–65), mathematician, physicist and astronomer, who at age 22 was Astronomer Royal of Ireland in the observatory in Dublin, which also hinted at personal connections between the families.[135] George Henry, who originally opposed his brother going to Cambridge where everybody was Protestant ('he should better go to Woolwich'), diverted the latter from his studies and from a promising career in analytical mathematical research. Instead, they 'plunged into the excitement of racing, hunting and horse training'.[136]

During these years both brothers developed impressive careers in horse-racing, winning several races and raising a number of champion horses. In 1841 George Henry, 'the best steeplechase rider of his day', was severely injured in a riding accident, and survived only due to his strong body,[137] but it was Augustus who met his death in April 1845, after being injured in a riding accident during the Grand National Race in Liverpool.[138] His grave is in the family cemetery, but his ashes were spread on Castle Island in Lough Carra, called by the locals 'Moore's Island'.

The high point of Moore's riding career was, undoubtedly, the victory of his horse Coronna in the Chester Gold Cup earning £17,000 (prize money and bets) on 6 May 1846. Moore used much of the money to alleviate the suffering of tenants on his estate, due to the Great Famine. With his friends and neighbors, Marquess of Sligo and Robert Blosse Lynch, he brought a cargo of 4,000 tons of maize from the United States on a chartered American ship and secured the population of his estate. He also chaired relief committees and established relief works.[139]

The situation in Mayo was among the worst. Already in 1846, 75 per cent of the agricultural holdings were valued at £4 per acre or less, meaning that tenants could not pay rent, and it all fell on the landlords. This caused even a very rich landlord the likes of the Marquess of Sligo, to go into heavy debt. Landlords faced two choices, both impossible: to evict their debtors or to be dispossessed by their creditors. The eviction rate in Mayo was of the highest, and it lasted until the early 1850s.[140]

The Great Famine was the turning point of G.H. Moore's life. Following Augustus's death and his fight against the famine, he entered politics and was elected Liberal MP for his native county in the following year. His deeds, along with his oratorical gifts, turned him into a leader of the Irish tenant-rights movement. His personal advantages were acknowledged by all of his contemporaries:

> [...] above all, and for every class of Irishmen, he had an inestimable advantage in being free from every thought and feeling which could have interfered with his combining all creeds and classes of Irishmen in the cause of their common country [...].[141]
> [...] a fine intellect, which was highly cultivated, and rhetorical gifts [...]. Among men whom he esteemed and who were his intellectual peers he was a charming companion, frank, cordial, and winning.[142]
> Moore [...], whose ample gifts of astuteness and generosity were inherited only in fragments by his more famous son [...], one of the most distinguished Irishmen of the century, combining liberal nationalism, great oratorical power, and acid wit, impressive land-holdings in west Mayo, and, a not inconsequential item of Irish prestige, the famous racing stable immortalized in his son's novel, *Esther Waters*.[143]

Moore became known for his struggles and efforts for Ireland, for its rights within Britain and its freedom, and for his distaste for the Irish representatives who, in his own words, 'went over to London and, at the first sounding of the trumpet of party, each dull old hack took the same dull old place in the same dull old ranks that he had occupied in every previous session'.[144]

His interesting parliamentary career continued until 1858, when he lost his seat. In 1861 he tried to initiate a national movement, something like the Italian movement, a volunteer organization which would work and even fight for the freedom of Ireland. He lost the battle for the people, who chose to join another national, secret movement, the Fenians.[145] Even in those years, so testified his son, George, riding a winning horse was the brothers' ultimate dream.[146] In 1868 he entered politics again and went to London, focusing his efforts on self-governance for Ireland. His sudden death on 19 April 1870 ended this move. He was laid to rest in the family's burial ground, with not many gentry attending the funeral, but with the poor coming from all over Mayo.

In 1851 he had married Mary Blake (1830–95), daughter of Maurice Blake of Ballinafad, and had three sons and one daughter.[147] The Blakes, one of the five noble Catholic families which had settled around Lough Carra, were close neighbors of the Moores. Moore also maintained his strong connection with 'Altamont', his old friend, third Marquess of Sligo, with whom he kept up intensive correspondence and ties.[148]

The chain of connections linking the Moores of Moore Hall with the Dead Sea ended just before the outbreak of the First World War, when Moore's second son, the novelist George Augustus, then over sixty years old, traveled to the region in order to take in the atmosphere for his book, *The Brook Kerith* (Wadi Quilt), 'the story of an unrisen Christ and his dramatic meeting with Paul twenty years after the crucifixion', published in 1916.[149]

Moore's memory is still alive in Mayo local oral history; even the county's internet site notes that G.H. Moore is 'still fondly spoken of in the area'.[150] Local myth retains some stories concerning his connection with the East. Mentioning his name in a Westport pub, I heard the rumor that he had an Egyptian wife, and that in Moore Hall, burnt in a fire caused in January 1923 by the IRA during the Irish Civil War, some of the Dead Sea scrolls were found!

As pointed out, the only actual publication deriving from their enterprise was the single page in the 1837 issue of the *JRGS*. Not being men of science, neither had the proper publication connections, but there was always Beek's brother, Charles Tilstone Beke (1800–74), who had already published and seemed to know the right people.[151] So their first step was a letter to Beke in Leipzig. The latter understood quite well that he was holding an important matter in hand. He forwarded the letter to at least two addresses: the secretary of the Royal Geographical Society for publication, and Carl Ritter in Berlin, who, Beke knew, was 'now engaged on that part of [his] valuable book which relates to Palestine & the vicinity'. The letter, Beke added, 'will be found to contain some new information respecting the vicinity of the gulf of Akaba', and an account of his own visit to the Dead Sea.[152] It should be added that this was not the first time Beke had approached Ritter. Actually he had been in contact with him at least three years earlier, asking the German geographer to substantiate the views and hypotheses he set forth in his *Origines biblicae*, mainly 'the new hypothesis which I have advanced as to the distinction between the Kingdom of Egypt & the country of the bondage of the Israelites'.[153]

William Beek left Moore in Jerusalem on 22 April. Beke forwarded the letter to Ritter on 2 June; in other words, the letter, which would have been written some weeks earlier, was probably written by Moore and Beek together, the latter instructing his brother to send it to the RGS. Consequently the RGS received the letter from Marseille, dated 22 August. It was received in London six days later, and the next day an answer was sent to Beek in Paris. The editor received it on 13 October.[154] The original letter, kept in the RGS archive, shows only slight editing, and actually it was published in full in the 1837 journal. On 25 March 1839 the RGS accepted another letter for publication from Beke in Leipzig, 'on an inscription found in Jerash in Palestine', naturally also by his brother.[155]

There is another unanswered question concerning Moore's publications. The *Proceedings of the Geological Society* of London in 1838 published a short report on the powerful earthquake of 1 January 1837, centered in the Galilee and in Lebanon. The paper is signed by a certain JH Moore, and, as G.H. Moore had been in the Hauran, at that time, there certainly exists the possibility that it is his report.[156]

Beek's case was very different from Moore's. 'Beek, William G., English Palestine-traveller, the companion of G.H. Moore on the sailing in the Dead Sea, 1837', these are all the details that could be found in the *Encyclopaedia of the Discoverers and Explorers of the Earth*. Schubert's claim, that Beek had been a lieutenant of the Navy, is not mentioned. However, there is one helpful comment, that '[i]n the German geographical literature, he is confused with Ch. T. Beek'.[157] This confusion is not accidental. First, they were brothers, William being the younger, a fact contained in the abovementioned letter which Charles Tilstone, then British acting consul in Leipzig, sent to Ritter, dated 2 June 1837.[158] The second reason is that only a few years later Charles Tilstone Beke had begun a career as an explorer in Africa which earned him no small amount of fame. He naturally became the subject of a number of biographies, and from these, minor details concerning his brother William can be gleaned. Their original name was Beck; Ch.T. changed to Beke ('being the *ancient* family name') in 1834, and we have no hint as to when and why his brother chose the form Beek.[159] A careful study of Beke's history and writings raises some points of interest concerning his influence on his brother's exploits in the East.

Captain William Cornwallis Harris had been chosen by the Governor and the East India Company to 'conduct a Mission which the British Government has resolved to send to Sáhela Selássie, the King of Shoa in Southern Abyssinia'. His instructions were to establish political and economic connections and to study the unknown country. After staying on African soil from May 1841 to March 1843, he returned to London with a 'Treaty of Amity and Commerce, made and concluded between His Majesty Sahela Selássie, King of Shoa, Efat, and the Galla, on the one part, and Captain Harris, under the authority of His Excellency the Governor of Bombay'.[160]

The delegation included seven more people, among them two young Germans, the natural historian Johannes Rudolf Roth (1815–58) and the painter Johann Martin Bernatz (1802–78) from Munich.[161] On reaching Shoa's capital, Ankobar, on July 1841, they met with two already well-known explorers, the Church Missionary Society emissary Johann Ludwig Krapf (1810–81) from Basel,[162] and Charles Tilstone Beke. The cooperation between Harris and Roth and Beke, the latter two serving mainly as sources of information, is attested to in their writings. It is quite remarkable that they were all connected with the Dead Sea-level debate, the Germans as participants in Schubert's delegation, and Beke on his brother's side.

Charles Tilstone Beke's biography is included in almost every British biographical collection. His signed books, sent courtesy of the author, can be found in many relevant libraries, like the one of the German Oriental Society in Halle. 'His passions were early Biblical history and the geography and exploration of northeast Africa.' He was a controversialist, 'and aired his views in public lectures, in correspondence, and in The Times with more energy than judgement', so summarized his biographer in the *ODNB*. He was well-educated, having studied law at Lincoln's Inn, but devoted his time to philological, historical and ethnological research, and he then turned to mercantile activity and trade. His first publication, in 1834, of the *Origines biblicae, or, Researches in Primeval History*,

> [...] set an intellectual framework for much of the rest of his life. He tried to harmonize recent scientific discoveries, especially those in geology, with a belief in the Bible as an inspired work of divine revelation. He was particularly interested in the geography of the Middle East as understood in the light of the Pentateuch and the principles of geological change.[163]

Treating biblical accounts literally, such as those of the Israelites crossing the Red Sea and their wanderings in Sinai, he sought to trace them on the nineteenth-century landscape of Palestine.[164] During the second half of the 1830s he issued some additional publications establishing his views concerning Babylon and the Persian Gulf.[165] For this, and for his African explorations and publications, he was elected to a variety of learned societies, most notably the Oriental Society of Germany, the Asiatic Society, and the geographical societies of London and Paris, with the University of Tübingen awarding him an honorary PhD.

In 1837 and 1838 he served for nine months as acting British consul in Saxony with his seat in Leipzig after the consul, Jacob James Hart, who was appointed in May 1836, was obliged to leave for a certain period.[166] During this time, at the request of John Bowring, Beke drew up a report on the city's commercial fair, which had traditionally been an important center for trade with the East. Beke's letters to the RGS prove that he was still in Leipzig in March 1839. He could have then met with Edward Robinson, who was working on his book in Berlin, Leipzig and Halle, and who sent a letter to the RGS from Leipzig on 28 January.[167] So far there is no direct confirmation of this hypothesis.

Convinced of the great importance of Ethiopia for commercial and other ties with interior central Africa, and also hoping to make some geographical discoveries such as the revelation of the sources of the Nile River, Beke traveled from November 1840 to May 1843 in Abyssinia, spending most of his time in the provinces of Shoa and Gojam.[168] His expedition resulted in his establishing the true physical structure of Abyssinia and of eastern Africa in general; discovering Lake Assal, a salt lake at 150 meters below sea level, inland of the Gulf of Tadjoura; fixing, by astronomical observations, the latitude of more than seventy stations; and mapping more than 70,000 square miles of country. He also proposed the establishment of a British mercantile settlement.[169] During his voyage he kept in constant contact, to the extent possible, with the RGS. Documents in the RGS archive reveal Beke's financial problems, as well as those of his wife, who remained in England and probably did not have much income. These letters also reveal his friendship with Washington as well as his relationship with Beaufort, with whom he consulted at the latter's Hydrographic Office while preparing his book.[170] In later years he was involved in disputes with the RGS, and in 1851 he publicly returned a gold medal he had received from the French geographical society. As a great expert on Ethiopia, he had also been sent as a mediator to attempt to procure the release of some prisoners held by the Ethiopian king.[171]

In 1861 and 1862 Beke, already over sixty, and his wife, traveled in Syria and Palestine, resuming the investigation of the issues of biblical geography he had first raised almost thirty years earlier in his *Origines*. Disembarking in Beirut, they continued on to Damascus and traveled continuously from the city to the fertile district east of it, which he claimed was the biblical Padan-Aram. Going southwest through the Hauran and the Gilead, they crossed the Jordan to Nablus, visited Jerusalem and sailed from Jaffa. When identifying localities, he referred to the works of Porter, Molyneux, Lynch, Kiepert and de Bertou, as well as to the later explorers Johann Gottfried Wetzstein (1815–1905, Prussian General Consul to Damascus 1848–62) and Richard Doergens (1839–1901), a Prussian surveyor.[172] In 1873 and 1874 the Bekes crossed Sinai and Midian, claiming that the real Mount Sinai should be located north of the Gulf of Akaba. The couple engaged in constant polemics defending Beke's views on biblical geography.[173] Following his death, his widow published his biography, especially mentioning his 'inadequately requited public services'.[174]

As for the Dead Sea traveler, William G. Beek, some details can be concluded. He spent several years traveling in the East. The fact that he had prior experience in measuring and that he carried some instruments with him, concurs with Schubert's claim that he was an English Navy lieutenant. In November 1834 he met Moore for the first time, in Tiflis, Georgia, so he must have also traveled in Persia and Asiatic Turkey. In addition to Syria and Palestine, he visited Egypt, from whence he crossed Sinai to Petra and then headed north to reach Baalbek. His first intention was to cross the desert to Baghdad, but he changed his mind due to the new plan with Moore. After their separation in Jerusalem on 22 April, he sailed, probably from Jaffa, reaching Marseille (from where he sent his letter to the RGS on 22 August 1837), continuing on to Paris (to where the response from the RGS was sent to him on 29 August) and to London. Before the end of that year, he quit London in order to reside in southern Italy. According to a letter of his, he was in Naples in April 1838, and in April 1841 he was still there,[175] as attested by another letter, dated 24 April (no mention of a year, though it is catalogued at the RGS under 1841) and mentioning that four and a half years had passed without hearing from Moore. But the same file holds another, short, letter from Beek, sent from Cambridge Heath, Hackney, on 10 April 1842, in which he writes that he hoped to come to London in the following days.[176]

The collaboration of George Henry Moore and William G. Beek remains a mystery in many respects. Although at least Moore's biography is well-known in detail, and considerable parts of their travels are well recorded, there remains a long list of unanswered questions concerning their wanderings and especially their scientific endeavors in the East. Why and when did they decide to study the natural history of the countries? Did they know Costigan; did they meet him before his death? Did they employ Costigan's Maltese servant, or at least interview him in Beirut? Who were their scientific contacts in Palestine and in the adjacent countries; from whom did they collect the scientific information? For which individual or institution did they collect the specimens, and had this been pre-planned? What was their scientific background in the fields they engaged in, that is, natural sciences (mainly geology), surveying and mapping? Who exactly was Beek, and what was his part in the expedition? Exactly what sort of fame did Moore hope to gain by fulfilling his mission? And how can the difference between his serious, almost scientific attitude in the East, and his return to his former capriciousness after his return to England, be explained?

Although this book claims to propose some solutions, many of these questions still await satisfactory answers. In the meanwhile, we must suffice with the facts we have gathered, showing, above all, Moore and Beek's important role in the early exploration of the Dead Sea, and not only as one of the first expeditions to establish its relative altitude. They understood that a study of the lake had to be conducted simultaneous to its mapping and to the research of the natural features of its surrounding areas, and did their best to work accordingly. Moore displayed strong determination to fulfill his research aims, sometimes to the point of extreme stubbornness (a characteristic which is demonstrated throughout his biography), but was thwarted by a combination of indifferent officials, dangerous security conditions, lack of means and less-determined companions.

5.2.1 G.H. MOORE: SCIENTIFIC WORK IN THE GOLAN AND THE HAURAN

George Henry Moore's diary of his travels in Syria, kept in the Manuscript Department of the Irish National Library in Dublin, is a thick document of 155 pages. The first date mentioned in it is 5 December 1836, and the last is 1 February 1837; still, it is clear that it contains some later entries. Though not explicitly mentioned, it is also obvious that the diary begins in Damascus. The excursion, which took Moore on a zigzag trail all the way south to Djerash, Petra and other ancient Transjordan cities, and then back north, ended when Moore reached Baalbek. Some parts of the document are difficult to read, as the handwriting, many times in pencil, tends to be very faint. It is also difficult to follow some of the place names mentioned, as the spellings used by Moore, repeating what he heard on his various stops, differ significantly from today's accepted versions.

Although it is not mentioned directly, there are many hints pointing to the fact that Moore went on this highly adventurous, inexplicable and almost delirious voyage, accompanied probably only by locals and his dog Feriss. The account of wages on the first page mentions a sum paid in advance, and another 'spent between Damascus' [and Baalbek?, HG]. The next fifteen pages contain a kind of English–Arabic handy dictionary, organized according to topics: foods, utensils, architecture and houses, family, geographical terms, adjectives, colors, human occupations, numbers, useful questions, and more of the same. In addition to the diary itself, some basic measuring devices and his drawing materials, Moore was also equipped with a *camera obscura* (literally, 'dark room'), a portable box device in which the picture, through a small hole, is imprinted on paper. Although there seems to be no existing photo taken by him, this camera makes him one of the earliest people known to have used such a device in the region, contradicting the so far accepted view that the earliest use of this early photographic instrument in our region was in 1839.[177]

All travelers' accounts stress the fact that the first Europeans to travel in these regions in the modern era were the two 'pioneers of exploration', Ulrich Jasper Seetzen and Johann Ludwig Burckhardt.[178] Seetzen's research had initially been published as individual letters in a little accessible periodical, and only in 1854 were the collected research papers issued in German and translated into English.[179] On the other hand, it seems that almost everybody had at their disposal Burckhardt's books, the first of which had been published in 1819[180] and did not fail to use and to cite these in preparation for, as well as repeatedly in the midst of, their travels.[181] It is also highly possible that they could see and use the book in one of the consular libraries – in Beirut, Damascus or Jerusalem.

In examining Moore's route in the Golan and Hauran, I will try to compare it to three other itineraries of the period, some also followed by maps. The first and earliest of these is Chesney and Robinson's journey, undertaken in November and December 1830 and described in an earlier chapter of this book.[182] As is the case in the record of Moore's journey, theirs is not accompanied by maps.

Robinson wrote in his book that it was Chesney who invited him to join the planned expedition. Chesney, for his part, wrote that the idea arose when he arrived in Damascus and found that he could not proceed with his original plan to continue to Iskanderun and then to the East. Instead he decided to check the practicability of Farren's idea to send Indian post to the town of Hit on the Euphrates, and from there to bring it to one of the harbors of the eastern Mediterranean. This would have to be done through one of the countries east of the Jordan, and it led him to study the village of Hit thoroughly when arriving with his raft.[183] It would not be outrageous to conjecture that Consul Farren was the contact man between the two, nor that, a few years later, he might have given Moore the idea to travel through the ruined and neglected cities of the Bashan.

The most contemporary description to Moore's is a map and a text, sketched and written by the French physician Charles Gaillardot (1814–83) from Lunéville in the Vosges region, one of the most significant French recruits of Mehemet Ali to serve and live in the Levant during the nineteenth century.[184] He lived and worked in the region for nearly fifty years, part of the time in Egypt, but mostly in Syria and Lebanon, where he combined careers as a physician and a soldier, scholar, teacher and tour guide. As a multi-disciplinary scholar, Gaillardot is emblematic of many of the European settlers in the Orient, mainly physicians, who were involved in the intensive scientific study of the region.[185] He made significant contributions to botanical, entomological, geological and archaeological research, as well as cartography and topography. Like many of his contemporaries, he was highly interested in the Dead Sea and its region, mainly in its geological history, and in 1844 published a long paper, to which he added some geological coups.[186]

Gaillardot's studies in the East began a relatively short time after his arrival there. His first scientific contribution was a small sketch-map of the Ledja area, published by Ritter in the 1846 issue of the journal of the geographical society in Berlin, the *MVGEB*.[187] The sketch, along with a cover letter dated Beirut, 16 August 1845, reached Ritter through the mediation of Anton Albert Heinrich Louis von Wildenbruch (1803–74), a military officer of a noble Berlin family, who served between 1843 and 1848 as the Prussian General Consul to Syria and Palestine, whose seat was in Beirut.[188] The Ledja (from the arabic *malja*, meaning 'shelter'), which begins about forty km from Damascus, was 'by far the most remarkable part of this interesting country', in the words of the Irish missionary Josias Leslie Porter who issued 'a map of Damascus, Hauran, Anti-Libanus &c.'.[189] Gaillardot sketched and described the area while serving as the personal physician of Sulaymân Paşa, who in 1838 joined Ibrahim Paşa in a long and difficult campaign against the rebelling Druze, which brought them to the latter's stronghold on the Druze Mountain (Jebel Druze).[190] The long and exceptionally detailed memoir accompanying the map, which is, in fact, Gaillardot's diary

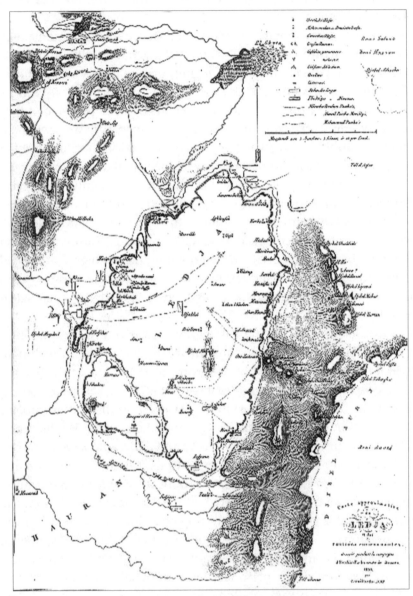

Fig. 39: Gaillardot, Map of the Ledja, 1838

describing the campaign, was published only in 1864 in a French geographic periodical.[191]

Another map of the region from the 1850s followed 'two discovery-travels in the east of the Jordan cities-desert by Consul Wetzstein (1858) and Cyril Graham (1857)'. The British explorer Graham (1834–95) and Consul Wetzstein had both been guided by Ritter, who would also undertake the publication of their itineraries and studies, including a map constructed by 'his' cartographer Heinrich Kiepert.[192]

J.L. Porter was born in Burt, County Doneghal, Ireland and died as president and vice-chancellor of Queen's College, Belfast. He was a leading scriptural geographer who left behind several books and papers concerning Palestine and its vicinity.[193] He was sent to the East as a missionary to the Jews by the Board of Missions of the Irish Presbyterian Church, replacing their first envoy, William Graham (1810–83), who in 1843 had established the station in Damascus and served there until 1847.[194] Porter served in Beirut and Damascus from December 1849 to 1859. 'While discharging his duty as a missionary,' wrote his biographer, 'he acquired, by frequent and extensive journeys, an intimate knowledge of Syria and Palestine, which he turned to good literary account.'[195] He is also known as the writer of Murray's first *Handbook for Travellers in Syria and Palestine*. Though not signed, it was dedicated to Reverend Henry Cooke (1788–1868), a highly influential minister of the Presbyterian Church in Ireland and Porter's stepbrother.[196]

In 1865 Porter published the first edition of a popular account of his voyages in the various areas of Syria, Lebanon and Palestine, entitled *The Giant Cities of Bashan and Syria's Holy Places*, including his travel from Damascus, along the eastern border of the Ledja, and south into the Hauran and Gilead.[197] As for the Hauran, the land of the deserted ruined cities, Porter's impressions are worth citing, as they undoubtedly represent the views of other travelers:

> Now there are no worshippers in those churches; and the people who for twelve centuries have held supreme authority in the land, have been the constant and ruthless persecutors of Christians and Christianity. But their power is on the wane; their reign is well-nigh at the end; and the time is not far distant when Christian influence, and power, and industry, shall again repeople the deserted cities, and fill the vacant churches, and cultivate the desolate fields of Palestine.[198]

I could scarcely get over the feeling, as I rode across the plain of Bashan and climbed the wooded hills through the oak forests, and saw the primitive ploughs and yokes of oxen and goads, and heard the old Bible salutations given by every passer-by, and received the urgent invitations to rest and eat at every village and hamlet, and witnessed the killing of the kid or lamb, and the almost incredible dispatch with which it is cooked and served to the guests – I could scarcely get over the feeling, I say, that I had been somehow spirited away back some thousands of years, and set down in the land of Nod, or by the patriarch's tent at Beersheba.[199]

The remarkable fact has already been pointed out: Porter chose to ignore his Irish predecessors, Costigan and Moore. This can only be described as deliberate, perhaps deriving from his membership in the Anglo-Irish Protestant Ascendancy, who arrogantly regarded themselves as the 'Irish Protestant nation' and actually denied the existence of the local Catholic population of Ireland.[200]

The outstanding memoir he published for his important map opens with the remark that 'no section of Syria had hitherto been so much neglected by the geographer as the environs of Damascus', which had received only brief notes by Burckhardt.[201] On planning his excursion in the Bashan, Porter used, in addition to the Bible and Josephus, the writings of Hadrianus Relandus (1676–1718, Dutch cartographer and philologist), Burckhardt, James Silk Buckingham (1786–1855, an English traveler and author who in 1813–18 traveled in Egypt, Palestine and Persia), and Ritter, as well as Burckhardt's and Berghaus's maps. He also possessed a map of the country between Damascus and Bussora, drawn by Fezzy Beg, Turkish Colonel of Engineers, which turned out mostly to be a copy of the Berghaus map.[202] The map and its accompanying memoir, devoted primarily to correcting Burckhardt's mistakes, were published in the 1856 issue of the *JRGS*. The map had been constructed from measurements and observations taken repeatedly in various travels between 1850 and 1855, using simple instruments (large compass, aneroid barometer) and taking as many bearings as possible. He began the construction by fixing the true positions of Damascus and Baalbek, and then adding all his data. Although not entirely accurate, Porter added, the map should be considered 'approximate as closely to the truth as possible'.[203]

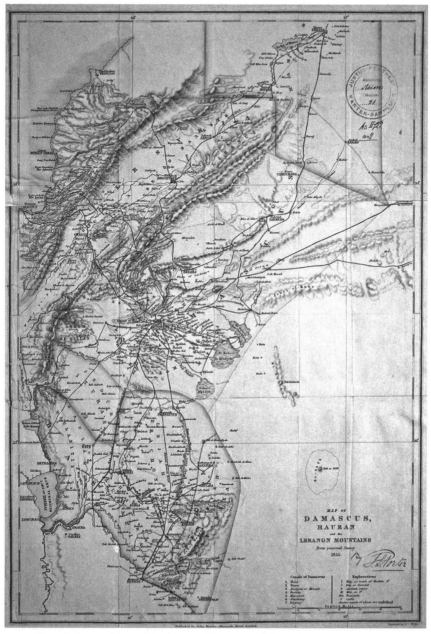

Fig. 40: Porter, Map of Damascus, Hauran and the Lebanon Mountains.
From personal Survey, 1855

While exploring the Hauran, Porter also copied many inscriptions, a dozen of which were published with annotations by the Royal Society of Literature.[204] Some of these inscriptions had already been copied by Moore, but of course were never published.

George Henry Moore preceded Porter by more than twelve years. Maurice Moore, briefly describing his father's travels, wrote that in a diary beginning 5 December 1836, Henry Moore had recorded traveling from Damascus to visit the ruins of Bussora, Djerash and Hauran. He added that his father described going through the Valley of the Thousand Gardens and arriving at Kiswee, three hours south-southwest of Damascus and from which Mount Hermon could be seen. Traveling from Kiswee ('which I guess H.M. considers home') to Moatbeen, where there are many Roman remains of private houses, he arrived at Jabob, which is six hours from Kiswee.

The first central place described by Moore after leaving Damascus was the village of Esrah (Moore: Ezraa; Gaillardot: Errâ; Wetzstein and Graham: Zara') at the southwestern edge of the Ledja, where he could find supplies such as 'rice & milk', and a 'Mootesellim' (Mutasallim) – a regional governor – to whom he could show his *firman*. Moore did not mention who had given him this document, probably permitting him to travel and to ask all the officials for help as needed, but it is logical that it had been signed by the Governor in Damascus, possibly even Ibrahim Paşa himself. The village of about 30–40 Greek-Orthodox Christians and 70–80 Muslim 'adult males', had been a place of great importance in antiquity and at the time was the site of an old church converted into a mosque.[205]

Passing some other villages, Moore reached 'Savaidah' (Soueida, Suweudeh) on 10 January 1837. The village – Moore even calls it a 'town' – was inhabited by Muslims, Christians and Druze. He studied and sketched a monument, 'probably a Roman tomb', and a 'great temple', measuring 35×47 ft, which he compared to the one in Baalbek. Contemplating the Greek inscriptions (copied, of course), he assumed that it had later been converted into a church. From soldiers he heard 'of another village called "Giniwat" where there were *Ahmood Kateer Kabeer* (many big columns) and the devil knows what'. This is also the first place in which he crossed the route of other travelers – Porter, for instance, who preferred the road east of the Ledja. Greatly impressed by what he saw there, Porter wrote that 'no city in Bashan – not even Bozrah, the Roman capital – surpasses Suweideh in the extent of its ruins.'[206]

Accordingly, Moore reached the village of 'Giniwat' (Qanaouat), to the northeast of Soueida, and described and sketched 'a very elegant temple a few hundred yards from this town'. About twenty years later, Porter described 'a small but a beautiful temple beside the town of Suleim [...] near Kunaivât',[207] identified with Kenath, a place mentioned in the description of the Israelite tribes' conquest of the country east of the Jordan.[208] Porter copied an inscription there, which is missing from Moore's report.

Returning to Soueida, among the numerous remains there, Moore mentioned an impressive gate which he compared to Baalbek, a theater, a 'building of water' and a Christian church. His route continued southward; the road was hilly and rocky, the land rich with pasture. On 14 January he reached Bussora, the next ancient site on his route, 'considered by the Arabs as ancient Damascus or Eskeh-Shum' (Bosra Eski Châm). Moore was deeply impressed by the ruins in this city, writing that 'Bussora must, in former times, both Roman and Saracene, have been a place of great importance.' He copied seven Greek and four Arab inscriptions, described the 'magnificent theatre, one of the finest in the world', the Saracenic fortifications, the mosques, a pillar that rocks in the breeze and issues a melancholy cry at night, a water reservoir, a gate and many other Roman remains.

Following these descriptions, Moore entered one of his philosophical moods, evoked by the impressive ancient remnants, writing:

It offers, in its stupendous remains, ample proof of the wealth, the taste and the population of the Roman city, in the heaps of accumulated ruins under which it is almost buried, of the successive generations which have rolled over its gradual decay; and in the immense fortifications which Saracene warfare has shown around it, of the strength and importance which in an after age, and hundreds of years after its glories had passed away, it still possessed. There is scarcely in the world a more interesting spectacle as regards the philosophy of history than is exhibited in this stupendous ruin. Here every gradation of human strength and human weakness, human wisdom and human degeneracy, human glory and human frustration lie buried in successive stratas, and in these layers of departed generations as in [?] any leaves of a volume, may the whole history of

Fig. 41: Syrian Diary: Copy of inscriptions; a Dolmen

the human race be read. Here are the footsteps of the most polished
life the most finished civilization that ever walked the world; and here
piled above them are these relics of moral and physical feebleness
into which that civilization debouched itself. Here again are both
girdled round with the proud and savage energy of semi barbarous
mind – and here are the wretched evidences of human nature in its
lowest mode of degeneracy; barbarism, feebleness and misery heaped
in wild accumulation over politeness and strength and wisdom and
glory. Is the historic volume to close here, or is another leaf to be still
added and to speak of this glorious regeneration of man?[209]

He visited a fortified theater, 'capable of containing four thousand
people'. The next pages in the diary reveal his deductive method,
arriving at conclusions after some – but hardly enough – reading and
scientific learning. An inscription in a subterranean colonnade of the
theater marks its construction date to the reign of Malek-ed-Daher, in
A.H. 610. Here Moore encounters some confusion as he tries to adjust
this date to what he remembers of English history. The Plantagenet
King Henry II died, according to his memory, in 1180, while the truth is
that he passed away in July 1189. His older son, Richard I 'the Lionheart'
(1157–99) succeeded him and reigned for ten years, a detail remembered
by Moore, including his participation in the third Crusade, from April
1191 to October 1192. As the year 610 is analogous to 1213, and Malek-
ed-Daher, Saladin, lived from 1137/8 to 1193, he wonders whether this
theater can have been constructed by Saladin: 'does history assign too
long a date to the life of Saladin?'[210]

For Moore, 'the fortification round this building' is the best proof
of the fact that 'the oldest part of the Castel Pisans at Jerusalem
fortifications [...] [has] no older date than the Saracenic conquest.' He
equates the size of the reservoir to the biggest of Solomon's Pools. The
improvised nature of Moore's excursion, certainly due to a basic lack of
background information concerning the area, is revealed by his next
step, taken at the suggestion of a local, 'rather intelligent', sheikh. It is
quite clear that Moore intended to continue southward, but instead he
went first to visit an area of ruined cities located to the east and east-
southeast of Bussora. 'Road to Salkhud lay along a Roman road which
my friend the Sheikh swears extended all the way to Baghdad.'[211]

On Saturday, 17 January, he arrived at the ruined and almost totally
deserted city of Salkhud, where he found a large Saracenic fortress 'on

the top of a high steep conical and volcanic looking hill', offering a beautiful view of the 'scene which lay at my feet bathed in the glories of the setting sun'. In 'Erman' (probably Ormane), a poor but inhabited small village, he witnessed Hauran towers and inscriptions. The area between Melan and Milah-h-Assaroor is described as 'a desert of garden mould'. Passing another deserted village, he returned to Erman, and the next day, Monday 19 January, he returned on the main road from Salkhad to Soueida.[212]

Moore was hoping to visit Shoahabah, but found that it lay seven or eight hours to the north and was inconsistent with his original plan to continue southward, to Djerash. He sent a letter to Consul Farren in Damascus asking for additional money and expressing his frustration and anger – 'I must really have a couple of pages for oaths and curses' – about his guards, servant and the sheikh 'for thus keeping me in ignorance of where I was going', and cursed himself 'for believing them or any one'. But on Tuesday he did continue to Shoahabah, the Roman Philippopolis,[213] where he spent the next day and a half observing, sketching and making plans of the walled city and its remains: an acropolis, an aqueduct, 'the finest roman baths of Syria, perhaps the finest anywhere', theater, etc. Porter, on his visit, had also been highly impressed by the city, which he called 'Shubba', 'almost entirely a Roman city', and even more so with the landscape revealed to him from the summit of a cup-shaped volcanic hill beside the city.[214]

It seems that Moore was now determined to begin heading southward, and on Thursday, 22 January, he set 'off early in the morning for Djirash'. He took the road leading to the southwest, in order to reach the main road connecting Damascus, Der'aa and Djerash (and Amman), and did not stop at the different villages on his way, so that his diary includes only names, directions and distances in time units. From Deraa he took the main road to the cross-roads in Hossn (El-Hosn), and on 24 January returned to Djerash. Throughout the excursion, his habits from back home are revealed on the rare occasion, as in his comment after spotting a herd of gazelles, that 'it would have been easy to side them down with good horses as the country stretched hard and unbroken for twenty miles in the direction of their flight.'[215]

During the eighteen days of his stay, he measured and sketched, although his diary entries begin to be very much shortened, with just a word or two for each day. He left the city and returned to Damascus in under three days, arriving there on 15 January 1837. He stayed in the city for two weeks, meeting people, such as F. (probably Farren), riding around and sketching.

The second part of the same booklet contains the diary of his journey from Damascus along the Barrada River to Baalbek, which lasted three days. Consul Farren accompanied him for an hour, and then they separated, 'with great regret, and impressed with feelings of the deepest esteem and the most cordial friendship'.[216] This time he did choose the beaten track – northwest along the river to the southern edge of the Anti-Lebanon mountains, and then, almost directly north, climbing to Zebedany, to the large ruined city. The last fifteen pages of the diary entail copies of inscriptions, measurements and sketches of stones, pillars, columns, the theater, a dolmen and more of the same.

The Syrian diary describes a period of about two months during the winter of 1836/7, from the beginning of December to the beginning of February. In many ways it is a unique document, and one can only regret the fact that it has not as of yet found the place it deserves within the scientific study of the Hauran and Golan regions. Its uniqueness and importance as a scientific document equals its significance as a personal, human and cultural source for understanding the thoughts, associations, ideas and beliefs of a young European wandering in an unknown, almost wild world, but one which was replete with history, antiquity and cultural associations.

5.2.2 MOORE AND BEEK'S DEAD SEA DIARY: DESCRIPTION AND EVALUATION

The document, a brown-covered notebook of 15×10.5 cm, contains 134 pages, most of them in manuscript.[217] It also includes some sketches, tables and compass roses. The first entry is from Beirut, dated 15 March 1837, while the last is from Jerusalem, dated 28 April. The diary supplies a thorough description of the adventures of the Dead Sea expedition.

In Beirut, Moore begins, 'we provide ourselves with a boat & two boatmen besides such stores as we considered necessary, also a light tent'.[218] They hired a vessel, which was to carry them and their equipment, including the boat, to Jaffa. They had to overcome some obstacles, mainly due to the Reis's (the ship's commander) refusal to sail, being backed by the owner of the vessel, a certain Edmund Guis who was also the French consul in the city.[219] They finally did sail from Beirut at sunrise, passed Saida (Sidon) and Tyre, and arrived in Acre by night. The next morning they 'took a stroll through the town, met Fessani and had a look at his horses',[220] left Acre the same morning, 'swept by the Cape of Carmel' and passed Athlit ('a picturesque mass of ruined buildings') and Tantura. A gale on the shore prevented them from disembarking at Caesarea, such that they arrived at Jaffa late at night. Against all warnings, the captain tried to enter the harbor steering through the rocks in the dark and the vessel almost sank. The passengers took a boat to shore, but had to wait until morning for the gates to open.[221] The party found a place to stay in the house of the consul, probably the English consular agent, Joseph Damiani. They had great difficulty in finding the means, the animals and the people necessary to transfer their baggage and boat to Jerusalem and to the Dead Sea. Although they possessed a *firman* from Mehemet Ali, they had to overcome complications raised by the muleteers, as well as by various officials, but after three and half days they succeeded in leaving Jaffa.[222]

The night of 21 March was spent in Ramleh, probably in the Franciscan monastery, although Moore mentions a Sardinian consul in the village. It took them another day to reach Jerusalem. In the entries made on the way, we find the first evidence of a scientific collection, when Moore wrote that they '[s]topped on the road to botanize'.[223] As the convent in Jerusalem – the Franciscan Casa Nova – was packed with pilgrims, they found accommodation in the homes of the local Protestant missionaries. George Backus Whiting (?–1855) and his wife Matilda S., née Ward (1805–73), missionaries for the American Board of Commissioners for Foreign Missions, had arrived in Beirut in 1830 and were sent to Jerusalem following the end of the rebellion against the Egyptian rulers in 1834. They established a mission school, but 'were forced to return to America because of Mrs. Whiting's poor health' in 1838. George Whiting returned to Syria before 1844, and died there eleven years later. The diary reveals the special relationship between Moore and the Whitings, whose friendly demeanor had been praised by many travelers. Moore visited them frequently, and they turned out to be his main allies in Jerusalem.[224]

The days in Jerusalem were spent both in exploring the city, mainly the Church of the Holy Sepulcher, as Easter was approaching, and arguing with the muleteers and the local governor about the ongoing demand to raise the fees. Moore also took some bearings, mainly from the Mount of Olives, and completed sketches. They left Jerusalem only on the morning of 28 March 1837.

There is a strange feature in the diary. Until page 29 the order is normal, and the handwriting is the same, surely Moore's. Pages 30–5 include sketches and bearings. Pages 36–8 and 40 are written in at least two different handwritings, and are much more difficult to read. The entries are considerably shorter, actually only comments. These begin in Jerusalem on the 9th, with the month – July – not being mentioned, and they include excursions in Palestine and a sail to Alexandria, ending in Jerusalem on the 9th of the following month. Page 39 is a continuation of page 35, after which comes page 41, which describes their last day in Jerusalem, before leaving for the Dead Sea.

The first visit they paid in Jerusalem was to the American missionary John Francis Lanneau, who joined the Whitings in the spring of 1836 and stayed there until 1839. Moore described him as 'the tall missionary we had seen on my last visit to Jerusalem [in October 1836, HG]', the first concrete testimony of Moore's previous visit to that city.[225] Moore's familiarity with Palestine literature is demonstrated in his mention of Henry Maundrell's description of the Passover ceremonies, including the Tenebrae, in the Holy Sepulcher.[226] Another name mentioned as a companion in Jerusalem is Holinski (or Holinsky). About a week later, the same person, accompanied by a Polish priest, came to visit Moore and Beek in their camp by the Dead Sea. Alexander Holinski and his brother, Stephan, joined the Polish poet Juliusz Slowacki (1809–49) on his travels in Egypt, Palestine and Syria in 1836–7. Their itinerary included Greece (September), Egypt (October) and Palestine. Holinski left the party in Jerusalem, while the others continued to Damascus, Lebanon and then returned to Italy.[227]

The following paragraph in the diary reveals the manner in which Moore financed his long stay, travels and endeavors in the East, as follows: 'went home and drew bills for £100 pounds which I sent to Farren to be negotiated thro' Black & Co.'. From this entry and other information in his diaries and letters, we learn that he could draw on his credit through English merchant-houses functioning in the various major cities in the East.[228] But since the money from Damascus did not arrive within two days, at a time when he needed to pay the Mutasallim of Jerusalem all his money in advance, Moore 'was obliged to go to other travellers, incidentally staying in Jerusalem, to request a loan'.[229]

As did most travelers, Moore received great assistance from the British consular representatives in the various countries and major cities that he visited. They helped him, albeit not always successfully, in his negotiations with the authorities as well as with the local population. Farren, the consul in Syria, in the autumn of 1834 initiated the first attempt to appoint a British consular representative in Jerusalem, which led, more than four years later, to William Tanner Young's appointment. The archives of the Foreign Office reveal a great deal of dislike and distrust for Farren and for his manners by his superiors.[230] On the other hand, he is repeatedly mentioned in Moore's diaries as a good friend and a source of support and help. Lindsay praises Farren for his hospitality, as well, writing: 'He is indeed the man of all others to represent the British nation in a country like this...'[231] He is also mentioned repeatedly in letters and diaries of participants of the Euphrates Expedition, as a person from whom they received untiring help and support.[232]

Lord Alexander William Crawford Lindsay (1812–80), 'British nobleman, traveller, and writer on art' who had graduated from Trinity College, Dublin, and held two earlships, spent his life in studious pursuits, in the compilation of a magnificent library and in travel. In 1836-7 he traveled in Egypt and Palestine accompanied by some friends. His letters, published in 1838, were described by the German Palestine-scholar Titus Tobler as 'für Jerusalem werthlos', but they are of much use for our study.[233] While traveling, his group was joined by some other Europeans who are mentioned by Moore. Dr. Wilson of Scotland is mentioned also by other contemporary travelers.[234] Lindsay described Captain Lacon as 'an intelligent officer who had joined our party'. Wilson and Lacon are also mentioned together on occasion in Moore's diary.[235] Impressed by the young Moore, Lindsay wrote that he met with 'a scientific gentleman, who was very courteous to us at Jerusalem', who 'was then surveying the lake'. He spares no words in describing his countryman:

> He is indeed a model for the travellers, so accurate and precise – I wish only he were a little more enthusiastic. But he is such a thorough gentleman – his feelings are all so good and honourable – his conduct towards his employers so conscientious – he is so cheerful, so uncomplaining under hardship and privation, that one cannot but love him – one cannot but regret that he will never be so extensively known as he deserves to be.[236]

Moore, 'an enthusiastic in architectural antiquities', strongly recommended that after leaving Jerusalem they 'extend [their] tour to the
Hauran'. Already an expert in that region, he proposed a route through
that country for them. [237]

The Scottish John Gardiner Kinnear reached the East for trade
purposes. Incidentally, he met with his fellow Scot, the painter David
Roberts (1796–1864) in Cairo, and joined him on his travels. Naturally
the visit to Petra was one of the highlights of their trip. A visit to the
Nabatean capital was problematic, and Stephens, as well as Lindsay's
group, whom he met, caved to the pressure of their Bedouin guides and
greatly shortened their stay, while Roberts's group insisted on staying
for a longer time, and the results can be seen in some magnificent
paintings.[238]

One of the interesting, important, but sometimes extremely difficult
missions of the present research has been trying to locate Moore's
acquaintances and encounters, as mentioned in his diaries. The
identification of the Europeans mentioned – diplomatic representatives,
missionaries, travelers – can shed light on this early stage of European
involvement in the Near East. On the other hand, it is difficult to
ascertain many facts concerning his local companions; as we recall,
Moore and Beek were the only Europeans in their party. Still, other
travelers mention some of these companions. As an example, 'Michali',
who is mentioned twice by Moore, might very well be identical to a 'Mr.
Micheli' whom Nathanael Burton met in March 1837, an Italian who
married in Cyprus and went to look for a job in Constantinople; or to
'Michele', who accompanied Allen's group about thirteen years later on
its travels in Lebanon and Syria: 'a Syrian dragoman, who spoke Turkish,
Greek, French, Italian, and English fluently'.[239]

Moore's next encounter in Jerusalem was a bit strange, but quite
typical of the city and its atmosphere in the first half of the nineteenth
century. He describes the American lady, a certain Miss Emlyn, as
'deplorably mad', traveling in the company of an Indian 'princess'
thinking about going to Mecca, with a Greek servant, a poodle and a
guitar. When they met again, about two weeks later, she was already in
the company of another American lady, equally mad, in his estimation.
Moore had to endure the company and life stories of both ladies, who
are repeatedly mentioned in the diary. The second, Harriet Livermore
(1788–1868), 'novelist, singer, poet, and revivalist preacher', a woman

of rare beauty, brilliant conversation and tempestuous character, turned to religion after a last-minute cancellation of her planned marriage. She made a career as a preaching evangelist, even speaking before the US Senate. Following the New Yorker Barbara Anne Simon's book, 'attempting to prove that the North and South American Indians were the descendants of the ten missing tribes of Israel',[240] Livermore decided to go to Jerusalem in order to await the Lord's coming. Between 1837 and 1862 she crossed the Atlantic ten times, attempting to establish an American colony. But instead, she ultimately found herself begging in the Jerusalem streets and, close to starvation, returning to the States. Her meeting with Moore seems to have been during her first visit to the city, and the descriptions of these encounters in the diary are quite piquant.[241]

Always interested in everything he heard, Moore did read one of the relevant books written by Simon, who 'shared the Ten Lost Tribe–American Indian connection and anticipated Indian conversion to Christianity and, by implication, return with all Jews to the Land of Israel'. He calls it a 'curious' book, though we cannot find a more in-depth reaction, as this page has no continuation.[242] Harriet Livermore was also described by another Irish traveler. While visiting the American missionaries in Cairo, Reverend Nathanael Burton learned about 'an extraordinary female' residing with them, who 'supposes that she is one of the witnesses' and causes much trouble; they did everything to get rid of her.[243]

In these beliefs, Harriet Livermore was following a theory cultivated by American eschatological preachers, as early as the seventeenth century, who claimed that there was a connection between American Indians and the lost tribes. As summarized by Gershon Greenberg, in his work about the main millennial advocates of this Christian eschatology in America:

> He believed in the truths of the Book of Revelation and the fall of the antichrist as Rome in particular. The *eschaton* was imminent, Jews would convert and be restored to their Land, and American Indians as descendants of the Ten Lost Tribes would be included.[244]

Together with Harriet Livermore, Moore mentions a certain Mr Johnson or Johnston, as someone with whom she repeatedly quarreled. Finally convinced of the 'Restoration of the Jews', Mr Bower Johnston retired from his business in England and settled in Jerusalem, aiming to unite his fate with them. Travelers who met him praised his mild manner and willingness to help and guide them.[245]

Moore's party left Jerusalem on 28 March. On the previous evening he had gone to the Franciscan cemetery on Mount Zion in order to pay his respects to Costigan, his forebear in the study of the Dead Sea. It was only natural for Irish travelers to visit the grave of their ill-fated countryman.

After staying overnight in Jericho, the expedition arrived at the mouth of the Jordan. On the way, Moore described some limestone formations and, for the first time, mentioned collecting soil and rock specimens ('Took some curious specimens of clayey formation near the banks of the Jordan'). They set up their camp near the Jordan's embouchure to the Dead Sea, and Moore started to measure ('Measured a beautiful base line of 900 & odd yards').[246] They were visited by Holinski and two others, who told them about 'a large party of Germans just arrived in Jerusalem from Cairo via Petra'. This was the first time they had heard about Schubert's group, as will be discussed in detail later.

The boat arrived on 31 March. On the same morning they began to realize the problem which they would face on their way to fulfilling their plan to travel around the lake. The Arab escorts declared that it was impossible for the mules to cross the Jordan. A short inquiry revealed the real reason. They claimed that due to problematic security conditions on the eastern side of the Jordan and of the lake, they could not assure the safety of the party. Instead, the party was forced to start moving westwards and then southwards along the shore, continuing to 'collect specimens', while coping with many signs of the unstable security situation that had also spread to the areas west of the Jordan. Moore spent the following days sketching the landscape, hunting with the help of his two dogs, sailing and collecting 'mineralogical, botanical and entomological specimens'.[247] Near the cliff from which he did his sketching, he spotted the ruins of a settlement, which their escort 'declared to be one of the guilty cities destroyed by the Almighty',[248] but which his party thought were the remnants 'of a modern and inconsiderable village'. Among the ruins, which he calls 'Bellet-e-Yaoudi', they found many graves, some of them quite recent.[249]

This name enables us to locate the site of their encampment. On his map of the Dead Sea published following his travels in 1850–1, the

French officer and scholar, Baron Louis Felicien Caignart de Saulcy (1807–80), located 'Kherbet-el-Yahoud' on the northwestern shore, a short distance south of 'Ayn-Fechkhah'. The description in his book is very detailed. He spotted the 'mass of ruins called Kharbet-el-Fechkhah' at the entrance of 'Ouad-Goumran'. Twenty-four minutes later, Saulcy's group arrived at their camp, which was situated two hundred yards north of the saltwater spring, Ein Feshcha. 'A little to the north of our camp, between it and the lake', he spotted the ruins which 'are known to the Arabs under the name of Kharbet-el-Yahoud'.[250] He spent several hours examining them, describing 'the distinguishable parts of this structure, which I do not hesitate in referring back to the period of Sodom and Gomorrah'.[251] The later excavations performed there by the French Dominicans from the École Biblique in Jerusalem revealed two facts concerning de Saulcy: on the one hand, he had extremely observant eyes which enabled him to trace the foundations of the large 'public building', but, on the other hand, his conclusions were usually mistaken, a kind of 'wishful thinking', as the ruins are dated to the period of the Second Temple. The settlement has much in common with Qumran, and flourished in the same period; de Saulcy identified Qumran with Gommorah.[252] This location is confirmed as well in Beek's sketch maps, kept in the map collection of the RGS (see fig. 43).

They spent the next few days traveling on the hills, collecting specimens and sailing. On 5 April, Moore and Beek meant to sail at sunrise in order to start their soundings in the sea. The amateur nature of their preparations was revealed in the fact that only then did they discover that 'there was no tallow for sounding'. The weight tied to the sounding cord, as well as the cord itself, needed to be smeared with tallow. After sailing for one and a half miles they discovered that their cord, 144 fathoms (267 meters) long, was insufficient for the depths they encountered.[253] Reaching the eastern shore, they explored the Arnon River (Wadi Mujib), which runs 'through a ravine the sides of which, composed of red sandstone something like of Petra though not so beautifully veined, are not 100 ft apart and rise perpendicularly 200 ft or more', and 'collected specimens of sandstone, slate and lava'.[254]

They moved their camp to another site, where the mountains are closer to the sea, probably in the area of Qumran. Moore 'went up the rocks to examine a cavern about one-half mile north of tent and about four or five hundred ft above the lake', which might coincide with de

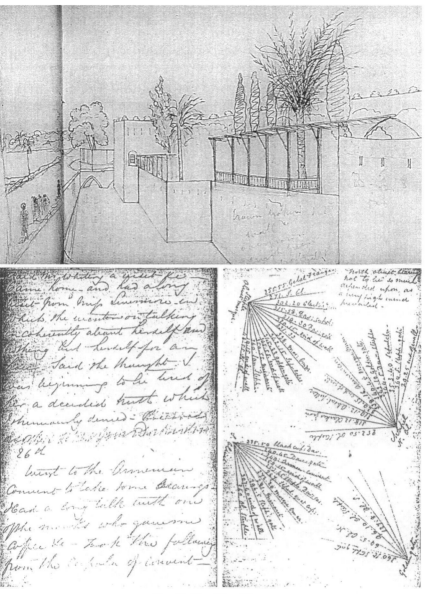

Fig. 42: Dead Sea Diary

Saulcy's cave 'of a square form', which 'bears the name of Morharrat-es-Saïd'.[255] Moore's long and detailed description contradicts the fact that he had no previous geological training. His colorful descriptions enable the reader to imagine the explorer, descending in the narrow and steep rocky passes, 'loaded with a quarter cwt of stones in one hand a bundle of botanical specimens in the other and an umbrella under [his] arm'.[256]

One of the companions, the sheikh, was sent to Jerusalem in order to put a box of geological specimens in the care of Mr Whiting and 'to buy a couple of hundred more fathoms of cord and other necessaries'. After collecting some small fish from a pool supplied with water from the spring, Moore 'tried some experiments upon them', putting some in the water of the lake; they were all dead within an hour.[257] Disregarding the rough condition of the sea, he went sailing again and 'arrived late and with enough salt in my beard and moustache to serve for dinner for a month'.

The news brought by the sheikh from Jerusalem described an increasingly dangerous situation at the southwestern side of the lake as well. This news seemed to discourage the entire party, with the exception of Moore. The Arabs even refused to take them to a nearby village, where 'according to the rumors [...], are oranges and lemons which no one can taste', most probably Ein Gedi. Determined to carry on his mission, Moore decided to ride to Jerusalem 'to see about all this'. It is also difficult to ignore his humorous remarks demonstrating his familiarity with the Bible, describing his horse, which lacked foreshoes, as walking 'like Agag delicately'.[258]

On the way through Wadi Kedron and the Greek monastery Mar Saba ('San Saaba' per Moore) to Jerusalem, he ceaselessly described the geological features at the expense of everything else, including the impressive monastery; we do not know if he even took the time to enter it. The approach to Jerusalem, on a spring Sunday afternoon, brought his poetic soul to the surface:

Never saw Jerusalem dressed in such gay colours. Everything was fresh and green the trees in full blossom and the view from the fountain of the Virgin struck me for the first time as beautiful [...] It was Sunday and the rocks rung with the songs of merry parties strolling about in the subdued sunshine of the evening. The birds caroled on the boughs, and as I approached the Jaffa gate the crowds of sauntering men and women gave new life and gladness to the scene.[259]

While waiting to meet the Mutasallim, Moore met the Germans and had to endure the company and life stories of the abovementioned 'two mad American ladies'. After some delays he succeeded in meeting the governor, but the reaction to his requests was very disappointing. Moore was told that there was nothing the governor could do. Instead, the latter suggested, Moore would do best to sail round the lake, avoiding the land.

Returning to the camp, Moore faced a strong sirocco eastern wind; the sea looked from the hills 'as the mouth of Acheron', and the mountains on the other shore 'like phantoms through the red haze'. The air was full of dust, the thermometer holding steady at 105°F (40°C), and 'the mosquitoes very distressing'.[260] The next day, 12 April, they set out again to the sea, which was calming down, and, although 'the lead proved too light for the deep soundings' and 'experiments very unsatisfactory', they performed some soundings which were recorded in a table. This table gives the wind strength and direction, the depth, time of sounding and a description of the bottom.[261] '5 minutes after 3 within one-half mile of shore, wind fresh, impossible to sound,' Moore wrote. 'About mid-way we met the sea rolling high, and when about two-thirds of the way found ourselves in the storm.' He described the wind as 'a perfect hurricane', and the waves as 'long billows rolling mountains high'. They had to fight the storm for several hours, and managed to reach shore – about six or seven miles south – only at ten o'clock at night.[262]

He was still waiting for a letter from Colonel Campbell, the British general-consul in Egypt, which he hoped would include a new *firman* from Mehemet Ali. The letters that awaited them in Jerusalem were brought to the camp on the next day. They included a letter from de Bertou, money and letters from the firm transferred by Moore's mother, a letter from Farren and an English newspaper from Malta. Moore did not bother to hide his disappointment at not receiving letters that would have been of greater importance to him – from Major Estcourt and mainly from Colonel Campbell.[263]

Moore still made all possible efforts to save his delegation. On 15 April, Beek was sent sailing to the northern shore, while Moore took the way to Jericho through the mountains. He visited the Muslim shrine in Nebi Moussa,[264] but – so typically – declined all invitations to go in and visit the place. Again, geology seems to be the only field of interest for him. He tried in vain to persuade the governor of Jericho to help them, and consequently, on 17 April, the whole group was obliged to return to

Jerusalem. The boat was left anchored in the lake, the heavy equipment in Jericho, and Moore and Beek left the Dead Sea. Moore was sure he would return, while Beek decided 'to cut the affair'.[265]

Their first encounter in Jerusalem was with Lord Lindsay's group, which had just returned from Petra – having faced no trouble at all on the way.[266] Moore decided to return to Djerash in order to stroll among the ruins. He was encouraged by the fact that he found two groups of travelers in Jerusalem preparing to go there. He started making the necessary preparations, wrote letters to his mother and Farren and then, on the 19th, again changed his mind.[267]

He spent the next days in Jerusalem, trying to make up his mind as to where to go and figure out what to do to get financial help and to obtain the necessary permits and licenses from the authorities. Beek instructed Moore on the use of the instruments he was leaving for him and left on 22 April. Explaining how he came to this decision, he claimed that it was reached only after being convinced that there was no chance to continue the work until June; only then was he 'determined to abandon the undertaking' as he had no intention of spending the hot summer months in the Jordan Valley. In the published letter, by contrast, it is claimed that 'Mr Beek has been obliged to return to Europe on occasion of the influence of the climate on his health.'[268]

Moore was a good student, at least at using the measuring instruments. He went to the Mount of Olives several times and to the Armenian Convent, at the southwestern edge of the city, and took bearings of many prominent points. The results are included in the diary, which ends on 27 and 28 April, two days spent with 'a good deal doing nothing'.[269]

During those ten days in Jerusalem, Moore was also busy sketching, meeting people and bargaining, mainly with the Franciscans about his room in their convent, and trying to solve his financial predicament. Help came from de Bertou, who wrote that he heard that 'we had been robbed of every thing we possessed on the Dead Sea', and enclosed an order from Consul Moore in Beirut to the procurator of the Franciscan convent 'for six thousand piasters to supply our immediate wants'.[270]

What happened in the following days is briefly described in the diary, and provided in detail in the (no longer extant) sections of diaries used extensively by Maurice Moore in his father's biography. In this original diary, which we have not been able to trace, George devoted only two pages to the story of the Dead Sea investigation, and continued the detailed description from 4 May.[271] Moore was still in Jerusalem, going through quite a difficult period and having too much spare time on his hands. His low mood is apparent from his diary, which includes only short comments from the days between 1 and 25 May. He still had some friends in Jerusalem, such as the Whitings and Holinski, but Lindsay's group, including Moore's friend Ramsay, had departed for Nablus on their way to Damascus, where the latter died of cholera on 8 June 1837.[272]

Moore's situation aroused nostalgic thoughts and reminiscences in him. Hinting at the disappointment engendered by his beloved married woman, Moore wrote to his mother:

> He whose heart and sword is mine to-day may desert me tomorrow, if his interest beckon him away [referring probably to Beek, HG]; and the love of a woman, that but yesterday seemed passionate and eternal, may to-day have passed, like a shadow on the waters, from her false and reckless heart; but a mother's love lives on alike through storms and sunshine, follows to the grave and the throne alike with unchanged and unchangeable devotion [...][273]

It took him ten more days to give up any hope of getting help from the local governors. He decided to go to Alexandria in order to 'lay the matter personally before the Pasha', Mehemet Ali himself. After more futile negotiation with Arabs from Hebron, who agreed to take him back to the Dead Sea, but only for six days ('In six days God made the world, but for me to get through my little task in the same time was, of course, out of question'), he went to Jaffa looking for a boat.[274] Being short of money for an 'express boat', he stayed there for a week, during which he proffered descriptions of the city and its inhabitants. Finding a boat and going on deck, he met Robert Pearce – 'the immortal', as Moore terms him – an adventurer and traveler whom he had first met two years earlier on the steamer that had taken both men to Syria, and about whom we failed to find any further material. This unexpected meeting led him to some philosophical remarks:

> When I first saw this singular being on the deck of the steamer that carried me to Syria how little did I dream that, nearly two years after, I should still be a wanderer beneath the same strange and burning sun. When the Mediterranean first bore me on its bosom with a heart as free and buoyant as its waves, surrounded by countrymen,

companions, friends, how little did I dream that, two years after, I should be still a solitary and gloomy stranger upon its blue waters, without a friend or companion save Robert Pearce![275]

Leaning over the bulwarks of the ship and gazing at the sea, he fell into one of his nostalgic moods, the thoughts causing him tears of happiness – only to be awakened by his notebook dropping into the water. 'My sketches, my memorandum, my compass bearings at Jerusalem – all gone.'[276]

After hearing from the English consul that the *firman* had been sent two days earlier he hurried back to Jaffa, where he had to stay in quarantine for two weeks, until 23 June. He used the time to meet and sketch people, especially the beautiful Helena, daughter of the Russian consul, and 'Sabkah the belly-dancer'. The *firman* arrived on 7 July, but the ensuing negotiations with the governor of Jerusalem were as futile as ever. The last entries in the diary were written in Jaffa on 14 July, and the next existing letter comes from London.[277]

The facts gathered and published in this book testify, above all, to Moore's important role in the early exploration of the Dead Sea, not only as one of the first to establish its relative level. He understood that a study of the lake would have to be conducted in tandem with the research of the natural features of its environs and while simultaneously surveying and mapping its shore, and he did his best to work accordingly.

Two sorts of results could have been expected from such an expedition: scientific reports, in the shape of articles and even a book, and a longer, more popular book that would tell the story of the voyage to the Dead Sea and Moore's other travels in the East. But Moore's letter to his mother, the one he sent from London in November 1837, and the lifestyle he conducted in the following years, point to his total denial of this chapter of his life, and to the strong lack of interest he showed in documenting his years in the East. But this was not a choice foretold or one made from the very moment he returned to England. As proved by some of the extant archival material, he did indeed busy himself with the scientific conclusions, especially regarding his most important finding – the level of the Dead Sea. But as time went on, he developed other interests, rejected all the pressures put on him to publish and destroyed most of his diaries and letters.

One of the questions arising from the diaries concerns the natural-history collections from the Dead Sea expedition. The diary includes evidence of an ongoing process of collecting specimens – geological, botanical and zoological. Moore also writes about boxes that were 'addressed to the care of Mrs. Whiting' in Jerusalem.[278] It is difficult to believe that Moore carried any of these collections with him; most of them must have been left in Jerusalem and long disappeared. Beek, on the other hand, did take some collections with him, and even fulfilled his intention, appearing in a letter, of depositing the minerals in the collections of the recently established Geological Society of London, another organization to which his brother contributed. According to a report given at the Annual General Meeting held on 16 February 1838, which lists the foreign specimens presented to the Society during the year 1837, 'specimens from the shores of the Dead Sea [were] presented by Henry [sic] Beek, Esq.'.[279]

The first objective of the expedition, as written in their letter to the RGS, was to perform 'a trigonometric survey of the Dead Sea'. Here they also only managed to achieve some beginnings, and maps were not mentioned in any of their diaries. Still, the proof that they did start to measure lies in three sheets (average size 53×65 cm), which are kept in the Map Room of the RGS.[280] They are not signed, and somebody, probably much later, added the supposition 'Moore's Survey of the Dead Sea?'.

These maps present different sections of the shore at the northwestern part of the Dead Sea, measured trigonometrically, and the line of the foot of the mountains. Some added written remarks on the maps provide evidence of two facts: first, that they are Moore's or Beek's drawings, and second, that they show the shores around Ein Feshcha. They mention, for example, 'pools of water where we found fish'. In his diary, Moore mentioned going to the lake 'to see a little pool where they told me were a quantity of little fish'.[281] Also marked on this sheet, presenting only a small region around Ein Feshcha, was their 'last station of tent', 'a heap of stones marks where stood the silk flag'. Another sheet presents the shore and mountain lines in a larger area. The only captions are 'Reed beds and springs of sweet water', referring to the area extending from Ein Feshcha to the south, and 'cavern', for the exact location of the cavern, mentioned repeatedly in the diary. This sketch gives the results of measurement along about five km from a little north of Ein Feshcha to the estuary of the Wadi Kedron.

The third map is of a smaller scale (scales are not mentioned, but the map is drawn in a scale close to 1:20,000). It describes the whole coast, from the northern part, somewhere west of the mouth of the Jordan, to the place where the mountains actually entered the sea in Ras Feshcha.[282] A break in the added line demarcating the foot of the mountains marks the canyon of Wadi Qumran. A text is added where the mountains reach the sea: 'Flag on rock; deep water close and no path below; 47 fathoms at 400 yd from shore; salt bottom'. The natural place to put a flag was this rock, which in those days was still protruding into the sea. This should be the site of the 'P.E.F. Rock', today west of the main road and south of Ein Feshkhah, where Masterman, the physician and director of the Anglican hospital in Jerusalem, marked the level of the sea for the PEF for fourteen successive years.[283]

Moore admitted in his diary that Beek was the expert in using the measurement devices, a fact that confirms Beek's claim that 'I had surveyed about a fifth [of the shore of the Dead Sea]'.[284] The same goes for another scientific achievement: the measuring of the longitudes of some important sites visited in their excursions, mainly not during the Dead Sea research. At the end of their letter to the RGS they added longitudinal measurements of the Convent of Mount Sinai, Akaba Fort, Petra, Hebron, Jerusalem, Djerash and Jaffa. These were taken by Beek on his tour from Egypt through Sinai and Akaba to Petra and the Hauran in the winter

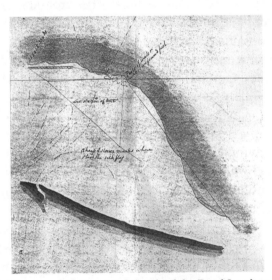

Fig. 43: Moore and Beek, partial sketch of the Dead Sea shore, detail

of 1836/7. Their significance, added the *JRGS* editor, confirming Beek's claim in his letter, lies in the fact that the measurement 'of Petra, we believe, [is] the first observation on record for that place'.[285]

Beek added in his letters that those were 'my observations', and they 'were made with Capt. Rater's repeating circle', which 'I used as a theodolite for triangulations & which served for observing latitudes. For ascertaining the heights of places I used a thermometer & boiling water'.[286] How does this correspond to Moore's letters to the secretary of the RGS on December 1838, where he writes about 'my observations' and 'my experiments'?[287]

How exactly did they go about performing the boiling-temperature measurements? The best description was given by Moore in his letter to the secretary of the RGS. They boiled 'common rain water, collected from a natural reservoir in the rock', in a tin which was intended for that purpose after a drawing in a pamphlet by a certain Colonel Sykes. The thermometer was inserted as nearly to the boiling point as possible, and the experiment was always repeated. In Jaffa and Beirut they received exact results of 212°F, by the Dead Sea 213°F, and at Jericho a 'somewhat superior' result.[288]

The suggestion to use thermometers for hypsometric measurements had first been raised in 1817, as the temperature of boiling water is of course dependent on the pressure of air on the water's surface. The problem in the beginning was that regular thermometers could, at most, be used to establish a general tendency, as in Moore and Beek's case. It would be necessary to develop special thermometers which were sensitive enough for this purpose.[289] The method was studied and tried for six years by Lieutenant-Colonel William Henry Sykes (1790–1872), an Indian Army officer and naturalist who between 1824 and 1831 held the position of 'Statistical Reporter', politician and ornithologist, an from 1834 was a member of the RS, who consequently published his results in the 1838 volume of the *JRGS*.[290] Sykes listed the problems and difficulties with the existing barometers (very costly, troublesome to carry, susceptible to accidents, unusable due to the escape of the mercury) and even with the newly invented thermometric barometer (very sensitive, very fragile, not fit for the rough work in the field). Attempting his methods during travels to Africa, Asia Minor and India, Sykes developed a way of using thermometers, always with at least two, in order to compare the observations. Three tables were developed in

India for the purpose of transferring the observations into heights, but Sykes provided his own table. According to his table, 213° equaled -507 ft, still to be corrected by multipliers according to the air temperature. The multiplier for 91°, the highest in the table, is 1.123, which brings us to a level of -569 ft.[291]

The other data which would enable us to estimate Moore and Beek's – as well as all other people's – contribution to the study of the Dead Sea is the comparison of their measurements with the latterly determined level of the Dead Sea during the relevant years, as drawn by Cippora Klein following very long and detailed work, and recently discussed by Revital Bookman and others. These detailed reconstructions of the fluctuations of the level between 1837 and 1848, which ranged between -400 and -395 meters, also enable us to establish and evaluate the various scientific projects discussed in this book.[292]

6 'The Chase After the Level': Dead Sea and Jordan Depression Surveys 1837–48, First Barometrical Measurements

At least five expeditions – groups or individual scholars – traveled to the Jordan Depression and its lakes in the years 1837 and 1838, equipped with barometers. It is difficult to imagine that this is mere coincidence, as some of them had heard the results of Moore and Beek's experiments even before these were published. Intrigued by the news and aware of its revolutionary importance, they made their way to the Dead Sea, trying to determine its exact level. They linked their results with the geo-religious significance of the region, i.e., the question of the ancient route of the Jordan and the obvious possibility of its having flowed into the Red Sea. If this were the case, so they believed, then the change, the interruption, must have been caused by the same geological-natural catastrophe that caused the destruction of Sodom, Gomorrah and the other punished cities, described so vividly in the book of Genesis.[1]

The first group, headed by Gotthilf Heinrich von Schubert (1780–1860) of Munich, reached the Dead Sea at the same time that Moore and Beek were conducting their research. Schubert was already one of the leading German natural historians, a distinguished scholar, whose work combined the influences of Romanticism with the so-called *Naturphilosophie*. He went on his long pilgrimage-exploration expedition accompanied by two of his young students, Michael Pius Erdl (1816–48) and Johannes Rudolf Roth, who were in charge of conducting the scientific work, carrying the instruments, performing the measurements and collecting specimens from the various natural-history fields; and the painter Johann Martin Bernatz. Schubert and company chose to reach Palestine from Egypt. Arriving from Jerusalem to Jericho and the Dead Sea, they also concluded that these sites were lower than the Mediterranean.[2]

They left Munich on 6 September 1836, sailing the Danube to the Black Sea and then to Egypt. Trying to establish the exact route of the Exodus, they crossed the Sinai Peninsula to Akaba and from there along the Arabah and to Petra. Returning west, they crossed the northern Negev to Hebron, Bethlehem and Jerusalem. After a long stay in the city with some small excursions, such as the one to the Dead Sea, they continued north in April 1837. Visiting Nablus, Nazareth, Carmel, Tabor and Tiberias, they crossed the Jordan at the Jacob Bridge to Damascus. Following excursions in Baalbek and Lebanon they sailed from Beirut to Italy. The voyage was extremely fruitful, yielding natural-history collections and numerous publications, a diary, a three-volume book, and various other scientific works.

Two outstanding achievements gave this exploration its relative importance. The first was their collection and purchase of numerous artifacts, mainly flora and fauna samples of a range never known before.[3] The second was their involvement in the earliest stages of revealing and publishing the fact that the Dead Sea, as well as other parts of the Jordan Rift Valley, were actually below sea level.

An interesting aspect of Schubert's descriptions is his expedition's encounters with local rulers and high officials as well as with fellow travelers and explorers. They also left some mementos, and Lindsay spotted Schubert's name scrawled on the wall of the Convent of the Forty Martyrs, on the path leading to the summit of Mount Sinai.[4] Naturally, they would also cross paths with Moore and Beek.

Moore's entry concerning the Germans is quite interesting:

They spent 20 days en route out of which they devoted 3 hours to the Ruins of Wady Mousa. One of them was a great natural history professor. Consequently the whole party thought of nothing but natural history. Two of the party married and slept with their wives in the same tent with the rest of the party with the exception of one unmarried lady who was allowed a tent to herself – a pity – why not let her see the fun.[5]

Moore, again in Jerusalem, met some of the Germans several days later. He remarked that they spoke neither French nor English fluently, an indication that Schubert himself was not present. The fact that within three years Roth and Bernatz would join an English expedition to Ethiopia, raises the unanswerable question of whom he actually met. Moore claims that they could hardly communicate. Seeing one of them skinning a porcupine for stuffing – a common natural-historian activity in this period – Moore added one of his cynical remarks: 'Can a dead porcupine awake sentimental feelings?'[6]

Schubert's reaction to the presence of the two Englishmen was completely different. In his book he recalled the 'somewhat extraordinary' sight of the brand new vessel his expedition spotted upon their arrival at the Dead Sea, flying the English flag with nobody around it. 'We looked at the boat with profound empathy,' wrote the Bavarian scholar, 'and were already then happy because of the future yield of scientific knowledge, which could justly be expected from this new, extraordinary sailing.' He added his regret at not being able to meet the 'two interesting travelers', who could have been of great help to him.[7]

The strange attitude demonstrated by the English travelers toward their German counterparts was not typical of the relationships among men of science from different European countries traveling and studying in the Near East during the first half of the nineteenth century. The negative attitude might have been understandable had it been displayed thirty or more years later, once science had become another tool in the struggle to inherit the dying 'sick man on the Bosporus'. The reason for Moore's attitude remains unclear, and he could of course not foresee the dispute which would soon develop between them.

A thorough examination of the respective timetables of the two groups raises the question of whether their meetings weren't more than coincidental and whether they did not in fact cooperate on a larger scale. How was it possible for Schubert's group to have spotted the boat, and not the tent that housed Moore and Beek and their relatively large delegation? Schubert's party arrived in Jerusalem on 28 March, the same day Moore's group left for the Dead Sea.[8] Moore was told about the Germans two days later, and he would meet them in Jerusalem on 9 April. After spending two days in Jerusalem he returned to the Dead Sea encampment, and spent 12 April sailing and fighting a storm.

The Germans stayed in Jerusalem until that date, when they left for Jericho. They reached the northern end of the Dead Sea on the next day, from the baptismal site known as the 'pilgrim's bath'. They rushed along the northwestern shore of the Dead Sea and, after finding that they had no provisions, left the shore and entered the desert mountains, spending the night in the Mar Saba monastery. One must therefore bear in mind that everything that Schubert wrote about the Dead Sea had been collected as impressions from a hurried ride, which could not have lasted more than a couple of hours.[9]

Moore wrote that he spent the whole day in the tent: '13th. The most laborious day of my life, the whole day spent in driving away the flies as we lay on our backs.' If the Germans spotted and described the boat – how could they have overlooked the camp and the people? The answer lies in the details of the route of the Germans, and the fact that the British encampment was rather farther north than the boat, which had been left by Moore after the storm. The Germans traveled along the shore, so it was possible that they did not spot the camp, which was a bit inland, probably in a hidden and shaded place. Schubert's group consequently did not notice the tent, but remarked the abandoned boat before entering Wadi Kedron. The Germans spent the next night in Jerusalem, and on 15 April continued their travel northward.

'Any preconceived opinion which I brought with me to the Dead Sea,' wrote Schubert, 'found itself after looking at it disappointed in a strange manner. I should have suspected the level difference, because of observations of earlier travelers, like Burckhardt, but this possibility did not cross my mind!'[10] He wrote about the seashore, 'rich with elevated beauties', about the taste and the specific weight of the water, about the influence of the level on the nature around it. He denied the possibility of a volcanic history of the region. Though not mentioning it directly, this is, in a way, reminiscent of Humboldt's theory of belts of plants. But most important for this book is his description of the barometers and their use. The party had left Germany with three barometers, but of course could not have expected such low levels. By the time they arrived in Jerusalem only one remained in satisfactory working condition. Already in Jericho they saw that their barometer was 'out of scale'; they even started suspecting its 'health situation'. Only after returning to Jerusalem, were they convinced that it did function well. Later, their results began to be confirmed by the observations of others.[11]

The results of the barometrical and meteorological observations performed by Schubert's group were published in various forums at different times. But it seems that one of the papers qualifies as its official publication. 'Please accept with forbearance this small, unsure contribution to the geography of Palestine,' wrote Roth in his cover letter to the editors of the *AEVS*, 'and you can be assured that, should God give us life and health, the geographers, and mainly you, could wait for more and heavier results.'[12] The paper, signed by Erdl, who actually performed the work, contains a list of 171 observations (Egypt, Sinai, Palestine from Akaba, Lebanon; many of them repeated several times). One barometer reached Munich 'in a thorough good situation and unchanged', so Professor Karl August Steinheil (1801–70) could perform the calculations and add a list of 65 levels.[13] His results concerning this study:

Jerusalem 2,472.9 Par. ft = 803.7 meters
    highest point on Mount of Olives 2,555.5 = 830.5 meters
Jericho [-]527.7 = -171.5
Sea level of the Dead Sea [-]598.5 = -195.5
Sea of Galilee [-]535.3 = -174
Jacob's Bridge 378.5 = 123

Schubert was blessed with both status and connections, and his excursion received great publicity in the contemporary press. A short summary of the scientific results of his expedition, published as early as March 1838 in the popular *Allgemeine Zeitung*, ends with a research plan:

Would they still carry out the project to bring a barge to the Dead Sea and to sail it to all its extension. How much interest would there be in an exact knowledge of the lake's depth, the temperature and contents of its water at a possible great depth, the knowledge of the grounds around it, steep mountain-walls, the creation of the asphalt, and more of the same.[14]

It is interesting to mention here that this report, published in March 1838, fails to mention those who had already tried to realize a similar program.

The French count, Jules de Bertou, 'whose biography is not known', in many ways followed in Callier's footsteps.[15] Some biographical details can be derived from Moore's letter of 3 December 1838 to the RGS, in response to Washington's inquiry as to 'who Mr. De Bertou is'. Moore described 'a Frenchman of very gentlemanly manners', who, since coming to Syria, probably in 1835, developed a close friendship with Consul Moore and even resided in his house. According to his own testimony, adds Moore, de Bertou served as aide-de-camp to Caroline Ferdinande Louise de Bourbon, Duchesse de Berri (1798–1870) 'during her memorable campaign in la Vendées [sic]' in 1832, and was of course a Carlist, seeking the establishment of a line of his family on the Spanish throne.[16]

Actually residing in Beirut for a considerable period, surely up to 1839 or even 1840, de Bertou initiated some interesting scientific explorations in addition to his intensive engagement in Dead-Sea and Arabah research, which will be discussed at length. One example is his study of Tyre and its ancient harbor, published in the *JRGS* in 1839.[17] William Wilde met 'the Count' in Jerusalem, claimed he was Swiss and testified that:

> M. de Bertou seems to have taken up this subject with great energy, and had petitioned the president of the Geographical Society at Paris, to prevail on the government to send out a diving bell, to explore these submarine ruins. Also I am not so sanguine as the Swiss traveler, yet the most interesting results may be anticipated.[18]

De Bertou was the first European in the new era to travel the entire length of the Arabah Valley and to establish the location of the watershed between the Dead Sea and the Red Sea. He was the first traveler to give a detailed account of the Ghor, the valley along the Jordan between the Sea of Galilee and the Dead Sea, and its side wadis. Callier, now representing the Parisian Société de Géographie, wrote that 'Nous avons signalé à M. Bertou l'importance de cette lacune', indicating the need for increased knowledge concerning the Jordan basin and its continuation into the Gulf of Akaba. Initially, de Bertou, who knew Moore and Beek personally, denounced their ostensible discovery because it contradicted the theory he was advocating, namely the historical flow of the Jordan into the Gulf of Akaba. It took him a while to change his mind, and another year to begin following their research. Yet, even as he set out for the Dead Sea, he continued to write that his aim was to establish whether the Dead Sea had a basin for itself, or whether it formed part of a larger one, connected with the Red Sea.[19]

Well acquainted with the region and the limitations caused by its severe climate, de Bertou waited for the next spring. Leaving Beirut at the beginning of March he hurried through Nazareth (7 March) to Jerusalem (10 March), and thence to Jericho (12 March, where they recorded -273m). The thirteenth of March 1838 was spent measuring the northern shore of the Dead Sea; he found out that it was -409m.[20] On the next day he returned to Jerusalem, and at the end of the month set out on another, month-long excursion, through Hebron and the southern end of the Dead Sea to Akaba (arriving 8 April), and back through the Arabah Valley and Petra.

De Bertou was determined to duplicate the experiment that had been conducted 'par un de mes amis, M. G. Moore', who claims to have found that the water started boiling at a temperature of 216° or 217° Fahrenheit (=102.22° or 102.77°C), and to endeavor to verify the results with his own barometer. Upon completion of the task, he published his results concerning the basin of the Dead Sea, namely, that it was 'beaucoup plus bas' than the Red Sea.[21] Following this first exploration, de Bertou issued some publications, mainly in his 'regular' periodical, the bulletin of the Parisian Geographical Society. He wrote to the Society that he had found the Latin Convent in Jerusalem to be 723.07m higher than the Mediterranean and 1,145.34m higher than the Dead Sea. Accordingly, the difference between the two seas was 422.27m.[22] Carl Ritter, who later summarized all the results, wrote that de Bertou measured 1,290 Parisian ft, the equivalent of 419.25m.[23] As will be described, de Bertou faced some difficulties in maintaining his barometer, and felt the need to vindicate its credibility in a letter to the Parisian society.[24]

Aware of the predominance of its London counterpart, he also hurried to write to the RGS, mentioning some of his results and promising to send his full account. John Washington, then RGS secretary, answered him on 3 June.[25] The main point raised by the latter was that much of de Bertou's data left room for doubt and, as he wrote in a letter to Consul Moore in Beirut, 'the Society is indebted to Mr. De bertou for his letter, but so far from having set the point at rest, he has made the point more complicated.'[26] He asked de Bertou why his observations concerning the level of the Dead Sea differed so greatly from those of Moore and Beek and from Schubert's, although their level for Jerusalem greatly corresponded, and why, according to his calculations, the difference between the Red Sea and the ocean was 630 feet, as 'surely this cannot be'. Additionally, the elevation of the north end of the Dead Sea, according to de Bertou's calculation, was 1340 feet below 'the level of the latter end', again, totally absurd, which made all of de Bertou's data very questionable. Washington's letter to Consul Moore acknowledges the receipt of de Bertou's report, sent on 12 May from Beirut. One should bear in mind that de Bertou had returned there only some days earlier.

De Bertou was always quick to write his reports and results, and in early 1839 the RGS received his manuscripts:

> No. 1: M. de Bertou's Journey from Jerusalem by Hebron and Zoar to 'Ain Arús between 12 March & 3 Apr. 38. recd 6 Dec 38.
>
> No. 2: M. de Bertou's Journey from 'Ain 'Arús along the Wadi 'Araba to 'Akaba and return to Wadí Arún & Petra from 3rd Apr. to 17th Apr. 38. rec. 6 Dec 38.
>
> No. 3: M. de Bertou's Journey from Wádi Hárún along Wadi 'Araba returning by a different route to Bír el Karyateïn from Ap. 18th to Ap. 23rd and return to Jerusalem May 1/38. rec. 6 Dec. 38.

A fourth manuscript, 'Notes on a Journey from Jerusalem to Hebron, the Dead Sea, El Ghór and Wádi 'Araba to Akaba & back [return, *JRGS* editors] by Petrá; in April 1838', a summary of the three reports, had been published in the *JRGS*, the editors adding that the manuscripts are kept in the RGS library for further reference.[27] The report in the *JRGS* of 1842 gave de Bertou's result as 1332.46 feet; if he meant English (and not Parisian) feet – this would be the equivalent of 406.13m.[28]

His second exploration of the region was conducted in the following year. Leaving Beirut in April 1839, he went to the sources of the Jordan, Lake Huleh and the Sea of Galilee, where he procured a boat and sailed around the lake. His claim that he was the first European in the modern era to sail on the Sea of Galilee is only half true, though he was surely the first one to report his sail, and it seems that he did not know about Costigan.[29] Continuing through Beth She'an to Jericho, he was again the first European to report on that unknown route. On this voyage he confirmed his previous observations, giving -315m for Jericho and -419m for the Dead Sea. This enabled him to be the first traveler to establish the topography of the entire length of the Jordan Rift Valley.[30] Here, de Bertou again exhibited an unusually effective method of publishing his findings. Two publications in French were directly followed by a paper, also in French, sent to the RGS, and published in its journal. Needless to say, all are dated the second half of 1839.[31] Lord Lindsay, who refereed the paper for the RGS, was not very critical, and mainly compared his own place names with those of de Bertou. He also added that 'Mr. Bertou's discoveries are so interesting in themselves & set forth so modestly that I must once more thank you for the pleasure you have given me in allowing me the perusal of them.'[32]

In his paper to the RGS, de Bertou compared his results in Jericho and the northern extremity of the Dead Sea from 1839 to those from the previous year. He determined again that the level was -419m. The detailed discussions and calculations are followed by a table, which includes some very interesting and pioneering observations. The table that appears below was copied directly from de Bertou's manuscript, whereas the editors of the BSG, where it was published, made a number of changes, in particular to site-names.[33]

La hauteur du Baromètre à Beyrout, sur le bord de la Méditerranée, évaluée à 28 pouces ou 757 mm, 96, a servi de base à tous les calculs (toutes les localités mesurées sont comprises entre 30° et 35° de latitude)

Lieux des observations	Thermomètre du Baromètre, centigr.	Thermomètre Libre, centigr.	Hauteur du Baromètre, millimeter	Elévation calculée en mètre	Heure de l'observation	Date
Ain ainoub	22.5	22.5	724.12	+399.3	10 am	
Beit el Din	15.31	15.31	694.80	+737.3	6 pm	
Djasine	15.25	15.25	683.52	+877.4	7 pm	
Kefarhouni	13.75	13.75	676.75	+957.7	3 pm	
E-leitanieh	17.5	17.5	726.38	+361.5	10 am	
Sources du Jourdain	21.25	21.25	742.17	+183.0	4 pm	
Banias	15.25	15.25	734.27	+263.2	5 pm	
Tel el Cadih	14.375	14.375	747.81	+105.0	6 am	
Ain-el-Blata	27.1875	26.25	755.70	+36.1	3 pm	
Caddès	15.25	15.625	721.86	+409.8	5 pm	
Bahr el houlé	25	23.75	759.09	-6.4	8 am	
Tibériade					6 pm 7 am	24 avril
					12	25 dito
Somme 79, 655	19.91	19.91	778.26	-230.3	12	3 mai
le ⅕	15.925				5 am	
Près de l'embouchu-re du Jourdain, dans le lac de Tibériade	22.5	21.875	780.52	-252.1		

Camp du Scheik Beschir	20	20	780.52	255.3	8 am	28 avril
Même latitude bord du Jourdain	15.25	15.25	787.29	334.7	6 am	2 mai
Wady el Fedjarith	23.75	23.75	785.03	301.3		
Même latitude plus prés du Jourdain	25	25	788.41	337.5		
Wady el Farah	22.5	22.5	786.16	315.2	9 am	1 mai
Même latitude bord du Jourdain	23.75	23.75	790.10	357.9	10 am	" "
Wady el abiad	15.25	15.25	789.54	359.3	5 am	29 avril
Même latitude bord du Jourdain	16.875	16.875	791.80	384.3	5 ¾ am	" "
Riha (Jericho) ½ somme... 17,875	22.334	22.334	786.16	315.2	1 pm 7 am	" " 30 "
Extrémité septentrionale de la mer morte	30.9375	30.9375	796.31	-419.8	4 pm	29 avril

The added observations describe weather conditions ('rain storm, black sky'; 'strong rain with no breaks') and measuring conditions ('both observations from the 25th before noon. Accepted through two barometers').

After meeting him in Jerusalem in 1838, Edward Robinson became quite critical of de Bertou's results and their implications. Various reasons, such as the bad relations between the Frenchman and his Bedouin guides, his employment of an ordinary and illiterate interpreter, and his neglect of accuracy, led to a list of points, 'which, as it seems to me, require either confirmation or correction'. Robinson did not keep his reservations to himself, and the RGS already knew about them in 1840, even before the publication of the latter's book.[34]

The RGS did not hide this criticism from de Bertou, but he rejected it. He admitted that he could not make use of the original instruments which he had brought from home, nor of others that were lent to him. He could use his barometer on the first excursion, but 'afterwards the heat melted the wax which joined the steel lock to the tube, the air entered, and I was deprived of the instrument upon which I had relied to establish the Levels from the south of the Dead Sea to the north of the Elanitic Gulf'. He was ready to give up the undertaking, but met a French traveler who 'lent me a very good Thermometer of Levebours', with which he took his measurements on his second exploration, 'from Hébron to Akába'.[35]

Van de Velde did not fully agree with Robinson's total dismissal of de Bertou's work. This was the first traveler, he wrote in his memoir, to describe the Ghor and all its side wadis, 'both large and small', between Tiberias and the Dead Sea. The Dutch cartographer made much use of this information in his map.[36]

The Austrian montanist (mineralogist and geologist) Joseph Russegger (1802–63) took his measurements of the Dead Sea and the Jordan Depression in late autumn 1838.[37] One of the leading Austrian montanists of these early stages of geology, he also became a pioneer of geological research in the Orient. Though less famous, his contribution to the study of the region, and of Palestine, is of huge importance, and probably equaled that of Titus Tobler, 'the father of the German study of Palestine'.[38]

Russegger was one of the European experts invited by Mehemet Ali, the Egyptian ruler, in the latter's efforts to develop and modernize his country.[39] He received the blessing of his Kanzler, Clement Lothar Wenzel, Fürst von Metternich (1773–1859), who showed much interest in the developments along the eastern shores of the Mediterranean, mainly since the Greek Revolt and the Egyptian conquest of Syria.[40] Russegger stayed in the East until 1839, exploring Egypt including parts of present-day Libya and Sudan, Sinai, Syria and Asia Minor. He then went to Greece, where he performed a similar research upon the invitation of King Otto I. After returning in 1841 to Vienna he published his seven-volume work, followed by an atlas, mainly of geology charts.[41]

Probably more than any other contemporary traveler, Russegger had been well educated and equipped for his studies and measurements. In a letter describing his early (1836) travels in Lebanon, he wrote about the various instruments in his possession:

[...] and, except for the Boussol-instruments [for measuring magnetic inclination] which had still not arrived [in Beirut] with azimuth-circle, telescope and altitude-curve, [I] am in possession of two

217

barometers for altitude measurements, many thermometers, one fotometer, thermohygrometer, hypsometer, some areometers [for measuring the weight and density of gas or liquid], electrometers [for studying the qualitative and quantitative electricity in the air], astatic needles, sextants, boussoles, telescopes, one microscope that enlarges up to 270,000 times in area, one electro-chemical and one thermo-electrical multiplicator, one inclinator, from essay-instruments [for chemical analysis], blowpipe apparatus, reagent-tubes-box, and a very strong magneto-galvanic apparatus with big horseshoe-magnets. All the instruments were produced in Vienna and [are] really of exceptional beauty and accuracy.[42]

This is quite an impressive professional list, if one compares it to the methods and instruments used, for example, by Moore and Beek.

Russegger's study of Palestine began after breaking his contract with the Egyptian ruler.[43] He began his journey in Suez, where, aware of the protracted discussion concerning the routes to India, he reported that a steamship came regularly every four weeks from Bombay, completing the voyage in 18 days such that the passengers could make their way to London in 36 days.[44] He crossed to Sinai ('after two years again Asian earth'), where he conducted diverse research on the seashore as well as in the high mountains ('the neighborhood of the [Saint Catherine] monastery is the wildest, which I've seen so far in my life'). In the monastery's visitors book he found the names of Schubert, Franz Ignaz Pruner (1808–82), a Bavarian physician who made a career in the service of Mehemet Ali, 'and mainly a lot of Englishmen'.[45]

Russegger's work laid the foundations for later geological studies of the whole region, including Syria and Palestine. His studies of the Jordan Rift, and especially the Dead Sea, are of significant value. Carl Ritter made great use of the work of the young Austrian in his *Vergleichende Erdkunde* and termed him, for example, 'the most reliable guide' for the study of the Sinai Peninsula. When describing the geological character 'of the country between Hebron, Bethlehem, Jerusalem, Jericho and the northern end of the Dead Sea', Ritter used, more than anything else, the work, data and results of 'my friend Russegger'. Russegger made it a point to climb all the Sinai mountains and supplied us with a list of eleven measured altitudes.[46]

A second list includes the results of his bearings from the Saint Catherine monastery through Wadi Arabah to Hebron. After visiting

Bethlehem, he arrived in Jerusalem ('Jerusalem has a mean height of 2,479 Parisian Feet'), where he stayed for a couple of weeks, and from whence he went to the Dead Sea. Though he admitted that 'I really did not go around the whole Dead Sea, that is 20 hours long and 7 hours on its widest spot', his report, including many measurements, is extremely interesting and of the highest value.[47] He described his last voyage in Palestine, in the Galilee, as 'one of the most interesting parts of my recent voyage'. The important result: The Sea of Galilee is 625 Parisian feet under the Mediterranean, and therefore 716 above the Dead Sea.[48]

In 1841, Russegger published a summary of his studies along 'the depression of the Dead Sea and the whole Jordan Valley'.[49] This was followed by the longest list at the time of levels in Palestine, and tables of many meteorological measurements in Jerusalem, Jaffa, Nazareth and other places.[50]

In 1845, Ritter published the tables including Russegger's climatological observations and the calculated relevant hypsometric data. Wilhelm Mahlmann (1812–48), Ritter's colleague and an expert on mathematical geography, added his comments to a letter which had been sent by Russegger, describing his measurements along the Jordan Rift Valley, where he also discussed Symonds's (erroneous for the Sea of Galilee) results.[51] Using an advanced mercury barometer he was able to establish quite accurate altitudes, such as that of the Jacob Bridge (378 Par. ft = 123m) or the Sea of Galilee (-625 Par. ft = -203.1m). The Dead Sea surface, he found, was 1341 feet or 435.8 meters below sea level.

Having already heard something about his contemporaries, their travels and surveys, Russegger wrote:

> As far as I know, there was, except for court counselor Schubert, only one traveler, an Englishman whose name I forgot, that claimed that the Dead Sea should lie deeper than the Mediterranean; as he had no instruments with him he could not supply definite data. Schubert was the first one to go there with instruments [...].
>
> I don't know Beke's determination, and the results of Bertou agree so closely with mine [...]; I don't know if Robinson himself made any observations.[52]

Russegger was the first to refute the accepted theory that all the area of the lake was of a volcanic origin and to acknowledge the important role of limestone in Palestine's geological formations.[53] He did not limit himself to his area of expertise – geology – and his reports, papers and books include a considerable amount of information in a vast range of fields relevant to the regions which he traversed. He contributed long lists of the existing written sources he had made use of, acknowledging them as one of the best available means for knowing a new country.[54] Due to his acquaintance with Ritter, he had ongoing close contacts with the scientific center in Berlin. He presented his studies before the geographical society, and also sent them collections of geological specimens.[55]

In Russegger's first report, which included the results of his hypsometrical measurements along the Jordan Depression, in Sinai and in other parts of Palestine, he explicitly stated that the surface of the Dead Sea was 1,319 Parisian ft (428.7m) lower than the Mediterranean, and 1,349 ft lower than the Red Sea, reminiscent of a similar error made by Napoleon's surveyors, which was corrected by Chesney. This altitude was changed in later reports to 1,341 ft (436m). Still, his work was greatly appreciated. One of his advantages over his predecessors was the constant re-taking of measurements at almost every location, so that his results could be better and more accurately calculated, being less influenced by occasional or incidental conditions.[56]

As in most fields of Holy Land studies, the American minister and scholar Edward Robinson also played a focal role in the efforts to establish the level of the Dead Sea and consequently to answer questions concerning earlier geological phenomena, including those described in the Old Testament. Robinson, 'the father of Palestine scientific research', conducted his 1838 studies of the biblical historical-geography, topography and toponomy of the country together with Eli Smith, a Presbyterian missionary and scholar residing in Beirut, who excelled in his knowledge of Arabic. The cartographer Berghaus could hardly find words to praise their work, as 'the observations of these two travellers are so full and comprehensive, their notes upon the form and features of the country so exact and definite'.[57] Their book, published simultaneously in German and English in 1841, became a cornerstone of the study of the Holy Land.[58] Receiving the RGS Patrons Medal ('being the Royal Donation of Her Most Gracious Majesty'),[59] Robinson maintained close, even intensive connections with the society, publishing continually in its journal and following all developments concerning the rift, as closely as he could.

Robinson and Smith 'entered Palestine from the south on 12 April 1838'. Two and a half months later, on 26 June, they 'rode into Beirut'. During this time Robinson became highly interested in the newly discovered unexpected depression of the Dead Sea and the other parts of the Jordan Valley. He went to the Dead Sea through the Judean Desert and reached Ein Gedi on 10 May.[60] Over the following eight years he was intensively involved with the question, talking to people and writing to them, lest the issue be consigned to oblivion.[61] Although he did not perform hypsometric measurements by himself, Robinson became deeply involved in determining the level, as well as in the general study of the Dead Sea and the Jordan Depression. He collected and published all the research done and the conclusions reached by other scholars, and did not hesitate to critique their results and cast doubt on their credibility.[62]

As mentioned above, Robinson became quite critical of de Bertou's findings and conclusions. Still in Germany, while writing his *Biblical Researches*, he chose the periodical of the Berlin Geographical Society as the platform for his immediate reaction to de Bertou's reports of 1839, which he also sent to the bulletin of the Parisian society and, in a concise English version, to the *JRGS*.[63] This reaction was repeated in all the editions of the *Biblical Researches*.

Following his return from his first exploration of the Arabah, de Bertou visited Robinson and Smith at their residence in Jerusalem, and told them about Moore and Beek's works and his tour and observations. Robinson's attitude was critical from the first moment. Various factors, such as the poor relations with his Bedouin guides (Robinson, employing the same Jehâlin Bedouins, heard their parallel complaints about de Bertou, and wrote that there was no way that they would have given him reliable oral information) his complete ignorance of the Arabic language and the use of a simple, illiterate interpreter ('I've been more than lucky in having Smith with me, who is fluent in the language and many of its dialects'), and neglect of accuracy, led in Robinson's opinion to a list of points which, as mentioned above, require 'either confirmation or correction', and made him question the credibility of the Frenchman in everything he said and wrote.[64] Robinson added some question marks concerning de Bertou's preparations and suitability for such a scientific mission. As an example, he mentioned the fact that de Bertou went to Petra without even looking once at the important and already famous album of his countryman, Léon de Laborde, which he was shown for the first time by the Americans in Jerusalem.[65]

Robinson checked every detail and report and, making the best use of his observations as well as comparisons with the itineraries of other explorers and travelers, all of them available for him in Berlin libraries, listed one by one the inaccuracies, inconsistencies and mistakes he found in them. 'The evidence of this deficiency on the part of M. de Bertou,' he concluded, 'appears in every page, which together with other circumstances cast a doubt on the extent of his own scientific knowledge as well as accurate observations.'[66] Later, rechecking the locations with his cartographer, Heinrich Kiepert, Robinson decided that he had been erroneous on one point and published another comment, and even apologized to de Bertou, saying that 'if I did Bertou an injustice, it happened against one's will'.[67]

Still, considering the inconsistency of the different results of the early explorers, as early as 1840 Robinson already suggested that the issue could not be resolved without ascertaining the difference through trigonometric measurement.[68]

7 Who Should be Crowned the Great Discoverer? Publications and Discussions Following Moore and Beek's Report

Who, thus far in our narrative, should be crowned the great discoverer of this unique geographical characteristic? Who were the creators of 'the drama of the scientific community's awareness of the depression of the Dead Sea'? Carl Ritter had no doubt: 'The reader's attention ought to be called particularly to the fact that it is to this [Moore and Beek's, HG] expedition that we owe the direct discovery of the depression of the Dead Sea.'[1] This view was not always accepted, even by some contemporaries and participants. The publication of Moore and Beek's revolutionary discovery, which found its way from London to the French and German papers, was followed by numerous discussions of various topics.

Charles Tilstone Beke's main interests lay in scholarship and research, although he supported himself through his commercial activity. His first publication, subtitled *Researches in Primeval History*, probably 'set an intellectual framework for much of the rest of his life'. The main idea behind his studies was 'to harmonize recent scientific discoveries, especially those in geology, with a belief in the Bible as an inspired work of divine revelation'.[2] He received his brother's letter concerning the Dead Sea about the time of its publication, and his reactions could be understood accordingly. First he wrote to the teleologist, Ritter,[3] which is surprising given the similarity of their approaches. In the year between his receipt of the letter and his departure on his African exploration, Beke served as an agent for the two explorers – his brother and Moore –

who were still on the road, among other things connecting them to the German and British scientific milieus.

As quoted by Beke, Schubert's group found 'the level of the Dead Sea to be 598 Parisian Feet lower than the Mediterranean'. The letter in the popular *Allgemeine Zeitung*, the largest and most influential German newspaper of that time, added that a boat should be transferred to the Dead Sea in order to explore the lake. Beke called the attention of the Germans to the fact that this had already been accomplished by his brother and Moore. According to a letter which he received from his brother, dated Jerusalem, 18 April 1837, 'the Dead Sea is at least 500 English Feet under the Mediterranean. Jerusalem, after my calculation, is 2,500 Feet above the sea level'.[4] Schubert's group, using barometers, found that 'the depression of the Dead Sea under the sea level of the Mediterranean is at least 598.5 or in round number 600 Parisian, i.e., close to 640 English Feet'.[5]

Schubert later claimed that, although the publication in the *JRGS* was obviously earlier, his team had in fact been the first to establish the fact that the entire valley, including the Jordan and the Sea of Galilee, was lower than sea level.[6] Erdl, who actually performed the observations, died in 1848. In the obituary for his brilliant young protégée, Schubert discussed the matter thoroughly in order to show his gratitude and to restore to the deceased some of his pioneering rights in establishing the Dead Sea level:

> Erdl was the first to bring this strange, unexpected fact to public mind; the first to measure this rift for all its length, from the Sea of Tiberias until the Dead Sea, and even more southwards from there to some points in the Araba. It was because of him that the attention was drawn, of Russegger and soon the participants and friends of Geography in all Europe, to a phenomenon that is probably unique in its kind and extension in the whole world.[7]

The issue developed into a debate between Beke and Schubert, which played itself out in 1838 for public consumption, through letters to the *Allgemeine Zeitung*. It took Schubert two days to react to Beke's letter. He wrote a short response, mainly expressing his hope that further studies by Moore and Beek would lead to more accurate information concerning the whole rift.[8] Beke's answer came on 11 June, and this time he added a surprising fact, a letter received lately from his brother, dated Naples, 15 April, 'in which he gives a more exact result of the levels, of the Dead Sea as well as of Jerusalem, and I am happy to say that they seem even more to agree with those of Mr. v. Schubert'. Beke claimed that while in London 'last October' (of 1837), he submitted these better results to the RGS: The Dead Sea is 700 feet lower than the Mediterranean, and about 200 feet lower than Jericho, and Jerusalem is about 2,700 feet above sea level. Two weeks later the editors received another letter from him, asking only to correct 'a small mistake': the level of the Dead Sea should have been given as -750, and not -700, English feet.[9]

It seems that Moore and Beek had lost contact directly after parting ways in Jerusalem. According to Beek's letter to the RGS in spring 1841, they had decided prior to separating that 'neither of us should, for a limited time, separately publish an account of his researches'.[10] This might also be one of the reasons that motivated Moore to refrain from publishing. By July 1839 Washington assumed that there would be no joint reaction from the two, as Beke had left England and Moore was too young '& I fear, too gay to write anything for us'.[11] In 1841 Moore was already deep into professional racing. 'George Moore and his brother, Augustus, had given up all else and devoted themselves heart and soul to racing and riding.'[12]

At that time, Beek gave up the hope of collaborating with Moore, claiming that, as four and half years 'without my companion having signified his intention of writing on the subject' have passed, he felt free to 'offer the public [my] notes'. Naturally, these were sent to the RGS – as a twelve-page memorandum which shows signs of editing but had never been published. The first part deals with the narrative of the expedition, but most of the document concentrates on Beek's theories as to the formation of the Dead Sea, which deeply contradicted those of de Bertou as published in the Journal of the Parisian Geographical Society of 1839.

This document also bears evidence of a disagreement between Moore and Beek. Whereas almost everywhere the discovery is ascribed to both, here Beek claims that it was Moore who agreed to carry all the expenses, but 'on my part I had to execute the survey', so 'I had, during the year 1837 been the first, I believe, to pronounce from actual obscuration in opinion of the depression of the level of the Dead Sea'. The original letter to the RGS bears only his signature, and we may never know whether it had been sent from both of them, or only at his private initiative.[13] At the beginning of 1838 the editors of the French geographical journal *Nouvelles Annales des Voyages* published an accurate French translation of the report in the *JRGS*.[14] Later that year, they also translated Charles Tilstone (erroneously identified as G.T.) Beke's letter to the *Allgemeine Zeitung*, which would become the opening shot in the heated argument with Schubert.

The differences between the British and the Germans were of relatively minor importance as they were similarly limited in terms of the methods and instruments used, and they yielded similar results. A considerably more significant debate developed between Moore and Beek and the two Frenchmen – their friend or at least acquaintance from Beirut, Count de Bertou, and Callier. The French scientific world followed the revolutionary development with much interest from its very beginning and, as mentioned above, Moore and Beek's letter to the RGS was translated and published, without any further comment, in a most important geographic journal.[15] Consequently the editor of that French journal received a letter from Charles Tilstone Beke in Leipzig, dated 29 March 1838, correcting some numbers and pointing out that both results, Moore and Beek's and those of Schubert, showed a depression of more than 500 Parisian feet, from which he concluded that the theory of the Jordan flowing into the Red Sea must be abandoned, with all its implications concerning the catastrophic event recorded in the Bible.[16]

The debate arose from a simple misunderstanding. In his report, de Bertou wrote that Moore, 'some months before me', had reached the conclusion that the Dead Sea was about 600 feet below the Mediterranean, and that, on the basis of barometric measurements, 'this difference of the levels should be doubled'.[17] However, in his analysis and publication a year earlier of the results of Beek's works, Callier had reached a different conclusion. Pointing out the enormous significance of the discovery of the impossibility that the Jordan could have flowed into the Red Sea, he wrote a long and detailed paper devoted to the problem of determining the level and to comparing the few results he had, such as the measurement by the Napoleonic engineers of the Gulf of Suez, Moore and Beek's survey of the Dead Sea and Jerusalem, and de Bertou's of all three points. Whereas de Bertou's barometrical measurements, when calculated, indicated a depression of 406 meters,

Callier determined that Moore and Beek's 102.5°C represented a level of 815mm63 on the barometer, denoting a depression of 607.8 meters.[18]

The detailed paper, which included numerous calculations, was published in the *NAVSG* with a shortened version in the *BSG*.[19] Simultaneously, Callier submitted his reports to the French Academy of Sciences, giving the same data: 216.5°F, equal to a depression of 2,220 feet or 608 meters. This publication found its way to western Ireland and reached George Henry Moore. It caused him, for the first – and probably the last – time since his return to discuss his expedition in public. The archives of the RGS hold two letters of his, both written in Moore Hall on the same day (3 December 1838), one a response to Callier, and the other a personal letter to 'my dear Sir', most probably Washington, who had been secretary of the RGS since 1836.[20] The second letter had been written as a reply to a letter dated 27 October, in which Moore was asked by the RGS about de Bertou, probably after they had received two manuscripts of his for publication. Both were consequently published in the following year.[21]

Moore's style, in both letters, was somewhat sarcastic, first casting doubt on Callier's authority to make such a statement, and then blaming him for twisting the facts. His and Beek's experiments, Moore corrected, which were repeated several times, showed that water had boiled at 213°F, and the only previously published data was that of a depression of 500 feet. Theirs should thus be considered the first record on that subject, and so far also the only one, 'for it is worse than childish to take into account the subsequent barometrical observations of M. de Bertou, as that gentleman distinctly states [...] that his barometer was out of order'. In spite of this fact, wrote Moore, Callier had chosen to use Bertou's results, revealing his ignorance in the following remark: 'It would be desirable to know whether M. M. Moore & Beke boiled fresh water or water of the Dead Sea.'

Moore offered a sound explanation for Callier's mistake. De Bertou had repeatedly asked Beek and himself about their experiments and results; Moore's Dead Sea diary reveals a strong connection between them. It seems that Callier's misunderstanding derived from a mistaken interpretation of the facts. De Bertou had been told by the Englishmen that they had sounded the depth of the sea, and in some places measured 2,220 feet without reaching the bottom; they had also tried to boil the sea water, and succeeded at 222°F. Both these facts were taken by Callier as evidence of the altitude of the surface of the Dead Sea – and of Moore and Beek's incorrect results. Moore ended his letter to the journal hinting at Callier's failure to establish the fact by himself, although he traveled in the region 'well provided with the instruments'. Would it not have been more beneficial to science, he wondered, had this gentleman performed his own observations, instead of 'mis-stating the observations of one who simply travelled for his own amusement [...]?'

At the end of both letters Moore repeated his preparedness to return to Syria and complete the mission at his own expense, but only on the condition of obtaining a *firman* from the authorities – Mehemet Ali – through the mediation of the British government. When presenting these letters, the RGS 'directed some enquiry to be made at the For[eign] Off[ice] respecting this point to be reported to the next meeting of the Council';[22] we have no evidence as to the results. In spring 1841, Beek also reacted to Bertou's paper of 1839. He sent to the RGS the twelve-page memorandum which had been 'Referred by Reported upon in the 28th June by M. Frere', but had never been published. The first part concerns the story of the expedition.[23]

Though this seemed to conclude Moore and Beek's involvement, the French continued in their intensive preoccupation with the possibility or impossibility of any ancient connection between the Dead and Red Seas. The longest, most detailed study was published in 1842 in German, in Berghaus's geographical periodical. Jean Antoine Letronne (1787–1848), an archaeologist, Hellenologist and Egyptologist, from 1831 professor of history and from 1838 of archaeology in the Collège de France, tried to assemble all the existing details and to reach a conclusion.[24] First Letronne decided to produce a chronological list and then to collect and study the existing papers and studies dealing with the topic, beginning with an 1835 paper of his own in which he had already raised the question, Callier's and de Bertou's longer reports and two other papers from 1836 dealing with the issue.[25] He devoted some research to the historical and contemporary connection between the Dead Sea and the Red Sea as well as the possibility of a canal connecting Suez with the Mediterranean.[26] He then summed up with a long part of a paper he published in 1817 concerning the difference in levels between the Red Sea and the Mediterranean. There he had reached the conclusion that a small difference was possible.[27]

One fact seems unquestionable in the aforementioned events and discussions: the *JRGS* was the first to publish the information that the society had received from Moore and Beek, and this publication catalyzed a period of intensive activity in the hypsometric measurements along the Depression, from the Gulf of Akaba in the south to the sources of the Jordan in the north. The leading geographers of the time, including the two 'fathers of modern geography' from Berlin, Alexander von Humboldt and Carl Ritter, followed the process closely, describing it in detail and evaluating its results.[28]

The discussion concerning the old course of the Jordan was, of course, of great significance, not only scientifically but also for theological perceptions, and involved numerous personalities – scientists, clergy and laymen. The Irish nobleman Frederick-William-Robert Vane-Stewart, Viscount Castlereagh, fourth Marquess of Londonderry (1805–72) traveled in the region in 1841, the period of British military involvement. He had been quite annoyed by those who so easily denounced the old and accepted traditions:

> I decline to subscribe to the opinion that the Jordan cannot have formerly passed down Wady Araba. [...] In the valley there are water-courses in every direction, as well towards Akaba as towards the Dead Sea, where it seems to be fashion to suppose that the Jordan in all times lost itself. [...] The position of the country seems to mark clearly the course of a great river down to the gulf of the Red Sea. I think some travellers have made up their minds beforehand to start new theories, and contradict all received opinions without good or sufficient grounds, and as there are explorers who have no traditions in their own countries, it does not seem unnatural that they should wish to attack those that may exist in others.[29]

8   Additional Surveys and Triangulation

At the beginning of the 1840s the exact altitude of the Dead Sea level was still unclear; it would have to be determined using more accurate and dependable methods and instruments, starting from the Mediterranean shore, going up to Jerusalem and continuing down to the Dead Sea. A similar geographical question, the 'long contested point' of the exact level of the Caspian Sea, which had been known to be lower than the Black Sea, had just been resolved. In 1836 a Russian expedition began the trigonometric leveling, and in 1838 Humboldt could already write to the RGS that the former was 94.9 Parisian feet lower than the latter.[1]

Symonds's triangulation from Jaffa through Jerusalem to the Dead Sea resulted in a difference of 1,607 ft. Beginning at the highest house in Jaffa, he estimated that the difference from the level of the Mediterranean would come to -1,400 English ft (-1,314 Parisian ft). Just like van de Velde, the RGS had to request the loan of 'Symonds' triangulation in Palestine' from the Navy.[2] The young military surveyor, already in England, forwarded his triangulation to the RGS, and it was published as follows: 'The Lake of Tabarie is 328.1 and the Dead Sea 1,311.9 ft. below the mean tidal mark of the Mediterranean at Acre and Jaffa which I have assured to be on the same level.' The original sketch is kept in the RGS archive, although I could find at least one more original – drawn on a scrap of parchment and signed by Symonds on 16 April 1842 – in Petermann's archive in Gotha.[3]

The triangulations, so significant for this study, were based on two measured base-lines, the first from Acre to the Sea of Galilee via Safed and the second from Jaffa to the Dead Sea via Jerusalem, connected by various intermediate points. In addition to levels, it also included distances given in yards. Accordingly, the direct distance between Jaffa and the castle of Acre was 115,400 yards (about 105.5 km); from the summit of Mount Hermon to Safed 137,300 yards (about 125.5 km); and from the 'Baths of Tiberias' to the Dead Sea (probably its northernmost point) 112,925 yards (about 103.26 km).[4] Another document, archived alongside the triangulation at the RGS, is a much lesser-known profile, also signed by Symonds. It follows both base-lines from the Mediterranean shore, to the 'Lake of Tabaria' (again, -328.1 ft) and to the Dead Sea (-1,311.9 ft), respectively.

Humboldt followed the developments in the leveling of the Dead Sea as closely as possible and acknowledged the unique importance of the geological problem of the lake, not merely because of theological considerations but mostly due to the French argument put forward by Letronne of the impossibility of the Jordan having connected the lake with the Red Sea in ancient times. In 1844 he summoned all of the information at his disposal. The numbers he used, in French (i.e., Parisian) ft, were:

Jerusalem +2,479 (816m)
Bethlehem +2,538 (846m)
Sea of Tiberias -625 (-104m)
Dead Sea -1,341 (-435m)

Humboldt could actually cite almost every account, and also possessed Symonds's and Alderson's texts, which were given to him by Washington on his 1842 visit to London.[5]

Another summary of the situation using Symonds's data had been made by Hamilton in his Anniversary Address for 1842. Counting all the former measurements and results (including those of painter David Wilkie), he pointed out the similarity in the results of de Bertou (-1,332.46 ft) and of Symonds (-1,311.9 ft).[6]

In 1843, Symonds was awarded the Gold Medal of the RGS for 'those who have distinguished themselves in advancing the cause of geographical science', at a ceremony held in his absence and attended by his father.[7] The decision to decorate him does not seem to have been an easy one, since he was almost constantly serving overseas and it was difficult, sometimes even impossible, to communicate with him. On 6 May 1843 Colonel Julian Jackson (1790–1853, RGS secretary from 1841 to 1848) wrote to William Richard Hamilton, by then president of the Society, asking him to 'approve of his [Symonds's] father being invited to receive the medal for him', and saying that he had written to Washington asking for information respecting the circumstances under which the triangulations had been undertaken.[8] Four days later he wrote to Symonds's father, posing a number of questions concerning the Palestine triangulation:

> When was it begun & how long did it take doing? Was it undertaken in the regular course of his duty or was it a voluntary and spontaneous labour of his own? Was he while engaged in those operations, acting under the directions of any superior officer or not? Did it occasion any expense defrayed by himself, or was it at the expense of the government? Was he prevented from carrying his triangulation over the whole of Syria from being recalled or otherwise?[9]

These questions testify to a certain lack of organization at the RGS, as the society had already received Symonds's letter of February, cited above, which includes answers to some of these questions.[10] Interestingly enough, it seems that Symonds, after hearing that his father had received the medal in his absence, expressed some doubts concerning the RGS's procedure. He told Jackson that the Society should have consulted the Board of Ordnance, his employers and the processors of the cartographic material. One can only assume that Symonds feared his colleagues in his endeavors would probably not have agreed to him getting all the fame for himself. Whatever the case may be, Jackson replied that there were already precedents for medals being awarded to officers in service without any preliminary permission, and the RGS was 'merely the judge as to the proper person to whom it should be given'. He urged Symonds to publish something in the journal, and regretted that the former was unable to stay in Syria long enough to complete his survey.[11]

What exactly were Symonds's achievements, according to the RGS?

> Finding himself in the course of service on the coast of Syria in 1840, [...]. Symonds, who had been early taught to spurn in glorious ease, and being now in a country full of the most stirring reminiscences, [...] was fortunate enough to be selected by his commanding officers to undertake the survey of a portion of Syria; and the result of his labours in the year 1841, notwithstanding the interruption occasioned by fever was the triangulation of the country between Jaffa and Jerusalem; and thence to the head of the Dead Sea on the S.; and from Cape Blanco to Saffet and the Lake Tiberias on the N.; these

two main lines being connected by intermediate triangles. [...] Whilst the operation was going on, Lieut. Symonds, being supplied with an 8-inch theodolite, was enabled to ascertain the difference of levels between the Dead Sea and the Mediterranean, and also between the Lake of Tiberias and the Mediterranean. [...] The solution of this problem, which has been a subject of discussion among geographers and travelers for the last ten years and more [...], forms an important era in the history of geographical knowledge.'[12]

Robinson, who had already suggested in 1840 that 'the question [of the level, HG] can never be decided with exactness, until the intervening country has been surveyed, and the relative level of the two seas trigonometrically ascertained', was happy to announce in the first volume of his new periodical, *Bibliotheca sacra*, that the realization of this goal was near at hand.[13] The altitude, according to the information he had received from his companion, Eli Smith, as transmitted to the latter personally by Symonds, was -1,312.2 ft (-426.5m).[14] This was accepted as Symonds's result and was repeated elsewhere, even by travelers who relied upon the aforementioned 'raised map of Palestine'.[15]

But the accuracy of the measurements was almost immediately questioned, by his fellow officers as well as by other scholars. Even Hamilton, in his 1843 Anniversary Address – given on the same occasion in which Symonds's father received his medal – hastened to question the measurements.[16] The confusion was compounded when the scholars began to suspect that Symonds had failed to determine the level of the Sea of Galilee. He had given a result of -328.1 ft (-106.6m), almost exactly half of the correct level. This error, once established, led the disappointed Robinson to completely discredit all of Symonds's measurements, albeit disguised in gentle words:

> I venture to suggest – not, certainly, in a spirit of doubt or want of confidence in the distinguished engineer, but solely in behalf of the interests of science – whether, after all, there may not be a possibility that some slight element of defect or inaccuracy may have entered into the observations or calculations, and thus have affected the correctness of the result?[17]

The work of Symonds and his fellow officers has been widely discussed and used. Alderson's *Notes on Acre*, a learned summary of the events in and around Acre from Napoleon onwards published in 1844 and including measurements performed, mostly in the city, said of the officers' work that it 'must be regarded as the hopeful first fruits of a golden harvest'.[18] George Williams devoted a special supplement in his book to their achievements, mainly the map of Jerusalem.[19]

Yet, skepticism regarding the accuracy of Symonds's measurements was expressed by Rochfort Scott when compiling the Map of Syria. So much so that van de Velde, also having Symonds's material in his possession, criticized Rochfort Scott for making such little use of it and modifying it so significantly, concluding that Scott's map 'is any thing but a faithful copy of the original'. The Dutch cartographer did not have access to all the other material that had been used for the construction.[20] The issue of the accuracy of Symonds's measurements was discussed in two reports from Robe, who had joined Rochfort Scott in compiling the map from the material collected from all his fellow officers in the 1840–2 delegation, for his employer, the Quartermaster General. Robe, still in Gibraltar, collected the material, checked and worked it into a rough sketch, and sent it to Britain for Rochfort Scott, who was responsible for adding his material, reducing the scale and producing the finished map.[21] Robe began with his own measurements in northern Palestine and southern Syria and Lebanon, where he measured two bases, one by Aleppo and the other near Beirut, although his damaged chronometer forced him to make use of material from the surveys of the Euphrates Expedition, furnished to him by Beaufort. The members of Chesney's expedition had had better barometers in their possession, such that their altitudes should be seen as exact. Notwithstanding the inaccuracies in his measurements, it is clear that Symonds had been using much better equipment than Robe and Rochfort Scott.

Robe did make use of Symonds's triangulation, but not before substantiating it with other measurements which he had received. Captain Thomas Graves RN (1802–56, murdered in Malta on the quay by a Maltese boatman), another Irishman serving in the Royal Navy and a well-known surveyor, had already been measuring in the Mediterranean from 1832. As commander of the steamer *Meteor,* he sailed from Malta to the Syrian coast equipped with numerous chronometers, to determine the meridian distances of several coastal points.[22] He supplied Robe with the longitudes and latitudes of 'Beyrout, Acre, Jaffa, Jerusalem, and other places'. Robe also received measurement data from two 'officers of great promise as surveyors', 'Lieutenant Ryder of HMS *Balvidiana* [sic] and his assistant Lieutenant Rayer', whose meridian distance from Jaffa to Beirut was consistent with Graves's. Alfred Phillipps Ryder, a graduate of the Royal Navy College in Portsmouth, served in the Mediterranean on the *Belvidera* (42 guns) in 1841–5.[23]

Comparing his data with Symonds's triangulation, Robe discovered some significant discrepancies, for example, in the distance between Jaffa and Acre, in which Symonds's diagram was approximately 'one in twenty' shorter. Robe did his best to reconcile the difference in the maps. 'From my knowledge of that officer's industry and talent,' Robe added, 'I should be very sorry to hazard' to determine that both his bases are in error.

The final, formal, long and detailed report along with the maps was sent by Rochfort Scott to the QMG:

> I have the honour to transmit herewith the maps and plans of Syria enumerated in the margin, constructed from the surveys and sketches made by some of the officers employed in that country in 1840–1, and the construction of which you were pleased to entrust to Major Robe and myself on our return to England.
>
> I respectfully venture to request that you would be so kind to transmit it to the inspection of His Grace the Commander in Chief and the [...] Honourable Secretary of State for Foreign Affairs, by whose direction the work was originally undertaken.[24]

This long, detailed handwritten report has not yet been used for the study of Palestine. The document thoroughly describes the 'Sea Coast and Forts' from Latakia in the north, to Beirut, Sidon, Tyre, Acre, Haifa, Jaffa, Gaza and el-Arish. It includes a description of the roads, some 'Inland Towns' and the rivers. Everything in it is presented from a military point of view, including 'Military lines of operations'.

Another fact concerning the officers' survey and its far-reaching implications is hinted at in a letter sent at the beginning of 1842 by Jackson, secretary of the RGS, to his French counterpart. Jackson pointed out that Chesney had been the one to give him the results of Symonds's triangulations concerning the depression of the Dead Sea, which Chesney received in a letter from Colonel Alderson.[25] This very important short letter alludes to the close ties between the two societies, but also to the fact that the Dead Sea had always been a factor in Chesney's arguments. Alderson, who probably knew the head of the Euphrates Expedition personally, hastened to send him the interesting data. Symonds's sketch had been signed by his superior only on 16 April of that year, a short time before the officer's departure from Palestine.[26]

From its foundation in 1830, the Royal Geographic Society was to serve also as the public arm of the various military and colonial governmental offices. The *JRGS* was the natural forum for the presentation of non-military data collected in projects executed by army personnel. All first secretaries of the society were military officers, trained in intelligence and strongly connected to the War Office. The reports were first read at the RGS meetings, and some were not even published, being considered to contain confidential material.[27]

The officials of the RGS, mainly its secretaries, turned out to be the most energetic advocates of research of the Jordan Depression and the Dead Sea, repeatedly raising the issue of its exact level and stressing the importance of the resolution to this question. Following Moore and Beek's letter, it would take almost ten years to solve the mystery of the exact level of both lakes, as well as that of the course of the Jordan between them. Already in early 1837 the journal told its readers about Moore, who 'we heard [...] has actually devoted the past year to a minute geographic examination of the Dead Sea and its shores'.[28] In the same year they would publish Moore and Beek's letter.

Not only was this matter initiated by members of the RGS; it was also expected of them to do something to solve the question. William Wilde, the Dublin physician, returned home from his travels in 1838, having become familiar with Costigan's story. Unaware of the subsequent explorers, he wrote in his account, first published in 1840, that 'now that the way has been opened, it is to be hoped' that the RGS 'will take up the matter, and send out some scientific person, with adequate means to complete what has been so advantageously begun'.[29]

The issue was mentioned in almost every Anniversary Address between 1838 and 1848, as described vividly by Barbara Kreiger in her *Living Waters*.[30] The RGS even tried, unsuccessfully, to initiate another barometrical measurement in order to find the exact level. Though the two able men charged with the task would not reach their destination, their barometer would, with the help of David Wilkie, as described later in this chapter.

There was no one more appropriate than John Washington to advocate the urgent need to do everything possible to resolve the riddle. He had already volunteered for the navy in 1812, serving mainly in North America before returning in 1816 to study at the Royal Navy College. Becoming an officer at 21, he sailed to almost all parts of the globe and his travels included journeys on foot and surveys. In 1836 he was appointed secretary of the Society (of which he was a co-founder), a position he held for five years, where 'with one clerk, he did the whole work of the society, the early success of which was largely due to his energy'. Sir John Barrow, then president of the RGS, selected Washington 'on account of his enthusiasm for Geography and his orderly and businesslike conduct of affairs'. Returning to active sailing in the 1840s following his resignation in 1841 from this position, Washington engaged mainly in coastal surveys. In 1845 Beaufort nominated him as 'Commissioner for inquiring into the state of the rivers, shores, and harbours of the United Kingdom'. First and foremost an intelligence officer, he was sent in 1853, just before the Crimean War, on an espionage mission to inspect some Russian harbors, and in 1855 he replaced Beaufort as chief hydrogapher. He held this position for only eight years, during which he prompted a significant change in British strategic thought, namely, the possibility of attacking Russia through its Baltic harbors. He guided hydrographic research to be in compliance with British strategic needs.[31] Like many of his military colleagues associated with exploration and mapmaking, Washington published frequently in the *JRGS*. He used the annual report of activities and achievements in explorative geography, presented by the president of the Society and published in its *Proceedings*, which also included a chapter devoted to 'Admiralty Surveys', to disseminate his ideas.[32]

Washington's central position within the geographical world is well documented. Humboldt, for example, referred to him as 'my friend' and 'my educated friend' and the two were in constant contact, even paying one another occasional visits. Every new piece of geographical data which reached Washington by virtue of his position was duly forwarded by him to Berlin.[33]

'But one object at this moment takes precedence of all others in interest: the difference of the level between the Dead Sea and the Mediterranean,' wrote Washington on June 1838 to Consul Niven Moore in Beirut, taking the opportunity also to ask the consul for further help.[34] Niven Moore's direct acquaintance with the region evidently led Washington to approach him for assistance in its systematic measurement. Not envisioning the feasibility of such a project in the near future, Washington reasoned that much data could be gathered from the 'accounts of various travelers in Syria and of their chief discoveries'. Accordingly, he sent Moore 'some hints for collecting geographical material', asking him to distribute these 'to any traveller who may be wandering in Syria'.[35] Washington continued to develop this idea of information-gathering via travelers and later, in the early 1860s, by this time Hydrographer of the Navy and following a short visit to the region, he produced a list of 'subjects that warrant attention and research in Palestine' and also made a 'list of geographical problems that require accurate solution'. He suggested that there should be someone to coordinate the research and direct the travelers. As always, he used the annual report to disseminate this idea. This text was also distributed as a circular, translated into German and published by Petermann, under the title 'Aufforderung an die Freunde der Geographie des Heil. Landes' ('Invitation to the Friends of the Geography of the Holy Land').[36]

One of the most striking incidents having to do with this method of publishing maps involved Washington and Heinrich Berghaus. Berghaus maintained strong contacts with the RGS. In a long and detailed letter dated July 1839, Secretary Washington politely rejected Berghaus's request for help in financing a new map of Syria, answering the former's inquiries point by point.[37] Washington first addressed one of Berghaus's important maps titled 'Part of Arabia Petraea and Palestine'. The original one, 'Karte von der Becken des Todten und des Rothen Meeres', had been published in Berghaus's periodical in 1842. This original map depicted the eastern part of the Negev desert and the route taken through it by the Americans, Robinson and Smith, in 1838. Berghaus's letter to the RGS, it seems, had been written mostly in order to praise Robinson and Smith's work and thus included only their route,[38] the map of it being attached to his letter to Washington.

The map subsequently published by the RGS under Berghaus's name, however, in addition to Robinson and Smith's route, showed the French de Bertou's route through this unknown desert region of southern Palestine. In London they had been preparing de Bertou's material for printing, and 'it became necessary to illustrate it by a

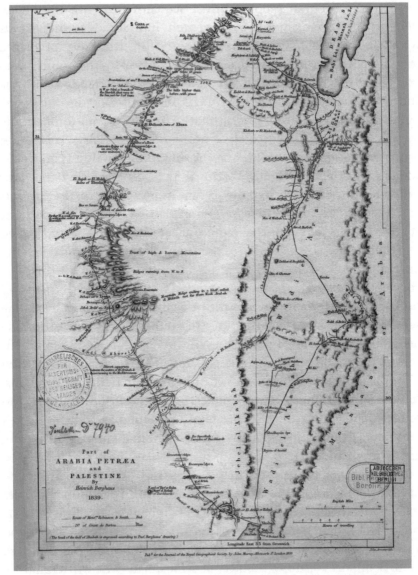

Fig. 44: Berghaus, Map, routes of Robinson/Smith and Bertou in the Negev

map.' As always trying to minimize expenses, 'we endeavour[ed] to make one map illustrate several routes'. So they simply added the route of the French count, most probably without even asking for Berghaus's permission. Consequently, the map also included the western half of the region.

240

It was in light of this publishing decision that Washington answered Berghaus's twelve questions. His responses dealt, among other things, with: Lindsay's travelogues ('extremely well written they do not contain much topographical knowledge'); Moore and Beek ('Mr. Moore is too young a man, & I fear, too gay to write anything for us'); positions on the Syrian Coast; Chesney's line from Iskanderun to Birejik; the book published in 1823 by the two naval captains, Irby and Mangles, who toured the East in 1816–18, partially accompanied by Banks and Legh, and issued an important sketch of the southern part of the Dead Sea;[39] Edward Rüppell's longitudes, mainly of Akaba, and the exact locations of Hebron and Gaza; the plan of Jerusalem made by the London artist and traveler Frederick Catherwood (1799–1854), who surveyed the Temple Mount in disguise;[40] and a final remark: asking Berghaus 'to write all Arabic names of places according to some fixed standard of orthography'.

'The exact level of the surface of the Dead Sea is a point of increasing interest not yet satisfactory cleared up,' declared William Richard Hamilton, president of the RGS during Washington's term as secretary, in his Anniversary Address for 1839, adding some comments concerning Moore's, Schubert's and Russeger's hypsometrical observations. 'Not unmindful of the interest attached to what appears to be one of the most remarkable features in the physical geography of the globe', he went on to place an excellent Newman barometer, which had been compared with the RGS standard, 'in the hands of two young Englishmen about to visit Palestine', asking them to perform the necessary observations.[41] Hamilton, like Washington, was a case of 'the right man in the right place'. After his return from his own travels and adventures in the East, he continued his impressive career from his seat in Europe. He served as one of the vice-presidents of the Society of Antiquaries from 1788 to 1813, and also replaced his father in 1811 as secretary of the African Association, where he remained until 1822. From 1809 he served as under-secretary of state for foreign affairs.[42] Between 1837 and 1849 he served three (not consecutive) two-year terms as president of the RGS, being, 'next to Barrow [...] probably the most valuable moulder of the forms and activities of the Society'. And, most important for this study, he was the leading figure behind the short-lived Syrian Society, later named the Palestine Association, established in London in 1804.[43]

The following year, in 1840, the new president, George Bellas Greenough (1778–1855), a geologist, co-founder and first president of the Geological Society of London ('he was proud of being a member of thirty-seven learned societies'), stated that 'the truth of the reported depression of the level of the Dead Sea below the Mediterranean' could not yet be satisfactory established, and that they still hoped for the accounts of that 'careful observer'.[44]

In 1841 the Society received the report of Edward Napier, who also offered to conduct the urgently needed survey of the Depression, needless to say asking for financial and organizational assistance in the matter.[45] Consequently Hamilton – again president – returned to the issue in his address for 1842, this time as a summary of the 'state of the art'. Among other things, he concurred with Robinson about the need for a trigonometric leveling and reported on Symonds's work and results. There is no mention of observers having been sent by the Society.[46] Having Symonds's triangulations in their possession, the RGS officials continued to be the most energetic advocates of this research, repeatedly raising the question and calling for its solution. The issue was mentioned in almost every Anniversary Address between 1839 and 1848.[47]

In a letter to the French geographical society, dated 25 January 1842, Secretary Jackson enumerated the results to date concerning the altitude of the Depression, mentioning Moore and Beek, de Bertou, Symonds and Russegger. But to these, he added interesting and important news which had reached him from the artist David Wilkie, writing from Jerusalem:[48]

> At Constantinople, on the 28th October last year you did me the honour to entrust to me your Barometer, with a request which I have never lost sight of hourly, that in the route of my reaching Syria I would make an observation of its altitude when placed on the level of the Dead Sea.[49]

Those who spend their time digging in the archives know that this can bring some unexpected surprises; finding the famous Scottish artist David Wilkie performing barometrical observations on the shore of the Dead Sea and on his way to Jerusalem is surely one of these. Wilkie, 55 years of age and already a well-established artist, well known for his paintings as well as for his travels, set out in 1840 on a voyage to the eastern Mediterranean countries.[50] Reaching the Ottoman capital at the end of that year, he and his fellow traveler, the London fine-art dealer William Samuel Woodburn (1786–1853), were detained there until the end of the war with the Egyptians. They left Constantinople on 13 January 1841 and, after a delay at Smyrna, landed at Beirut on 8 February. One month later, Wilkie wrote his surprising letter from Jerusalem.

Staying in the Holy City as a guest of British Consul Young, the painter was quite impressed – not always favorably – by the Franciscan Father Bonaventura, an Irish compatriot called 'M'Lauchlan' (MacLaughlin), penitentiary apostolic from 1840, also mentioned as being in Jerusalem as late as 1860.[51] Wilkie and his friend traveled to the Dead Sea accompanied by the American missionary Elias Root Beadle (1812–79), fluent in Arabic, who stayed in Beirut from spring 1839 and after two years moved to Aleppo.[52] Four of Wilkie's paintings from the voyage have a direct bearing for this book. In Beirut he painted Mrs. Moore, wife of the British consul, in an Arab dress, as well as the consul's dragoman. He also painted the sheik who escorted him and his party to the Dead Sea and the Jordan, and Mehemet Ali – his last painting before dying during the sail back home.[53]

Wilkie's letter was sent to a certain John Harvey, who, already aware of Wilkie's death, forwarded a copy to the secretary of the RGS, then probably still Washington. He added another interesting comment, saying that:

> ...when prevented by illness at Constantinople from going myself to Syria, I entrusted my Barometer [to Wilkie, HG]. I wrote at the time to the Society that I have been compelled to give up the undertaking in consequence of ill health. I regret this important communication should have been so long delayed from reaching the Society but am only just returned from abroad.[54]

Harvey had thus probably been one of the 'two young Englishmen' mentioned above, supplied by the RGS secretary with a most modern barometer, in order to resolve the question.[55] As for Wilkie, the artist found himself fulfilling a scientific mission for the Royal Geographical Society. Wilkie received Harvey's barometer on 28 November, but due to the war had to stay in Constantinople. He used the time for meetings

(Sir Moses Montefiore on his second voyage) and paintings, including a portrait of Sultan Abdülmecid (fig. 4).[56]

Back in Britain, Harvey contacted the Society. The letter, dated 8 March 1841, was read at the Society's meeting on 3 September. Wilkie had made nine observations, twice a day on successive days in Beirut, finding 'mean Barometer 30.133 Thermometer 58.722'; one in Jaffa (Barometer 29.490 Thermometer 56); and then, from 1 March to 6 March, one each in Jerusalem, the Dead Sea, Jericho and then again in Jerusalem:

March 1st			
Morg	27.490		56
Eveng	27.460		56
2nd Morn	27.432	Fine weather	56
Eveng			
3rd Morn	27.386	Grey morning	55.5
Even	27.400		56
4th	27.438	Fine morning	55.5
	29.358		

Examining in convent St. Saba on the way to the Dead Sea, threatening rain, Therm. 86.

March 5th On reaching the Dead Sea, about 11 o'clock, sky overcast and threatening rain – Barometer inserted in the shingle close to the salt water in the open air

	Barometer 31.372		Thermometer 68

Evening in a Tent pitched at the entrance to the mountains a little above Jericho – during rain and wind

	Barometer 30.575		Thermometer 76

6th after two hours ascend in the mountains. Fogges – open air

	29.106		67 ½

At another stage of the ascent – open air – sun shining

	28.406		70

On again reaching Jerusalem

	27.278		56 ½

'Being greatly impressed with the party around me with the elevation of the Barometer on the shore of the Dead Sea,' he added, 'I made a hasty drawing of its exact appearance to which the following attestation in my note book was subjoined.' All three signed the letter,

> On the banks of the Dead Sea this 5th day of March 1841 weather cloudy and threatening rain. We the undersigned attest the above representation of the state of the Barometer ... as its elevation to be correct.
> The Thermometer being at 68 Fahrenheit
> (signed) William Samuel Woodburn
> E. R. Beadle
> David Wilkie R.A.[57]

But the decision-makers in London were not so confident of these results. On the back page of the letter, somebody – probably Secretary Jackson – added, that '[t]hese observations were made at such distant intervals, that, any thing like precision being out of the question, a close computation is useless. I w[oul]d therefore recommend it to be withheld, and the general Results only given along with the two letters.' The only mention in the report of 1842, was that 'calculations from the data furnished by the late Sir David Wilkie make it 1,200 feet'[58] – which of course is quite accurate!

David Wilkie died at sea on his way home, and his body was consigned to the depths in the Bay of Gibraltar. He was never married, but there is good evidence that during the 1820s or even earlier, he tried to conquer the heart of Miss Emerilda Fraser (?–1840), whose father served in the garrison in Guernsey. This fact might not be of any interest for this book, but, as mentioned before, Wilkie's rival was a young, short but determined, Irish artillery officer, Francis Rawdon Chesney. Emerilda Fraser turned Chesney down three times, and this was one of his reasons for undertaking the 1829 journey to Turkey. Finally, in April 1839, the 46-year-old woman, very ill, married Chesney; she died after eighteen months.[59]

Louis von Wildenbruch, Prussian General-Consul in Syria and Palestine between 1843 and 1848, who resided in Beirut, supplemented his diplomatic duties with intensive scientific activity.[60] Personally acquainted with the leading geographers in Berlin, the officer consistently sent his scientific reports and results to the *Gesellschaft für Erdkunde*, where they were read (at its meetings) and published (in its periodical). One of his important contributions, published in 1845, was 'Profilzeichnungen nach barometrischen Nivellements in Syrien', a detailed sketch which included three profiles. The first showed the levels from Jaffa through Jerusalem to the Dead Sea, which he noted as 1,351.6 Parisian ft (439.27m) below the Mediterranean.[61] Wildenbruch's letter, sent to Ritter and dated 16 August 1845, included a list of measurements made by him, to which he added comments concerning Schubert's hypsometry. His measurements also included some very interesting spots along the Jordan Rift, from Tel el Kadi (526.8m in the list, 503.9m in the profile) and Jacob's Bridge (84.4m), through Tiberias and all the way to Jericho and the Dead Sea.[62]

In 1849 Wildenbruch was already back in Berlin, and he addressed a letter to his countryman, the young cartographer August Petermann, who was then residing in London. In this letter, which was read at the RGS and published in its journal in 1851, Wildenbruch commented at length about different points which he had studied in Syria and Palestine, 'although I have left all my books and papers in Syria'.[63] It is not surprising that the letter had been addressed to Petermann, who, two years earlier, had published his own paper concerning the slope of the Jordan, and who was gaining a reputation worldwide as an advocate of explorative geography.[64] It is also highly possible that Widenbruch and Petermann were personally acquainted.

'I confess that the appearance [of the Dead Sea from the Mount of Olives, HG] scarcely justifies our assuming so great a depression as it really proves to be,' wrote Wildenbruch at the beginning of his letter. On the other hand, the Sea of Galilee, from the top of Mount Tabor, did seem to him to be very deep; and indeed it was much deeper than Symonds's calculated 328 ft. He described how he tried to establish the levels of the whole Jordan Valley and the Arabah. Adding a detailed description of the vicinity of Jacob's Bridge, he presented one of the earliest and more accurate descriptions of the Huleh Valley and Lake, the surrounding villages, various points of interest and bearings from different spots, for example from 'Castle Banias, in Jebel Sheikh', which refers to Nimrod's Castle.[65] The only thing comparable to this pioneering work is Robe's map of the sources of the Jordan, which preceded Wildenbruch's by three or four years.[66] Since Robinson failed to visit this area in his 1838 travels due to the security conditions, these two relatively unknown surveys form the earliest scientific study of the sources of the Jordan and of the Huleh Valley, and are of tremendous importance to the study of the entire Jordan Rift Valley.

Wildenbruch continued his letter, describing the eastern sectors of the Golan region, the Lebanon and Anti-Lebanon mountains, and the Litani River and its bridges. He added much hypsometric data calculated according to his observations along the Jordan as well as in Lebanon, advocating their accuracy because they were taken in 1846 'by means of two hypsometers, which were constructed at Vienna by Ekling, under the direction of Professor Baumgärtner, [...] One of these instruments was observed five times in the day by Mr. Blanche....' The references are to Andreas Freiherr von Baumgärtner (1793–1865), a celebrated scientist, and Isidore Blanche, a French diplomat and amateur botanist associated with Gaillardot, who contributed to the early herbariums from Syria and Palestine.[67]

One more of Wildenbruch's achievements should be mentioned at this point, namely, his active role in the publication of Gaillardot's rare and important 'Map of the Ledja'.[68] The sketch and a cover letter, dated Beirut, 16 August 1845, reached Ritter through the mediation of Wildenbruch, then still in Beirut. Being well acquainted with Ritter, and probably his student at the military academy in Berlin, Wildenbruch would send his tutor much of the material he accumulated, for publication in Ritter's geographic journals.[69] In his letter to Ritter, Wildenbruch described Gaillardot as 'a scientifically efficient learned man. [...] Unfortunately so far he published nothing of what he possesses.' The map, drawn in 1838, was still in Gaillardot's possession, and Wildenbruch, whom he could only have met after 1843, showed much interest in it. After receiving the manuscript, it was naturally sent to Ritter in Berlin. I fully agree with Wildenbruch's claim that the map was certainly the best of this area executed until then.[70]

9 Conclusive explorations: Molyneux and Lynch

The question of the course and slope of the Jordan seemed to be a relatively uncomplicated one. Possessing the actual altitudes of the Sea of Galilee and the Dead Sea, as well as the exact distance between them, it should have been very easy to calculate the average slope of the river. Assuming a relatively direct course of the Jordan between both lakes (Carne: 'the Jordan's course [...] being perfectly straight'),[1] Charles Tilstone Beke wrote, as early as 1838, that 'there is nothing in the about 60 to 70 English miles of route of this river between both [lakes, HG], that could cause a remarkable difference in their relative levels'.[2] No real attention was paid to his letter at the time, but things changed when, four years later, the scientific world learned about Symonds's triangulation results. In his Anniversary Address for 1843 given on the same occasion as the ceremony in which Symonds's father received his medal, Hamilton already questioned the possibility of 'a difference of nearly 1000 feet between the lake of Tiberias and the Dead Sea, a distance in direct line of little more than one degree of latitude, which implies (the Jordan not being a meandering stream) a fall of more than 16 feet in every mile of its course.'[3]

Five years passed until the issue was brought up again, this time by Edward Robinson. Relying mainly on data he had gathered from the *JRGS*, he actually reproduced Hamilton's calculations. Accepted worldwide as one of the leading scholars in the study of Palestine, his words sounded very convincing:

> Yet in the 984 feet of its descent in 60 geographical miles, there is room for THREE CATARACTS, each equal in height to NIAGARA, and still to leave to the river an average fall equal to the swiftest portion of the Rhine, including the cataract of Schaffhausen![4]

Received on 27 October 1847, the paper was read at the RGS meeting of 22 November, refereed on 10 January and sent for printing after only a week – remarkable speed, even for a paper with almost no corrections.[5]

One response came at the following meeting, on 28 February 1848, from the young German cartographer August Heinrich Petermann, a respected fellow of the Society who worked in London from 1847 to 1854. Petermann gave a paper critiquing Robinson, the experienced scholar and leading authority, arguing that there was nothing unique in the slope of the Jordan, which was equal to that of some famous English rivers. He added that Robinson's calculations were all the more problematic since they accepted Symonds's incorrect leveling of the Sea of Galilee, consequently calculating a difference of about 300 rather than 200 meters. A more accurate calculation of a drop of 8 feet per mile would not be at all unusual. Another point he made demonstrates 'how deceptively the length of the course of a river is diminished in maps on a small scale'.[6] Hamilton, the president, responded in an address delivered in May 1848, in which he pointed out two mistakes in Robinson's data. First, according to Russegger and Wildenbruch, the Sea of Galilee was actually much lower, and second, according to Russegger, the distance between the two lakes was greater, so the calculated slope should indeed be only 8, instead of 16 feet per mile.[7]

But within a short time all would be able to breathe a sigh of relief that the question of the slope of the Jordan had been satisfactorily resolved. The answers were included in a paper that was read at the meeting of 27 March, just one month after Petermann's, and published in the *JRGS* directly following both Robinson's and Petermann's papers. It was Hydrographer of the Navy Francis Beaufort, who 'communicated to us an interesting paper, drawn up by the late Lieutenant Molyneux, of H.M.S Spartan', in which the meandering character of the Jordan between the two lakes was scientifically established for the first time.[8] It had taken twelve years after the first research-boat had sailed in the Dead Sea to establish the meandering route of the Jordan and thus to determine that the actual flowing distance was more than double the direct one. Eagerly following all the developments from Berlin, Ritter could write, quite happily, that 'the route of the stream and the nature of its valley [...] are not a secret any more!'[9]

Thomas Howard Molyneux (1822–47), an English naval officer, sailed in August 1847 from the Sea of Galilee along the Jordan to the

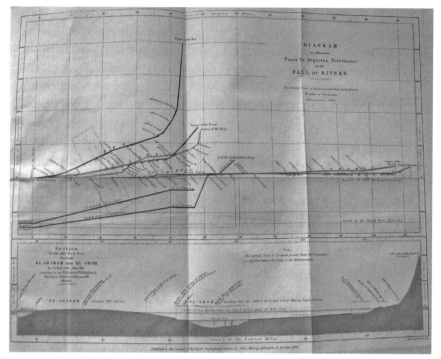

Fig. 45: Petermann, Slope of the Jordan and some rivers in the UK

Dead Sea, dying soon afterwards due to after-effects of the obstacles and difficulties he had faced during his voyage, which included security and weather conditions, salt water and other complications.[10] The 24-year-old English lieutenant entered the navy at age 15, saw nine years of active service on a number of ships, passed his examination in 1843, served on a gunship in Portsmouth, then studied for one year in a college and was promoted to lieutenant on 27 July 1846. Attached to the Mediterranean Squadron for a year, he sailed under the command of Captain (later Admiral Sir) Thomas Matthew Charles Symonds (1813–94). Symonds, the older half-brother to John Symonds, commanded the *Spartan*, a frigate of 22 cannons serving in the Mediterranean, from 1846 to 1849. Both officers were sons of Admiral Sir William Symonds, Surveyor of the Navy from 1832 to 1847, Thomas being one of the highly skilled naval officers chosen by his father to command 'his' battleships.[11]

In his report, which he managed to compose on the *Spartan* before his death, Molyneux wrote that 'our objects were to examine the course of the Jordan, as well as of the valley through which it runs, and especially to measure the depth of the Dead Sea.'[12] This evidence of detailed research goals explains the expedition's choice of the 'northern route', which began at the Sea of Galilee. Another point discussed by scholars in their descriptions of the expedition were the exact roles played by Symonds and Molyneux. Molyneux's report buttresses Boggis's claim, almost a century later, that Symonds had been the initiator of the research, that it was he who, perhaps as a continuation of his brother's triangulation, planned a thorough study of the river and both lakes and did 'everything in his power to promote and further them'. Molyneux, for his part, showed great interest and enthusiasm and volunteered to perform the work.[13]

The report contains a mixture of scientific observations and detailed descriptions of difficulties, obstacles and problems faced by the expedition. It is based on his journal, written intermittently during the voyage. Aware of its importance, Captain Symonds hurried on 13 September 1847 to send a letter to his personal acquaintance, Beaufort, telling him to await 'the Dead Sea soundings' soon.[14] Twenty days later, on 3 December, he forwarded the journal of 'the noble fellow [who] fell a victim to Typhus fever'. As it was a military document, Beaufort's authorization was necessary to make it available to the public.[15] Beaufort forwarded Molyneaux's texts and sketches to the RGS, where they were read and subsequently published. Interestingly enough, the text was published in full, but the editors did not publish the accompanying sketch-map.[16]

This sketch-map is a very detailed and extremely important document. Dated 7 December 1847, more than a month after Molyneux's death, its title declares that it is a 'true copy' of the latter's sketch made by Captain Thomas Symonds. It gives the 'soundings obtained in Lake of Tiberias August 23rd & Northern extremity of Lake by observation', estimated distances between different points, and soundings in the Dead Sea. It includes many comments and additions, such as 'latitude of northern extremity', 'thermometer in shade', directions, buildings, bridges, etc. along the Jordan and in the main settlements in the surrounding country.

In addition to various espionage missions, in which he served as a reliable expert in the evaluation of foreign navies (for example, in 1841, when he was sent to the Black Sea to report on the Ottoman and Russian fleets), William Symonds's greatest achievement was the introduction of some very important changes in the British fleet, 'giving his ships

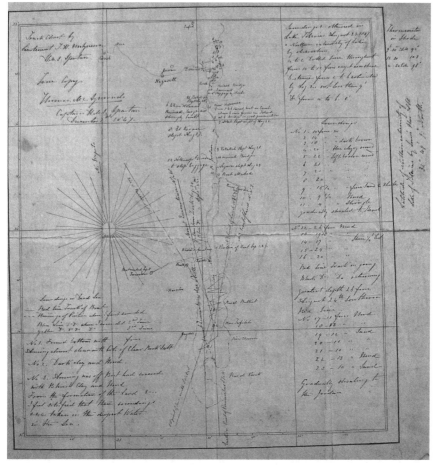

Fig. 46: Molyneux, sketch-map, 1837

greater beam and a more wedge-shaped bottom, thus obtaining greater speed and stability, and, by requiring less ballast, increasing the stowage and permitting heavier armaments'.[17] By his first wife (out of three), he had one daughter and four sons. The eldest, William Cornwallis (1810–41), an army officer and expert in surveying, is known as the founder of Auckland, New Zealand, and the surveyor-general of the island. He was drowned in a gale while trying to bring medical supplies to a sick missionary's wife.[18]

Thomas Matthew Charles Symonds enlisted in the navy on 25 April 1825, was promoted to lieutenant on 5 November 1832 and served in the Mediterranean and in the East Indies. On 21 October 1837 he was made commander and returned home. From 27 August 1838 he commanded the sloop *Rover* (18 guns) in the North America and West Indies station until he was promoted to captain on 22 February 1841. In May 1846 Symonds was appointed to the *Spartan* on the Mediterranean, and commanded the ship until 1849. He continued to serve in the Mediterranean, participated in the Crimean War and, early in 1855, returned home, where he was amply rewarded. He continued to be promoted and was eventually knighted, serving at home in various positions of command. According to Andrew Lambert in the *ODNE*, 'Symonds's career was made by his father's post at the Admiralty, both his promotion to commander and, critically, that to captain being rewards for Sir William's services from his political friends. Like his father, he was a difficult man to work with – opinionated, argumentative, and obstinate.'[19]

During 1847, the *Spartan* repeatedly crossed the eastern Mediterranean from her base in Malta to various harbors in the east. Most of the time the crew reported on the port cities (Beirut: 'The Port is in a shameful condition not a wharf or landing place of any description'; Jaffa: 'The town is a miserable assemblage of dirty houses, the Gardens in the neighborhood are very fine').[20]

Captain Symonds was, of course, aware of the story of the leveling of the Dead Sea. He was probably only too happy to find someone as enthusiastic as himself to carry out his plan to launch a boat in the Sea of Galilee and sail down the Jordan to the Dead Sea, in order 'to obtain an account of anything interesting in the course of the Jordan, and the valley through which it runs, and more especially to discover, if there was any, and at what depth, soundings may be obtained in the Dead Sea'. The editors of the *JRGS* made some changes, mainly in writing that the main objective was 'to measure the depth of the Dead Sea'.[21] The captain and another officer rode horses, supplied by the British vice-consul, from Acre to Nazareth and Tiberias, where they themselves sailed on the lake and assisted Molyneux and his party in their preparations, before parting ways with the small group, comprised of an officer, 'three good volunteer seaman' and a Beirut dragoman.[22]

It had not been an easy task to convey the boat and all other provisions, loaded on 'four good camels', from Acre to Tiberias, the most difficult part being the descent from the mountains to the valley by the Sea of Galilee.[23] Finding that 'a coil of deep sea lead line and a Hand Lead and Line had by some mistake been left behind', they sent someone to bring it from the ship, and in the meantime could launch their boat and sail to the northern extremity of the lake. Already there, Molyneux reiterated that 'we felt extremely hot' and 'it was now so boiling hot that we landed and got under the shade of a willow tree'.[24]

The boat was launched in the Sea of Galilee on 23 August 1847 and, according to the map, sailed to a point which had been estimated by Molyneux as the center of the lake, then to the eastern shore and back to Tiberias. 'It appears to me that the lake as marked on the maps is too small,' he concluded.[25] After a zigzag sailing and some depth measurements on the second day, the small expedition entered the Jordan on Wednesday, 25 August, and began making its way south in two parallel groups. The three able sailors joined by the dragoman sailed the boat, while Molyneux and other accompanying persons went by land, fixing meeting points when necessary. The report is important for the study of the region, as Molyneux kept good records and provided thorough and accurate descriptions. From the moment they entered the Jordan, these are also full of long descriptions of incidents with Arabs and Bedouins. It might be useful here to quote Molyneux:

> I had bother enough to-day to drive any reasonable person mad: Almost every minute of it I was expecting that we should come to blows; but happily I had seven barrels about my person, which I took good care to let them know; for it is still the fact that throughout the country of Ishmael 'every man's hand is against every man'.[26]

His most important observation was already made after two days of sailing. 'It would be quite impossible to give any account of the various turnings of the Jordan [...]; it was well and quaintly described in a newspaper I saw the other day as "the crookedest river wot is".'[27] It is quite remarkable that both scientists, Robinson and Petermann, probably did not see this piece of evidence before writing their papers.

In 1873, while the Survey of Western Palestine was in progress, Major Wilson of the PEF read a paper describing 'recent surveys in Sinai and Palestine' at a meeting of the RGS. He also dealt with the problem of the slope, giving the numbers which were accepted by the surveyors, showing how simple the answer to Robinson's question was, given the exact distances and altitude differences:

From Tell el Kady to El Huleh there is a fall of 328 feet in 11.9 miles [a slope of about 5.5‰, HG], from El Huleh to the Sea of Galilee a fall of 898.75 feet in 11.1 miles, and from the Sea of Galilee to the Dead Sea a fall of 665.75 feet in 65.9 miles [~2‰]. From the Dead Sea to the water-parting there is a rise of 2073 feet in 67.9 miles, and from the water-parting to the Gulf of 'Akaba there is a fall of 781 feet in 40.7 miles.[28]

Regarding the expedition, after some difficult and, primarily, exhausting adventures, Molyneux reached the conclusion that it would be impossible to carry out his plan to reach the Dead Sea in four or five days, as 'it was almost like moving an army in an enemy's country'.[29] In the area of the Damia Bridge and Wadi Zerka, the boat failed to arrive at the meeting point with the land expedition, as it had been attacked and robbed and the sailors had disappeared. After some fruitless searches, Molyneux rode to Jerusalem and returned with Consul Finn and some Ottoman soldiers to search, in vain, for the missing men. Only then, fatigued and sleepless, did he reach the Dead Sea.

All these details, so painfully described in his report, were confirmed by Finn at the 11 January 1850 meeting of his literary society.[30] Accompanied by 'a Maltese servant' who came with Finn from Jerusalem, Molyneux sailed on the lake for two and a half days but, not being able to endure 'this misty furnace' and the 'well-heated oven', he decided to stop the sailing. The map reveals a zig-zag sail from the northern shore up until a point about halfway between Ein Gedi and the northern end of the Lisân. He did perform many soundings, which are listed on the right side of the map. 'As soon as we reached the shore we took all things out of the boat', and began moving northward. There he received a letter from Finn, telling him that the lost sailors had reached Tiberias safely. Going through Jericho, the small expedition climbed to Jerusalem, and on 12 September returned to the *Spartan* in Jaffa. Having fallen ill, and although he was much better treated than Costigan had been, Molyneux died in Beirut on 3 October 1847.[31]

Finn's report, an interesting document which has already been used by Masterman, Eriksen and myself, includes some important observations – concerning Ottoman soldiers, the natural landscape of the river banks and more. He also writes that at one point in their search for the soldiers, they met with two colleagues, the Prussian consul in

Jerusalem, Ernst Gustav Schultz, and his cousin Theodor Weber (1816–93), later Prussian consul in Beirut, who 'had come from Jerusalem to investigate a particular spot in the neighbourhood'. The Germans declined the request to join the search for the missing soldiers, claiming that their horses were too tired and not capable of participating.[32]

Molyneux was buried in Beirut, but his boat would eventually find its way back to the Dead Sea, again through Vilnai's initiative. Sir Thomas Symonds, already a retired admiral, 'evidently [...] regarded it as his own property' and transferred the boat to his estate – 'Sunny Hill on the Warberries' by Torquay – his home until his death in 1894. 'This boat was built 1836, visited Acre, Cana of Galilee, Lake of Tiberias, Jordan, Dead Sea, Jerusalem Joppa – 1847'; this inscription on a long strip of metal, probably added by Symonds, was attached to the boat. On the estate the boat served as the roof of a brick summerhouse, where Boggis saw it in the 1930s. He added that the oak sternboard was preserved in the hall of that summerhouse, bearing the inscription 'Jerusalem'. This would not be brought over with the boat.

Vilnai later testified that he learned about the existence of the boat from Boggis's book, published in 1939 after the latter sailed the Jordan in a canoe in 1932. Vilnai used his connections to search for it and, in 1962, visited the estate and succeeded in getting permission to bring the boat to the Dead Sea Works Museum.[33] A contemporary Israeli newspaper report linked the story to Agatha Christie, but the facts are probably as Vilnai described, in a personal newspaper report as well as in his book.[34] The museum has since closed and the boat, quite neglected,

Fig. 47: Molyneux, Boat

has stood for many years in the yard of the Dead Sea Works awaiting restoration and proper display.[35]

It is rather symbolic that on the same day the members of the RGS in London were carefully listening to the Molyneux report, the next expedition left Beirut on its way to Acre, the Sea of Galilee, the Jordan and the Dead Sea. Lynch's American expedition was on its way to answer most of the questions that had been left unsolved by former explorers. Lynch was also going to honor his predecessor's memory, naming the southern extremity of the Lisân 'Point Molyneux', facing Point Costigan.

Molyneux was not a scientist, and he had only two limited objectives. Along with his predecessors, he paved the way for the most ambitious American expedition, led in 1848 by the American naval officer William Francis Lynch. This was one of a number of scientific explorations sent by the US government beginning in 1838.[36] Lynch and his expedition have been studied extensively, and recently were the subjects of a long and well-researched book written by a veteran US naval pilot.[37] Lynch had joined the US Navy at the age of 18 as midshipman; in May 1828 he was promoted to lieutenant, and it was in this capacity – twenty years later – that he proposed the idea of the exploration. A devout Christian as well as a fearless adventurer who acknowledged the importance of the scientific study of unknown regions, Lynch's interest in the expedition apparently derived from both qualities. His study was very scientific, exact and detailed, but his narrative is also filled with descriptions of the emotions and religious associations aroused by the river and the lake.[38]

The expedition stayed in the Dead Sea area during the spring of 1848, eleven years after Moore and Beek's and Schubert's groups, and ten years after de Bertou and Russegger. They produced the first accurate maps of the Jordan between both northern lakes (Huleh and Sea of Galilee) and the Dead Sea, and of the Dead Sea itself. The difference of levels, as given in Lynch's official report, based on barometrical measurements, was 1,234.589 ft (401.24m), as documented in his report of 20 April.[39] On 29 May, reaching the Mediterranean again, he wrote his final conclusions:

> The results give 1316.7 feet as the depression of the level of the Dead Sea below the Mediterranean. Jerusalem is 2610.5 feet above the latter, and 3927.24 feet above the former sea. Its elevation above

the last being almost exactly the multiple of its height above the Mediterranean, and the difference of level of the two seas.[40]

Lynch was promoted to the rank of commander in 1849 and captain in 1856. Later he participated in the Civil War as naval commander in the Confederate Army.

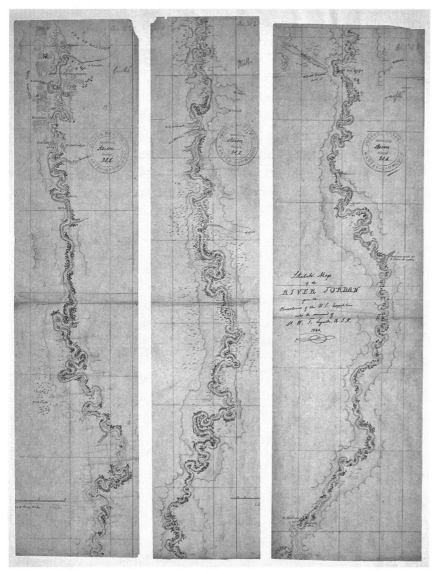

Fig. 48: Lynch, Sketch of the Jordan

Trying to make use of Lynch's map, of which he had great expectations, van de Velde was deeply disappointed. 'From an expedition so well organized,' he wrote, 'something more accurate and less sketchy might have been expected; and such serious errors, as those which occur in this map, are doubly to be regretted, when a work bears the official stamp.' Had Lieutenant John B. Dale, Lynch's second-in-command and his best surveyor, lived to draw up the map, most of the mistakes in Lynch's map could have been avoided. But Dale, the third victim of Dead Sea exploration, died in Beirut on 24 July 1848.[41] Notwithstanding, fifteen years later, Wilson pointed out that the error had been van de Velde's and that Lynch's map was 'quite accurate' in one of the important points in discussion, the embouchure of Wadi Zerka.[42]

Lynch's expedition marked the end of the first stage in the scientific study of the Dead Sea and its environs – the general exploration and the collection of facts and data. This was the stage during which scholars looked for answers to the traditional questions and curiosities surrounding the Jordan Depression and the lake. There is probably no

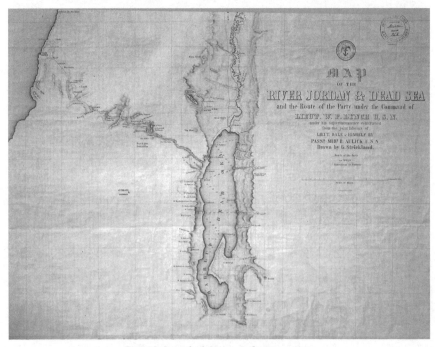

Fig. 49: Lynch, Map, southern section

one more deserving to sum up the description of these ten turbulent years in Dead-Sea research, nor more authoritative, than Carl Ritter, who, although he never visited the Holy Land, took a leading part in its study.[43] In the middle of the century, in 1850, he presented his lecture entitled 'The Jordan and the Sailing on the Dead Sea', which was published that same year. Applying his geographical method, Ritter gave a full summary of the history of the explorations and research conducted, of all the facts and data that had been accumulated and the conclusions reached to date:

> Certainly these were so far only boats brought there from England and North America [...]. These seafaring nations tried what was unheard of before, to send some supplied missions to the Jordan and the Dead Sea, with the help of their governments, in order to bring to an end the up till now disgraceful lack of knowledge of many neighbouring European cultural people about the formation of that valley. They had no idea how difficult such a mission was. The energy applied to fulfilling this task was demonstrated by the three repetitive starts [most probably referring to Costigan, Molyneux and Lynch, HG], that were needed to overcome the forces against them![44]

Concluding Remarks

Who were the creators of 'the drama of the scientific community's awareness of the depression of the Dead Sea'? Ritter's clear opinion has already been presented: 'The reader's attention ought to be called particularly to the fact that it is to this [Moore and Beek's, HG] expedition that we owe the direct discovery of the depression of the Dead Sea.'[1]

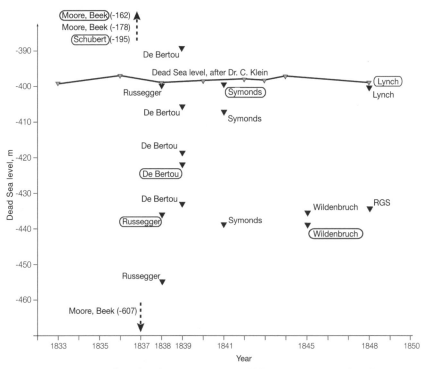

Fig. 50: Dead Sea level measurements 1837–1848, compared with Klein's calculated level

In order to fully answer this question, I have tried to summon up the various measurements and their respective publications. As previously described, these reports differ, sometimes significantly, from one another, even if they refer to the same hypsometry. All altitudes are, naturally, under sea level, given in English feet (= 304.8mm) or Parisian feet (= 325mm). The years mentioned relate to the publication, and not necessarily (usually not, in fact) to the date the measurement was performed.

The actual Dead Sea levels in the period discussed, according to Klein, were (in meters, below sea level):[2]

13 October 1836 – 397.5
12 May 1838 – 399.5
21 April 1840 – 399
7 July 1842 – 398.5
March 1843 – 398.5 / 399
Summer 1844 – 397.5
April 1848 – 399.5

Though later studies have criticized parts of Klein's reconstruction, they too admit that 'the high-resolution historic record presented by Klein [...] is undoubtedly the most detailed record proposed' and that 'the curve should be used cautiously and the data reevaluated before such use.'[3]

In addition to the illustration, the following list of measurements of the levels and published results testifies to the fact that there are considerable discrepancies between the different results of any given measurement, published in different places and at different times. The measurements dealt with here were conducted by Moore and Beek in March–April 1837; Schubert in April 1837; de Bertou in March 1838 and May 1839; Russegger in November–December 1838; Symonds in May–June 1841; Wildenbruch in 1845; and Lynch in April–May 1848. All measurements are below sea level.

Dead Sea (see also fig. 50):

1838:   500 ft – Moore and Beek according to Moore[4]
      598 ft – Schubert according to Moore[5]
      406m – de Bertou according to Callier[6]
      607m – Moore and Beek according to Callier[7]
      422.27m (1145.34–723.07) – de Bertou[8]

1841: 1,341 ft – Russegger[9]
1842: Between 500 and 600 ft – Moore and Beek according to Hamilton
       598.5 ft – Schubert according to Hamilton
       1,400 ft – Russegger according to Hamilton
       1,332.46 ft – de Bertou according to Hamilton[10]
       598.5 Par. ft – Steinheil's calculation from Erdl's data[11]
       1,200 ft – de Bertou according to David Wilkie[12]
       1,311.9 ft – Symonds, as well as Hamilton[13]
1843: 1,337 and 1,312.2 ft – Symonds according to Robinson[14]
       1,312.2 ft – Symonds, RGS[15]
1845: 1,341 Par. ft – Russegger
1846: 1,351.6 Par. ft - Wildenbruch[16]
1848: 1,340 ft – *JRGS*[17]
       419m = 1,374.7 ft – de Bertou according to Petermann
       1341 Par. ft = 1,429.2 Eng. ft – Russegger according to Petermann
       1,351.6 Par. ft = 1,446.3 Eng ft – Wildenbruch according to
       Petermann
       1,312.2 ft – Symonds according to Peterman[18]
1849: 1,312 ft - Humboldt[19]
1850: 1,351 Par. ft – Symonds according to Ritter
       1,341 Par. ft – Wildenbruch according to Ritter
       1,231 Par. ft – Russegger according to Ritter
       1,290 Par. ft – de Bertou according to Ritter[20]
       1,235 Par. ft – Lynch according to Ritter[21]
1852: 1,235.589 ft = 401.24m – Lynch[22]

Sea of Galilee:[23]

1841: 625 ft – Russegger[24]
1842: 328.1 ft – Symonds according to Hamilton[25]
       535.5 Par. ft – Erdl[26]
1843: 84 and 328.1 ft – Symonds according to Robinson[27]
1846: 774.1 and 812.6 Par. ft – Wildenbruch in two different
       measurements
       625 Par. ft – Russegger according to Ritter
       535 Par. ft- Schubert according to Ritter[28]
1848: 625 Par. ft – Russegger according to Hamilton
       793 Par. ft – Wildenbruch according to Hamilton[29]
       755.6 ft = 230.3m – de Bertou according to Petermann

625 Par. ft = 666.1 Eng. ft – Russegger according to Petermann

793.3 Par. ft = 845.5 Eng. ft – Widenbruch according to Petermann

328.1 ft. – Symonds according to Petermann[30]

1849: 666 ft – Humboldt[31]

1850: 612 Par. ft – Lynch according to Ritter[32]

The data can also be organized, not chronologically, but by those who performed the measurements, their reports, and others' reports about them. For the Dead Sea, Moore and Beek's results are reported as between 500 and 607 feet below sea level, whereas Schubert's are always accepted as 598 and 598.5 feet. De Bertou's reported calculations vary from 406 to over 422 meters, whereas Russegger's are usually accepted as 1,341 Parisian feet, with two exceptions (1,400 and 1,231). Symonds's accepted result was 1,311.9 or 1,312.2 feet, with two exceptions (1,337 feet and an erroneous 1,351 Parisian feet). Wildenbruch measured 1,351.6 Parisian feet, but Ritter reported 1,341, and Lynch – 1,234.589 English, or 1,235 Parisian, feet.

These lists also provide evidence of the interest aroused in certain scientific circles concerning the main question, namely, the exact altitudes of the levels of both lakes. They also demonstrate some of the problems of communication and discourse between different parts of the scientific world, while, on the other hand, indicating the existing contacts and the fact that scholars received and read periodicals from foreign countries and sent their material for publication not only by their 'home society' and in their 'home forum'. It also testifies to the personal connections of some of the scholars with colleagues in other countries, some of them also members of their own national scientific associations. The progress of the research towards the solution to this question, compared with what can be reconstructed based on Klein's research, is demonstrated in fig. 50.

The study of the Dead Sea and the Jordan Rift Valley cannot be described simply as geographical, historical, botanical or geological. This field of study constituted a complicated and multifaceted scientific inquiry. David Livingstone looked at the 'historical geography of science and religion' as part of what he characterized as the 'historical geography of ideas', calling for a stronger use 'of space and geography in *all* social theory'.[33] And indeed, the scientific study of the Dead Sea, in particular during the period discussed in this book, constitutes one of the best illustrations of what he terms 'the story of encounters between scientific claims and religious convictions'. All of the research questions posed by the various explorers, scientists and scholars, whether or not they physically set foot there, derived from historical-religious associations, narratives and memories, Old Testament tales and myriad legends and curiosities, all strengthened by the lake's mysterious nature, the tremendous difficulty in reaching it and its unique, desolate, sweltering and anything but friendly atmosphere and surroundings. From the present study, it might even be possible to conclude that all Dead-Sea research up until the second half of the nineteenth century was aimed only at understanding and verifying its important scriptural narrative.

'The chase after the level', as I have chosen to call it, is, not coincidentally, inspired by another expression, 'the chase after the Bible', which I coined in an earlier paper about the early development of Palestine studies in the nineteenth century and its unavoidable connection with the Scriptures.[34] The discussions in the book have proven how much these two pursuits had in common. The Jordan and the Dead Sea play a highly significant role in numerous scriptural narratives. Both have developed meanings which go far beyond their geographical names and which greatly surpass their size and appearance. Among other things, they represent the manifestation of God's wrath in the Great Flood and in the destruction of Sodom and Gomorrah, the crossing of the Jordan into the Promised Land and the site of the baptism of Jesus. Moore and Beek's discovery was the start of a revolutionary scientific process, which directly affected other fields, not the least of which were theology and Bible studies. It altered the accepted understanding of the geography and topography described in the Scriptures and their agreement with the existing landscape. So typical of the nineteenth-century Christian study of the Holy Land, Ritter's and Robinson's approach, also accepted by French scholars such as Letronne, considered the Scriptures to be a reliable historical-geographical source. Consequently, for them the topography of the Holy Land should be investigated in accordance with these sacred historical descriptions. The Dead Sea and the entire Jordan Valley formed not only a test case, but probably *the* test case.

One of the important arguments in this book, however, is that the geo-religious 'revolution' must also be approached and perceived as a purely scientific process, one typical of the nineteenth-century geographical world with its respective national geographical societies, its international cooperation and scientific discourse, the bevy of scholars, explorers and 'scientific agents' in the field and the constant competition to uncover new, revolutionary findings.

Another considerable part of this book's inquiry is devoted to the role of Dead-Sea research within the geo-political realities of the eastern Mediterranean and the Near East, all the way to Persia, Arabia and India. The study of the Jordan and the Dead Sea was performed within a relatively short period of considerable change and renewed intensivity in the European geo-political approach to the Near East. Britain, France and Russia, primarily, were competing for wealth and influence; they were mainly interested in building and safeguarding their colonial empires. The Austro-Hungarian monarchy as well as a burgeoning Prussia, were also a constant presence, but only in the second line. In any case, and as demonstrated in the book, these considerations placed the entire Jordan Rift Valley within the limits of the space which was considered geo-politically important.

The first stage of the topographic study of the Rift and its lakes was conducted by individual investigators trained in science and geodesy, as well as by travelers and adventurers who entered the field as amateurs, sometimes by sheer coincidence. Although many of them worked independently, others had been sent by scientific organizations or governmental or military agencies. Though most of the study of the Dead Sea originated, as indicated above, from a combination of geo-religious motivations and perceptions of modern geographic research, such formal involvement derived, at least in part, from the European powers' race for influence, economic control, military superiority and empire-building. These political and military efforts were manifested in two directions: forwarding their interests and gaining advantages, but at the same time blocking the advance and minimizing the achievements of their competitors. It was a global fight, undertaken according to perceived needs, and when necessary, ignoring ethical obstacles. The Near East, governed by the declining Ottoman Empire which was on the constant verge of dissolution, became one of the main battlefields, particularly from the beginning of the nineteenth century. To quote John Marlowe:

> Both France and Britain were concerned to prevent the dissolution
> of the Ottoman Empire since such dissolution would have meant a

Russian occupation of Constantinople. This would both threaten France as a Mediterranean Power and increase the threat to British communications with India already presented – in the eyes of the British Government – by the beginnings of Russian overland expansion in central and south-west Asia.[35]

The study of the Dead Sea as part of the entire Jordan Rift Valley was strongly related to other events in the global game in the Near East. The period in question followed international events such as the French occupation of Algeria, the Greek Rebellion and another one in the series of wars between Russia and the Ottomans in which the latter continued to lose territories. Britain and Russia were competing, again with military intervention, in Persia, and both were also fighting in other areas such as Afghanistan. It was a period during which the after-effects of the almost twenty years of ongoing Napoleonic wars were felt everywhere in Europe and in the Near East. The third, but mostly the fourth and fifth decennia of the nineteenth century also turned out to be crucial for the history of the countries bordering the Mediterranean to the east. One need only recall that the Jordan Valley was a potential route for a Russian attack on Egypt in order to understand the urgent need for a proper geographical reconnaissance of the area and the issuing of an up-to-date map which would be sufficiently accurate for whoever needed it – whether for military, scientific, or commercial purposes.

Yet, as has been said, the geographical research in the eastern Mediterranean countries around the Holy Land often also went hand in hand with geo-religious studies. The narratives of Chesney, Callier and Lvov offer three outstanding examples of what Driver terms 'geography militants': geographically trained officers who toured the region in the early 1830s, performing military-geographic research quite typical of the period, combined with often simultaneous, geo-religiously inspired studies. The Royal Geographical Society and the Hydrographic Office of the Navy were deeply involved in its study, as were, though to a somewhat a lesser extent, the French and Russian military information-gathering authorities – the French Dépôt de la Guerre and the H.I.M. Quarter-Master Suite.

Even if they did not meet personally, Callier, Chesney and Lvov were very familiar with one another and undoubtedly understood just how much they had in common. Participants in Chesney's expedition repeatedly met with Europeans who were traveling in the East at the same time, such as Moore and de Bertou. The list of connections, as demonstrated over and over again in this book, is much longer, and strongly supports another of its central arguments, namely, concerning the role played by individuals and individual ties and communication in the events and processes described.

In a previous study I argued that a survey of Palestine was never a priority of the government in London, and for that matter, of any other government in Europe. Herbert Horatio Kitchener (1850–1916), who, due to Claude Reignier Conder's (1848–1910) illness, in effect commanded the final stages of the British Ordnance Survey of Western Palestine and the preparation of the maps published in 1880, was appointed Britain's minister of war during the First World War. In 1915 he reported to the cabinet that he thought that Palestine was of little value, strategic or otherwise, and that it had not even one worthy port.

Accordingly, Palestine's primary significance during most of the nineteenth century was indeed rooted in its religious tradition, and this provided the pretext for studies of a more limited scope by individuals or associations, with only little involvement of their governments. The fact is that beyond the plans for a peaceful Christian occupation of the holy places – the 'Peaceful Crusade' – which originated mainly in the early 1840s, Palestine did not constitute an object of imperialistic aspirations. Hence, there was no special need to invest means and effort in mapping it. Indeed, this was delayed until the development of the special local and regional constellation that made possible the actualization of such a project.[36]

This point has been argued throughout the book. To gain some perspective, one need only compare the expenditures made on the Survey of Western Palestine in the 1870s with the huge projects and investments of the British Empire in Mesopotamia during the 1830s and 1840s. Chesney's measurements were continued by Lynch, and the entire project was formally completed in 1842. Chesney estimated in 1834 that the cost of his expedition would reach £13,000, but this increased considerably and reached a total of £43,000. This sum should be compared with the means invested in the SWP. Over the first 25 years of its activity, the Palestine Exploration Fund spent £51,000 to fund all of its research in Palestine, an average of slightly more than £2,000 a year. Exactly one third of this amount, £17,000, was spent on the Survey of Western Palestine, which was conducted from 1871 to 1877, again about £2,000 per year. But was this actually the entire cost of the survey and its publication? The answer to these questions can be found in John James Moscrop's *Measuring Jerusalem*, published in 2000, which deals with the PEF and its history, using the wealth of material kept in the organization's archives in London. In his conclusion to the chapter on the SWP, he begins with an unequivocal statement:

> The Western Survey [i.e., the Survey of Western Palestine, HG] was born of a very real desire by Fund members and subscribers, [...] to map the Holy Land. It came of an idealistic imperial religious wish to possess the land for the British Empire, to symbolize the achievements of the world's greatest Protestant Christian Empire. *It also came from a very real need for Britain to map the Jordan Valley to protect both Suez and India against both France and Russia* [my emphasis, HG].[37]

The story of the survey actually provides some of the most significant support for this claim, as can be seen in a letter sent from the British War Office in May 1877, which expressly stated that it was military-strategic considerations and no other interest that led to the completion of the survey. It was added that, although there were other reasons, of a sentimental nature, that might perhaps be of some weight in completing the survey, it was preferable 'to base any recommendation on the enormous military value of a good map of the country to us'.[38]

In 1870, when the French began mapping the Galilee, Charles Wilson of the Royal Engineers, who had already conducted some studies in Palestine, was appointed to a senior position in the Topographical Department of the London War Office Intelligence Department. The English certainly did not intend to leave the work of mapping Palestine to the French. Furthermore, the general geo-political situation in the region, pointing clearly at another imminent war between Russia and the Ottoman Empire, led to English recognition that this stretch of land between the Jordan and the Mediterranean nevertheless bore strategic importance for them. The history of the survey indicates that the campaign would not have succeeded without the cooperation, or more correctly, the support and financial backing, provided by the War Office to the PEF. The society certainly did not have the financial means to conduct such a survey.[39] Nor could the PEF finance the preparation and publication of the maps. The War Office was involved in all stages of the project, with Wilson serving as the de facto liaison between the government and the PEF Executive Committee. The construction of the Suez Canal, reawakening worries about a Russian advance into Mesopotamia or towards Egypt, imminent war between Russia and the Ottoman Empire (which indeed erupted in 1876) and British involvement in the political struggles between the European powers – all these factors had a major influence on the performance of the work and the speed with which the map was completed.

But this had not been the situation forty years earlier, at least not in and around Palestine. Governmental financing had gone to other projects in the region, Chesney's expedition, of course, being the best and most salient example. The danger of a Russian advance on Egypt was always there, but its actuality was considered of a lesser degree than that of an advance towards India, which well explains Britain's priorities. The case of the study of the Dead Sea and the Jordan was no different. For 'the early spies', this had been another area of possible interest and accordingly deserving of some study, though never too intensive; other regions received much greater time and effort. The importance of the Jordan Rift Valley derived mainly from its abovementioned strategic value as a possible route for a Russian invasion, a consideration which had always been there, but certainly not one of the immediate threats to the British Empire. It had never been important enough to warrant a government-initiated and -sponsored project.

But once it was performed – and mainly due to its exciting apparent conclusions – this scientific study became the object of official attention, and even, in some cases, encouragement. There were people doing the work in the field; the scientific milieu showed great interest, as did the highly influential religious world. Joining them would bring significant advantages to the interested power. For Britain, it fit perfectly into the establishment of its 'imperial knowledge' of the Near East.

To sum up, the book has hopefully sufficiently established and demonstrated the connection between exploration, cartography and imperial interests in the study of the Dead Sea as part of Palestine, and Palestine as part of the Near East. It is very much a narrative of powers, interests, international diplomacy, influence, ambition, economy and trade. But this research testifies that it also concerns people, their encounters, their discourse, their exchange of ideas deriving from the general environment on the one hand, and their beliefs on the other.

The last issue to be dealt with in this summary is the role of the Irish – what I term 'the Irish connection' – in the study of the Holy Land in British imperialism, precisely during the 1830s and the 1840s:

> Irish perspectives (both Protestant and Catholic) [for supporting the empire, HG] were shaped by various political ideologies and attitudes, by Irish pragmatic goals, and by various non-English senses of identity. Furthermore, Irish colonizers, both Catholic and Protestant, played important roles in shaping British identity in the colonies.[40]

Jennifer Ridden, who wrote these lines in a paper published in 2004, talks openly of 'the network of connections and movements of Irish people' throughout the empire, such that people in Ireland 'became increasingly aware of the ways in which the language of imperial Britishness could be turned to their advantage', in particular for a kind of self-governance.[41]

The first to establish this narrative link in the case of the Holy Land was the Franciscan Father Eugene Hoade, well known for his contribution to the study of the country and himself, of course, an Irishman. His 1952 paper, 'Ireland and the Holy Land', was published in the annual of his Alma Mater in Multyfarnham, a thirteenth-century Franciscan monastery in central Ireland. He names some early and medieval travelers, counts the number of the Irish serving in the Franciscan Custodia Terrae Sanctae and adds material concerning other compatriots, such as Costigan.[42] In 1974 he was succeeded by Con Costello, who published his most informative book concerning Irish links with the Levant, mainly the Holy Land, from the earliest times he could trace. The book has been of tremendous importance for me, as it depicts the impressive Irish participation in British activities in the region, as well as Irish travelers, missionaries, clergy and others who were present in the frame of space and time dealt with in my book.[43] Highly valuable for my study were his fourth (on missionaries in Syria), fifth (on nineteenth-century explorers) and sixth ('Officers and Scholars, Ladies and Gentlemen travellers') chapters. Undoubtedly, the long list revealed in his book as well as in my study, is one of the best demonstrations of the special link between the Irish people and the eastern Mediterranean countries, of which Syria, Palestine and Egypt held a central place. Certainly I did not deal with the Irish connection with India, nor did I study their part in the building of that most important British colony, but I did show the acquaintances and the possible encounters and exchanges generated by the Irish participation in both areas.

The list of Irish people mentioned in my study as active participants in both 'routes' – the Jordan Rift Valley/Dead Sea route, on the one hand, and the Euphrates 'road to India', on the other – is impressive: Costigan, Moore, Chesney, the Lynches, Porter, to name only the important ones. To this one must add the dozens of other travelers who visited the East, many of whom are mentioned in this book and whose travelogues provided valuable information concerning their compatriots. The same goes, of course, for missionaries and clergymen who lived in the East for various periods. Many names were mentioned in this book, in some cases also complementing Costello's list. In addition to those Irish-born protagonists in this narrative, the 'Irish connection' should also include some people who studied in Dublin, usually at the influential Trinity College. The best example of these might be Michael Solomon Alexander (1799–1845), a Posen-born Jewish rabbi who converted to the Anglican Church and became the first Protestant Bishop of Jerusalem (1842–5) and upon whom 'it was usual for visitors from Ireland to call'.[44] The claim that 'affinity with the East had long been part of the Irish temperament', that the Irish were fascinated by the new environment and often submerged in it, some of them ending up by being converted to Islam, might have some factual basis, although it must be stressed that many of them acted simply as part of their service to the Empire. Earlier studies pointed out that 'the number of Irish soldiers, missionaries, and administrators going to India grew tremendously in the nineteenth century', and this must also be true for nearer parts of the East, including Egypt, Syria and Palestine. All these far-away and exotic countries offered the Irish adventure as well as employment opportunities. The participation in imperial projects was probably one of the only avenues open for Irishmen to develop a career, with more prospects than existed locally or in England. But on the other hand – to use the colorful image of the mingling of Saxon and Celtic blood – it was also the best way to achieve Irish–English parity.[45]

Another process which might have had an impact on the intensiveness of the Irish connection to the Holy Land, especially in the 1820s, was the Catholic emancipation in Ireland, which was reaching its climax in those years. From 1823, a lawyer, Daniel O'Connell (1775–1847), led a popular campaign against English law, also applied in Ireland, which prevented all non-Anglicans from holding public office. O'Connell advocated home rule for Ireland, and as the campaign progressed, he fought all other anti-Catholic legislation. In April 1829 the Catholic Emancipation Act was enacted in the British Parliament, and one result was that Catholics could now become MPs; George Henry Moore was certainly one of these. There must have been a connection between such a movement, which tried to realign Ireland with Catholic Britain and with the continent, and the new wave of Irish interest in the Holy Land.

From the end of the seventeenth century, the East India Company recruited the Irish as soldiers and low-level civil servants. The numbers and percentage of Irish troops recruited by the company are impressive, approaching 40 per cent. Anglo-Irish aristocrats gained access to the highest positions. The Irish constituted one quarter of the Indian Civil Service. It is also only natural that the mid-1840s saw a tremendous increase of Irish recruits, seeking relief from the famine. In 1855, the civil service and the army in India were thrown open to accepting more Irish into their ranks, and Trinity College began tailoring its curriculum to the civil service exams. These developments hold true for permanent settlers, as well; in addition to soldiers and missionaries, between 1815 and 1910, the Irish constituted about one third of the white settlers in the British Empire. It is also clear that the elite and the gentry were highly represented in this respect.[46] Networks developed based on prior acquaintance, family connections (as, for example, the Lynch family in the Indian Navy), mutual interest, and a kind of *landsmannschaft*, based on common origins and culture, and the feeling that one could have more confidence in one's compatriots, primarily in such far away countries.

Therefore, it is no wonder that contemporary voices in Ireland advocated active Irish participation in the Empire. One example was a paper read in a Dublin club by a veteran of the Bengal civil service, and subsequently published in 1878, condemning those who rebelled against the Empire, in each part of which one could find 'Irishmen as leaders of thought and foremost in administration'. Therefore, he said, people who were under the impression that the colonies were 'places to which the poor can emigrate', and that India was 'whither young men of the middle class go out as cadets, and whence they come home colonels', should delve more deeply into the study of this glorious, 'vast experiment of freedom and equal law for all, and of self government wherever it can be had'.[47]

This approach fits into Lennon's long discussion, citing many early Irish writers, concerning the use of Irish–Indian analogies, based on Celtic–Oriental semiotics, mainly among the group of academic or semi-academic Irish orientalists. But these processes, where non-English immigrants could develop an impressive career in the imperial colonies, were relevant only for the later years, mainly the second half of the nineteenth century.[48]

About two-thirds of the members of Chesney's expedition were Irish. It is difficult to establish the reason, although it might not have been with prior intention, as Chesney chose his people according to their proven capabilities and availability. Chesney does not reveal any form of Irish pride in his many writings. On the contrary, he wrote about 'that unhappy country Ireland, about which everyone is greatly alarmed'.[49]

The British Empire and its interests, the Holy Land and its sacredness, the Jordan Rift Valley and the Dead Sea and their scientific revelation – these three narratives meet in the story told in this book. And within this story, it was the people, mainly those in the field, who turned it into one of the most exciting narratives in the history of Palestine, the beginning of a hundred years that would lead to its total transformation and bring it into modernity.

Notes

PREFACE AND ACKNOWLEDGEMENTS, INTRODUCTION

1   Heim, Tobler, 59; Tobler, Topography, I, iii–v; Furrer, Tobler, 54. Cf. Robinson, Researches; Goren, Zieht hin, 83–91, 222–43; Makdisi, Artillery, 171–4, 193–9.
2   Schur, Dead Sea, 4; Vardi, Height, 23–5.
3   Costello, Ireland; idem, Costigan; idem, Explorers. Lt. Colonel Costello, who recently passed away, was renowned for his lifetime dedication to the recording and preservation of the heritage and history of County Kildare.
4   Eriksen, Costigan; idem, Molyneux; idem, Illness; idem, Explorers.
5   Kreiger, Waters.
6   Elath, Chesney; idem, Routes.
7   Guest, Expedition.
8   Life of Chesney, vi–v. Lambert, Franklin, deals intensively with the role of this personal activity, these views and contexts, in Arctic exploration.
9   Edney, Mapping. Cf. also Livingstone, Tradition.
10   Edney, Mapping; Godlewska, Geography.
11   Dunbar, Compass. Cf., as examples of the vast literature: Driver, Geography; Lester, Geographies; Miller and Reill, Visions; Home, Royal Society, 307–9, and bibliography in nn. 1–2 on page 328.
12   See, e.g.: Pyenson, Mission; Heffernan, Scholarship; Mignolo, Renaissance, 259–314. See also Livingstone's detailed discussion (Tradition, 155-76).
13   Ben-Arieh, Pioneer; idem, Rediscovery; idem, Perceptions. Cf. Goren, Ritter.
14   Day, Admiralty, 61.
15   Van de Velde, Memoir, 15, and on him see Frederiks, Velde; Ben-Arieh, Rediscovery, 130–1; Bartlett, Mapping, 113–18. Cf. Napoleon, Guerre d'Orient; Godlewska, Survey; idem, Egypt; Jacotin, Carte; idem, Carte topographique; Gichon, Napoleon, passim. About Jacotin and mainly his relations with the Cassinis, the pioneers of French cartographic survey, cf. Godlewska, Geography, 77–8. For the French measurements in Palestine: Berghaus, Memoir, 1–4; Karmon, Jacotin: Godlewska, Survey, passim; idem, Geographers. For Napoleon's invasion: Laurens, Expedition; Lord, England, 146–62.
16   Watson, Fifty Years, 65–80; Ben-Arieh, Rediscovery, 209–18; Silberman, Digging, 113–23; Moscrop, Measuring.

PART 1
Chapter 1

1 Eugene Rogan, 'Mehmet Ali', *ODNB,* 53764; see e.g., Lord, England, 46–9, 125–32; Marlowe, Relations, 13–14.
2 For an interesting contemporary detailed description of 'the first Egyptian Campaign', see Olberg, Geschichte. Naturally, the campaign is dealt with in all studies dedicated to the Eastern Mediterranean in the 1830s; for contemporary studies, based also on Ottoman documents, see Kutluoğlu, Question, 61–107; Fahmy, Mehmed Ali.
3 Vereté, Palmerston, 143–4, citing a dispatch from Consul-General Barker; Alderson, Acre, 39: 3,500 cavalry and 18,000 infantry. For a detailed study of the army, see also Fahmy, Mehmed Ali, passim.
4 Olberg, Geschichte, 63–81, pl. I. Kutluoğlu, Question, 63, gives the difficult to accept number of 2,500 men.
5 Olberg, Geschichte, 64, 77–8; Kutluoğlu, Question, 62.
6 Alderson, Acre, 39–46, a detailed description of the battle; Olberg, Geschichte, 94–100; Kutluoğlu, Question, 64–8 (citation), 71–3; Schur, Acre, 253–4.
7 Rochfort Scott, Rambles, I, 6–19; Kutluoğlu, Question, 40–1.
8 Olberg, Geschichte, 101–202, pl. II, III, IV; Kutluoğlu, Question, 61–82. The Egyptian admiral, commanding the fleet between 1831 and 1833, deserted in 1833 to the Ottomans and died some months later in Constantinople (Rochfort-Scott, Rambles, I, 6–8).
9 David Steele, 'Temple, Henry John', *ODNB,* 27712; Lambert, Battleships, 2–8, 34–8.
10 Webster, Policy, certainly the most detailed discussion of the issue. See also Kutluoğlu, Question, passim; Lambert, Battleships, esp. 91.
11 Webster, Policy, I, 82–7, 255–346, II, 619–776; Kelly, Mehemet Ali, 350. The long and detailed paper describes in detail all the Egyptian eastern efforts.
12 Lambert, Gates, chapter three, 4.
13 Marlowe, Suez, 33–6 (citation, 35); Webster, Policy, I, 82–7.
14 Webster, Policy, I, 255–332 (detailed discussion of British involvement in the events of 1830 to 1834); Kutluoğlu, Question, 83–7; Guest, Expedition, 33–4.
15 Rochfort Scott, Rambles, I, xi.
16 Vereté, Palmerston, 145–7; cf. Webster, Policy, I, 273–7.
17 Muriel E. Chamberlain, 'Canning, Stratford, Viscount Stratford de Redcliffe', *ODNB,* 4558; Webster, Policy, I, 320–32.
18 W.P. Courtney, *rev.* H.C.G. Matthew, 'Adair, Sir Robert', *ODNB,* 84.
19 Muriel E. Chamberlin, 'Gordon, George Hamilton', *ODNB,* 11044; idem, 'Gordon, Sir Robert', *ODNB,* 11080.
20 Vereté, Palmerston, 147–50.
21 Webster, Policy, I, 320–32.
22 Webster, Policy, II, 540–3.
23 Kutluoğlu, Question, passim., probably the best and most informative study from the Ottoman point of view.
24 Stafford, Murchinson, 94. For the full discussion cf. Webster, Policy.
25 Lambert, Canon, 79. Cf. Webster, Policy, II, 619–776; Kutluoğlu, Question, 131–88.
26 Marlowe, Relations, 15, citing Dundas, British Minister of War. Cf. Invasions of India; Fontanier, Narrative, 288–90.
27 'French and Russian intrigue in the East', Herbert Taylor to President (Hobhouse), Feb. 9/37, BL OIRR, MSS Eur. F213/1.
28 Atkin, Diplomacy, 60–5.
29 Atkin, Diplomacy, 67.
30 Atkin, Diplomacy, 68–70.

31   Atkin, Diplomacy, 72–4; Marriott, Relations, 102–3.
32   Chaudhuri, Disturbances, 118–20; Marlowe, Suez, 26–7.
33   Graham, Britain, 262–5.
34   Lorimer, Gazetteer, 173–4; Markham, Persia, 392–3.
35   Markham, Persia, 393–7; Marriott, Relations, 104–6; Graham, Britain, 265–7.
36   Guest, Expedition, 7–10; Elath, Routes, 27–42. The ancient projects are described, for example, in the report of the Select Committee, 458–61.
37   For example Taylor in Baghdad, Kelly, Britain, 269–70.
38   Low, Afghan War; Jackson, Pomp, 39–57; Marriott, Relations, 107–9; Lorimer, Gazetteer, 222–5; Webster, Policy, II, 743–52; Tuchman, March; P.J. Marshall, 'Eden, George', ODNB, 8451. Probably realizing the connection between the campaigns in Palestine and in Afghanistan, Alderson, Acre, brings sketches from the English Garrison in Jellalabad and sections of its fortifications, drawn in 1842.
39   Jackson, Pomp, 29.
40   Marriott, Relations, 106–10.
41   Wood, History, passim.; Bent, English, 655–7, 663.
42   Marlowe, Suez, esp. 10.
43   Robin A. Butlin, 'Maundrell, Henry', ODNB, 18378.
44   Wood, History, 157–78 ('Decline'), 179–204 ('The End'); Bent, English, 662–3.
45   Wood, History, 186. For the Company and the Gulf and Arab countries cf. Lorimer, Gazeteer, passim.
46   Chaudhuri, Disturbances, passim. Harlow and Carter, Imperialism, 4–5, depict a critical approach towards the Company and its methods. For texts of both acts and constitution: 9–20. For the Company's history, policy, deeds, and interests, see also e.g., Hutchins, Illusion; Sutton, Lords; Carter and Harlow, Archives, 27–88; Guest, Expedition, 2–4.
47   Lorimer, Gazeteer, passim, esp. 171–7, 213–20 (history of British residencies), 440–69, 633–93; Belgrave, Pirate; Markham, Persia, 425–6.
48   Belgrave, Pirate; Markham, Persia, 426–30.
49   Graham, Britain, 271–5, 297–9. See there, 282–304, for a detailed discussion of Aden's importance, history, and mainly its development as a British auxiliary port until its conquest.
50   Wellsted, Book, 400; Fontanier, Narrative, 120–3. Cf. F. Beauvois, 'Fontanier', NBG, 18 (1858), 117; Pfullmann, Entdeckerlexikon, 211.
51   Markham, Persia, 435.
52   Xenophon, Anabasis 1867; Xenophon, Anabasis 2001; cf. Ainsworth, Ten Thousand; Fox, March.
53   Williams, Policy, 133–4.
54   Thomas, Treaties, 46–7; Kelly, Britain, 110–11, 139, 219, 269–70, 317–18.
55   Williams, Policy, 134. Cf. Miles Taylor, 'Urquhart, David', ODNB, 28017.
56   Graham, Britain, 267–71; Webster, Policy, 525–81.
57   ODNB, 28017. For his studies of the Turks and their habits see Avicioğlu, Urquhart.
58   Urquhart, Russian Progress; idem, Russia (citation: 380); idem, Transactions.
59   Urquhart, Lebanon, passim (citation: I, v).
60   There is a vast literature, containing contemporary eye-witness reports (from both sides), later reports, and modern studies. Alderson, Acre, 21–38, used mostly French sources and added many maps and sketches; Kelly, Syria, 345–6. Cf. Gichon, Napoleon, for a detailed survey of Napoleon's Palestine campaign.
61   Marlowe, Suez, 5. See also his detailed discussion interweaving French and British interests and moves, ibid., 1–29.
62   Fontanier, Narrative, iii, 2–3, 120–5 (in Bombay).
63   Fontanier, Narrative, 168–70, 288–340; Guest, Expedition, 112–28.

64 Raguse, State, 223; idem, Voyage, II, 261–3, 278; Lamartin, Pilgrimage, 352–8.
65 Armstrong, Essay.
66 Lardner, Steam; Barber, Letter.
67 Grindlay, View, vi–vii.
68 Grindlay, View, 8–12.
69 Lardner, Steam, citation 74.

Chapter 2

1 Marlowe, Suez, 18–9.
2 Frumin, Rubin and Gavish, Russian; Frumin, Russian.
3 Godlewska, Survey; idem, Geographers. Cf. Outram, Politics.
4 Beaufort, Karamania. Cf. Dawson, Memoirs, I/II, 1–14, esp. 2–3; Friendly, Beaufort; Courtney, Beaufort; Day, Admiralty, 44–67; J.K. Laughton, *rev.* N.A.M. Rodger, 'Beaufort, Sir Francis', *ODNB,* 1857; Landy, Beaufort. Founded in London in 1826, the society encouraged publishing inexpensive scientific material for the wider public: Cain, Society. Lambert, Franklin, passim, stresses Beaufort's central role in the study of the Arctic and in the development of its cartography, as well as in the intensive studies of earth magnetism, and Driver, Geography, 34, 62-3, establishes his connections with the RGS.
5 Dawson, Memoirs, I/II, 3–4.
6 Day, Admiralty, 44–6 and passim.
7 Dawson, Memoirs, I/II, 5–11; See here the recent discussion of Della Dora, Landscapes, dealing with the cartography of the Dardanelles and the isthmuses of Suez and Mount Athos.
8 I deeply thank Yoland Hodson and Andrew Cook for their stimulating ideas and information concerning this issue.
9 *PGS,* 3 (November 1838-June 1842), 47 (meeting 15 Feb. 1839).
10 Since 1870 'Topographical and Statistical Depot of War Office'. Cf. Andrews, Landscape, 1–2.
11 Courtney, Beaufort, 191–5.
12 Herschel, Manual.
13 Herschel, Manual, iv. Cf. Michael J. Crowe, 'Herschel, Sir John Frederick William', *ODNB,* 13101.
14 Driver, Geography, 49–67; Herschel, Manual; Manley and Rée, Salt, passim; Dawson and Uphill, 188; Mill, RGS, 38–9; Fagan, Rape, 80–90; Hallett, Penetration, 358.
15 Fagan, Rape, is a good example of a modern approach to this phenomenon.
16 Marshall-Cornwall, Soldiers, 357–9; Alastair W. Massie, 'Koehler, George Frederick', *ODNB,* 15804; J.M. Wagstaff, 'Leake, William Martin', *ODNB,* 16242; Wagstaff, Leake; Wagstaff, Pausanias. Cf. Marlowe, Relations, 16.
17 *ODNB,* 16242; Cf. Della Dora, Landscapes, 515-16.
18 R.E. Anderson, *rev.* R.A. Jones, 'Hamilton, William Richard', *ODNB,* 2147; William St Claire, 'Bruce, Thomas', *ODNB,* 3759; Mill, RGS, 38–9; Searight, British, 196; Dawson and Uphill, 188; Fagan, Rape, 80–90; Jackson, Pomp, 20–8.
19 Lamartine, Pilgrimage, 4. Cf. Léo Joubert, 'Lamartine', *NBG,* 29 (1854), 78–100, esp. 86–7; Said, Orientalism, passim, esp. 170–81. He sailed from Marseille in July 1832 and left Syria on his return in May 1833.
20 For biographies see *DBF,* VII, 900–1; EEEE, I, 480–2; Broc, 73–5. On the *ingénieurs-géographes,* who were attached to the Dépôt de la guerre, and their responsibilities in times of war and peace, see Bonato, Chypre, 113, n. 2.
21 Broc, 328–9; Poujoulat, 'Michaud', *NBG,* 35 (1861), 330–4, esp. 332; Michaud, Crusades.

22 Bonato, Navarin, 107 (from the Bibliothèque Nationale, Department of Manuscripts, NAF23762). My gratitude to Yehuda Levi for his translations of French documents.
23 'Poujoulat', *NBG*, 40 (1862), 922–3. Broc, 73, does not bother mentioning him at all.
24 Walckenaer, Voyages; Callier, Kleinasien; biographies in note 20. Cf. Bonato, Navarin; idem, Chypre.
25 Letter by Callier and Stamaty, Izmir, 23. Feb. 1831, File 3M378 - 4ème liasse, (archive de Service Historique de l'Armée de Terre). Dorit Ayalon found this document and generously allowed me to use it.
26 Callier, Kleinasien, 923.
27 For a detailed itinerary see Broc, 73–4.
28 Callier, Note , citations 88–9.
29 Indication de la route parcourue par le Cap. Callier, coloured manuscript, RGS, Map Room, Israel, S/S 21.
30 Berghaus, Letter. For the map and Bertou see discussion, pp. 237–8.
31 Reinach, Inscriptions.
32 Callier, Kleinasien; idem, Reise.
33 Callier, Map; Fischer, Geschichte, 45–6. A copy: JPMC, Asien, 29 II.
34 Saul and Thobie, Militaires.
35 Reinach, Inscriptions, 49; Kutluoğlu, Question, 139–41. Cf. Ernouf, 'Soult', *NBG*, 44 (1865), 241–53; and for his part in the Ottoman–Egyptian crisis cf. Kutluoğlu, Question, 144–52; Webster, Policy, II, 625–71.
36 EEEE, I, 481; Progress 1836–7, 183, note. For Ritter and the study of the Holy Land: Goren, Ritter; Goren, Zieht hin, 68–83.
37 Callier, Map; see Reinach, Inscriptions, 49–50, nn. 1 and 2.
38 Said, Orientalism, passim; G.R., 'Sacy', *NBG*, 42 (1863), 987–93; Dawson and Uphill, 391–2.
39 Hase, Callier, 281–2.
40 Hase, Callier, 282.
41 Callier, Note; idem, Mémoire; Letronne, Trennung, 213–17.
42 Biographies: Stanley Lane-Poole, *rev.* Roger T. Stern, 'Chesney, Francis Rawdon', *ODNB*, 5230; Life of Chesney; Elath, Chesney; idem, Routes; Guest, Expedition; Chesney, Chesney.
43 Chesney, Expedition; idem, Narrative; Ainsworth, Narrative.
44 Elath, Chesney; idem, Routes; Hoskins, Routes.
45 Guest, Expedition; Naumann, Queen.
46 Life of Chesney, ix; cf. England and the East, 2202. According to his uniform, his height was 4 feet 9 inches (Guest, Expedition, 23, note), or 5 feet 1 inch (*ODNB*, 5230). Cf. Guest's evaluation of Chesney personality – 'Chesney was a visionary' – Expedition, 151.
47 Chesney, Portrait, 574–5.
48 Elath, Routes, 49–57.
49 Chesney, Narrative, 4–141; Life of Chesney, 166–250; Guest, Expedition, 22–30.
50 Life of Chesney, 166–67; see above, pp. 240–3.
51 Memo regarding Capt. Chesney, NA, FO 352/26(1), 86–7; Francis Rawdon Chesney, Diary 1829-, PRONI D3480/52/1. This is a rather long (over 900 pages) document, in which pp. 42-77 are dedicated to the travels in Egypt and Palestine. See also Elath, Expedition, 35–6, 49–50; Life of Chesney, 168–70; Guest, Expedition, 23–4. For Smith: Roger Morris, 'Smith, Sir (William) Sidney', *ODNB*, 25940.
52 Memo regarding Capt. Chesney, NA, FO 352/26(1).
53 Chesney to Stratford Canning, Blackheath 14 August 1833, NA, FO 352/26.
54 Above, n. 25.

55 Chesney to Stratford Canning, Blackheath 14 August 1833, NA, FO 352/26; Chesney, Narrative, 3.
56 Chesney, Narrative, 3.
57 Robinson, Syria, 7, 141–2, 376, n. 2.
58 Guest, Expedition, 1–10. For Peacock see, e.g., Felton, Peacock; Nicholas A. Joukovsky, 'Peacock, Thomas Love' ODNB, 21681.
59 Guest, Expedition, 4–5 Naumann, Queen, 11–13. The document includes an examination of the possibilities of a Red Sea–Mediterranean canal. For Ellenborough: David Steele, 'Law, Edward', ODNB, 16143; Lambert, Battleships, 47–50. Cf. England and the East, 2201–2.
60 Elath, Routes, 41.
61 Barker, Syria; Arthur H. Grant, rev. Lynn Milne, 'Barker, John (1771–1849)', ODNB, 1405.
62 Bindoff, Representatives, 165; Wood, History, 181–3.
63 Ottoman firman and its translation, Barker, Syria, II, 321–23.
64 Barker, Syria, I, 99–117.
65 Barker, Syria, I, 108–9.
66 Manley and Rée, Salt, 242–73; Barker, Syria, II, 1, 200, 285.
67 Arthur H. Grant, rev. Elizabeth Baigent, 'Barker, William Burckhardt', ODNB, 1419. For the explorer Johann Ludwig Burckhardt see Ben-Arieh, Pioneer, 103–6; Goren, Zieht hin, 48–55, and the bibliography there.
68 Barker, Notes, this report in the JRGS of a voyage in summer 1835 (though the title is September 1834...), exactly when Costigan reached the Dead Sea, includes an annex: a report of Consul Moore on the strong earthquake of 1.1.1837, which actually destroyed the cities of Tiberias and Safed; idem, Lares. Cf. ODNB, 1419 (also the citation). For Ainsworth: Elizabeth Baigent, 'Ainsworth, William Francis', ODNB, 242.
69 Harford, Caravan; Wood, History, esp. 75–6, 126–7, 162–3, Appendix II (list of consuls from 1580).
70 Harford, Caravan, 109 n. 25.
71 Memo regarding Capt. Chesney, NA, FO 352\26 (1), 86–7. For texts of the reports and memos, see Memories by Captain Chesney on the Euphrates, with remarks on the first by the envoy at the Court of Persia, PRONI, D3480/52/2.
72 Chesney, Narrative, 4–5.
73 E.I. Carlyle, rev. Todd M. Endelman, 'Wolff, Joseph', ODNB, 29836; Hopkins, Wolff; Klein-Franke, Wolff; Crombie, Zion, 16–17; Costello, Ireland, 68; Pfullmann, Entdeckerlexikon, 455–6. See Crombie, Alexander, 28–9, for Wolff's tour in Ireland, where he was accompanied by Michael Solomon Alexander, later first Protestant Bishop in Jerusalem.
74 Dawson and Uphill, 364: consul for Tuscany. For Galloway see p. 88.
75 Paxton, Letters, 239; Dawson and Uphill, 169, Fagan, Rape, 267–9.
76 Francis Rawdon Chesney, Diary 1829-, PRONI, D3480/52/1, 43–7. For descriptions of his travels and reports: Chesney, Narrative, 5–11, 364–73; Life of Chesney, 188–202; Elath, Routes, 50–3. Suez citation: Madden, Travels, II, 141.
77 Francis Rawdon Chesney, Diary 1829-, PRONI, D3480/52/1, 43; Life of Chesney, 192. The sources describe him as a Pole or Austrian.
78 Captn. Chesney Report to Sir R. Gordon, Bushire July 27/31 – Tabriz 10th Oct/31, NA, FO 352/26(1), 72–3. The Polish involvement in the East during the 1830s is still awaiting a thorough study. For Abbas Mirza and British policy and involvement: Webster, Policy, II, 739–41.
79 Memories by Captain Chesney on the Euphrates, with remarks on the 1st one by the envoy at the Court of Persia, No. 8 page 1 to 29: Jaffa 2 September 1830, Letter to His Excellency Sir Robert Gordon on Steam by the Red Sea, PRONI,

D3480/52/2. Cited in: Chesney, Narrative, 372–3. Cf. Elath, Routes, 51; *ODNB*, 5230; Guest, Expedition, 25; Della Dora, Landscapes, 534.

80   Cf. Della Dora, Landscapes, 533-4; e.g. Wilson, Lands, I, 139–42; Chesney, Chesney, 338.

81   Marlowe, Suez, 5–10, 17–22.

82   Memo regarding Capt. Chesney, NA, FO 352/26(1), 86–7.

83   Chesney, Narrative, 4–5. Peacock died in 1866, the book was published two years later.

84   Chesney, Narrative, 50–141. Cf. Guest, Expedition, 25–30; Elath, Routes, 54–6.

85   Chesney, Narrative, facing p. 70.

86   Guest, Expedition, 23, citing a document in the PRONI (D.3480/52/12). The Kelek used to sail the rivers was constructed of several rows of air-filled skins of mutton or goat, with boards as the deck.

87   Maundrell, Journey; Bent, English, 658–9; *ODNB*, 18378; Wood, History, 235–6.

88   Ainsworth, Narrative, I, 50.

89   Thomas, Treaties, 46–7; Belgrave, Pirate, 32, 86, 95, 179; Guest, Expedition, passim. For the residency in Basra cf. Belgrave, Pirate, 87–92, 196–7.

90   See, e.g., a list of his reports: Memo regarding Capt. Chesney, NA, FO 352/26(1), 86–7; Chesney, Campaigns (summary of his views concerning the Russian danger).

91   NA, FO 352/26(1), different documents.

92   Tresse, Installation, 360–7. E. Guis was the French Consul (his brother, H. Guis, was consul in Tripoli), Raguse, State, 223; idem, Voyage, II, 261–3, 278.

93   Chesney to 'My Dear Sir', Pera, 13 June 1832, NA, FO 352/26(1).

94   Chesney to 'My Dear Sir', Pera, July 1832, NA, FO 352/26(1). Capt. Kelly could presumably be identified with the Irish Walter Keating Kelly (1806–73), who travelled and published intensively, both about Syria and the Holy Land (Kelly, Syria).

95   Chesney, Narrative, 12–49; Life of Chesney, 203–25. Guest, Expedition, 25, devotes two-and-a-half lines, saying that Chesney simply 'awaited the Ambassador's approval of his plans' concerning the Euphrates; Elath, Routes, 54 – half a page.

96   Francis Rawdon Chesney, Diary 1829-, PRONI, D3480/52/1, 48; Alderson, Acre, 29; Randolph Cock, 'Oldfield, Thomas', *ODNB*, 20682 (citation); Gichon, Napoleon, 127, 132–3. General Louis Alexandre Berthier, later marèchal de France and prince de Neufchâtel et de Wagram (1753–1815). British consuls were still busy with Oldfield's tomb in 1838 (Memo of a letter to Mr. Moore at Bayrout, 22 August 1838, PRONI, D/3480/52/6), and his name is commemorated until the present on a memorial plaque in Acre (see fig 15).

97   Chesney, Expedition, 12–13; Life of Chesney, 194; Guest, Expedition, 25.

98   Chesney, Expedition, 13.

99   Francis Rawdon Chesney, Diary 1829-, PRONI, D3480/52/1, 50–5.

100   Robinson, Travels; Robinson, Syria; Naumann, Queen, 24; Francis Rawdon Chesney, Diary 1829- , PRONI, D3480/52/1, 57. For Farren: Tresse, Installation; Vereté, Consulate, 319–35, esp. n. 2 on 325–6.

101   Francis Rawdon Chesney, Diary 1829-, PRONI, D3480/52/1, 58–9; Chesney, Narrative, 22–3, 30–3.

102   Much more information can be obtained in Robinson's book (Robinson, Syria).

103   Francis Rawdon Chesney, Diary 1829-, PRONI, D3480/52/1, 67–77; Chesney, Narrative, 48–9.

104   Life of Chesney, 204–6.

105   Chesney to Stratford Canning, Blackheath, 14 August 1833, NA, FO 352/26(1), his report in Art. XI.

106 Home, Royal Society, 318, 325.
107 Valentine Blake, 12th Baronet of Galway (1780–1847); John Martin (-1846).
108 Costello, Ireland, 94; Marlowe, Suez, 40–2; Elath, Routes, 56–82; Jones and Grissom, Chesney.
109 Ged Martin, 'Grant, Charles', *ODNB*, 1249; Guest, Expedition, 33–50; Jones and Grissom, Chesney, 191–5.
110 Elath, Routes, 68–70.
111 Select Committee, 481.
112 Select Committee, 466.
113 Rochfort Scott, Rambles.
114 Rochfort Scott, Rambles, I, 6–23, 41–3.
115 Rochfort Scott, Rambles, II, 77–87.
116 Kutluoğlu, Question, 87–97. In 1830 General Muravyev's brother Andrej Nikolaevich made a pilgrimage to the Holy Land and met Mehemet Ali.
117 In 1819–21 Michail Petrovich Lazarev commanded the sloop *Mirnyy* ("Peaceful") during the Russian circumnavigating expedition in which Antarctica was discovered.
118 Lvov, Syria, 226. Probably meaning Colonel Auguste Schultz, see p. 98.
119 Duhamel, Autobiography.
120 'Eastern Anatolia and part of Turkish Kurdistan', RSAMH, fund 450, list 1, file 535, parts 1–3; Lvov, Syria. The original (full) text: RSAMH, fund 444, list 1, file 51.
121 RSAMH, fund 450, list 1, file 535, part 1.

Chapter 3

1   Chesney to Hobhouse, Euphrates Steamer, Aña, 28 May 1836, NA FO 352\26(1), 22.
2   John Hobhouse to Herbert Taylor, Windsor Castle, July 27/36, BL OIRR, MSS. Cf. Chesney, Narrative, 251–76; Life of Chesney, 326–32.
3   John Hobhouse to the King, Indian Board, July 27/36, BL OIRR, MSS. For Hobhouse see Peter Cochran, 'Hobhouse, John Cam', *ODNB*, 13404; Mansel, Grand Tour, 55–6; for his central part in the expedition, cf. Guest, Expedition, passim. See also Michael Brock, 'William IV', *ODNB*, 29451.
4   John Hobhouse to Herbert Taylor, Windsor Castle, October 24/36, BL OIRR, MSS.
5   Richardson, Loss.
6   Elath, Routes, 55–6; Guest, Expedition, 29–30.
7   E.g. Art. XI (in the *Qurterely Review* of 1833); Select Committee; Elath, Routes, 56–82; Guest, Expedition, 35–6.
8   Firman and Viziral Letters issued by the Porte relative to the Navigation of the Mesopotamian Rivers, Tigris and Euphrates, by British Vessels, 29 December 1834, NA, FO 881/2460, 383; Thomas, Treaties, 849–50: Imperial Firman of Protection for the English Steam Vessels destined to navigate the River Euphrates, 29th Dec 1834, pp. 848–49 (A true Translate, signed R. Taylor, Lieut. Col., P.A., Turkish Arabia, Translate of a Booyooroldi by H.H. Alee Reza, Pacha of Bagdad &c. &c. &c., to the Turkish Officers on the Euphrates, from Aanah to Bussora, 13th of Shuval, 1250, or 11th Feb 1835); Hurewitz, Diplomacy, I, 111–12.
9   Reports on the Navigation, 374. For Ponsonby in the High Porte and his role in the Eastern crisis and the British 'Russian Diplomacy', cf. Webster, Policy, II, 596–617, 624–737.
10 Fontanier, Narrative, 288; Marlowe, Suez, 41.
11 Williams, Policy, 98; Guest, Expedition, 12–19, 43–4 (detailed discussion of steamships and navigation, advantages and disadvantages, technologies, early projects to and in India, specifications for the expedition boats);

Naumann, Queen, 31–4. For Laird's part in the Euphrates Expedition, which included engineers from the company, two of them losing their lives: Guest, Expedition, 44, 73, 90, 118, 121, 144. The three steamers arriving in 1840 were also manufactured by Laird (Clowes, History, VI, 195–6). Cf. J.K. Laughton, *rev.* Lionel Alexander Ritchie, 'Laird, John', *ODNB*, 15894; John Flint, 'Laird, Macgregor', *ODNB*, 15895; Herman, Scots, 318–19.

12   Life of Chesney, vii-viii.
13   I find here Guest, Expedition, 51–73, as the best analysis.
14   England and the East, 2210–11: all the difficulties were caused by the Paṣa, Mehemet Ali.
15   All works devote a long, detailed description, to the event as well as to its implications. See, e.g., Ainsworth, Narrative, I, 387–400; Guest, Expedition, 83–93; Naumann, Queen, 208–20.
16   Chesney, Expedition. Also published: Ainsworth, Narrative; Chesney, Narrative (1868); Nostiz, Travels (an interesting report by Pauline Helfer, the only female participant); Elath, Chesney; idem, Routes. William Patrick Andrew, Chairman of the Euphrates and Scinde Railway Companies, used all of Chesney's reports and results in his book, advocating the constructing of a railway through Mesopotamia to India (Andrew, Memoir, 18–43). As example of Chesney's contemporary reports of the immense obstacles, see Letter from Chesney to Hobhouse, Euphrates Steamer, 18 March 1836, NA, FO 352\26(1), 19.
17   PRONI, D3480/52/6, Letterbooks 1838–1842; John Washington to Chesney, RGSA, 3 Sept 1838, 1b-2; Arrowsmith to Washington, 3 September 1838, trying to estimate Chesney's expenses, RGSA, 2B-3; Chesney to Beaufort, 27 December 1839, RGSA, 65–65B.
18   Elath, Chesney; idem, Routes; Guest, Expedition; Naumann, Queen.
19   Chesney to Hobhouse, 2 March 1839, PRONI, D3480/52/6, Letterbooks 1838–42, 30–31b; Guest, Expedition, 41.
20   RGSA, Council Minute Book, Oct. 1830–July 1841, 247; John Washington to Chesney, 23 April 1838, RGSA, RGS Letter Book 1836–40, 205.
21   Ainsworth, Narrative, I, viii-ix.
22   Stafford, Murchinson, 94.
23   Washington, Sketch, 249–50.
24   Cf. the detailed discussion by Lambert, Franklin, 82–9, 167–99, for Sabin and his magnetic measurements as a central issue in the Arctic and Antarctic exploration.
25   Chesney, Narrative, 549–51; Guest, Expedition, passim; Lambert, Franklin, 153–62, 279–82.
26   E.g., Extract of a letter from Chesney to Hobhouse, Alexandretta, 26 January 1836, NA, FO 352/26(1), 17.
27   Lynch, Lynch, 341; Charlewood, Passages, 27–9; cf. Fontanier, Narrative, 304.
28   Paxton, Letters, 47, 206–7. For Paxton see pp. 153–5.
29   GRO D1571, F 451-F 457.
30   GRO D1571, F 465.
31   Estcourt to Father, Orfa, 23 May 1835(?), GRO D1571, F 451, 1554, F553 1834–36; Chesney, Narrative, 545; Guest, Expedition, 73.
32   Estcourt to Edmund, Aleppo, 15 May 1835, GRO D1571, f 457, 1544, 1547; Burton, Narrative, 62.
33   Estcourt to Father, Malta, in quarantine, 11 March 1837, GRO D1571, f 457, 1531; Estcourt to President, Beyrout, 25 February 1837, Malta, 10 March 1837, 3 April 1837, BL OIRR, MSS. Eur. F213/1; Guest, Expedition, 132–48. For his biography see John Sweetman, 'Estcourt, James Bucknall Bucknall', *ODNB*, 8892; Chesney,

Narrative, 251–76, 322–6, 542–3, 547–8 (biography, citation); Beechey, Address 1856, clxxv (obituary); Elath, Routes, 91; Fontanier, Narrative, 298–301; Charlewood, Passages, 43–55; Guest, Expedition, 41, and passim, Naumann, Queen, cites many of his letters.

34   Cf. Chesney, Chesney, 340.
35   Chesney, Narrative, 251–76, 547–8.
36   Bence-Jones, Guide, 231.
37   Burke, Ireland, 741; Burke, Gentry, 423–4; Melvin, Galway, 330–5 (citation 331). See Lynch, Record, 140–3, for the origins of the Lynch family in Ireland; 'Genealogy of the Lynch Family', manuscript from the Dictionary of Irish Biography (forthcoming); my gratitude to Linde Luney for her tremendous help. One interesting narrative relates that James Fitz Stephen Lynch (†1519), three times mayor of Galway, hung his own son out of a window of his Mayoralty house for murdering his girlfriend's lover, though a judiciary refused to try the popular young man, 'the start of the family Law–Lynching'.
38   Berry, Partry.
39   Cf. for example Carter and Harlow, Archives, 203–48; McLaren, India.
40   H.M. Chichester, rev. Elizabeth Baigent, 'Lynch, Henry Blosse', ODNB, 17254; Chesney, Narrative, 547–8; Lynch, Record, 72–6; EEEE, 3 (1993), 312–13; Guest, Expedition, 40–1.
41   Chesney to Hobhouse, 26 October 1836, BL OIRR, European Manuscripts, Eur F 213/5, 236–7, cited by Guest, Expedition, 79.
42   Henry Blosse Lynch to Hobhouse, Bagdad, 28 February 1838, NLI, Acc. No. 5475. Cf., for example, Lynch, Note; idem, Memoir.
43   Henry Blosse Lynch to Hobhouse, Bagdad, 28 February 1838, NLI, Acc. No. 5475.
44   Graham, Britain, 281–82; Guest, Expedition, 140–7; cf. Lynch, Memoir.
45   Longrigg, Iraq, 293. He mentions, probably erroneously, four steamers brought by Michael Lynch.
46   Lynch to Secret Committee, 25 June 1842, BL OIRR, Political and Secret Dept Records 9/13, cited by Guest, Expedition, 147; Lorimer, Gazetteer, 236; Stafford, Murchinson, 95.
47   In the words of his older brother, John F., who in 1844 published in the DUM his brother's journals from a mission in 1839–40 to Afghanistan: Lynch, Journal. C.B. = 'Companion of the Most Honourable of the Bath'.
48   Chesney, Narrative, 547–8; Hamilton, Address 1842, lxi-lxii; EEEE, III, 312–13; Elath, Routes, 120–35; Longrigg, Iraq, 293–96.
49   Geographical Discovery (Letters, extracts from the Address of the President of the Royal Geographical Society in London).
50   RGSA, Council Minute Book, Oct 1830–July 1841, 260 (28 January 1839), 262 (route from Bagdad to Tabriz); Reports on the meetings of the Bombay Geographical Society, September 1841 to May 1844, 169–86; x: Meeting 4 May 1843, Commander H.B. Lynch as one of twelve Resident Members. For the maps, e.g., Lieut. H.B. Lynch Note on [the] Part of the River Tigris, RGSA, JMS 9/43; Greenbough, Address 1841, xlviii-xlix.
51   Rawlinson, Address 1873, cited (with slight mistakes) by Lynch, Record, 76.
52   The Governor of India to Lieutenant E.P. Lynch, 16th Regiment Bombay Infantry, 18th January 1838, HBL, informing him that he had been nominated to serve with the British Detachment to Persia under Major General Sir Henry Bethume; Burke, Ireland, 741; H.M. Chichester, rev. Roger T. Stearn, 'Lynch, Patrick Edward', ODNB, 17257.
53   File holding about 200 pages describing his voyage [signature: General Edward Patrick Lynch (1809–84)], 1, HBL.

54 Major General Lynch to the Editor of Dublin University Magazine, Partry House, 4 February 1834, File, no signature, containing manuscript of his journey, about 200 pages, HBL. Cf. Lynch, Record, 108; Major E.P. Lynch, Journey from Baghdad to Tabriz, RGSA, JMS 9/42; Elizabeth Baigent, 'Lynch, Thomas Kerr', ODNB, 17261.
55 Guest, Expedition, 144-6.
56 ODNB, 17261; Lynch, Record, 134-5.
57 Lynch, Visit; Lorimer, Gazetteer, 226-7.
58 Lynch, Navigation; idem, Mesopotamia.
59 Costello, Ireland, 134-8.
60 Chesney, Narrative, 543-5; Fuller, Kerrymen, 69-70; Guest, Expedition, 41-2, 117-18.
61 Andrews, Landscape, 35-208; Doherty, Survey, 14-32; Edney, Mapping, 245-87 and passim.; Elizabeth Baigent, 'Colby, Thomas Frederick', ODNB, 5837. The bars were needed to compensate for the variations which could be caused by the metal measuring chains, used for distances in base-lines: Andrews, Landscape, 44-7. For the confusion while trying to adopt them into the Indian survey: Edney, Mapping, 246-7.
62 Fontanier, Narrative, 305-6.
63 Chesney, Narrative, II, 552; Guest, Expedition, 42-3.
64 ODNB, 242; Ainsworth, Obituary, 98; Guest, Expedition, 43.
65 Chesney, Narrative, 553-4.
66 Ainsworth, Narrative, I, vii-ix.
67 Ainsworth, Narrative, passim.
68 Denis Wright, 'Rassam, Hormuzd', ODNB, 35677. He was a younger brother of Christian Anthony.
69 RGSA, Council Minute Books, Oct 1830 – July 1841, 239 (The RGS [was] ready to contribute 500£, spread over two years, to explore the country of the Nestorian Christians in Kurdistan), 241, 244, 245, 250, 253, 255, 257, 262, 275, 280; Stafford, Murchinson, 95-7 (citation).
70 Ainsworth, Narrative; idem, Researches; idem, Travels.
71 Ainsworth, Ten Thousand, vii.
72 Guest, Expedition, 49, 81, 154; Ainsworth, Narrative, 36.
73 J.K. Laughton, rev. Elizabeth Baignet, 'Wellsted, James Raymons', ODNB, 29022; Dawson and Uphill, 437; Pfullmann, Entdeckerlexikon, 448-51.
74 Guest, Expedition, 17; J.K. Laughton, rev. Andrew Lambert, 'Malcolm, Sir Charles', ODNB, 17861; Robert Eric Frykenberg, 'Malcolm, Sir John', ODNB, 17864; Home, Royal Society, 324; Herman, Scots, 300-1; Lambert, Battlefleet, 184-6. For the most detailed study of Sir John Malcolm and his career, and of the Scottish influences and 'school of thought', see Mclaren, India, passim.
75 Dawson, Memoirs, I, 127-8, II, 55 (on lieutenant T.G. Carless), 195 ('an admirable survey'); EEEE, 3 (1993), 535-6 (citation); Searight, Charting; Bartlett, Edom, 20.
76 Elath, Routes, 80.
77 Wellsted, Memoir; Dawson, Memoirs, II, 38-40; Robin Bidwell, 'Haines, Stafford Bettesworth', ODNB, 37502; Pfullmann, Entdeckerlexikon, 239-40. Lieutenant Haines acted as chief surveying assistant to various captains in the survey of the gulf from 1820 to 1830.
78 Wellsted, Memoir; idem, Travels; idem, Book, 401; Markham, Persia, 431; Kelly, Britain, 371-4; Washington, Sketch, 247; Home, Royal Society, 318, 325.
79 Wellsted, Book, 401.
80 Ormsby, Narrative.
81 Elath, Britain, 55; Guest, Expedition, 21-2, 26.
82 Guest, Expedition, 28.

83 Guest, Expedition, 62–3, 163 note 1 (his sources).
84 Ainsworth, Narrative, I, 87.
85 Ainsworth, Narrative, I, 89.
86 Guest, Expedition, 28–9, 62–4, 80–3, 90–2, 154.
87 Dawson, Memoirs, II, 88–90 (citation); Kelly, Britain, 466–575.
88 Dawson, Memoirs, 89–90; J.K. Laughton, *rev.* Andrew Lambert, 'Jones, James Felix', *ODNB*, 15049; Burell, Preface; Jones, Journal (example of his scientific contributions); Jones, Baghdad.
89 Madden, Travels, I, 118–9; cf. J.M. Rigg, *rev.* Lynn Milne, 'Madden, Richard Robert', *ODNB*, 17753; Bartlett, Travellers.
90 David Steele, 'Temple, Henry John', *ODNB*, 27712; Webster, Policy, I, 82–7 (beginning of the Eastern Question), 255–346 (first Egyptian War), II, 523–776 (development of the Eastern Question and second Egyptian War).
91 Marlowe, Suez, 32–5.
92 Rochfort Scott, Rambles, II, 229. Cf. Webster, Policy, II, 543, 545; Perrier, La Syrie, 69; Prokesch-Osten, Mehmed-Ali, 67–73, 156–7; Carré, Voyageurs, 279–84; Hofman, Administration, 321; Kutluoğlu, Egypt, 40–1. Saul and Thobie, Militaires, 174–86 (a paper dealing with French military serving the Egyptians). For Hüsrev Paşa see Kutluoğlu, Egypt, 26–8, 44 n. 2.
93 Webster, Policy, II, 543, 545; Jochmus, Krieg, 11–13 (citation).
94 See for example Kutluoğlu, Question.
95 Vereté, Palmerston, 143–5. For the British consular service: Platt, Cinderella, esp. 125–79; Middleton, Administration, esp. chap. IX.
96 Tresse, Installation. Cf. Williams, Policy, 424–7.
97 Dawson and Uphill, 82; Bindoff, Representatives, 38–9; Eliav, Britain, 23–5 (his part in nominating a consul in Jerusalem). He is mentioned by many of the visitors and travellers. For his activity in Egypt see Kutluoğlu, Question, 99–129.
98 Moore started his career as *cancellier* to the embassy at Constantinople in 1822, served later as acting Consul-General in Syria and received the naval medal and a Turkish decoration: Boase, II, 952. See also: Bird, Bible, 317; Vereté, Consulate, 323–4, 331–2. Lindsay, Letters, iv, calls him 'Nathanael Moore, Esq.'. Cf. Wilkie's drawings of his wife in Arab dress and of his dragoman, Wilkie, Sketches, no. 13, 14; Eliav, Britain, 24–6, 114 n. 2.
99 Hurewitz, Dilomacy, I, 110–11; Williams, Policy, 294–6.
100 John Bowring, 'Report on the Commercial Statistics of Syria', in: Reports from the Commissioners, XXI (1840), 237–380, BL SPIS, B.S.Ref. 1. 1840[278.]XXI; Williams, Policy, 300–1. On Bowring: Gerald Stone, 'Bowring, Sir John', *ODNB*, 3087.
101 General Index to Accounts and Papers, &c., 1801–1852, 969, BL, Social Policy Information Service.
102 Bowring, Report (above, n. 100), 283–5.
103 Farah, Politics, 30–51; Kutluoğlu, Question, 151–5.
104 Vereté, Consulate, 319–35; cf. also idem, Restoration; Eliav, Britain, 21–30.
105 Vereté, Consulate; Eliav, Britain, 64–9.
106 Vereté, Consulate, 334–5; Carmel, Russia.
107 Vereté, Consulate, 335.
108 Vereté, Consulate, 336–41; idem, Restoration.
109 Graham, Britain, 274–8; Kelly, Mehemet 'Ali.
110 Elath, Routes, 100; http://weekly.ahram.org.eg/2003/658/chrncls.htm; Train From Cairo, 190–3, and pl. VII; Marlowe, Suez, 42–3 (names him R.H. Galloway); Hoskins, Routes, 231–2, 238–9, 292–5 (names him J.R. Galloway).
111 Train from Cairo, 193–4.
112 Train from Cairo, 195. For Harris: H.M. Chichester, *rev.* James Falkner, 'Harris, Sir William Cornwallis', *ODNB*, 12428.

113 Train from Cairo, 196–200.
114 Jochmus, Krieg, 28; H.M. Chichester, 'Michell, Edward Thomas (1786–1841)', *rev*. James Falkner, *ODNB*, 18654 (also for Jochmus); J.K. Laughton, *rev*. Andrew Lambert, 'Stopford, Sir Robert', *ODNB*, 26588.
115 Webster, Policy, II, 722–6. Jochmus published his own history of the events between 1840 and 1848 (Jochmus, Krieg), as well as a rather long report on 'a journey in the Balkan' he performed in 1847, where he – not surprisingly – added a 'Sketch of the Marches of Darius & Alexander, to the Danube, and the Passage of the Balkan' (Jochmus, Notes). Schur (Acre, 266) claims he was a converted Jew.
116 Heigel, 'Otto', *ADB*, 24 (1887), 691–9.
117 Jochmus, Krieg, 1–3; Webster, Policy, II, 722–6.
118 My thanks to Eran Dolev, who, interested in the grave of the British physician and pathologist Thomas Hodgkin (1798–1866, Cf. Amalie M. Kass, 'Hodgkin, Thomas', *ODNB*, 13429), who died of dysentery while escorting Moses Montefiore, took me to the cemetery; Acton, Letters, 33–5.
119 See fig. 15.
120 Kelly, Syria, 345; cf. Alderson, Acre, 26–38; Lord, England, 152–63. Joachim Prince Murat (1767–1815), Maréchal de France. Cf. the discussion of Oldfield's death, above, p. 47.
121 Sparrow, Secret Service, 191.
122 Alderson, Acre, 27, 30–1; Sparrow, Secret Service, 186–8, 190–1; Gichon, Napoleon, 127–43 and n. 14 on p. 264; Schur, Acre, 219–20, 225.
123 Sparrow, Secret Service, 192–3.
124 Marlowe, Relations, 18–22; Sparrow, Secret Service, 191–6; David Gates, 'Abercromby, Sir Ralph, of Tullibody', *ODNB*, 45.
125 Marlowe, Relations, 22–8.
126 Jackson, Pomp, 30–3; idem, Relations, 33–4.
127 Marlowe, Relations, 34–5.
128 Napier, Reminiscences; Marriott, Question, 237–45; Anderson, Question, 100–6; Breycha-Vauthier, Österreich, 20–5; Webster, Policy, I, 619–776. Cf. Clowes, History, VI, 310–23.
129 Lambert, Canon; Farah, Politics, 30–51; Kutluoğlu, Question; Said, Orientalism.
130 Clowes, History, VI, 252–61; Lambert, Battlefleet, 91–3.
131 Kutluoğlu, Question, 26–31, registers Hüsrev's enemies.
132 Farah, Politics, 32–3, 41–2; Kutluoğlu, Question, 167–70; G.C. Boase, *rev*. H.C.G. Matthew, 'Ponsonby, John', *ODNB*, 22499; Andrew Lambert, 'Napier, Sir Charles', *ODNB*, 19747.
133 Farah, Politics, 35–8.
134 Jochmus, Krieg, 2; Farah, Politics, 34–8 (Palmerston's speech, cited); Kutluoğlu, Question, 131–60.
135 *ODNB*, 26588; Jochmus, Krieg, 9. For a description in the formal history of the navy: Clowes, History, VI, 308–23; Lambert, Battlefleet, 38.
136 A personal description of Napier, the highly uncommon officer: Clowes, History, VI, 313, note 5; Jochmus, Krieg, 16–9; Kutluoğlu, Question, 167–82.
137 *ODNB*, 19747; Lambert, Battleships, 38, 91; Jackson, Pomp, 62. For the second Earl of Minto (1782–1859): Alsager Vian, *rev*. H.C.G. Matthew, 'Kynymound, Gilbert Elliott Murray', *ODNB*, 8662.
138 Clowes, History, VI, 312.
139 Jochmus, Krieg, passim; Lambert, Canon; Farah, Politics, 37–8 and n. 63.
140 Clowes, History, VI, 322.
141 Of the many detailed descriptions, see Prokesch-Osten, Mehmed-Ali, 156–7; Kutluoğlu, Question, 169–74.

142 R.H. Vetch, *rev.* James Falkner, 'Smith, Sir Charles Felix', *ODNB*, 25785.
143 Alderson, Acre, 47–57; Prokesch-Osten, Mehmed-Ali, 166–7; Clowes, History, VI, 314–22; Jochmus, Krieg, 19–21; Rustum, Notes; Lambert, Canon; Andrew Lambert, 'Napier, Sir Charles', *ODNB*, 19747; idem, Battlefleet, 90.
144 *ODNB*, 19747.
145 Jochmus, Krieg, 19–22; Lambert, Battlefleet, 38, 107; idem, Battleships, 15.
146 Matuszewicz, Notice; Rustum, Notes, 29–31 (and passim, a detailed description of Acre's fortifications); Schur, Acre, 261, 266–8.
147 Farah, Politics, 42–5.
148 Lambert, Battlefleet, 101–4 ('HMS *Excellent* and the profession of naval gunnery').
149 Alderson, Acre, 51 and n. 17, 59–60. Cf. J.K. Laughton, *rev.* Andrew Lambert, 'Hastings, Sir Thomas', *ODNB*, 12586.
150 Lambert, Battlefleet, 95.
151 Charlewood, Passages, 52; Clowes, History, VI, 315. Cf. Chesney, Narrative, 548–9; Guest, Expedition, passim, esp. 153.
152 2nd Lieutenant 1833; Lieutenant 1836; 2nd Captain 1845; Captain 1846; died at Argostall, Cephalonia, 8 August 1852.
153 Jones, Surveys.
154 Rochfort Scott, Rambles.
155 Acton, Letters, 33–4.
156 NA, WO 78/1000.
157 NA, M.P.K. 294, WO78/1000 (former signature M.R. 161).
158 Ben-Arieh, Maps, 69–71; cf. Van de Velde, Memoir, 5; Alderson, Acre; Jones, Surveys, 60–2.
159 Williams, City, Supplement, 9–13; cf. P. Courtney, *rev.* Triona Adams, 'Williams, George (1814–1878)', *ODNB*, 29505.
160 Williams, City, Supplement, 9. For early plans for an organized trigonometric measurement of Palestine see Goren, Sacred, 92–100.
161 O'Byrne, II, 1152; Sharp, Symonds; Andrew Lambert, 'Symonds, Sir William', *ODNB*, 26893 (citations); Boase, III, 860; Clowes, History, VI, 181 passim; Lambert, Last Sailing, 67–87; and most detailed, concerning his contribution to the development and change of British battleships: idem, Battleships, passim; idem, Battlefleet, esp. 67–87.
162 Alderson, Unterschied.
163 Symonds to Washington, 4 Somerset Place, Somerset House 21 February 1842, RGSA, RGS corr block 1841–50: Symonds, Lt. Thomas F. L.
164 Hamilton, Address 1842, lx–lxi.
165 Map of Syria, cf. Jones, Surveys, 38–9. Arrowsmith was also fellow founder of the RGS: Elizabeth Baignet, 'Arrowsmith, John', *ODNB*, 701. Cf. NA WO 78/1000 (24), for Rochfort Scott's 'Military Report on Syria', which came with the map.
166 Goren, Pioneer.
167 Robinson, Researches Palestine, 10. It seems that none of them had already been a member of the society, and Robinson's mistake derives probably from the fact that Symonds received the Society's Gold Medal.
168 Alderson, Acre.
169 Relief Map, Maps Collection, BL, Maps R.M. 88. See: Murchinson, Address 1845, cviii.
170 Ritter, Comparative, II, 85.
171 Ritter, Entdeckungen; Robinson, Researches Palestine, 11–15. Cf. Goren, Pioneer, 112–23.
172 Alderson, Acre; see 54 for details from Symonds' survey of the city walls.
173 Cf. Goren, Zieht hin, 104–10; Goren, Petermann; Elizabeth Baignet, 'Petermann, August Heinrich', *ODNB*, 41218.

174 Goren, Kiepert.
175 Kiepert, Map 1842.
176 Van de Velde, Memoir, 1, 16. Cf. Frederiks, Velde; Ben-Arieh, Rediscovery, 130–1; Vries, Kaart; Bartlett, Mapping, 113–18.
177 Zimmermann, Schulz; idem, Analyse, 5. Cf: Goren-Morag, Mapping; Goren, Zieht hin, 194–201.
178 Gelber, Pre-Zionist; Goren, Zieht hin, 262–9.
179 Zimpel, Jerusalem; idem, Plan. For Emmerich: Brentano, Leiden.
180 Van de Velde, Memoir, 4–6.
181 Van de Velde, Memoir, 1.
182 Van de Velde, Memoir, 4–6, 22.
183 Goren, Zieht hin, 222–43.
184 Tobler, Planography, 16–19.
185 J.K. Laughton, *rev.* Andrew Lambert, 'Codrington, Sir Henry John', *ODNB*, 5797 (citation); J.K. Laughton, *rev.* Roger Morris, 'Codrington, Sir Edward', *ODNB*, 5796. For the *Asia* and its part in Navarino see Lambert, Battlefleet, 100, 178–9.
186 George Biddlecombe to Beaufort, H M Ship Talbot, Corfu, 8th April 1840, Constantinople, 23rd Nov 1840, January 5th 1841, 1st March 1841, July 4th, 1841, HON, Incoming letters prior to 1857 B, 124, 128, 129, 142, 143. Cf. Dawson, Memoirs, II, 80–1; Lambert, Battlefleet, 96. For the map see also Zvieli, Galili and Rosen, Acre, 65–7.
187 This sketch was used by Alderson for the 'Plan of St. Jean D'Acre' on his description of the bombardment (Alderson, Acre, 46–8, pl. X).
188 Remarks made on board HM Steam Vessel Cyclops Between the 1st of January and 31st of December 1842, by James Thomas Russell Master, HON, Miscellaneous Papers 83, 231–6.
189 H.M. Chichester, *rev.* James Falkner, 'Napier, Edward Delaval Hungerford Elers', *ODNB*, 19750.
190 Napier to Hamilton, Jaffa, 21 January 1841, Napier to Staunton, on the Nile near Cairo, 10 February 1841, RGSA, RGS corr. Block 1841–50: Napier, Major E; Hamilton, Address 1842, lix-lx.
191 Wilde, Narrative. For Wilde, Oscar W.'s father, and his voyage, cf. Tobler, Bibliographia, 161 ('an exact and well-educated observer'); Costello, Ireland, 104, 132–4; James McGeachie, 'Wilde, Sir William Robert Wills', *ODNB*, 29403.
192 Mill, RGS, 16–41; Fleming, Barrow; Richard Davenport-Hines, 'Staunton, Sir George Thomas', *ODNB*, 26325; Lambert, Franklin, passim.; J.M.R. Cameron, 'Barrow, Sir John', *ODNB*, 1544.
193 Napier, Reminiscences.

PART 2

Chapter 4

1 Seché, Entstehung; Horowitz, Jordan, esp. 1–34; Bookman et al., Quaternary.
2 Allen, Dead Sea, I, vi. Cf.: Elath, Routes, 115. Manuscript: RGSA, No. 1853 (2): Captain W. Allen R.N.; Allen, Obituary; Williams, Policy, 99–100 (commercial aspects of his Africa delegation). For his biography: Dawson, Memoirs, II, 61–2; Boase, I, 53; J.S. Keltie, *rev.* Andrew Lambert, 'Allen, William', *ODNB*, 393.
3 Allen, Dead Sea, 238.
4 Allen to Palmerstone, Athenaum Club, 15 July 1853, NA, HO 45/4946; The copies of a printed paper containing details of a proposed ship canal through the Dead Sea, by Captain W. Allen RN, 1854, NAM, Outram Papers, 9210\127–55.

5   Allen, Dead Sea.
6   Allen, Dead Sea, I, 318–37. All these explorers are dealt with in this book.
7   Allen, Watershed; idem, Attempt.
8   Allen, Dead Sea, 343.
9   Humboldt, Asien, 544–5; idem, Cosmos, 301 and note. For his part in the geographic study of the Holy Land see Goren, Zieht hin, passim. Livingstone, Geographical Tradition, 113-38, and Driver, Geography, 11–17, 34–7, are mainly concerned with the influence of Humboldt and 'Humboldtian science' on Geography and the RGS.
10   Ritter, Jordan, 1. For Ritter and his place in the study of Palestine: Goren, Ritter; idem, Zieht hin, 68–83.
11   Ritter, Jordan, 9–15.
12   Boggis, Jordan, 14–21.
13   Gaillardot, Note, 859; cf. Goren, Chase.
14   Judith Bronkhurst, 'Hunt, William Holman', ODNB, 34058; Ben-Arieh, Painting, 116–26.
15   Lynch, Narrative, 310–11.
16   Van de Velde, II, 124–5.
17   Van de Velde, Narrative, II, 116–18.
18   Van de Velde, Map. Cf. Fischer, Geschichte, 65–8.
19   N. Perrin, Forward, in: Kreiger, Waters, 8.
20   Maundrell, Journey, 16–17; Fischer, Geschichte, 19–20. For the 'Island' see, for example, Fischer, Geschichte, 63, 51 ('the Island rudschm el-bahr is missing by Robinson and by Kiepert'); Klein, Fluctuations; Horowitz, Jordan; Bookman et al., Quaternary.
21   Aiken, Geography, 89–132; Thomas Hamilton, rev. H.C.G. Matthew, 'Porter, Josias Leslie', ODNB, 22574; Reed, Cabinet, 207; Porter, Giant Cities, 112.
22   Seché, Entstehung; Klein, Fluctuations (for 1800–30: N126–N142); Horowitz, Jordan, 25–42, esp. 28–31.
23   Wright, Notes, 252.
24   Werblowsky, Meaning, 1. Cf., e.g., Van de Velde, Narrative, II, 124–5.
25   Gollwitzer, Palästinafahrten, 288–9; Said, Orientalism, 168–77; Goren, Zieht hin, 33–4 (Michaelis behind Niebuhr's expedition); 56 (Büsching's Holy Land studies).
26   Schubert, Erdl, 892. Cf. Robinson, Depression, 15 (citation); Bookman et al., Quaternary (the whole discussion).
27   For discussions of the Dead Sea in historical sources, and what can be learnt and used in current studies, cf. Klein, Fluctuations; idem, Evidence; idem, Fluctuations of the Level; Horowitz, Jordan; Bookman et al., Quaternary.
28   Bekenmeier, Reisen, 72–5; Fischer, Geschichte, 63, 13–14; Bartlett, Mapping, 43–8.
29   Shaw, Travels, 346. Italics in the original. Cf. Peta Rée, 'Shaw, Thomas', ODNB, 25269; Bartlett, Mapping, 95.
30   Shaw, Travels, 347.
31   Tobler, Bibliographia, 119–20; Ish-Shalom, Travels, 30–1.
32   Egmont and Heyman, Travels, I, 340–1.
33   Busching, Beschreibung; idem, Erdbeschreibung, 249–346 (esp. 249).
34   Bannister, Survey, 135–7. For Banks as a 'geographical collector' cf. Miller, Banks; Livingstone, Tradition, 126–33, 156–60; Driver Geography, esp. 27–37; Mackay, Agents. For an early discussion of the history of the examination of Dead Sea water specific weight, beginning already with Aristototeles and Vespasian, see Klein, Fluctuations, N16-N17.
35   Irby and Mangles, Travels, 139. Cf. Manley and Rée, Salt, passim; Ben-Arieh, Rediscovery, 52–5, 79–84; Fischer, Geschichte, 39–40; Bartlett, Edom, 17–19;

J.K. Laughton, *rev.* Andrew Lambert, 'Irby, Charles Leonard', *ODNB*, 14443; J.K. Laughton, *rev.* Andrew Lambert, 'Mangles, James', *ODNB*, 17933; Ben-Arieh, Maps; Dawson and Uphill, 29 (Bankes), 214–5 (Irby), 245 (Legh), 273 (Mangles).

36 Kreiger, Waters, 38.
37 Ehrenberg, Untersuchung. Cf. Humboldt, Ehrenberg; Goren, Zieht hin, 60–2, and bibliography there.
38 M. Bertou, Jerusalem, Ap. 29, rec. 15 June 38, to the President of the Geographical Society, RGSA, RGS Cor. Block 1834–40: Bertou, J. de.
39 Goren, Zieht hin, 169–72.
40 Ehrenberg, Untersuchungen, 191–2.
41 Nissenbaum, Studies; idem, Chemical; idem, Analyses.
42 Nissenbaum, Studies. Cf. F. Hoeffer, 'Lavoisier', *NBG*, 30 (1859), 2–19.
43 Perry, Experiments; Nissenbaum, Analyses, 279; Klein, Fluctuations, N16. Perry collected water samples also from the hot springs in Tiberias and from Hamam Farun in the Sinai Peninsula. Cf. Elizabeth Baignet, 'Perry, Charles', *ODNB*, 76839.
44 Tuchman, Bible, 156–7; Costello, Ireland, 109–13. Cf. Elizabeth Baigent, 'Pococke, Richard', *ODNB*, 22432; Bartlett, Travellers, n.p.; idem, Mapping, 95, 100.
45 Pococke, Beschreibung, II, 52–6.
46 Nissenbaum, Studies, n.p.; idem, Chemical, 281.
47 Klaproth, Analysis; idem, Untersuchungen; Weishaar, Untersucuhung, 1–3; Nissenbaum, Chemical, 298.
48 Forbin, Voyage, 404–6; Gay-Lussac, Analyse; Essai de l'eau; Weishaar, Untersuchung, 5–6; Gmelin, Resultate; Klein, Fluctuations, N16–N17; Nissenbaum, Chemical, 285. Cf. J. Lamoureaux, 'Gay-Lussac', *NBG*, 19 (1858), 758–75; L. Louvet, 'Forbin', *NBG*, 18 (1858), 151–7; Dawson and Uphill, 153. Arago – French Catalan mathematician, physicist, astronomer and politician.
49 Weishaar, Untersuchung, 6. Cf. Ladenburg, 'Gmelin', *ADB*, 9 (1879), 266. No biographical details concerning the other two.
50 Madden, Travels, II, 251, 254–60, cited also by Costello, Ireland, 107, 128–9.
51 J.Y. Mason, Report of the Secretary of the Navy, with a Report made by Lieutenant W. F. Lynch…, BSOG, Ob 1428, 88.
52 Kawerau, Amerika, passim; Oren, Power, 122–33; Makdisi, Artillery, passim.
53 Bird, Notice, 21–4 (citation p. 21); idem, Notice Hall; idem, Notices; Hall, Description.
54 Fischer, Geschichte, 92.
55 Ben-Yehuda, Eretz Israel; Brawer, Centenary; Klein, Klein, Fluctuations, 14–20; Kreiger, Waters, 53–60; Vardi, Review, 34–5; Horowitz, Jordan, 25–34.
56 Goren, Level. The following discussion is, naturally, based on this paper.
57 Brawer, Centenary.
58 Van de Velde, Memoir, 168.
59 Vardi, Heights.
60 Schur, Dead Sea.
61 Kreiger, Waters.
62 L. Louvet, 'Marmont', *NBG*, 32, 867–99; Saint Marc, Marmont; Dawson and Uphill, 277.
63 Raguse, Voyage, II, 331–2; idem, State, v-vi.
64 Raguse, Voyage; idem, State (citation: iv).
65 Raguse, State, 298–334.
66 Raguse, State, 223; idem, Voyage, II, 259–63.
67 Raguse, State, 265–6, 269–94.
68 Raguse, Voyage, III, 3–113, 8 to 29 September 1834.
69 Raguse, Voyage, III, 9.

70 Raguse, Voyage, III, 23-5, 38-9. General Jean Baptiste Kléber (1753-1800) had been left as the commander when his superior returned to France, and was killed by an Egyptian assassin.
71 Raguse, Voyage, III, 79-84.
72 Raguse, Voyage, III, 67-78.
73 Fischer, Geschichte, 63, 42, 93.
74 Raguse, Voyage, III, 84-5.
75 Ritter, Comparative, II, 80-1; Van de Velde, Memoir, 15-16; Fischer, Geschichte, 43-5 (detailed list of Berghaus' sources). For Berghaus: Engelmann, Berghaus.
76 Berghaus, Map; Berghaus and Stülpnagel, Palestine; Engelmann, Atlas. Cf. Wilson, Surveys, 212; Fischer, Geschichte, 43-5; Goren, Zieht hin,92-5.
77 Berghaus, Memoir; idem, Memoir Arabia. Cf. Goren, Zieht hin, 92-5.
78 Van de Velde, Memoir, 15-16; Wilson, Surveys, 212 (citation). For Wilson see R.H. Vetch, rev. J.R. Smith, 'Wilson, Sir Charles William', ODNB, 36951.
79 Berg Sinai. For Rüppell: ADB, 29 (1889), 707-14; Dawson and Uphill, 368; Goren, Zieht hin, 48-50.
80 Manley and Rée, Salt. In addition to the story of Salt, the book reveals an intensive study of his connections with Burckhardt.
81 Koner, Antheil, 392; Schur, Travellers, 64-5; Goren, Zieht hin, 48-50; cf. Rüppell, Itinéraire. The society was named after its founder, the physician J.C. Senckenberg.
82 First published in the periodical of the Gotha observatory: Rüppell, Observation; idem, Carte. So, for example, d'Anville's map of the 1760s (fig. 35), which shows a mountain range (Gebbel Dahab) separating both bays. Cf. Ritter, Comparative, I, 46-51.
83 Berghaus, Memoir Arabia, 7, 23. The editorial of the AEVS gives 7,047 feet (Berg Sinai, 176), i.e., 2,168.3 metres.

Chapter 5
1 Ritter, Jordan, 15, 21-4; Ben-Arieh, Pioneer; Goren, Zieht hin, 36-48; Schäbler, Seetzen; Schienerl, Seetzen, 59-63; Bartlett, Edom, 15-16; Pfullmann, Entdeckerlexikon, 402-8.
2 Kruse, Seetzen, I, 426-9.
3 Kruse, Seetzen, II, 217-74.
4 Kruse, Seetzen, II, 239.
5 Kruse, Seetzen, II, 293-385; Ritter, Jordan, 21-7; Fischer, Geschichte, 63, 32-3; Schur, Dead Sea, 3-4.
6 Carne, Letters, II, 14 ('Mr. H.'); idem, Syria, 70. Cf. G.C. Boase, rev. Elizabeth Baignet, 'Carne, John', ODNB, 4714; Dawson and Uphill, 213.
7 Fischer, Geschichte, 63, 34.
8 Kruse, Seetzen, II, 241.
9 Kruse, Seetzen, II, 242-3. For 'the Linnaean travel' cf. Koerner, Purposes.
10 Kruse, Seetzen, II, 371-3.
11 Seetzen, Map. Cf. Ritter, Jordan, 15, 21-4; Fischer, Geschichte, 63, 35-6; Bartlett, Mapping, 104-7.
12 Lindenau, Seetzen.
13 Lindenau, Seetzen, 545-6; cited in Berghaus, Memoir, 7-8.
14 Kruse, Seetzen, II, 363.
15 Kruse, Seetzen, II, 330.
16 Lindenau, Seetzen, 542; D'Anville, Map. Cf. Fischer, Geschichte, 63, 27-9; Godlewska, Geography, 47-8; Bartlett, Mapping, 100-3.
17 Burckhardt, Syria, 390.

18 Stebbing, Christians, 182.
19 Arthur Burns, 'Stebbing, Henry', *ODNB*, 26337.
20 E.g.: Vilnay, Dead Sea, 29–31; idem, Costigan; Kreiger, Waters, 53–60; Costello, Explorers, 91–4; Eriksen, Explorers, 11–51; Goren, Nicolayson, 65–72, 89–94; Bartlett, Travellers.
21 Corcoran, Clongowes, 174 (John, Silvester and Christopher Costigan studied there 1819–26); Costello, Costigan; idem, Explorers; idem, Ireland, 97–104; Eriksen, Costigan; idem, Illness; idem, Explorers, 11–33; Boggis, Jordan, 22 (citation).
22 TCD MS 869/1: The papers of Major Henry Charles Sirr (1764–1841), 59–116.
23 John Costigin to Beaufort, Magdalene St. Drogheda, Ireland, 5 July 1834, HON, Incoming letters prior to 1857, C 722. For Edgeworth: W.J. McCormack, 'Edgeworth, Maria', *ODNB*, 8476; cf. Landy, Beaufort, 328. The letter mentions Captain Ross, probably James Clark R. (1800–62), 'who wrote on steam warfare and took the steam powered Victory to the Arctic', and Costigan's propeller patent. My gratitude to Andrew Lambert, citation from his mail.
24 Masterman, Explorations; idem, Explorers; Costello, Explorers; idem, Costigan, 214; idem, Ireland, pp. 97–104; Eriksen, Illness; idem, Explorers, 11–51; Kreiger, Waters, 53–60.
25 Information supplied by Linde Luney, Dictionary of Irish Biography, Royal Irish Academy.
26 Webber Smith, Athos; John Washington to Lieutenant Webber Smyth, 6 March 1837, RGSA, Letter Book, 1836–1840, 81; Webber Smith, Map; 'Wyld, James', *DNB* 21, 1148–9.
27 Stephens, Incidents, II, 30, 201–2, 213–5; Hagen, Maya. For a detailed description of Stephens' map see Vilnay, Dead Sea, 32–3; cf. also Bartlett, Edom, 20–1.
28 Masterman, Explorations, 407–12; Eriksen, Explorers, 35–42; Goren, Nicolayson, 65–72, 89–94 [English text].
29 Burton, Narrative, 49. Cf. Costello, Ireland, 132.
30 Paxton, Letters, 18, 233–4, 261–3.
31 Robinson, Syria, 2. Eliav (Britain, 91) mentions a Giuseppe (Jusuf) Matback, first British vice-consul in Jaffa, holding the post from 1834 to 1847.
32 Ainsworth, Narrative, I, 66.
33 Allen, Dead Sea, I, 10–11.
34 Hagen, Maya, 28–30; Kreiger, Waters, 53.
35 Volney, Voyage; M. Avenel, 'Volney', *NBG*, 46 (1866), 347–51; Dawson and Uphill, 427–8; Said, Orientalism, 168–71. Cf. Hagen, Maya, 31–42.
36 Laborde, Journey; cf. Walckenaer, Rapport; Bartlett, Edom, 19–20. Biographies: L.L., 'Laborde', *NBG*, 28 (1859), 387–90; P., 'Linant', *NBG*, 31 (1860), 246–7; Dawson and Uphill, 256–7; Pfullmann, Entdeckerlexikon, 176–8, 286; Kurz and Linant de Bellefonds; Linant de Bellefonds, Cairo.
37 Marlowe, Suez, 42–4; Della Dora, Landscapes, 534–5.
38 Hagen, Maya, 50; Finnie, Pioneers, 152–60; Kreiger, Waters, 53–4.
39 Stephens, Incidents, II, 47–66; Hagen, Maya, 50–5; Finnie, Pioneers, 167–8.
40 Stephens, Incidents, II, 71.
41 Mentioned by almost every traveller. E.g., Lindsay, Letters, 246.
42 Lindsay, Letters, 201.
43 Lindsay, Letters., 202. Von Hagen, Stephens' biographer, mistakenly wrote that he did sail on the lake, and cites as proof a letter from W.F. Lynch to his compatriot, which included instructions for the needed gear for a such a sailing (Hagen, Maya, 55–6; Lynch, Narrative, Preface, vi).
44 Stephens, Incidents, II, 201–2, 213–5. Also partly cited by Masterman, Explorations, 407–14; cf. Kreiger, Waters, 54–7. For an interesting description of the village, dating from September 1834, see Raguse, Voyage, III, 74–7.

45   Hagen, Maya, XIII.
46   Macalister, Masterman; Shwake, Krankenhauswesens, I, 166, 185–7; Crombie, Friedman, 28–9. For a most detailed description and evaluation of his times and activities in the Holy Land see Perry and Lev, Medicine, 86–102.
47   Masterman, Summary. The periodical reports: Masterman, Observations; Macalister, Gleanings. Cf. Watson, Fifty Years, 171; Underhill, Levels; Raz, Dead Sea, 16; Klein, Fluctuations, 54–5.
48   Gray Hill, Dead Sea; Wilson, Dead Sea. Cf. Wahrman, Gray Hill.
49   Macalister, Observations; Masterman, Observations, 34 (1902), 155. Macalister wrote Masterman's obituary (Macalister, Masterman) and dedicated his book to him (idem, Excavation). Cf. Brian Fagan, 'Macalister, Robert Alexander Stewart', ODNB, 57475.
50   PEF, (Jer)/5: Minutes of the Transactions of the Jerusalem Literary Society, Founded November 20. 1849; Macalister, Gleanings, esp. 40 (1908), 52.
51   Masterman, Explorers, 13.
52   Masterman, Explorations; idem, Explorers, 13–19. Cf. also idem, History.
53   Eliav, Britain, 69–81; Deborah Manley, 'Finn, Elizabeth Ann', ODNB, 50902.
54   Finn, Stirring Times, II, 89–124; Macalister, Gleanings, 40 (1908), 39.
55   PEF, (Jer)/5, 254–63.
56   Schwake, Krankenhauswesens, I, 103, 113–14; Gidney, History, 119–21; Costello, Ireland, 66–8; Perry and Lev, Medicine, 28–30, 60–1. For the LJS, its history and activity in Palestine, see Gidney, History; Crombie, Zion.
57   Carmel, Christen, 17–24; Crombie, Zion, 20–5, 47–85; Schwake, Krankenhauswesens, I, 117–52; Lieber, Purchase.
58   PEF, (Jer)/5.
59   Goren, Nicolayson, 67–72, 94–89.
60   Masterman, Explorers, 14.
61   Boggis, Jordan, 25, 94; Hoade, Ireland, 72; Vilnai, Costigan; idem, Dead Sea, 31, 34–5; Benvenisti, Cemeteries, 122–5; Costello, Ireland, 101–2. The stone had been recently moved and is displayed in the yard of the Franciscan museum in the Flagellatio.
62   Costello, Ireland, 97.
63   Lynch, Narrative, 310–11 (due to its significance, part of this is cited for the second time); J.Y. Mason, Report of the Secretary of the Navy, with a Report made by Lieutenant W. F. Lynch..., BSOG, Ob 1428, 16.
64   Wilde, Narrative, note on 549–50. Cf. also Weber Smith, Athos, citation 64.
65   Carne, Syria, 71–2; Costello, Ireland, 103.
66   Joshua 2.
67   Stebbing, Christians, 182–3; Eriksen, Explorers, 48.
68   Gadsby, Wanderings, I, 508; Dawson and Uphill, 159. The Armenian Cemetery borders on the Franciscan.
69   Boggis, Jordan, 22–5.
70   Eriksen, Illness.
71   Jampoler, Lynch.
72   Michael Friedlaender to Andrew Jampoler, 12 Oct 2003, author's collection.
73   Ritter, Jordan, 17.
74   Wilde, Narrative, 549 note.
75   Egmont and Heyman, Travels, I, 342.
76   Chateaubriand, Itinéraire, I, 355; cited also by Kreiger, Waters, 53.
77   Eriksen, Explorers, 30–2.
78   Carne, Letters, II, 1–23, citation 14.

79 Paxton, Letters. Interestingly enough, he is not mentioned in books dealing with American missionaries in the East (e.g., Kawerau, Amerika, list of missionaries, 650).
80 Shanks, Anti Slavery, 133 and passim.
81 Paxton, Memoir, 296–9.
82 Paxton, Letters, 160–1; Kawerau, Amerika, esp. 254–7.
83 Paxton, Letters, 162.
84 Paxton, Letters, 224–6. For Lindsay and Wilson see 189–96.
85 Paxton, Letters, 162–3.
86 For all details concerning Moore and Beek's expedition see below.
87 Progress 1836–7, 183.
88 RGSA, RGS Correspondence 1834–40: Beek, W. (citation); RGSA, JMS 9/9.
89 Dead Sea.
90 Ritter, Comparative, III, 127 note 1.
91 Kreiger, Waters, 60–1. The same description is repeated in some Israeli studies, e.g. Vardi, Height, 23–5.
92 See above, pp. 224–6.
93 Moore, Gentleman; R.V. Comerford, 'Moore, George Henry (1810–1870)', ODNB, 19114.
94 Moore 1837, MS 3509 – Dead Sea Diary; MS 3510 – Syrian Diary, NLI. The first diary was mentioned by Costello in his pioneering paper: Costello, Explorers, 96. He used parts of it in his book: idem, Ireland, 105–7. The diaries were also intensively used by Moore's son, Colonel Maurice G. Moore, for the biography of his father (Moore, Gentleman, n. 15). My deepest gratitude to Dr. Noel Kissane, former manager of the Department of Manuscripts in the National Library of Ireland, for supplying me with the microfilm, and to the late Prof. Kenelm V. Gow from Halifax, Canada, grandson of Nina Louisa Mary, fourth child of G.H. Moore, for permitting me to use the material in my publications.
95 Schubert, Erdl, 891.
96 William Beek to RGS, 24th April (1841?), RGSA, RGS Journal Mss. Middle East, 1837 & 1841; Moore to Mother, London, 13 November 1837, NLI, Ms 890: G.H. Moore II.
97 The whole project is described in detail in the Dead Sea Diary (MS 3509). See also: Moore, Gentleman, 32–43 (the travels), 44–72 (the story of the Dead Sea exploration).
98 Robinson, Syria, 4–5.
99 Moore, Gentleman; idem, G.H. Moore; Hone, Moores; Kevin Coyne, 'The Moores of Moorehall', doon.mayo-ireland.ie/moores.html, 4.
100 Freeman, Portrait, 8–29; Hone, Moore, 16–43; Kevin Coyne, 'The Moores of Moorehall', doon.mayo-ireland.ie/moores.html, 3–4; Edwin Gilcher, 'Moore, George Augustus', ODNB, 35089.
101 Burke, II, 2640; Burke, Gentry, 492. My gratitude to Patricia (great granddaughter of G.H. Moore) and Philip Deane of Steyning, West Sussex, for the family tree, which goes back to Judge Sir Thomas More (1451–1530).
102 Moore, Gentleman, 1–6.
103 Certificate, 12.12.1780, John Moore of Moore Hall Esqre. to Alexander McDonnell Attny., The King against John Moore Esqre., 5th Septembre 1798, NLI, Ms. 889: G.H. Moore I.; Pedigree in Spanish of the family of Moore of Moore Hall, co. Mayo, NLI, Ms 9012; A Map of Moorehall, in the Barony of Carra, Co. Mayo, by order of George Moore, by Richard Crisham, May 1809, NLI, Ms 10, 165; Kevin Coyne, 'The Moores of Moorehall', doon.mayo-ireland.ie/moores.html.

104 All the descriptions from drawings made according to the reminiscences of two people employed in Moore Hall, kept in the Community Room, St. Mary Catholic Church, Carnacon. My deepest gratitude to Art Ò Súilleabháin, who first revealed to me the secrets of Moore Hall, and whose knowledge of the history of the region is of crucial importance for this study. Cf. Bence-Jones, Guide, 210–11.

105 A document dated c. 1870, lists the 'Property owners County Mayo': Major-General Edward P. Lynch, Partry House, Ballinrobe 1237 Acres; George A. Moore, Moorehall, Ballyglass 12371 Acres; The Marquess of Sligo, Westport House, Westport 114,881 Acres; Sir Robert Lynch Blosse, bart., Atrhavallie House, Balla, 17,555 Acres (http://www.cmcrp.net/Mayo/Landowner1.html).

106 Letters to 2nd Marchioness and Lord Altamont [3rd Marquess] from his Brothers, WEP. I thank Birgid Clesham for the information. For a thorough study of Western Ireland landowners 'tribal families', see Melvin, Galway.

107 Letters to 2nd Marchioness and Lord Altamont [3rd Marquess] from his brothers, Lord John Browne, Royal Navy and Lord James Browne, 9th Lancers, NLI.

108 Cf. Ridden, Britishness.

109 Letters from Moore to his parents, St. Mary's College, Oscott, January 1826–June 1827, NLI, Ms. 889: G.H. Moore I, 10–26; ODNB, 19114.

110 Hone, Papers, 34–5.

111 Money recruited for G.H. Moore Esqre from 1 May 1832 to 1 May 1839, NLI, Ms. 890: G.H. Moore II. In these 6¼ years, which included all his voyages, he spent £3,712 and received only £2,500, leaving him in a deficit of £1,212. Cf. Hone, Moores, 61–3.

112 Moore to Mother, May 1833, NLI, Ms. 890: G.H. Moore II., 72.

113 Louisa Moore to Lord Sligo, Moore Hall, 23 and 28 November 1833, TCD MS 7762–72, 206 (citations), 208; NLI, Ms. 890: G.H. Moore II, 54–80; cf. Hone, Papers, 35–9. The Most Noble, the Marquess of Sligo, owned, in addition to the Westport House, co. Mayo, also Brownstown Lodge, co. Kildare and 2 Mansfield Street, London (Jane Lyons, 'From Ireland', http://www.from-ireland.net/history/offauth/mayo1834. html).

114 Chambers, Granuaile. Sligoville, called after him, was the first free village in Jamaica.

115 Moore to Mother, Cheltenham 1833, NLI, Ms. 890: G.H. Moore II, 77. Cf. Mansel, Grand Tour.

116 Jane Lyons, 'From Ireland', http://www.from-ireland.net/history/offauth/mayo 1834.html; Melvin, Galway, 344–8 and pl. 10.3 presenting Dalgan House; Hone, Moores, 67.

117 Kutluoğlu, Question, 105–7.

118 Moore, Gentleman, 28; Hone, Moores, 72. Alexej Fedorowitsch Orlów (1787–1861), military commander and diplomat, was engaged in the wars against the Ottomans as well as in the treaties signed with them.

119 Hugh Hammersley to Mrs. Moore, London, 2 January 1835, NLI, MS 890: G.H. Moore II, 55, 82; cited also by Hone, Moore, 71–2; Hone, Moores, 71–2.

120 DSD, 135.

121 NLI, Ms 890: G.H. Moore II, 83; DSD, 60.

122 Kirwan, Notes, title. The regiment gained fame for its part in the first Anglo-Afghan war.

123 Moore, Gentleman, xvii; Hone, Papers, 43–4.

124 Hone, Moore, 85–6; idem, Moores, 74–100 (the most detailed description of the development of the relationship between Edgeworth and the Moores); Edgeworth, Memoir, III, 178–85. Maria Edgeworth is mentioned intensively

in Louisa Moore's letters; e.g., Louisa Moore to Prof. William Hamilton, Observatory, Dublin, Moore Hall, 19 July 1836(?), TCD MS 7762-72, 572. Her first visit to Western Ireland was in late 1833 (*ODNB*, 8476).

125 Edgeworth, Memoir, 185, in a letter dated 15 April 1837, i.e., before Moore's return; cf. Landy, Beaufort, 328.
126 Hone, Moore, 87; Freeman, Portrait, 12 (citations).
127 Moore, Gentleman, xiii-xvii, 303-4.
128 DSD, 60.
129 DSD, 60-1.
130 NLI, MS 890: G.H. Moore II, no. 83. My thanks to Milka Levy-Rubin for the translation.
131 Moore, Gentleman, 33-43.
132 DSD, entries.
133 Moore to Mother, London, 13 November 1837, NLI, MS 890: G.H. Moore II. Cited in Moore, Gentleman, 71.
134 Driver, Geography, 93-106, citation 93. Cf. Hargreaves, Reade.
135 Letters to Prof. William Hamilton, Observatory, Dublin, 1834-1836, TCD MS 762-72, 390, 397, 402, 405, 423, 429, 431 (Moore, Augustus), 514, 571 (Moore, Louisa); Hone, Papers, 39-42. Cf. Albert C. Lewis, 'Hamilton, Sir William Rowan', *ODNB*, 12148.
136 Moore to Mother, Bath, 22 February 1833, NLI, Ms. 890: G.H. Moore II, 63; Moore, Gemtleman, 73; Hohn, Moore, 89.
137 Moore, G.H. Moore, 19-20.
138 Moore, Gentleman, 97-8, 101-2. Of the three sons, two – Augustus and John – died in riding accidents.
139 Moore, G.H. Moore, 20; Kevin Coyne, 'The Moores of Moorehall', doon.mayo-ireland.ie/moores.html, 2-3.
140 Donnelly, Landlords, 336-41.
141 Moore, G.H. Moore, 18.
142 *ODNB*, 19114; Moore, G.H. Moore, 27-32.
143 Brown, Politics, 129.
144 Moore, G.H. Moore, 20-2.
145 Moore, G.H. Moore, 22-7.
146 Moore, Confessions, 6.
147 Notice of assignment of mortgage Debt of £2,817.15 and securities for the same for securing £1,100 and interest. To the Most Noble John Marquis of Sligo and Mark Blake Esquire trustees of the settlement made on the marriage of George Henry Moore and Miss Mary Blake. Dated this 18th day of December in the year of our Lord 1852, NLI, File: Legal corresp re M/S G.H. Moore & Mary Blake. My gratitude to Patricia (great-granddaughter of G.H. Moore) and Philip Deane of Steyning, West Sussex, for the family tree. The WEP hold a solicitor's notice to 3rd Marquess concerning the marriage settlement of George Henry Moore and Mary Blake; my gratitude to Birgid Clesham for the information.
148 WEP, various letters.
149 *ODNB*, 35089; Moore, Kerith. Cf. Freeman, Portrait, 185-91, who shows that Moore was deeply influenced by the Frenchman Ernest Renan; Hone, Moore, 312-7 (including a letter describing the short voyage in Palestine), 332-42 (discussion of the novel).
150 'Images of Mayo', http://www.castlebar.ie/imagemayo/moore.htm.
151 Donald Crummey, 'Beke, Charles Tilstone', *ODNB*, 1974.
152 Beke to Ritter, Leipzig, 2 June 1837, SBPK, Nl. Ritter.
153 Beke to Ritter, Asiatische Gesellschaft, London, 19 July 1843, SBPK, acc. Darmst.
154 RGSA, JMS 9/9.

155 RGSA, Council Minute Books, Oct. 1830 – July 1841, 263.
156 Moore, Earthquake.
157 EEEE, I, 218–19.
158 SBPK, Nl. Ritter: Beke, Charles Tilstone.
159 Boase, I, 223; EEEE, I, 223–4; *ODNB*, 1974; Beke, Summary, 4 (citation).
160 Treaty between Her Majesty the Queen of England and the King of Shoa, 16th Nov 1841, Thomas, Treaties, 674–7; Harris, Highlands. Cf. EEEE, 9 (1982), 463–4.
161 Wagner, Roth, 33–5; Roth, Harris. Cf. Goren, Zieht hin, 124–39.
162 Baumann, Apostelstrasse, 20–3; Carmel, Christen, 162–7.
163 *ODNB*, 1974; Beke, Origines; cf. idem, Summary, 4.
164 Beke, Localities; idem, Notes JRGS, 76–7.
165 Beke, Evidence; idem, Persian Gulf; idem, Alluvia.
166 C.T. Beke to Chevalier Winter, Chief Justice of the Town of Leipzig, British Consulate, 29. June 1837, SAL, Kap. 68 A Nr. 11: Das Großbritanische Konsulat; Beke, Summary, 6.
167 RGSA, Council Minute Books, Oct. 1830–July 1841, 259 (from Mr. Beke in Leipzig, 28 January), 260 (from Mr. Robinson in Berlin, 28 January), 261 (from Dr. Robinson at Leipzig, 25 February), 263 (from Mr. Beke at Leipzig, 25 March).
168 E.g. Beke, Countries. The tremendous interest raised is reflected in the publication in London of three volumes dealing with travels in Ethiopia in 1843 and 1844, including the one by Harris: Abyssinia – Mission.
169 Williams, Policy, 108. See *ODNB* 1974, for a summary of the travels, research, publications and achievements, and Beke, Summary, for all his publications.
170 Secretary Jackson to Mrs. Beke, 13 December 1842, and to Dr. Beke, 11 May 1843, RGSA, Letter Book 1841–1844, 162, 206, 245; C.T. Beke to Beaufort, 6 November 1843 and 8 April 1844, HON, Incoming letters prior to 1857 B 1–300, 245, 246.
171 Beke, Reasons; idem, Statement.
172 Beek, Notes; idem, Notes JRGS (map); idem, Summary, 12–14. For Wetzstein and Doergens and their mutual work and publications cf. Goren, Zieht hin, 185–93.
173 Beek, Jacob; idem, Idol; idem, Discoveries.
174 Beke, Summary; for his public services 'in respect of the Abyssinian Expedition': 15–21.
175 Beke, Meer und See, 1221; Schubert, Erdl, 891; William Beek to RGS, 24 April (1841?), RGSA, RGS Journal Mss. Middle East, 1837 & 1841.
176 RGSA, JMS 9/66.
177 SD, 76; Nir (Beginnings, 68–70), claims that Alexander Keith was the first to use this technique in Palestine in June 1839.
178 About them see Ben-Arieh, Pioneer; Goren, Zieht hin, 36–55, and the detailed bibliography there; *ODNB*, 3957.
179 Reference is to the *MCEHK*; Kruse, Seetzen. Cf. Goren, Zieht hin, 47.
180 Burckhardt, Nubia (1819, and German trsl. 1820); idem, Syria (English and German 1822).
181 E.g., Robinson, Syria, 146, 153–4, 158–9, 166–7, and passim.
182 Chesney, Narrative, 21–8 (Hauran), 28–49 (continuing south to Jerash, Amman, es-Salt, etc.); Robinson, Syria, 141–230.
183 Chesney, Narrative, 21–2, 76–9.
184 Cf. Guémard, Gaillardot; Shehade, Gaillardot; Goren, Gaillardot.
185 Hofman, Administration; Shamir, Egyptian Rule; Solé, L'Égypte, 220.
186 Gaillardot, Note.
187 Ritter, Gaillardot. Cf. Goren, Ritter.
188 Priesdorff, Führertum, 6 (1938), 575; Goren, Zieht hin, 181–5.
189 Porter, Memoir. I thank Yinon Shivtiel for the information.

190 Perrier, La Syrie; Prokesch-Osten, Mehmed-Ali, 71–81. Cf. Paxton's description of the campaign (Letters, 220–1).
191 Gaillardot, Relation.
192 Ritter, Wetzstein; Graham, Explorations; Kiepert, Note. Cf. Goren, Zieht hin, 187–8.
193 The latest comprehensive study: Aiken, Geography, 89–132; ODNB, 22574; Reed, Cabinet, 207; Thomas Hamilton, rev. David Huddleston, 'Graham, William', ODNB, 11227; Eiken, Faith; Costello, Ireland, 73–82, 144–5 (many citations from Porter's books). For his bibliography see also Tobler, Bibliographia, 189, and Röhricht, Bibliotheca, 467–8, Following Röhricht, Schur (Travellers, 205–6) wrongly calls him John Leech P., a mistake copied later by several others. Costello (Ireland, 73) calls him James Leslie.
194 Hutchinson, Salvation; Costello, Ireland, 71–9.
195 Hamilton ODNB (above, note 193).
196 Porter, Handbook; Aiken, Geography, 93–8; Cf. Finlay Holmes, 'Cooke, Henry', ODNB, 6168; Eiken, Faith, 2.
197 Porter, Giant Cities, 20–96; cf. Röhricht, Bibliotheca, 467–8; Aiken, Geography, 95–7.
198 Porter, Giant Cities, 17.
199 Porter, Giant Cities, 18.
200 Wessels, Nationalism, 246–7.
201 Porter, Map; idem, Memoir, 43; cf. Bartlett, Mapping, 115–8; Aiken, Geography, 109–17.
202 Porter, Memoir, 48–9; Van de Velde, Memoir, 18. For Buckingham: G.F.R. Barker, rev. Felix Driver, 'Buckingham, James Silk', ODNB, 3855; and for his travels: Buckingham, Travels. For Relandus' maps of Transjordan: Bartlett, Mapping, 88–95.
203 Van de Velde, Memoir, 18–21.
204 Hogg, Porter.
205 SD. There is no original numbering to the pages. They had to be rearranged in chronological order, and numbering was then added in order to facilitate the following discussion.
206 Porter, Giant Cities, 56.
207 Hogg, Porter, 3–4.
208 Numbers 42, 32.
209 SD, 56–8.
210 Thomas K. Keefe, 'Henry II (1133–1189)', ODNB, 12949; John Gillingham, 'Richard I (1157–1199)', ODNB, 23498; SD, 59–60. Malek-ed-Daher was actually Saladin's son.
211 SD, 74–5, 79.
212 SD, 76–90; citation: 84.
213 SD, 92–7. The native hamlet of Philip the Arab, emperor of Rome in 244, who built it as a metropolis and is said to have wanted to turn the city into a replica of Rome.
214 SD, 97–109; Porter, Giant Cities, 36–8.
215 SD, 109–24 (citation: 122).
216 SD, 130.
217 DSD. There is no original numbering to the pages. They had to be rearranged in chronological order, and numbering was then added in order to facilitate the following discussion.
218 RGSA, RGS Jorn. Mss. Middle East, 1837 & 1841, 2.
219 The Reis, the 'head', meant the captain. Guis and the Austrian Loretta, whose son also accompanied the Duc on his tour, are both mentioned in Raguse, State, 223; idem, Voyage, II, 261–3, 278; Tresse, Installation, 360–1, 366.

220 DSD, 3. My efforts to find details about Fessani did not bear fruit.
221 DSD, 3-7.
222 DSD, 7-15. For the family Damiani as consuls of various European countries in Jaffa, see Eliav, Austria, 36-7, nn. 13-14 (citation of a colourful description of 'the old Damiani' by Russegger).
223 DSD, 17.
224 Tibawi, American, 57-62, 74, 111, 130; Abu-Gazaleh, Missions, 23-5; Kawerau, Amerika, 254-7; Burton, Narrative, 106-7.
225 Bird, Bible, 317; Taylor, Mission, 82-3; Abu-Gazaleh, Missions, 24-5; Kawerau, Amerika, 256-7.
226 Tenebrae – the popular name for the special form of prayers for the last three days of the Holy Week: Cross, 1349.
227 DSD, 23, 47. Cf. Bystron, Polacy; Weryho, Slowacki.
228 DSD, 24-5.
229 DSD, 29-30.
230 Vereté, Consulate, on Farren 319-35, esp. n. 2 on 325-6.
231 DNB, 11, 1164-5; Dawson and Uphill, 257; Lindsay, Letters, iv, 315, 330, 364 (citation). See also: Elath, Routes, 54.
232 Appendix No. 2: Journey from the Bay of Orontes to Damascus, 1835, by the late Major General Estcourt, GRO, D1571, F 458.
233 Hugh Brigstocke, 'Lindsay, Alexander William Crawford', ODNB, 16686; Lindsay, East; Tobler, Bibliographia, 159. Burton, a possible acquaintance from Dublin, met him in Alexandria (Burton, Narrative, 27). Cf. Paxton, Letters, 211-12.
234 Paxton, Letters, 210.
235 DSD, 108-9, 114; Lindsay, Letters, 17. Reference is, most probably, to Commander (from 1842) Henry James L. (born 1810), a naval officer, who served in 1835 and later in the Mediterranean (EBR after O'Byrne).
236 Lindsay, Letters, 247-9.
237 Kinnear, Cairo, 133, 167.
238 Krystyna Matyjaszkiewicz, 'Roberts, David', ODNB, 23746; Ben-Arieh, Painting, 79-106.
239 DSD, 114-5; Burton, Narrative, 179; Allen, Dead Sea, II, 4.
240 DSD, 31; Oren, Power, 143. For the theme and its development see Greenberg, Indians.
241 DSD, 25-7, 79, 82-3, 86-7, 110-15, 111-23. Cf. Hoxie, Livermore; Oren, Power, 143-5; Kark, Consuls, 215 ('How am I to act when any crazy and distressed citizen of the U.S. comes into this country', the Consul in Beirut, 1843).
242 DSD, 124; Simon, Tribes. For Simon: Greenberg, Indians, 140-2, wrote that 'little is known about Simon'.
243 Burton, Narrative, 56-7. Cf. Costello, Ireland, 132.
244 Greenberg, Indians, citations 134, 141.
245 DSD, 79, 83, 87; Burton, Narrative, 95-6, 99, 122, 131-2. The role of the British Evangelical movement in the preaching for the restoration of the Jews has been discussed in many studies, e.g., Vereté, Consulate; idem, Restoration; Kedem, Eschatology; Kochav, Movement.
246 DSD, 34-6, 44-5.
247 DSD, 47.
248 For the 'Biblical connection' cf. Goren, Chase.
249 Balat and also Kasr, a site which fits the forthcoming description. I thank Prof. Amnon Cohen for the information.
250 Saulcy, Narrative, II, 35-6; idem, Esquisse. Cf. 'Saulcy', NBG, 43 (1864), 353-5; Dussaud, Envers.
251 Saulcy, Narrative, II, 37-9.

252 Vaux, Fouilles; idem, Qumran, 1362–3.
253 1 fathom = 1/1000 nautical mile = 1.853 metres.
254 DSD, 58–9. The description is very accurate. They sailed quite a long distance, as the Arnon, the biggest stream entering the Dead Sea from the east, reaches the sea at a point parallel to Ein Gedi, about 28 km south of Qumran.
255 DSD, 62–5; Saulcy, Narrative, II, 35.
256 DSD, 66. Cwt = Centweight or Hundredweight, the term used in England and the USA for Zentner (Quintal = 50 kg.).
257 DSD, 67–72.
258 DSD, 73–5. Cf. I Samuel 15, 32
259 DSD, 77–9. The Fountain of the Virgin, Christian name of the Fountain of Gichon in the Kedron Valley, to the west of the City of David and close to the village of Siloam.
260 DSD, 87–9.
261 DSD, 89–92.
262 DSD, 93–7.
263 DSD, 98
264 Lindsay, East, 138.
265 DSD, 99–106.
266 DSD, 108. The names mentioned: Dr. Wilson and Lacon.
267 DSD, 108–11.
268 RGSA, JMS 9/9; Beek to the JRGS, 24 April (1841?), RGSA, RGS Journal Mss. Middle East, 1837 & 1841, p. 3.
269 DSD, 114–23, the bearings: 120, 122.
270 DSD, 118.
271 DSD, 128, 132, 134; Moore, Gentleman, 44–70.
272 William Wardlaw Ramsay was Lindsay's 'friend and near relation', and 'companion of the greater part of my tour': Lindsay, Letters, iv. Lindsay describes his 'excellent abilities and sound judgement', 'singular genius for music and drawing', 'sweetness of temper, a warm, kind heart', etc. He is mentioned in many places in the book, when Lindsay quotes his journal. His death is described on pages 328–9.
273 DSD, 133; Moore, Gentleman, 46.
274 Moore, Gentleman, 49.
275 Moore, Gentleman, 52. All my efforts to locate Pearce, or any details about him, did not bear fruit.
276 Moore, Gentleman, 55.
277 Moore, Gentleman, sketches facing 60, 66; Chesney, Narrative, 251–76, 547–8.
278 DSD, 67.
279 Beek to the secretary of the RGS, 22 August 1837, RGSA, RGS Correspondence 1834–40: Beek, W.; PGS, 2/55 (1838), 344 (CT Beke, meeting 19 February 1836), 609. I thank Prof. Gordon L. Herries Davies for this information, for his continuous support, for ideas and information he gave me, as well as for his friendship and real interest. It is difficult to decide whether Henry is a mistake or another relative of the brothers.
280 RGS, Maps Room, Jordan S/S. 3.
281 DSD, 71.
282 The scale measured in comparison to Sheet 10 (Jerusalem) of 1:100,000 Palestine, revised and printed 1953.
283 Masterman, Summary. A photo of the rock: idem, History, 251.
284 DSD, 114; Beek to secretary of the RGS, 22 August 1837, RGSA, RGS Correspondence 1834–1840.
285 On the Dead Sea. Original letter: RGSA, Beke 1837.

286 Beek to secretary of the RGS, 22 August 1837, RGSA, RGS Correspondence 1834–
     1840; Beek to the JRGS, 24 April (1841?), RGSA, RGS Journal Mss. Middle East,
     1837 & 1841, p. 3. A Repeating Theodolite has a horizontal circle, able to rotate
     freely, or to be secured, either to the alidade or to its support, so as to permit
     cumulative reading.
287 RGSA, Moore, Geo. H., RGS Correspondence 1834–40.
288 RGSA, Moore, Geo. H., RGS Correspondence 1834–40.
289 'Höhenmessung', *MKL*, 8 (1889), 632–3.
290 Sykes, Thermometers. Cf. B.B. Woodward, *rev.* M.G.M. Jones, 'Sykes, William
     Henry', *ODNB*, 26871; Home, Royal Society, 325.
291 Sykes, Thermometers, 440–1.
292 Klein, Fluctuations; Bookman et al., Quaternary, 166–7, figures A and B.

Chapter 6

1   Mainly Genesis, 19: 24–9.
2   Schubert, Reise; Erdl, Barometer. Cf. Goren, Roth; idem, Zieht hin, 117–24.
3   Schubert, Results; cf. Goren, Zieht hin, 122.
4   Lindsay, Narrative, 191.
5   DSD, 48–9.
6   DSD, 80.
7   Schubert, Reise, III, 93.
8   For his itinerary: Erdl, Barometer. DSD, 31, 37, 75, 80, 87, 97.
9   Schubert, Reise, III, 84–93.
10 Schubert, Reise, III, 85; idem, Results, 630; idem, Fündlinge, 357.
11 Schubert, Reise, 86–7; idem, Erdl, 893–4; idem, Fündlinge, 358–60.
12 Erdl, Barometer, 267. Cf. Schubert, Results, 629.
13 R. Knott, 'Steinheil', *ADB*, 35 (1893), 720–4.
14 Schubert, Results, 630.
15 Broc, 28–9; EEEE, 1 (1978), 255–6.
16 Moore to Washington, Moore Hall, 3 December 1838, RGSA, RGS
    Correspondence 1834–40, second letter. Cf. 'Berry', *NBG*, 3 (1843), 674–5.
17 Bertou, Tyre; idem, Réponse; idem, Extract.
18 Wilde, Narrative, II, 139, 154.
19 M. Bertou, Jerusalem, Ap. 29, rec[ieved] 15 June 38, to the president of the
    Geographical Society, RGSA, RGS Cor. Block 1834–40: Bertou, J. de; Callier,
    Note. Bertou's route is given in the map: Heinrich Berghaus, Part of Arabia
    Petraea and Palestine, 1839, a map attached to Berghaus, Letter (fig.44). Cf. also
    Van de Velde, Memoir, 50.
20 For a detailed itinerary, measurements and studies: M. Bertou, Jerusalem, Ap.
    29, rec[ieved] 15 June 38, to the president of the Geographical Society, RGSA,
    RGS Cor. Block 1834–40. Broc, 28, gives -406m.
21 Callier, Note, 92–7; idem, Mémoire; Bertou, Voyage; idem, Extraits; idem, Notes;
    idem, Itinéraire; idem, Extrait; idem, Note; idem, Mont Hor. Cf. Robinson,
    Bemerkungen; Delcros, Notice.
22 Bertou, Voyage; idem, Extraits, 242.
23 Ritter, Erdkunde, 704.
24 Bertou, Extraits, 240–4. For a summary of his results see also Fischer, Geschichte,
    38–47.
25 Washington to Bertou, 3 June 1838, RGSA, RGS Letter Book 1836–40, 218–20;
    and also all the letters in RGSA, RGS Cor. Block 1834–40: Bertou, J. de.
26 Washington to H. Moore Esq, H.M. Consul, Beïrut, 30 June 1838, RGSA, RGS
    Letter Book, 1836–1840, 220–1.

27 RGSA, JMS 9/31: Bertou (1) 1839; Bertou, Notes, 286 note.
28 Hamilton, Address 1842, lx. 1 Parisian foot = 324.84 mm; 1 British foot = 304.79 mm (a rate of 1.066:1).
29 Ritter, Comparative, II, 238.
30 Broc, 28–9.
31 Bertou, Itinéraire; idem, Voyage; idem, Notes; idem, Dépression; Delcros, Notice. On the depression of the Valley of the Jordan and the Dead Sea by the Count Jules de Bertou with a section, Paris 12 Nov/ accepted 21 Nov 39, RGSA, JMS 9/32.
32 Lord Lindsay to Hamilton, n.d., RGSA, RGS Corr. Block 1834–40: Lindsay, Lord.
33 On the depression of the Valley of the Jordan and the Dead Sea by the Count Jules de Bertou with a section, Paris 12 Nov/ accepted 21 Nov 39, RGSA, JMS 9/32, last page; Bertou, Extrait, 166; Delcros, Notice, 336–8.
34 Robinson, Researches, II, 659–99; Greenbough, Address 1840, lviii.
35 Bertou to John Washington, Beirut, 6 August 1838, RGSA, RGS Cor. Block 1834–40: Bertou, J. de.
36 Bertou, Dépression, 12 (1839), 151–8; Van de Velde, Memoir, 50.
37 Russegger in Palästina; Mahlmann, Russegger; Russegger, Übersicht, 70. Cf. Goren, Zieht hin, 253–6.
38 Koner, Antheil, 384; Ben-Arieh, Rediscovery, 79; Gollwitzer, Palästinafahrten, 305; Goren, Zieht hin, 222–43. For Austrian Montanists serving Mehemet Ali see also Prokesch-Osten, Mehmed-Ali, 69–70.
39 Hofman, Administration; Shamir, Egyptian Rule.
40 For Metternich's policy in the East see Gelber, Question, 46–9, 53–5; Eliav, Austria, 33–47 and passim (documents); Webster, Policy, passim.
41 Russegger, Reisen; Koner, Antheil, 384–5; Ritter, Russegger.
42 Russegger, Libanon, 170.
43 Russegger, Reisen 1. This letter should serve as an important document in learning about Mehemet Ali's ideas and ruling system.
44 Russegger in Palästina, 381.
45 Russegger in Palästina, 381–2, 389–90. For Franz Prunner-Bey see Schäfer, Pruner; Goren, Zieht hin, 152–3.
46 BLO, 27 (1874), 292–7; Ritter, Russegger; Fischer, Geschichte, 55–6; Goren, Zieht hin, 253–6.
47 Russegger in Palästina, 406–7; cf. Schur, Dead Sea, 4–5.
48 Russegger in Palästina, 693. For a detailed report on his voyage in Galilee, in an early professional geological paper edited by his friend Karl Cäsar von Leonhard (1779–1862), professor of Mineralogy from Heidelberg, to whom he sent many of his letters and findings: Russegger, Brief. It was also translated and published in the periodical of the French Geological Society: Russegger, Lettres.
49 Russeggert, Depression, 179–81.
50 Russegger, Depression, 185–94.
51 Ritter, Russegger; Mahlmann, Russegger. Cf. Goren, Zieht hin, 78–9, 182–3.
52 Russegger, Depression, 179–80.
53 Cf. Fraas, Todte Meer, 6; Ritter, Comparative, I, 55–6.
54 Russegger, Reisen, II\I, 760, 838–74.
55 Russegger, Uebersicht; Ehrenberg, Russegger, 187.
56 Russegger in Palästina, 407; Russegger, Depression, 186; Ritter, Russegger; Delcros, Notice, 339.
57 Berghaus, Letter, 308–9. Cf. Smith and Hichcock, Robinson; Appleton, Cyclopaedia, V (1888), 561–2.
58 Robinson, Researches. Cf. Ben-Arieh, Rediscovery, 85; Goren, Zieht hin, 83–91.

59 Robinson, Extracts; Jackson to Revd. Dr. E. Robinson, 29 May 1842, RGSA, Letter Book 1841–1844, 130; RGSA, Council Minute Books, Oct. 1830–July 1841, 260 (from Robinson in Berlin, 28 January 1839), 261 (from Robinson in Leipzig, 25 February).
60 Bliss, Exploration, 197. For the itinerary and route: Robinson, Journal, II, 569, 571; Berghaus, Letter.
61 Robinson, Bemerkungen; idem, Nachschrift; idem, Depression; idem, Depression etc.; idem, Dead Sea; idem, On the Depression.
62 Robinson, Depression; Williams, City, I, Supplement, 128–30.
63 Bertou, Dépression, 1839; idem, Itinéraire; idem, Notes; Robinson, Bemerkungen; idem, Nachschrift. Manuscript of his letter to the RGS: 'On Mr. de Bertou's Statements referring the Valley of Araba', RGSA, JMS 9/34.
64 Robinson, Bemerkungen, 192–3; idem, Researches, II, 659–99; Detailed manuscript in Robinson's handwriting is kept in the RGS/IBG Archives London.
65 Robinson, Researches, 660–1; Laborde, Journey.
66 'On Mr. de Bertou's Statements referring the Valley of Araba', RGSA, JMS 9/34, 2–3.
67 Robinson, Nachschrift, 21. For Kiepert and his work on and in Palestine: Goren, Zieht hin, 95–104; Goren, Kiepert.
68 Robinson, Depression, 16; idem, Depression etc.

Chapter 7
1 Ritter, Comparative, III, 127 n. 1.
2 *ODNB*, 1974.
3 Goren, Zieht hin, 71–2; idem, Ritter, with bibliography.
4 Beke, Meer; idem, Dépression, 372–3.
5 Schubert, Reise, III, 86–7; Erdl, Barometer, 273.
6 Schubert, Fündlinge, 357–9.
7 Schubert, Erdl, 890–1.
8 Schubert, Meer.
9 Beke, Meer und See; idem, Niveau.
10 William Beek to RGS, 24 April (1841?), RGSA, RGS Journal Mss. Middle East, 1837 & 1841.
11 Washington to Dr. Berghaus, 5 July 1839, RGSA, RGS Letter Book 1836–40, 274.
12 Moore, Gentleman, 82.
13 RGSA, RGS journal mss Beek 1841; JMS 9/9.
14 Notes Mer Morte.
15 Notes Mer Morte.
16 Beke, Dépression.
17 Bertou, Itinéraire, 328.
18 Callier, Mémoire; idem, Note, 94–9.
19 Callier, Mémoire; idem, Note.
20 RGSA, RGS Correspondence 1834–40: Moore, Geo. H. For Washington: Dawson, Memoirs, II, 93–111; Morris, Admiralty; Sainty, Admiralty, 77, 156.
21 Bertou, Note; idem, Extract.
22 RGSA, Council Minute Book, Oct. 1830–July 1841, 256.
23 Beek to Hamilton, RGSA, JMS 9\66. William Frere (1775–1836), academician, serjant-in-law and later college master and vice-chancellor of Cambridge University: Alsager Vian, 'Frere, William (1775–1836)', *ODNB*, 10176.
24 Letronne, Trennung. For his biography: L.J., 'Letronne', *NBG*, 18 (1858), 1015–21.
25 Letronne, Trennung, 202–3.
26 Letronne, Communication; idem, Suez; idem, Séparation; idem, Séparation I.
27 Letronne, Différence; idem, Trennung, 242–9.

28 Humboldt, Asien, I part II, 543–9; idem, Cosmos, I, 301; Ritter, Jordan; idem, Comparative, III, 125–8, 150–1.
29 Castlereagh, Journey, I, 202.

Chapter 8
1 Humboldt, Difference.
2 Jackson (RGS Secretary) to Inspector General of Fortifications, RGSA, Letter-Book 01.07.1841–05.05.1844.
3 Symonds to 'My Dear Sir', Southampton, 10 Waterloo Place, 16 April 1842, RGSA, RGS corr block 1841–50: Symonds, Lt. Thomas F.L.; Symonds, Rough Sketch of a portion of the Triangulation of the Southern District of Syria, 16 April 1842, RGSA, OBS 155: Symonds (fig. 30); JPMC, Asien, 30 II; Hamilton, Address 1843, lx.
4 Calculated 1 yard = 3 feet = 36 inches = 91.44 cm.
5 Humboldt, Asien, 544–7; Lettrone, Trennung.
6 Hamilton, Address 1842, lx-lxi.
7 Presentation Medals.
8 Jackson to Hamilton, 2 May 1843, RGSA, Outgoing Letter-Book for 1841–1844. My deepest gratitude to Francis Herbert for locating this letter, and for his intensive help and long friendship. For Jackson: Mill, RGS, 52–57; Goudie, Jackson; Elizabeth Baignet, 'Jackson, Julian', ODNB, 14540.
9 Jackson to Sir Wm Symonds, 6 May 1843, RGSA, Letter Book 1841–1844, 203.
10 Symonds to Washington, 4 Somerset Place, Somerset House, 21 February 1842, RGSA, RGS corr block 1841–50.
11 Jackson to Lieut Symonds RE, 23 May 1843, RGSA, Letter Book 1841–44, 215–6.
12 Presentation Medals, xi-xii.
13 Robinson, Researches, II, 222; idem, Depression, 16–17.
14 Idem, Depression etc.
15 Hamilton, Address 1843, lxxiv; Murchinson, Address 1845, cviii; Wilson, Lands, II, 24.
16 Hamilton, Address 1843, lxxiv-lxxv; Jones, Surveys, 34.
17 Robinson, Depression, citation 84. Cf. Kreiger, Waters, 62–3, 69–70; Jones, Surveys, 20, 36–7.
18 Alderson, Acre; citation: Williams, City, 10.
19 Williams, City, Supplement.
20 Van de Velde, Memoir, 5–6.
21 Fred. H. Robe to Sir Jas. Willoughby Gordon Bt. GOCB, Quarter Master General, Gibraltar, 3 February and 25 April 1845, NA, WO 78/1000 (2), WO 78/1000 (24).
22 Dawson, Memoirs, II, 20–1; Ritchie, Admiralty, 269.
23 J.K. Laughton, rev. Andrew Lambert, 'Ryder, Sir Alfred Phillipps', ODNB, 24393.
24 Charles Rochfort-Scott to General Sir J.W. Gordon Bart, Q.C.B., Quarter Master General etc. etc. etc., Military Report on Syria, Carmarthen 14 November 1846, NA, WO 78/1000(24).
25 Jackson, Extrait, 142.
26 Fig. 30: Rough Sketch of a portion of the Triangulation of the Southern District of Syria, JPMC, Asien, 30 II.
27 Of many papers, see, for example, Freeman, RGS, for its role in the development of Geography. I thank Andrew Cook and Andrew Lambert for their illuminating comments on the subject. For the formal history of the RGS see Mill, Record. Out of the numerous studies dealing with the organization, its activities and influence, cf. Livingstone, Tradition, 155–76; and mainly Driver, Geography, passim.
28 Progress 1836–7, 183.

29   Wilde, Narrative, 550 note.
30   Kreiger, Waters, 61–3.
31   Dawson, Memoirs, II, 93–111; Day, Admiralty, 67–80; J.K. Laughton, *rev.* R.O. Morris, 'Washington, John (1800–1863)', *ODNB*, 28807; Ritchie, Admiralty, 281–3.
32   Mill, Record, 41–2, 53; Dawson, Memoire, II, 94.
33   Humboldt, Cosmos, 301 note; idem, Asien, 545 note.
34   Washington to H. Moore Esq, H.M. Consul, Beïrut, 30 June 1838, RGSA, RGS Letter Book, 1836–1840, 220; Washington, Sketch, 250.
35   Washington, Sketch, 250.
36   Ripon, Surveys, 150–2; Petermann, Aufnahmen; Goren, Sacred, 95–7.
37   Washington to Dr. Berghaus, 5 July 1839, RGSA, RGS Letter Book 1836–40, 272–7.
38   Letronne, Trennung, pl. II; Berghaus, Letter.
39   Ben-Arieh, Rediscovery, 52–5, 79–84; Fischer, Geschichte, 39–40; Bartlett, Edom, 17–19; Irby and Mangles, Travels; J.K. Laughton, *rev.* Andrew Lambert, 'Irby, Charles Leonard', *ODNB*, 14443; J.K. Laughton, *rev.* Andrew Lambert, 'Mangles, James', *ODNB*, 17933; Ben-Arieh, Maps; Goren, Zieht hin, 57–60 (for Rüppell); Dawson and Uphill, 29 (Bankes), 86 (Catherwood), 214–5 (Irby), 245 (Legh), 273 (Mangles).
40   Dawson and Uphill, 86; Ben-Arieh, Maps.
41   Hamilton, Address 1839, lxiv.
42   *ODNB*, 12147; Dawson and Uphill, 188 ; Mill, RGS, 38–9; Fagan, Rape, 80–90; Evans, Antiquaries, 200; Hallett, Penetration, 358.
43   Minutes of the Transactions of the Syrian Society Established on Saint George's day In the Year of our Lord 1805, RGSA, ar GB402 PAL: Palestine Association 1805–1808; Mill, RGS, 38–9.
44   Greenough, Address 1840, lviii. Cf. Mill, RGS, 35–40; John Wyatt, 'Greenough, George Bellas', *ODNB*, 11432.
45   Napier to Staunton, on the Nile near Cairo, 7 February 1841, RGSA, RGS corr. Block 1841–50: Napier, Major E.
46   Hamilton, Address 1842, lx-lxi.
47   Kreiger, Waters, 61–3.
48   Jackson, Extrait.
49   Wilkie to Harvey, copy, Jerusalem, 8 March 1841, RGSA, J. Mss. Middle East 1841: Wilkie. The letter copied by Cunningham, Wilkie, 405–7.
50   Hamish Miles, 'Wilkie, Sir David', *ODNB*, 29413; Cunningham, Wilkie; Ben-Arieh, Painting 106–13,
51   Costello, Ireland, 63–5 (64 on MacLaughlin), 135–6 (description by Acton); Hoade, Ireland.
52   Cunningham, Wilkie, 408–11 (Wilkie to his wife, Jerusalem, 9 March, 1841). For Beadle: Kaweraw, Amerika, 243–4, 258, 43.
53   Wilkie, Sketches, nos. 13, 14, 17; Weeks, Face.
54   John Harvey, on the back page of the letter, RGSA, J. Mss. Middle East 1841: Wilkie; cf. Cunningham, Wilkie, 402.
55   Hamilton, Address 1839, lxiv.
56   Cunnigham, Wilkie, 284–392.
57   The low temperatures he measured in March are remarkable: in Jerusalem always 13°-14°, at the Dead Sea about 19° and never more than 25°.
58   On the back page of the letter, RGSA, J. Mss. Middle East 1841; Jackson, Extrait, 140–1; Hamilton, Address 1842, lx.
59   Life of Chesney, 166; Guest, Expedition, 23–4, 150–1.
60   Priesdorff, Führertum, 6, 575; Goren, Zieht hin, 181–5.
61   Ritter, Wildenbruch; idem, Jordan.
62   Ritter, Wildenbruch. Cf. Fischer, Geschichte, 62.

63 Petermann, Wildenbruch.
64 Petermann, Jordan, see next chapter. Cf. Goren, Zieht hin, 104–10; Goren, Petermann.
65 Petermann, Wildenbruch, 228–30.
66 Ritter, Entdeckungen; Goren, Pioneer; above, chap. 3.2.
67 Petermann, Wildenbruch, 235; Blanche and Gaillardot, Catalogue; Deflers, Notice, 1–2, 6: 'Blanche et Gaillardot, Plantes récoltées en Syrie et en Palestine, 2500'. Cf. Weiss, 'Baumgartner', *ADB*, 2 (1875), 164–5. The mistake is Wildenbruch's, the a in his name is certainly without an *Umlaut*.
68 Ritter, Gaillardot. Cf. Goren, Gaillardot.
69 Ritter, Wildenbruch; Wildenbruch, Profilzeichnungen.
70 Ritter, Gaillardot, 249–50.

Chapter 9

1 Carne, Letters, II, 20.
2 Beke, Meer und See.
3 Hamilton, Address 1843, lxxiv-lxxv.
4 Robinson, Depression, 85. Original emphasis.
5 RGSA, JMS/9/87.
6 Hamilton, Address 1848, xxxv.
7 Petermann, Jordan; Hamilton, Address 1848, xxxv-xxxvi. Cf. *ODNB*, 41218; Goren, Zieht hin, 104–10.
8 The journal of Lieut. Thomas Molyneux relating to the British naval expedition to the Dead Sea, RGS/IBG Archives London. Published as Molyneux, Expedition.
9 Ritter, Jordan, 12.
10 Masterman, Exploration, 412–16; idem, Explorers, 19–26; Vilnay, Dead Sea, 31, 34; Eriksen, Molyneux; idem, Explorers, 53–86; Goren, Nicolayson, 73–6, 88–77 [English text].
11 For biographies: O'Byrne, II, 1151–2; J.K. Laughton, *rev.* Andrew Lambert, 'Symonds, Sir Thomas Matthew Charles', *ODNB*, 26891. Cf. Lambert, Battlefleet, 71, 84.
12 Molyneux, Expedition, 104.
13 Molyneux, Expedition, 104; Boggis, Jordan, 26–7.
14 Symonds to Beaufort, Beirut, Spartan 13 September 1847, HON, Symonds 707; Symonds to the RGS, H.M.S. Spartan, Beirout, 3 December 1847, RGSA, RGS corr block 1841–50: Symonds, Lt. Thomas F.L.
15 Symonds to Beaufort, H.M.S. Spartan, Beirut, 3 December 1847, RGSA, RGS corr block 1841–50: Symonds, Lt. Thomas F.L.
16 Track Chart by Liutenant T.H. Molyneux H.M.S. Spartan, 1847, DALM, Vz7/40/2 (my deepest gratitude to Peter Collier for supplying me with excellent scans); RGSA, OBS 155 (sketches); Beaufort to Secretary of the RGS, 11 Gloucester Place, June 26/48, and copy of Molyneaux Journal, RGSA, JMS 9/85; Molyneaux, Expedition.
17 *ODNB*, 26893.
18 He had strong connections with the RGS, who, through the meditation of Beaufort, sent him measuring instruments and other material (Washington to Captain Symonds, 27 May 1839, RGSA, RGS Letter Book 1836–40, 265–6).
19 *ODNB*, 26891.
20 James Bodie (Master), Remark Book, H.M. Ship 'Spartan'. Between 1 January and 31 December 1847, HON, H O Ships Remarks Book, H-W(1).
21 Copy of Molyneux Journal by Symonds, RGSA, JMS 9/85; Molyneux, Expedition, 104.

22 Copy of Molyneux Journal by Symonds, RGSA, JMS 9/85, 1–2, 5.
23 Copy of Molyneux Journal by Symonds, RGSA, JMS 9/85, 2–4.
24 Copy of Molyneux Journal by Symonds, RGSA, JMS 9/85, 5–6.
25 Molyneux, Expedition, 107.
26 Molyneux, Expedition, 113.
27 Molyneux, Expedition, 113.
28 Molyneux, Expedition; Hamilton, Address 1848, xxxvi; Wilson, Surveys, 210 (citation).
29 Molyneux, Expedition, 115.
30 English exploring expedition to the Jordan and the Dead Sea: Archbishop Gobat, etc., PRO FO 226/97. The RGS might have made a mistake, as the correspondents – in Arabic – were the British Consul (Finn) and the Governor of Jerusalem. In his answer to Finn's request, the latter wrote that Molyneux had failed to coordinate his exact program with the governor of Acre, but he was still sending forty soldiers to help search for the missing men. In his short answer, Finn only corrected the number, fourteen and not forty. My thanks to Mustafa Abbassi who translated the documents.
31 Eriksen, Explorers, 59–62 (detailed chronology of the expedition), 85–6 (Maltese servant); Boggis, 26–35.
32 Masterman, Explorers, 21–2. Interestingly enough, Schultz claimed that he went to Jericho in order to meet Molyneux (Van de Velde, Memoir, 17–18 n. 2). For Schultz and Weber: Goren, Zieht hin, 184–5, 194–201; Goren – Morag, Mapping.
33 Boggis, Jordan, 32–3; Vilnai, Dead Sea, 34.
34 Ben-Zvi, Source; Vilnai, Fate.
35 The boat had been recently transferred for restoration and study to the laboratory of the Leon Recanati Center for Maritime Studies in the University of Haifa.
36 Jenkins, Expeditions. On Lynch: 461–517.
37 Jampoler, Lynch; and cf. Ben-Arieh, Lynch; Kreiger, Waters, 76–94; Silberman, Digging, 53–62; Rook, Lynch. For his biography: Lynch, Record, 138–9; Jampoler, Lynch, passim.
38 Lynch, Narrative; idem, Report; Montague, Narrative.
39 J.Y. Mason, Report of the Secretary of the Navy, with a Report made by Lieutenant W.F. Lynch..., BSOG, Ob 1428, 12. Lynch, Report; Ritter, Jordan.
40 J.Y. Mason, Report of the Secretary of the Navy, with a Report made by Lieutenant W.F. Lynch..., BSOG, Ob 1428, 23. Cf. Fischer, Geschichte, 62–4.
41 Goren, Ritter.
42 Ritter, Jordan, 17.
43 Jampoler, Sailors, 217–41.
44 Van de Velde, Memoir, 17; Wilson, Surveys, 214.

Concluding Remarks

1 Ritter, Comparative, III, 127 note 1.
2 Klein, Fluctuations; idem, Evidence; idem, Fluctuations of the Level.
3 Bookman et al., Quaternary, 166–7.
4 Moore to RGS, RGSA, RGS Correspondence 1834–40: Moore, Geo. H.
5 Moore to RGS, RGSA, RGS Correspondence 1834–40: Moore, Geo. H.
6 Calculated by Callier after de Bertou's measurements: Callier, Note, 94.
7 Calculated by Callier after Moore and Beek's boiling temperatures: Callier, Note, 99.

8   Bertou, Extraits, 242.
9   Russegger, Depression, 186.
10   Four results after Hamilton, Address 1842, lx.
11   Erdl, Barometer, 279.
12   Hamilton, Address 1842, lx.
13   Rough Sketch of a portion of the Triangulation of the Southern District of Syria, JPMC, Asien, 30 II; Hamilton, Address 1842, lx.
14   Robinson, Depression etc.
15   Hamilton, Address 1843, lxxiv; Murchinson, Address 1845, cviii.
16   Wildenbruch, Profilzeichnungen, 270.
17   Hamilton, Address 1848, xxxvi.
18   Four results after Petermann, Jordan, 90.
19   Humboldt, Cosmos, I, 301
20   Four results after Ritter, Erdkunde, 704.
21   Ritter, Jordan, 38.
22   Lynch, Report.
23   Cf. Gal and Merkel, Level, as the first and only attempt, so far, to establish the levels in historical times and compare them to the 'red line', which marks the minimum level of the lake at its driest point.
24   Russegger, Depression, 186.
25   Hamilton, Address 1842, lx.
26   Erdl, Barometer,
27   Robinson, Depression etc.
28   Three results after Ritter, Wildenbruch, 271.
29   Two results after Hamiltom, Address 1848, xxxv.
30   Four results after Petermann, Jordan, 90.
31   Humboldt, Cosmos, 301.
32   Ritter, Jordan, 38.
33   Livingstone, Science, esp. 367–8, 371–4. See also the detailed discussions in the recently published PhD thesis of his student, Edwin Aiken: Aiken, Geography, passim.
34   Goren, Chase.
35   Marlowe, Suez, 34.
36   Goren, Sacred. To the 'Peaceful Crusade' see Goren, Crusade.
37   Moscrop, Measuring, 123.
38   Moscrop, Measuring, 119, after PEF, Letter Book entry, 29.
39   Moscrop, Measuring, 95–125.
40   Ridden, Britishness, 88. For background cf. Cullen, Diaspora.
41   Ridden, Britishness, 88–90.
42   Hoade, Ireland.
43   Costello, Ireland, 63–160.
44   Costello, Ireland, 68–70; Crombie, Alexander, esp. 212–3; Yaron Perry, 'Alexander, Michael Solomon', *ODNB*, 334.
45   Lennon, Orientalism, 169–71.
46   Lennon, Orientalism, 171–6; Ridden, Britishness, 88, 91. In her paper, she deals with two 'case studies' from 'a group of intermarried liberal Protestant families' of Counties Limerick and Clare.
47   Robertson, Empire.
48   Lennon, Orientalism, 183–203.
49   Chesney to 'My dear Sir', n.d. [1833?], NA FO 352/26(1).

Bibliography

ARCHIVES

BL OIRR = British Library, Orient / India Reading Room

BL SPIS = British Library, Social Policy Information Service

BSOG = Bibl. Soc. Orie. Germ. (Library of the German Oriental Society, Halle)

DALM = Discrete Admiralty Library Manuscripts, Portsmouth

GRO = Gloucestershire Record Office, Gloucestershire County Council

HBL = Henry Blosse-Lynch Private Archive, Longcross House, Headley (Berkshire)

HON = Archive, The United Kingdom Hydrographic Office (UKHO), Taunton

JPMC = Justus Perthes Maps Collection, Gotha
   (Universitäts-und Forschungsbibliothek Erfurt/Gotha, Sammlung Perthes, Kartensammlung)

NA = The National Archives, London (The Public Record Office until 2003)
   NAM = National Army Museum, Department of Archives Photographs Films and Sound

NLI = National Library of Ireland, Manuscripts reading room
   DSD = Moore 1837, MS 3509 – Dead Sea Diary
   SD = MS 3510 – Syrian Diary

PEF = Palestine Exploration Fund Archive, London

PRONI = Public Record Office of Northern Ireland, Belfast

RGS = Royal Geographical Society, London, Map Room
   RGSA = RGS/IBG Archives London
   Moore, Geo. H., RGS Correspondence 1834–40
   RGS Journal Mss. Middle East, 1837 & 1841
   J. Mss. Middle East 1841

RSAMH = Российский сударственный Военно-Исторический Архив (РГВИА) [Russian State Archive of Military History]

SAL = Stadtarchiv Leipzig

SBPK = Staatsbibliothek Preussischer Kulturbesitz, Berlin, Handschriftenabteilung

TCD = Manuscript Department, Trinity College Library, Dublin

WEP = Westport Estate Papers [not sorted]

ABBREVIATIONS OF PERIODICALS AND NEWSPAPERS

A = Das Ausland
AAAG = Annals of the Association of American Geographers
ABAZ = Außerordentliche Beilage zur Allgemeinen Zeitung
ACP = Annales de Chimie et de Physique
AEVS = Annalen der Erd–, Völker– und Staatenkunde
AJSA = American Journal of Science and Arts
AP = Annalen der Physic
APC = Annalen der Physic und Chemie (Poggendorffsche Annalen)
BAB = Bericht über die zur Bekanntmachung geeigneten Verhandlugen der Königlich-
*   Preussischen Akademie der Wissenschaften*
BAZ = Beilage zur Allgemeinen Zeitung
BS = Bibliotheca sacra
BSG = Bulletin de la Société de Géographie de Paris
BW = The Biblical World
DUM = The Dublin University Magazine
EHR = The English Historical Review
ER = The Edinburgh Review, or Critical Journal
GABA = Gelehrte Anzeigen herausgegeben von Mitgliedern der k. bayerischen Akademie der
*   Wissenschaften*
GJ = The Geographical Journal
IEJ = Israel Exploration Journal
IG = Irish Geography
IM = Imago Mundi
JDEIA = Jahrbuch der Deutschen Evangelischen Instituts für Altertumswissenschaft des
*   Heiligen Landes*
JMH = The Journal of Modern History
JRGS = Journal of the Royal Geographical Society
JS = Journal des Savan(t)s
LEPMJ = The London and Edinburgh Philosophical Magazine and Journal
MCEHK= Monatlische Correspondenz zur Beförderung der Erd– und Himmels-Kunde
MES = Middle Eastern Studies
MVGEB = Monatsbrerichte über die Verhandlungen der Gesellschaft für Erdkunde
*   zu Berlin*
NAVSG = Nouvelles Annales des Voyages et des Sciences Géographiques
NJMGGP = Neues Jahrbuch für Mineralogie, Geognosie, Geologie und Petrefaktenkunde
NRRSL = Notes and Records of the Royal Society of London
PEFQS = Palestine Exploration Fund, Quarterly Statement
PEQ = Palestine Exploration Quarterely
PGS = Proceedings of the Geological Society of London
PM = (Petermanns) Mittheilungen aus Justus Perthes' geographischer Anstalt über wichtige
*   neue Erforschungen aus dem Gesammtgebiete der Geographie*
RDM = Revue des Deux Mondes
TBGS = Transactions of the Bombay Geographical Society
TIBG = Transactions of the Institute of British Geographers
ZAE = Zeitschrift für (die) allgemeine Erdkunde, Berlin

ZGEB = Zeitschrift der Gesellschaft für Erdkunde zu Berlin
ZDPV = Zeitschrift des deutschen Palästina-Vereins

ABBREVIATIONS AND BIBLIOGRAPHY

Abu-Gazaleh, Missions = Adnan Abu-Gazaleh, *American Missions in Syria: A Study of American Missionary Contribution to Arab Nationalism in 19th Century Syria*, Brattleboro, VT: Amana Books, 1990.

Abyssinia – Mission = 'Abyssinia – The mission to Shoa', *DUM*, 24 (1844), pp. 253–68.

Acton, Letter = John Acton, *A Letter Adressed to a Namesake and Relative, Residing in Castlebar: Containing a Sketch of His Travels through the Most Celebrated Portion of the Holy Land*, Castlebar: The 'Telegraph' Office, 1841.

ADB = *Allgemeine Deutsche Bibliographie* (Bayerische Akademie der Wissenschaften, Historische Komission), I-LVI, Leipzig (& München): Duncker, 1875–1912.

Aiken, Geography = Edwin James Aiken, *Scriptural Geography: Portraying the Holy Land* (Tauris Historical Geography Series), London and New York: I.B. Tauris, 2010.

Ainsworth, Letters = William Francis Ainsworth, Letters [unsigned], *Literary Gazette*, 1836, pp. 443–4, 522–3, 713–14; 1837, pp. 95–6, 288–9.

Ainsworth, Narrative = William Francis Ainsworth, *A Personal Narrative of the Euphrates Expedition*, I-II, London: Kegan Paul, Trench & Co., 1888.

Ainsworth, Obituary = 'William Francis Ainsworth, Ph.D., F.S.A.', *GJ*, 9 (1897), pp. 98–9.

Ainsworth, Researches = William Francis Ainsworth, *Researches in Assyria, Babylonia, and Chaldæa: Forming Part of the Labours of The Euphrates Expedition*, London: John W. Parker, 1838.

Ainsworth, Ten Thousand = William Francis Ainsworth, *Travels in the Track of the Ten Thousand Greeks: Being a Geographical and Descriptive Account of the Expedition of Cyrus and of the Retreat of the Ten Thousand Greeks, as Related by Xenophon*, London: John W. Parker, 1844.

Ainsworth, Travels = William Francis Ainsworth, *Travels and Researches in Asia Minor, Mesopotamia, Chaldea, and Armenia*, I-II, London: John W. Parker, 1842.

Alderson, Acre = Ralph Carr Alderson, *Notes on Acre and Some of the Coast Defences in Syria* (Papers on Subjects Connected with the Duties of the Corps of Royal Engineers, VI), London: John Weale, 1843.

Alderson, Unterschied = Ralph Carr Alderson, 'Unterschied des Wasserspiegels des Todten Meeres und des Wasserspiegels des Mittelländischen Meeres', AEVS, 1 (1842), pp. 249–50.

Allen, Attempt = William Allen, 'An attempt to account for numerous appearances of sudden and violent drainage on the sides of the basin of the Dead Sea', *JRGS*, 23 (1853), pp. 163–6.

Allen, Dead Sea = William Allen, *The Dead Sea, a New Route to India, with Other Fragments and Gleanings in the East*, I-II, London: Longman, Brown, Green, and Longmans, 1855.

Allen, Obituary = 'William Allen, R.N., F.R.S.', *DUM*, 1/1 (1878), pp. 539–40.

Allen, Watershed = William Allen, 'The watershed of Wadi el Arabá', *JRGS*, 23 (1853), pp. 166–71.

Anderson, Question = Matthew Smith Anderson, *The Eastern Question 1774–1923: A Study in International Relations*, London: Macmillan, 1966.

Andrew, Memoir = William Patrick Andrew, *Memoir of the Euphrates Valley Route to India*, London: Wm. H. Allen, 1857.

Andrews, Landscape = John Harwood Andrews, *A Paper Landscape: The Ordnance Survey in Nineteenth-Century Ireland*, Oxford: Clarendon Press, 1975.

Appleton, Cyclopaedia = James Grant Wilson and John Fiske (eds.), *Appleton's Cyclopaedia of American Biography*, I-VI, New York: D. Appleton, 1888–9.

Armstrong, Essay = Robert Armstrong, *A Practical Essay on Steam Boilers*, [London?] [1836/7?].

Art. XI = 'Art. XI. – 1. *Reports on the Navigation of the Euphrates.* Submitted to the Government by Captain Chesney, of the Royal Artillery. London. 1833. 2. *An Account of Steam-Vessels...* Compiled by G. A. Prinsep. Calcutta. 1830. 3. *Eastern and Egyptian Scenery... with Remarks on the Advantages and Practicability of Steam-Navigation from England to India.* By Captain C. F. Head', *The Quarterely Review*, 49 (April & July, 1833), pp. 212–28.

Atkin, Diplomacy = Muriel Atkin, 'The pragmatic diplomacy of Paul I: Russia's relations with Asia, 1796–1801', *Slavic Review*, 38/1 (1979), pp. 60–74.

Avcioğlu, Urquhart = Nebahat Avcioğlu, 'David Urquhart and the role of travel literature in the introduction of Turkish baths to Victorian England', Starkey, Interpreting, pp. 69–80.

Bannister, Survey = John Thomas Bannister, *A Survey of the Holy Land; Geography, History, and Destiny: Designed to Elucidate the Imagery of Scripture, and Demonstrate the Fulfillment of Prophecy*, Bath: Binns and Goodwin; London: Simpkin, Marshall, and Co., 1844.

Barber, Letter = James Barber, *A Letter to the Right Hon. Sir John Cam Hobhouse, Bart, M.P., President of the India Board &c.&c.&c., on Steam Navigation with India, and Suggesting the Best Mode of Carrying It into Effect viâ the Red Sea*, London, 1837.

Barker, Lares = William Burckhardt Barker, *Lares and Penates; or, Cilicia and Its Governors: Being a Short Historical Account of that Province from the Earliest Times to the Present Day...*, ed. William Francis Ainsworth, London: Ingram, Cooke, and Co., 1853.

Barker, Notes = William Burckhardt Barker, 'Notes made on a journey to the source of the River Orontes in Syria, in September, 1834', *JRGS*, 7 (1837), pp. 95–102.

Barker, Syria = Edward B.B. Barker (ed.), *Syria and Egypt under the Last Five Sultans of Turkey: Being Experiences, during Fifty Years, of Mr. Consul-General Barker, Chiefly from His Letters and Journals*, I-II, London: Samuel Tinsley, 1876.

Bartlett, Edom = John Raymond Bartlett, *Edom and the Edomites*, Sheffield: Sheffield Acad. Press, 1989.

Bartlett, Mapping = John Raymond Bartlett, *Mapping Jordan through Two Millenia* (The Palestine Exploration Fund Annual, X), Leeds: Maney, 2008.

Bartlett, Travellers = John Raymond Bartlett, 'Irish travellers and archaeologists in the Near East', [unpublished manuscript].

Baumann, Apostelstrasse = Andreas Baumann, *Die Apostelstrasse: Eine außergewöhnliche Vision und Ihre Verwirklichung*, Giessen and Basel: Brunnen, 1999.

Beaufort, Karamania = Francis Beaufort, *Karamania: A Brief Description of the South Coast of Asia Minor*, London: Hunter, 1817.

Beechey, Address 1856 = Frederick William Beechey, 'Anniversary Address', *JRGS*, 26 (1856), pp. clxxi-ccxxxiv.

Beke, Alluvia = Charles Tilstone Beke, 'On the alluvia of Babylonia and Chaldæa', *LEPMJ*, 14 (June 1839), pp. 426–32.

Beke, Countries = Charles Tilstone Beke, 'On the countries south of Abyssinia', *JRGS*, 13 (1843), pp. 254–68.

Beke, Dépression = [Charles Tilstone Beke], 'Dépression de la Mer Morte', *NAVSG*, 2 (1838), pp. 372–4.

Beke, Discoveries = Emily Beke (ed.), *The Late Dr. Charles Beke's Discoveries of Sinai in Arabia and of Midian*, London: Trübner, 1878.

Beke, Evidence = Charles Tilstone Beke, 'On the geological evidence of the advance of the land at the head of the Persian Gulf', *LEPMJ*, July 1835.

Beke, Idol = Charles Tilstone Beke, *The Idol in Horeb: Evidence that the Golden Image at Mount Sinai Was a Cone, and Not a Calf*, London: Tinsley Brothers, 1871.

Beke, Jacob = Emily Beke, *Jacob's Flight; or a Pilgrimage to Harran and Thence into the Promised Land*, London: Longman, Green, Longman, Roberts, and Green, 1865.

Beke, Localities = Charles Tilstone Beke, *Localities of Horeb, Mount Sinai, and Median, in Connexion with the Hypothesis of the Distinction between Mitzraim and Egypt*, London 1835.

Beke, Meer = Charles Tilstone Beke, 'Das todte Meer', *ABAZ*, 20.4.1838, pp. 833–4.

Beke, Meer und See = Charles Tilstone Beke, 'Das todte Meer und der See Tiberias', *BAZ*, 11.6.1838, p. 1221.

Beke, Niveau = Charles Tilstone Beek, 'Das Niveau des todten und des Mittelmeeres', *BAZ*, 27.6.1838, p. 1341.

Beke, Notes = Charles Tilstone Beke, *Notes on an Excursion to Harran, in Padan-Aram, and Thence over Mount Gilead and the Jordan, to Sechem*, London: W. Clowes, 1862.

Beke, Notes JRGS = 'Notes on an excursion to Harrān, in Padan-Aram, and thence over Mount Gilead and the Jordan, to Sechem, by Charles T. Beke...', *JRGS*, 32 (1862), pp. 76–100.

Beke, Origines = Charles Tilstone Beke, *Origines biblicae; or, Researches in Primeval History*, London: Parbury, Allen and Co., 1834.

Beke, Persian Gulf = Charles Tilstone Beke, 'On the former extent of the Persian Gulf, and on the non-identity of Babylone and Babel; in reply to Mr. Carter', *LEPMJ*, July 1837.

Beke, Reasons = Charles Tilstone Beke, *Reasons for Returning the Gold Medal of the Geographical Society of France, and for Withdrawing from Its Membership*, London: James Madden, 1851.

Beke, Statement = Charles Tilstone Beke, *A Statement of Facts Relative to the Transactions between the Writer and the Late British Political Mission to the Court of Shoa in Abessinia*, London: James Madden, 1846.

Beke, Summary = Emily Beke, *Summary of the Late Dr. Beke's Published Works, and of His Inadequately Requited Public Services*, Tunbridge Wells: A.K. Baldwin, 1876.

Bekenmeyer, Reisen = Anemone Bekenmeier (ed.), *Reisen nach Jerusalem: Das Heilige Land in Karten und Ansichten aus fünf Jahrhunderten, Sammlung Loewenhardt*, Wiesbaden: Dr. Ludwig Reichert, 1993.

Belgrave, Pirate = Charles Belgrave, *The Pirate Coast*, London: G. Bell and Sons, 1966.

Ben-Arieh, Exploration = Yehoshua Ben-Arieh, 'The geographical exploration of the Holy Land', *PEFQS*, 104 (1972), pp. 81–92.

Ben-Arieh, Lynch = Yehoshua Ben-Arieh, 'William F. Lynch's expedition to the Dead Sea, 1847–48', *Prologue: The Journal of the National Archives*, (Spring 1973), pp. 14–21.

Ben-Arieh, Maps = Yehoshua Ben-Arieh, 'The first surveyed maps of Jerusalem', *Eretz-Israel: Archaeological, Historical and Geographical Studies*, 11 (1973) (I. Dunayevsky Memorial Volume), pp. 69–71 [Heb.].

Ben-Arieh, Painting = Yehoshua Ben-Arieh, *Painting the Holy Land in the Nineteenth Century*, trsl. Zipora Brody and Ethel Broido, ed. Yohai Goell, Jerusalem: Yad Izhak Ben-Zvi, 1997.

Ben-Arieh, Perceptions = Yehoshua Ben-Arieh, 'Perceptions and images of the Land of Israel in the writings of nineteenth-century western travellers', Shmuel Almog et al. (eds.), *Transition and Change in Modern Jewish History: Essays Presented in Honor of Shmuel Ettinger*, Jerusalem: Zalman Shazar Center, 1987, pp. 89–114 [Heb.].

Ben-Arieh, Pioneer = Yehoshua Ben-Arieh, 'Pioneer scientific exploration in the Holy Land at the beginning of the nineteenth century', *Terrae Incognitae*, 4 (1972), pp. 95–110.

Ben-Arieh, Rediscovery = Yehoshua Ben-Arieh, *The Rediscovery of the Holy Land in the Nineteenth Century*, Jerusalem: Magnes, Israel Exploration Society, and Detroit: Wayne State University Press, 1979.

Ben-Yehuda, Eretz Israel = Eliezer Ben-Yehuda, *Sefer Eretz Israel*, Jerusalem: Y.M. Salomon, 1883 [Heb.].

Ben-Zvi, Source = Reuven Ben-Zvi, 'The source of information: Agatha Christie', *Ma'ariv*, 8.9.1963 [Heb.].

Bence-Jones, Guide = Mark Bence-Jones, *A Guide to Irish Country-Houses*, London: Constable, 1988.

Bent, English = James Theodore Bent, 'The English in the Levant', EHR, 5 (1890), pp. 654–64.

Benvenisti, Cemeteries = Meron Benvenisti, *The Jerusalem Cemeteries*, Jerusalem: Keter, 1990 [Heb.].

Berg Sinai = 'Wie hoch ist der Berg Sinai?', *AEVS*, 5 (1832), p. 176.

Berghaus, Letter = 'Extract from a letter of Professor Berghaus', *JRGS*, 9 (1839), pp. 308–10.

Berghaus, Map = Heinrich Berghaus, *Karte von Syrien, den Manen Jacotin's und Burckhardt's gewidmet* (Berghaus' Atlas von Asien, 5), Gotha: Justus Perthes, 1835.

Berghaus, Memoir = Heinrich Berghaus, *Geographisches Memoir zur Erklärung und Erläuterung der Karte von Syrien* (No. 5. von Berghaus' Atlas von Asia), Gotha: Justus Perthes, 1835.

Berghaus, Memoir Arabia = Heinrich Berghaus, *Geo-Hydrographisches Memoir zur Erklärung und Erläuterung der General-Karte von Arabia und dem Nil-Lande* (No. 6 von Berghaus' Atlas von Asia), Gotha: Justus Perthes, 1835.

Berghaus and Stülpnagel, Palestine = Heinrich Berghaus and Friedrich von Stülpnagel, *Palästina nach den zuverlässigsten alten und neuen Quellen*, mit Text von Karl von Raumer, Gotha: Justus Perthes, 1844.

Berry, Partry = Henry Fitzpatrick Berry, 'The Partry private cemetery, Townland of Cloonlagheen, and Parish of Ballyovey', *Journal of the Association for the Preservation of Memorials to the Dead in Ireland*, 8/2 (1910), pp. 130–4.

Bertou, Dépression = Jules de Bertou, 'Dépression de la vallée du Jourdain et du lac Asphaltite', *BSG*, 12 (1839), pp. 113–58; 15 (1849), pp. 219–20; 17 (1842), pp. 139–43.

Bertou, Extract = Jules de Bertou, 'Extract from a notice on the site of ancient Tyre', *JRGS*, 9 (1839), pp. 286–94.

Bertou, Extrait = 'Extrait d'une autre lettre de M. Bertou, datée de Beyrout, le 25 novembre 1838', *BSG*, Deuxième Série, 11 (1839), pp. 166–9.

Bertou, Extraits = 'Extraits de deux letters de M. le comte J. de Bertou, sur son voyage dans la Palestine', *BSG*, Deuxième Série, 10 (1838), pp. 240–6.

Bertou, Itinéraire = Jules de Bertou, 'Itinéraire de la mer Morte à Akaba par les Wadys-el-Ghor, el-Araba et el-Akaba, et retour à Hébron par Petra', *BSG*, Deuxième Série, 11 (1839), pp. 274–331.

Bertou, Mont Hor = Jules de Bertou, *Le Mont Hor, le tombeau d'Aaron, Cades: étude sur l'itinéraire des Israëlites*, Paris: B. Durpat, 1860.

Bertou, Notes = Jules de Bertou, 'Notes on a journey from Jerusalem to Hebron, the Dead Sea, El Ghór, and Wádi 'Arabah to 'Akabah, and back by Petra; in April, 1838', *JRGS*, 9 (1839), pp. 277–86.

Bertou, Réponse = Jules de Bertou, 'Réponse à une question de M. Poulain de Bossy sur l'emplacement de Tyr', *BSG*, Deuxiéme Série, 11 (1839), pp. 150–66.

Bertou, Tyre = Jules de Bertou, 'Extract from a Notice on the Site of Ancient Tyre', *JRGS*, 9 (1839), pp. 286–94.

Bertou, Voyage = Jules de Bertou, 'Voyage de l'extrémité sud de la Mer Morte à la pointe nord du golfe Elanitique', *BSG*, Deuxiéme Série, 10 (1838), pp. 18–32.

Bindoff, Representatives = Stanley Thomas Bindoff, Elizabeth Frances Malcolm Smith and Charles Kingsley Webster (eds.), *British Diplomatic Representatives 1789–1852*, London: Royal Historical Society, 1934.

Bird, Bible = Isaac Bird, *Bible Work in Bible Lands: or, Events in the History of the Syria Mission*, Philadelphia: Presbyterian Board of Publication, 1872.

Bird, Notice = Isaac Bird, 'Notices of Minerals, etc., from Palestine, Egypt, etc.', *AJSA*, ser. 1, 10 (1826), pp. 21–9.

Bird, Notice Hall = Isaac Bird, 'Notice of various facts relating to Palestine; in a letter [...] to Prof. Hall', *AJSA*, ser. 1, 12 (1827), pp. 145–7.

Bird, Notices = Isaac Bird, 'Notices of Palestine, etc.', *AJSA*, ser. 1, 15 (1829), pp. 374–8.

Blanc, Narrative = Henry Blanc, *A Narrative of Captivity in Abyssinia: with Some Account of the Late Emperor Theodore, His Country and People* (Cass Library of African Studies: Travels and Narratives, 65), London: Frank Cass, 1970.

Blanche and Gaillardot, Catalogue = Isidore Blanche and Charles Gaillardot, *Catalogue de l'herbier de Syrie*, Paris: Mme. Ve. Dondey-Dupré, 1854.

Blanckenhorn, Sodom = Max Blanckenhorn, 'Noch einmal Sodom und Gomorrah', *ZDPV*, 21 (1898), pp. 65–83.

Bliss, Exploration = Frederick Jones Bliss, *The Development of Palestine Exploration: Being the Ely Lectures for 1903*, New York: Charles Scribner's Sons, 1907.

BLO = Constant von Würzbach (ed.), *Biographisches Lexicon des Kaiserthums Oesterreich, enthaltend die Lebensskizzen der denkwürdigen Personen, welche seit 1750 in den Österreichischen Kronenländern geboren oder darin gelebt und gewirkt haben*, I–LX, Wien, 1856–1891.

Boase = Frederic Boase, *Modern English Biography*, I–VI, London: F. Cass, 1965 (1st ed. 1892–1921).

Boggis, Jordan = James Edmund Boggis, *Down the Jordan in a Canoe*, London: Society for Promoting Christian Knowledge, 1939.

Bonato, Chypre = Lucie Bonato, 'Camille Callier: un officier instruit de l'armée française qui explora Chypre en 1832', *Thetis*, 10 (2003), pp. 113–41.

Bonato, Navarin = Lucie Bonato, 'Navarin, Nauplie, Athènes: Les trois escales grecques de l'ingénieur-géographe Camille Callier en route verse l'Orient en 1830', *Thetis*, 10 (2003), pp. 107–12.

Bookman et al., Quaternary = Revital Bookman et al., 'Quaternary lake levels in the Dead Sea basin: Two centuries of research', Yehuda Enzel, Amoz Agnon and Mordechai Stein (eds.), *New Frontiers in Dead Sea Paleoenvironmental Research* (Geological Society of America, Special Paper 401), Boulder, CO: Geological Society of America, 2006, pp. 155–70.

Brawer, Centenary = Avraham Jacob Brawer, 'Centenary to the finding of the depression of the Dead Sea', *Hateva Veha'aretz*, 4/9 (1937), pp. 444–5 [Heb.].

Breycha-Vauthier, Österreich = Arthur Carl von Breycha-Vauthier, *Österreich in der Levante: Geschichte und Geschichten einer alten Freundschaft,* Wien and München: Harold, 1972

Brentano, Leiden = Clemens Brentano, *Das bittere Leiden unseres Herrn und heilandes Jesus Christus: Nach den Betrachtungen den Augustinerin von Dülmen* (Leben und Lehre Jesu Christi, 5), Stein am Rhein: Christiana, 1996 (17th ed., 1st pub. 1833).

Broc = Numa Broc, *Dictionnaire illustré des explorateurs et grands voyageurs Français du XIXe siècle*, II: *Asie*, Paris: C.T.H.S., 1992.

Brown, Politics = Malcolm Brown, *The Politics of Irish Literature: From Thomas Davies to W. B. Yeats*, London: George Allen & Unwin, 1972.

Buckingham, Travels = James Silk Buckingham, *Travels among the Arab Tribes Inhabiting the Countries East of Syria and Palestine, Including a Journey from Nazareth to the Mountains beyond the Dead Sea, and from Thence through the Plains of the Hauran to Bozra, Damascus, Tripoly, Lebanon, Baalbeck, and by the Valley of the Orontes to Seleucia, Antioch, and Aleppo*, London: Longman, Hurst, Rees, Orme, Brown and Green, 1825.

Burckhardt, Nubia = John Lewis Burckhardt, *Travels in Nubia*, London: J. Murray, 1819.

Burckhardt, Syria = John Lewis Burckhardt, *Travels in Syria and the Holy Land*, London: J. Murray, 1822.

Burell, Preface = R.M. Burell, 'Preface', *Memoirs by Commander Felix Jones, I.N.* (Selections From the Records of the Bombay Government, XLIII-New Series), Bombay: Bombay Education Society, 1857, pp. iii-xxxiii.

Burke = Charles Mosley (ed.), *Burke's Peerage & Baronetage*, 106th edition, Crans-sur-Céligny (Switzerland), 1999.

Burke, Gentry = Bernard Burke, *A Genealogical and Heraldic History of the Landed Gentry of Ireland*, new ed., rev. Arthur C. Fox-Davies, London: Harrison & Sons, 1912.

Burke, Ireland = *Burke's Irish Family Records*, 5th ed., ed. Hugh Montgomery-Massingberd, London: Burke's Peerage, 1976.

Burton, Narrative = Nathanael Burton, *Narrative of a Voyage from Liverpool to Alexandria, Touching at the Island of Malta, and from Thence to Beirut in Syria, with a Journey to Jerusalem, Voyage from Jaffa to Cyprus and Constantinople...*, Dublin: John Yates, 1838.

Busching, Beschreibung = Anton Friedrich Busching, *Beschreibung des todten Meers in Palästina*, Hamburg: Johann Carl Bohn, 1766.

Busching, Erdbeschreibung = Anton Friedrich Busching, *Neue Erdbeschreibung von Asia: Erste Abteilung, welche die Turkische Länder in diesem Welt-Theil, Arabien, Mesopotamien, Syrien und das Gelobte Land in sich begreift*, Schaffhausen: Benedict Hurter, 1769.

Butlin, Historical Geography = Robin A. Butlin, *Historical Geography: Through the Gates of Space and Time*, London etc.: Edward Arnold, 1993.

Bystron, Polacy = Jan Stanislaw Bystron, *Polacy w Ziemi Swietej, Syrii I Egypcie 1147–1914*, Krakow: Orbis, 1930.

Cain, Society = Mead T. Cain, 'The maps of the Society for the Diffusion of Useful Knowledge: A publishing history', *IM*, 46 (1994), pp. 151–67.

Callier, Kleinasien = 'Camille Calliers Reise in Kleinasien, Syrien, Palästina und im peträischen Arabien', *A*, 8/231–2 (1835), pp. 923–4, 928.

Callier, Map = Camille Callier, *Carte de la Syrie Méridionale et de la Palestine, dressée en 1835, d'après les ordres du Directeur du Dépot-général de la guerre Lieut.–Général Pelet*, [Paris], 1840.

Callier, Mémoire = Camille Callier, 'Mémoire sur le dépression de la Mer Morte et de la valée du Jourdain', *NAVSG*, 21 (1839), pp. 5–38.

Callier, Note = Camille Callier, 'Note sur le voyage de M. le Comte de Bertou, depuis le Lac Asphaltite jusqu'a la Mer Rouge, par le Ouadi-èl-Araba', *BSG*, Deuxiéme Série, 10 (1838), pp. 84–100.

Callier, Notes = Camille Callier and Poulain de Bossay, 'Notes sur quelques explorations à faire en Syrie, en Palestine et dans l'Arabie Pétrée', *BSG*, Deuxiéme Série, 11 (1838), pp. 40–7.

Callier, Reise = 'Reise des Stabskapitäns Callier von Jerusalem nach Akabah am rothen Meere', *A*, 7/137–8 (1834), pp. 546–8, 551–2.

Callier, Voyage = Camille Callier, 'Voyage en Asie Mineure, en Syrie, en Palestine et en Arabie-Pétrée', *BSG*, Deuxiéme Série, 7 (1834), pp. 5–22, 239–62.

Carmel, Christen = Alex Carmel, *Christen als Pioniere im Heiligen Land: Ein Beitrag zur Geschichte der Pilgermission und des Wiederaufbaus Palästinas im 19. Jahrhundert*, Basel: Friedrich Reinhardt, 1981.

Carmel, Russia = Alex Carmel, 'Russian activity in Palestine in the nineteenth century', Richard I. Cohen (ed.), *Vision and Conflict in the Holy Land*, Jerusalem: Yad Ben-Zvi, 1985, pp. 45–77.

Carne, Letters = John Carne, *Letters from the East, Written during a Recent Tour through Turkey, Egypt, Arabia, the Holy Land, Syria, and Greece*, I-II, London: Henry Colburn, 1826[2].

Carne, Syria = William Henry Bartlett, Thomas Allom, etc. (paintings), John Carne (text), *Syria, the Holy Land, Asia Minor &c. Illustrated*, I-III, London and Paris: Fisher, Son & Co., 1838.

Carré, Voyageurs = Jean-Marie Carré, *Voyageurs et écrivains Français en Égypte*, I: *Des pèlerins du Moyen Âge à Méhémet-Ali*, 12th ed., Cairo: Institut Français d'archéologie orientale, n.d (1st ed. 1932).

Carter and Harlow, Archives = Mia Carter and Barbara Harlow (eds.), *Archives of Empire*, I: *From the East India Company to the Suez Canal*, Durham and London: Duke University Press, 2003.

Castlereagh, Journey = Viscount Castlereagh (Frederick-William-Robert Vane-Stewart), *A Journey to Damascus through Egypt, Nubia, Arabia Petraea, Palestine, and Syria*, I-II, London: Henry Colburn, 1847.

Chambers, Granuaile = Anne Chambers, *Granuaile: The Life and Times of Grace O'Malley, c. 1530–1603*, Dublin: Wolfhound, 1998.

Charlewood, Passages = Edward Philips Charlewood, *Passages from the Life of a Naval Officer*, Manchester: Cave & Sever, 1869.

Chateaubriand, Itinéraire = François-René de Chateaubriand, *Itinéraire de Paris a Jérusalem*, I-II, Paris: Firmin-Didot, 1856 (1st ed. 1811).

Chaudhuri, Disturbances = Sashi Bhusan Chaudhuri, *Civil Disturbances during the British Rule in India (1765–1857)*, Calcutta: The World Press, 1955.

Chesney, Campaigns = Francis Rawdon Chesney, *The Russo-Turkish Campaigns of 1828 and 1829: With a View of the Present State of Affairs in the East*, London: Smith, Elder & Co., 1854.

Chesney, Chesney = Helena C.G. Chesney, 'General Francis Rawdon Chesney, 1789–1872', John Wilson Foster and Helena C.G. Chesney (eds.), *Nature in Ireland: A Scientific and Cultural History*, Dublin: Lilliput, 1997, pp. 337–42.

Chesney, Expedition = Francis Rawdon Chesney, *The Expedition for the Survey of the Rivers Euphrates and Tigris, Carried On by Order of the British Government, in the Years 1835, 1836, and 1837...*, II, New York: Greenwood, 1969 (1st ed. London: Longman, Brown, Green, and Longman, 1850).

Chesney, Narrative = Francis Rawdon Chesney, *Narrative of the Euphrates Expedition, Carried On by Order of the British Government during the Years 1835, 1836, and 1837*, London: Longman, Green, and Co., 1868.

Chesney, Portrait = 'Our Portrait Gallery. – No. XXIV, Lieutenant-Colonel F. R. Chesney, Royal Artillery, F.R.S. and F.G.S.', *DUM*, 18 (1841), pp. 574–80.

Clowes, History = William Laird Clowes, *The Royal Navy: A History from the Earliest Times to the Present*, I-VII, London: Little, Brown, Sampson Low and Marston, 1897–1903.

Corcoran, Clongowes = Timothy Corcoran, *The Clongowes Record 1814 to 1932*, Dublin: Browne and Nolan, [1832].

Costello, Costigan = Con Costello, 'Christopher Costigan, explorer of the Dead Sea', *IG*, 11 (1978), 214.

Costello, Explorers = Con Costello, 'Nineteenth-century Irish explorers in the Levant', *IG*, 7 (1974), pp. 88–96.

Costello, Ireland = Con Costello, *Ireland and the Holy Land: An Account of Irish Links with the Levant from the Earliest Times*, Alcester and Dublin: C. Goodfile Neale, 1974.

Courtney, Beaufort = Nicholas Courtney, *Gale Force 10: The Life and Legacy of Admiral Beaufort*, London: Review, 2003.

Crombie, Alexander = Kelvin Crombie, *A Jewish Bishop in Jerusalem*, Jerusalem: Nicolayson's, Christ Church, 2006.

Crombie, Friedman = Kelvin Crombie, 'A real son of Zion: Ben Zion Friedman and the Jewish Mission at Safed', *Mishkan*, 15/2 (1991), pp. 25–36.

Crombie, Zion = Kelvin Crombie, *For the Love of Zion: Christian Witness and the Restoration of Israel*, London, Sydney and Auckland: Hodder & Stoughton, 1991.

Cross = Frank Leslie Cross, *The Oxford Dictionary of the Christian Church*, 2nd ed., eds. Frank Leslie Cross and Elizabeth Anne Livingstone, Oxford: Oxford University Press, 1988.

Cullen, Diaspora = L.M. Cullen, 'The Irish diaspora of the seventeenth and eighteenth centuries', Nicholas Canny (ed.), *Europeans on the Move: Studies on European Migration, 1500–1800*, Oxford: Clarendon Press, 1994, pp. 113–49.

Cunningham, Wilkie = Allan Cunningham, *The Life of Sir David Wilkie: With His Journals, Tours, and Critical Remarks on Works of Art; and a Selection from His Correspondence*, I-III, London: John Murray, 1843.

D'Anville, Map = Jean Baptiste Bourguignon d'Anville, *Palestine*, London (1771?).

Dawson and Uphill = Warren R. Dawson and Eric P. Uphill, *Who Was Who in Egyptology*, M.L. Bierbrier, 3rd revised ed., London: The Egyptian Exploration Society, 1995.

Dawson, Memoirs = Llewellyn Stiles Dawson, *Memoirs of Hydrography: Including Brief Biographies of the Principal Officers Who Have Served in H. M. Naval Surveying Service between the Years 1750 and 1855*, I: *1750 to 1830*, II: *1830 to 1885*, Eastbourne: Henry W. Keay, 1885.

Day, Admiralty = Archibald Day, *The Admiralty Hydrographic Service, 1795–1919*, London: Her Majesty's Stationary Office, 1967.

DBF = Michel Prevost et al. (eds.), *Dictionnaire de Biographie Française*, I-XVII, Paris: Letouzey et Ané, 1927–8.

Dead Sea = 'On the Dead Sea and some positions in Syria', JRGS, 7 (1837), p. 456.

Deflers, Notice = Albert Deflers, *Notice sur l'herbier Gaillardot*, Cairo: Imprimerie Hindié, 1898.

Delcros, Notice = Francois-Joseph Delcros, 'Notice sur la dépression de la Mer Morte et du cours du Jourdain jusqu'au nord du lac de Tibériade, et discussion des résultats des observations barométriques de MM. De Bertou et Russegger qui constatent unedépression au-dessus de la surface genérale d'équilibre des mers', *Bulletin de la Société de Géologie de France*, 14 (1843), pp. 336–9.

Della Dora, Landscapes = Veronica Della Dora, 'Geo-strategy and the persistence of antiquity: Surveying mythical hydrographies in the Eastern Mediterranean', *JHG*, 33/3 (2007), pp. 514-541 DNB = Leslie Stephen and Sidney Lee (eds.), The Dictionary of National Biography: from the Earliest Times to 1900, I-XXI + supplement, London: Oxford University Press, 1921-1922.

Doherty, Survey = Gilian M. Doherty, *The Irish Ordnance Survey: History, Culture and Memory*, Dublin: Four Courts, 2006.

Donnelly, Landlords = James S. Donnelly, Jr., 'Landlords and tenants', William Edward Vaughan (ed.), *A New History of Ireland*, V: *Ireland under the Union, I, 1801–70*, Oxford: Clarendon Press, 1989, pp. 333–49.

Driver, Geography = Felix Driver, *Geography Militant: Cultures of Exploration and Empire*, Oxford and Malden, MA: Blackwell, 2001.

Duhamel, Autobiography = Alexander O. Duhamel, 'Автобиография', Русский Архив, 1885, номер 4 ['Autobiography', *Russian Archive*, 1885, vol. 4].

Dunbar, Compass = Gary S. Dunbar, '"The compass follows the flag": The French scientific mission to Mexico, 1864–1867', *AAAG*, 78/1 (1988), pp. 229–40.

Dussaud, Envers = René Dussaud, 'L'envers d'un voyage archéologique en Palestine (1850–1851)' *Mémorial Lagrange* (Cinquantenaire de l'école biblique et archéologique française de Jérusalem), Paris: Librairie Lecoffre, 1940.

EBR = Warren E. Preece et al. (eds.), *Encyclopedia Britannica*, I-XXIII, Chicago etc.: William Benton, 1967.

Edgeworth, Memoir = [Maria Edgeworth], *A Memoir of Maria Edgeworth, with Selection from her Letters*, ed. by her children, I-III, London: private ed., 1867.

Edney, Mapping = Matthew H. Edney, *Mapping an Empire: The Geographical Construction of British India, 1765-1843*, Chicago and London: The University of Chicago Press, 1997.

EEEE = Dietmar Henze, *Enzyklopädie der Entdecker und Erforscher der Erde*, I-V, Graz: Akademische Druck- u. Verlagsanstalt, 1978-2004.

Egmont and Heyman, Travels = Johann Aegidius van Egmont and John Heyman, *Travels through Part of Europe, Asia Minor, the Islands of the Archipelago, Syria, Palestine, Egypt, Mt. Sinai, etc.*, trsl. from the Low Dutch, I-II, London: L. Davies & C. Reymer's, 1759.

Ehrenberg, Russegger = Christian Gottfried Ehrenberg, 'Mittheilungen über eine bisher unbekannte sehr grosse Verbreitung der mikroskopischen Lebens als Felsmassen im centralen Nordamerika und im westlichen Asien', *BAB*, 1842, pp. 187-8.

Ehrenberg, Untersuchung = Christian Gottfried Ehrenberg, 'Ueber mikroskopische Untersuchung des Jordanwassers und Bodens des Todten Meeres', *BAB*, 1849, pp. 187-93.

Eiken, Faith = Edwin Eiken, 'Placing Faith: Spatial Apologetics in Victorian Palestine' [ms., n.d.].

Elath, Chesney = Eliahu Elath, 'Francis Rawdon Chesney and the Search for Shorter Routes to India', Dissertation, Manuscript [n.d.].

Elath, Routes = Eliahu Elath, *Britain's Routes to India: British Projects in 1834-1872 for Linking the Mediterranean with the Persian Gulf by Steam Navigation on the Euphrates and by Euphrates Valley Railway*, Jerusalem: Magnes, 1971 [Heb.].

Eliav, Austria = Mordechai Eliav (and Barbara Haider), *Österreich und das Heilige Land: Ausgewählte Konsulatdokumente aus Jerusalem 1849-1917* (Fontes Rerum Austriacarum: Österreichische Geschichtsquelle, 2te Abt.: Diplomataria et Acta, 91), Wien: Österreichischen Akademie der Wissenschaften, 2000.

Eliav, Britain = Mordechai Eliav, *Britain and the Holy Land 1838-1914: Selected Documents from the British Consulate in Jerusalem*, Jerusalem: Yad Izhak Ben-Zvi and Magnes, 1997.

Engelmann, Atlas = Gerhard Engelmann, 'Der Atlas von Asien des Heinrich Berghaus', *PM*, 104 (1960), pp. 311-29.

Engelmann, Berghaus = Gerhard Engelmann, *Heinrich Berghaus: Der Kartograph von Potsdam* (Acta Historica Leopoldina, Nr. 10), Halle/Saale 1977.

England and the East = 'England und der Orient', *ABAZ*, 19.10.1838, pp. 2201-2, 20.10.1838, pp. 2210-11.

Erdl, Barometer = Michael Pius Erdl, 'Barometer- u. Thermometer-Beobachtungen, angestellt auf einer Reise durch Arabia Peträa, Palästina und Syrien', *AEVS*, 1 (1842), pp. 267-80.

Eriksen, Costigan = Erik Olaf Eriksen, 'Christopher Costigan (1810-1835): Irish explorer of the Dead Sea', *Holy Land*, (Spring 1985), pp. 41-9.

Eriksen, Explorers = Erik Olaf Eriksen, *Holy Land Explorers*, Jerusalem: Franciscan Printing Press, 1989.

Eriksen, Illness = Erik Olaf Eriksen, 'The illness of Christopher Costigin - A case of heat stroke', *Dublin Historical Record*, 39 (June 1986), pp. 82-5.

Eriksen, Molyneux = [Erik Olaf Eriksen], 'Lt. Molyneux, British explorer of the Dead Sea', *Holy Land*, (Fall 1985), pp. 162-6.

Essai de l'eau = 'Essai de l'eau du Jourdain', *ACP*, 11 (1819), pp. 197-8.

Evans, Antiquaries = John Evans, *A History of the Society of Antiquaries*, Oxford: Oxford University Press for the Society of Antiquaries, 1956.

Fagan, Rape = Brian M. Fagan, *The Rape of the Nile: Tomb Robbers, Tourists, and Archaeologists in Egypt*, New York: Charles Scribner's Sons, 1975.

Fahmy, Mehmed Ali = Khaled Fahmy, *All the Pasha's Men: Mehmed Ali, His Army, and the Making of Modern Egypt*, Cambridge: Cambridge University Press, 1997.

Farah, Politics = Caesar E. Farah, *The Politics of Interventionism in Ottoman Lebanon, 1830–1861*, Oxford: Center for Lebanes Studies, and London and New York: I.B. Tauris, 2000.

Felton, Peacock = Felix Felton, *Thomas Love Peacock*, London: G. Allen and Unwin, 1972.

Finn, Stirring Times = James Finn, *Stirring Times, or Records from Jerusalem Consular Chronicles of 1853 to 1856*, ed. Elisabeth Anne Finn, I-II, London: Kegan Paul, 1878.

Finnie, Pioneers = David H. Finnie, *Pioneers East: The Early American Experience in the Middle East*, Cambridge, MA: Harvard University Press, 1967.

Fischer, Geschichte = Hans Fischer, 'Geschichte der Kartographie von Palästina', *ZDPV*, 62 (1939), pp. 169–89; 63 (1940), pp. 1–111 (Bd. II, pp. 43–5).

Fleming, Barrow = Fergus Fleming, *Barrow's Boys*, New York: Grove, 1998.

Fontanier, Narrative = Victor Fontanier, *Narrative of a Mission to India, and the Countries Bordering on the Persian Gulf, &c., by Way of Egypt, and the Red Sea, Undertaken by Order of the French Government*, I, London: Richard Bentley, 1844.

Forbin, Voyage = Louis Nicolas Phillipe Auguste, Comte de Forbin, *Voyage dans le Levant en 1817 et 1818*, Paris: Delaunay, 1819².

Fox, March = Robin Lane Fox (ed.), *The Long March: Xenophon and the Ten Thousand*, New Haven: Yale University Press, 2004.

Fraas, Todte Meer = Oskar Fraas, *Das Todte Meer*, Stuttgart: Steinkopf, 1867.

Frederiks, Velde = Johannes Godefridus Frederiks, *Biographisch woordenboek der Noord- en Zuidnederlandsche letterkunde*, Amsterdam 1888, p. 39.

Freeman, Portrait = John Freeman, *A Portrait of George Moore in a Study of His Work*, London: T. Werner Laurie, 1922.

Freeman, RGS = Thomas Walter Freeman, 'The Royal Geographical Society and the development of geography', Eric Herbert Brown (ed.), *Geography Yesterday and Tomorrow*, Oxford: Oxford University Press, 1980, pp. 1–17.

Friendly, Beaufort = Alfred Friendly, *Beaufort of the Admiralty*, London: Hutchinson, 1977.

Frumin, Russian = Mitia Frumin, 'Russian navy mapping activities in the eastern and southern Mediterranean (late 18th century), *Journal of the Washington Map Society*, 13 (2004), pp. 13–26.

Frumin, Rubin and Gavish, Russian = Mitia Frumin, Rehav Rubin and Dov Gavish, 'A Russian naval officer's chart of Haifa Bay 1772', *IM*, 54 (2002), pp. 125–8.

Fuller, Kerrymen = J.F. Fuller, 'Two Forgotten Kerrymen', *Journal of the Cork Historical and Archaeological Society*, 27 (1921), pp. 69–72.

Furrer, Tobler = Konrad Furrer, 'Dr. Titus Tobler', *ZDPV*, 1 (1878), pp. 49–60.

Gadsby, Wanderings = John Gadsby, *My Wanderings: Being Travels in the East in 1846–47, 1850–51, 1852–53*, I-II, London: Gadsby, 1860.

Gaillardot, Note = Charles Gaillardot, 'Note sur la Mer Morte et la Valée du Jourdain', *Annales de la Societé d'émulation des Vosges*, V, 3é c. (1848), pp. 859–77.

Gaillardot, Relation = Charles Gaillardot, 'Relation de la campagnes des égyptiens dans le Hauran, Syrie Orientale 1838. Extrait du journal d'expédition', *NAVSG*, 6 Sér., 10 (1864, II), pp. 309–64.

Gal and Markel, Levels = Yitzhaki Gal and Doron Markel, 'Were the historical minimum levels of the Sea of Galilee in the historical past lower than the "red line"?', *Water, Fluids and Irrigation Engineering*, 1 (1999), pp. 23–8 [Heb.].

Gay-Lussac, Analyse = Joseph Louis Gay-Lussac, 'Analyse de l'eau de la Mer Morte', *ACP*, 11 (1819), pp. 195–7.

Gelber, Question = Nathan Michael Gelber, 'The question of Eretz-Israel in the years 1840 and 1842', *Zion (Literary Organ)*, 4 (1930), pp. 44–64.

Gelber, Pre-Zionist = Nathan Michael Gelber, 'A pre-Zionist plan for colonizing Palestine: The proposal of a non-Jewish German-American in 1853', trsl. Guido Kisch, *Historia Judaica*, 1/2 (1939), pp. 81–90.

Geographical Discovery = 'Geographical discovery in the East, Euphrates & Persia', *TBGS*, 6 (1844), pp. xvii-xviii.

Gichon, Napoleon = Mordechai Gichon, *Napoleon in the Holy Land*, ed. Effi Melzer, Reut: Effi Melzer, 2003 [Heb.].

Gidney, History = William Thomas Gidney, *The History of the London Society for Promoting Christianity Amongst the Jews, from 1809 to 1908*, London: London Society for Promoting Christianity Amongst the Jews, 1908.

Gmelin, Resultate = Christian Gottlob Gmelin, 'Resultate der Analyse des Wassers vom todten Meere', *AP*, 85/1 (1827), pp. 177–8.

Godlewska, Egypt = Anne Godlewska, 'Map, text and image: The mentality of enlightened conquerors: a new look at the *Description de l'Egypt*', *TIBG*, NS 20 (1995), pp. 5–28.

Godlewska, Geographers = Anne Godlewska, 'Napoleon's geographers (1797–1815): imperialists and soldiers of modernity', Anne Godlewska and Neil Smith (eds.), *Geography and Empire*, Oxford: Blackwell, 1994, pp. 34–53.

Godlewska, Geography = Anne Marie Claire Godlewska, *Geography Unbound: French Geographical Science from Cassini to Humboldt*, Chicago: University of Chicago Press, 1999.

Godlewska, Survey = Anne Godlewska, *The Napoleonic Survey of Egypt: A Masterpiece of Cartographic Compilation and Early Nineteenth-Century Fieldwork* (ed. Edward H. Dahl, *Cartographica* 25/1&2 [1988], Monograph 38–39), Toronto: University of Toronto Press, 1988.

Gollwitzer, Palästinafahrten = Heinz Gollwitzer, 'Deutsche Palästinafahrten des 19. Jahrhunderts als Glaubens- und Bildungserlebnis', Bernhard Bischoff and Wolfgang Stammler (eds.), *Lebenskräfte in der Abendländischen Geistesgeschichte: Festschrift für Walter Goetz zum 80. Geburtstag*, Marburg: Simons, 1948, pp. 286–324.

Goren, Chase = Haim Goren, 'The chase after the Bible: individuals and institutions – and the study of the Holy Land', Ute Wardenga and Witold J. Wilczyński (eds.), *Religion, Ideology and Geographical Thought* (WSP Kielce Studies in Geography, 3), Kielce: Wydawnictwo JENOŚĆ, 1998, pp. 103–15.

Goren, Crusade = Haim Goren, '"The Peaceful Crusade": The Crusades and Eretz-Israel in the Nineteenth Century', *Cathedra*, 135 (2010), pp. 63-88 [Heb.].

Goren, Gaillardot = Haim Goren, 'Charles Gaillardot, Renan's man-in-the-field: physician and scholar', Michel Abitbol (ed.), *France and the Middle East: Past, Present and Future* (World Powers and the Middle East, The Harry S. Truman Institute), Jerusalem: The Hebrew University Magnes Press, 2004, pp. 99–124.

Goren, Kiepert = Haim Goren, 'Heinrich Kiepert in the Holy Land, spring 1870 – sketches from an exploration-tour of an historical cartographer', Lothar Zögner (ed.), *Antike Welten Neue Regionen: Heinrich Kiepert 1818–1899*, Berlin: Kiepert KG, 1999, pp. 45–62.

Goren, Level = Haim Goren, 'How low is the lower point on earth? The story of determining the level of the Dead Sea', Jacob D. Maos, Moshe Inbar and Deborah F. Shmueli (eds.), *Contemporary Israeli Geography* (Horizons in Geography, 60–1), Haifa: Department of Geography and Environmental Studies, University of Haifa, 2004, pp. 147–62.

Goren, Nicolayson = Haim Goren, 'Nicolayson and Finn describe the expeditions and deaths of Costigan and Molyneux', *Cathedra*, 85 (October 1997), pp. 65–94 [Heb. and Eng.].

Goren, Petermann = Haim Goren, 'August Petermann and Palestine cartography', Sebastian Lenz and Ferjan Ormeling (eds.), *Die Verräumlichung des Welt-Bildes: Petermanns Geographische Mitteilungen zwischen "explorativer Geographie" und der "Vermessenheit" europäischer Raumphantasien* (Beiträge der Internationalen Konferenz auf Schloss Friedenstein Gotha, 9.–11. Oktober 2005, Friedenstein Forschungen, 2), Stuttgart: Steiner, 2008, pp. 75–87.

Goren, Pioneer = Haim Goren, 'Pioneer surveying and mapping of the Galilee and the Hauran: The map of the sources of the Jordan River (1841) and the map of the *Ledja* (1838)', *Cathedra*, 96 (July 2000), pp. 111–30 [Heb.].

Goren, Ritter = Haim Goren, 'Carl Ritter's contribution to Holy Land research', Anne Buttimer, Stanley D. Brunn and Ute Wardenga (eds.), *Text and Image: Social Construction of Regional Knowledge*, Leipzig: Institut für Länderkunde, 1999, pp. 28–37.

Goren, Roth = Haim Goren, 'Johannes Rudolph Roth: Ein Leben für die Palästinaforschung', *JDEIA*, 5 (1997), pp. 22–44.

Goren, Sacred = Haim Goren, 'Sacred, but not surveyed: Nineteenth-century surveys of Palestine', *IM*, 54 (2002), pp. 87–110.

Goren, Zieht hin = Haim Goren, *"Zieht hin und erforscht das Land": Die deutsche Palästinaforschung im 19. Jahrhundert*, trsl. Antje Clara Naujoks (Schriftenreihe des Instituts für deutsche Geschichte der Univesität Tel Aviv, 23), Göttingen: Wallstein, 2003.

Goren – Morag, Mapping = Haim Goren and Orli Morag, 'To the story of the mapping of the Galilee: Zimmermann's map after Schultz's routes', Yoram Bar-Gal, Nurit Kliot and Ammatzia Peled (eds.), *Eretz Israel Studies – Aviel Ron Book*, Haifa: Department of Geography and Environmental Studies, Haifa University, 2004, pp. 307–23 [Heb.].

Goudie, Jackson = Andrew S. Goudie, 'Colonel Julian Jackson and his contribution to geography', *GJ*, 144/2 (1978), pp. 264–70.

Graham, Britain = Gerald Stanford Graham, *Great Britain in the Indian Ocean: A Study of Maritime Enterprise 1810–1850*, Oxford: Clarendon, 1967.

Graham, Explorations = Cyrill C. Graham, 'Explorations in the desert east of the Hauran and in the ancient land of Bashan', *JRGS*, 28 (1858), pp. 226–63.

Gray Hill, Dead Sea = J. Gray Hill, 'The Dead Sea', *PEFQS*, 32 (1908), pp. 273–82.

Greenberg, Indians = Gershon Greenberg, 'American Indians, ten lost tribes and Christian eschatology', Bryan F. Le Beau and Menachem Mor (eds.), *Religion in the Age of Exploration: The Case of Spain and New Spain*, Omaha, NE: Creighton University Press, 1996, pp. 127–48.

Greenough, Address 1840 = George Bellas Greenough, 'Address at the anniversary meeting, 25th May, 1840', *JRGS*, 10 (1840), pp. xliii-lxxxiii.

Greenough, Address 1841 = George Bellas Greenough, 'Address at the anniversary meeting, May 24, 1841', *JRGS*, 11 (1841), pp. xxxix-lxxvii.

Grindlay, View = Melville Grindlay, *A View of the Present State of the Question as to Steam Communication with India*, London: Smith, Elder and Co., 1837.

Guémard, Gaillardot = Gabriel Guémard, 'Deux grands Lorrains d'Égypte: les Gaillardot', *Mémoires de l'Academie de Stanislas*, 6th series, 25 (1927–8), pp. 59–67.

Guest, Expedition = John S. Guest, *The Euphrates Expedition*, London and New York: Kegan Paul, 1992.

Hagen, Maya = Victor Wolfgang von Hagen, *Maya Explorer: John Lloyd Stephens and the Lost Cities of Central America and Yucatan*, Norman, OK: University of Oklahoma Press, 1948.

Hall, Description = F. Hall, 'Description of minerals from Palestine', *AJSA*, ser. 1, 9 (1825), pp. 337–51.

Hallett, Penetration = Robin Hallett, *The Penetration of Africa: European Enterprise and Exploration Principally in Northern and Western Africa up to 1830*, I: *To 1815*, London: Routledge & Kegan Paul, 1965.

Hamilton, Address 1839 = William Richard Hamilton, 'Anniversary address', *JRGS*, 9 (1839), pp. xlvii-xxii.

Hamilton, Address 1842 = William Richard Hamilton, 'Address to the Royal Geographical Society of London: Delivered at the anniversary meeting of the 23rd May, 1842', *JRGS*, 12 (1842), pp. xxxv-lxxxix.

Hamilton, Address 1843 = William Richard Hamilton, 'Address at the anniversary meeting, May 22, 1843', *JRGS*, 13 (1843), pp. xli-cx.

Hamilton, Address 1848 = William Richard Hamilton, 'Address to the Royal Geographical Society of London: Delivered at the anniversary meeting on the 22nd May, 1848', *JRGS*, 18 (1848), xxxi-lxxii.

Harford, Caravan = Frederic D. Harford, 'Old caravan roads and overland routes in Syria, Arabia, and Mesopotamia', *The Nineteenth Century and After*, 84 (1918), pp. 97–113.

Hargreaves, Reade = John D. Hargreaves, 'Winwood Reade and the discovery of Africa', *African Affairs*, 56 (1957), pp. 306–16.

Harlow and Carter, Imperialism = Barbara Harlow and Mia Carter (eds.), *Imperialism & Orientalism: A Documentary Sourcebook*, Malden, MA and Oxford: Blackwell, 1999.

Harris, Highlands = William Cornwallis Harris, *The Highlands of Ethiopia*, I-III, London: Longman, Brown, Green, and Longmans, 1844.

Hase, Callier = Raoul-Rochette Hase, Antoine-Jean Letronne and Charles-Athanase Walckenaer, 'Voyages de M. Camille Callier en Asie-Mineure, en Syrie, en Palestine et dans l'Arabie Pétrée', *NAVSG*, 65 (1835), pp. 280–6.

Heffernan, Scholarship = Michael J. Heffernan, 'A state scholarship: the political geography of French international science during the nineteenth century', *TIBG*, New Series 9:1 (1994), pp. 21–45.

Heim, Tobler = Heinrich Jakob Heim, *Dr. Titus Tobler der Palästinafahrer: Ein appenzellisches Lebensbild*, Zürich: Friedrich Schultheß and Trogen: J. Schläpfer, 1879.

Herman, Scots = Arthur Herman, *The Scotish Enlightment: The Scots' Invention of the Modern World*, London: Fourth Estate, 2002.

Herschel, Manual = John F.W. Herschel (ed.), *A Manual of Scientific Enquiry, Prepared for the Use of Officers in Her Majesty's Navy, and Travellers in General*, London: J. Murray, 1851.

Hoade, Ireland = Eugene Hoade, 'Ireland and the Holy Land', *The Franciscan College Annual*, 20 (1952), pp. 69–77.

Hofman, Administration = Yitzhak Hofman, 'The administration of Syria and Palestine under Egyptian rule', Moshe Ma'oz (ed.), *Studies on Palestine during the Ottoman Period*, Jerusalem: Magnes, The Hebrew University Institute of Asian and African Studies, and Yad Izhak Ben-Zvi, 1975, pp. 311–33.

Hogg, Porter = John Hogg (ed.), 'Greek inscriptions from Syria and the Hauran, discovered by the Rev. J. L. Porter, M.A.', *Transactions of the Royal Society of Literature*, Second Series, 5 (1856), pp. 243–74.

Home, Royal Society = Roderick Wire Home, 'The Royal Society and the Empire: The colonial and commonwealth fellowship, Part 1. 1731–1847', *NRRSL*, 56 (3) (2002), pp. 307–32.

Hone, Moore = Joseph M. Hone, *The Life of George Moore*, London: Gollancz, 1936.

Hone, Moores = Joseph M. Hone, *The Moores of Moore Hall*, London: Cape, 1939.

Hone, Papers = Joseph M. Hone, 'Moore Hall papers', *The Dublin Magazine*, 14/3 (1939), pp. 34–44.

Hopkins, Wolff = Hugh Evan Hopkins, *Sublime Vagabond: The Life of Joseph Wolff – Missionary Extraordinary*, Worthing: Churchman, 1984.

Horowitz, Jordan = Aharon Horowitz (et al.), *The Jordan Rift Valley*, Lisse etc.: A.A. Balkema, 2001.

Hoskins, Routes = Halford Lancaster Hoskins, *British Routes to India*, New York: Frank Cass, 1966.

Hoxie, Livermore = Frederick E. Hoxie, 'Livermore, Harriet', Edward T. James, Janet Wilson James and Paul S. Boyer (eds.), *Notable American Women 1607–1950: A Biographical Dictionary*, Cambridge, MA: Belknap, 1971, pp. 409–10.

Humboldt, Asien = Alexander von Humboldt, *Central Asien: Untersuchungen über die Gebirgsketten und die vergleichende Klimatologie*, trsl. William Mahlmann, I/II, Berlin: Klemann, 1844.

Humboldt, Cosmos = Alexander von Humboldt, *Cosmos: A Sketch of a Physical Description of the Universe*, trsl. E.C. Otté, I, London: Henry G. Bohn, 1849.

Humboldt, Difference = Alexander von Humboldt, 'On the difference of level between the Black Sea and the Caspian', *JRGS*, 8 (1838), pp. 135–6.

Humboldt, Ehrenberg = Alexander von Humboldt, 'Rapport sur le voyage fait par MM. Ehrenberg et Hemprich en Égypte, Dongola, Syrie, Arabie, et à la pente orientale du plateau de l'Abyssinie, de 1820 à 1824', *NAVSG*, 36 (1827), pp. 369–97.

Hurewitz, Diplomacy = Jacob Coleman Hurewitz, *Diplomacy in the Near and Middle East: A Documentary Record: 1535-1914*, I-II, New York: Octagon, 1972.

Hutchins, Illusion = Francis G. Hutchins, *The Illusion of Permanence: British Imperialism in India*, Princeton: Princeton University Press, 1967.

Hutchinson, Salvation = L. Hutchinson, 'The salvation of Israel: the story of the Jewish mission', Jack Thompson (ed.), *Into All the World: A History of 150 Years of the Overseas Work of the Presbyterian Church of Ireland*, Belfast: Overseas Board, PCI, 1990, pp. 125-43.

Invasions of India = *Invasions of India from Central Asia*, London: Richard Bentley and Son, 1879.

Ish-Shalom, Travels = Michael Ish-Shalom, *Christian Travels in the Holy Land: Descriptions and Sources on the History of the Jews in Palestine*, Tel Aviv: Am Oved and Dvir, 1965 [Heb.].

Irby and Mangles, Travels = Charles Leonard Irby and James Mangles, *Travels in Egypt and Nubia, Syria, and the Holy Land: Including a Journey Round the Dead Sea, and through the Country East of the Jordan*, London: John Murray, 1844.

Jackson, Extrait = 'Extrait d'une letter addressée à M. D'Avezac par M. le colonel Jackson, secrétaire de la Société royale géographique de Londres', *BSG*, 2nd ser., 17 (1842), pp. 139-43.

Jackson, Pomp = William Jackson, *The Pomp of Yesterday: The Defence of India and the Suez Canal 1798-1918*, London and Washington: Brassey's, 1995.

Jacotin, Carte = Pierre Jacotin, 'Carte de l'Égypte', Emde-François Jomard (ed.), *Description de l'Égypte*, Paris: Dépôt general de la guerre, 1818.

Jacotin, Carte topographique = Pierre Jacotin, *Carte topographique de l'Égypte et de plusieurs parties des pays limitrophes levee pendant l'expédition de l'Armée Française*, 47 sheets, Paris 1810.

Jampoler, Lynch = Andrew C.A. Jampoler, *Sailors in the Holy Land: The 1848 American Expedition to the Dead Sea and the Search for Sodom and Gomorrah*, Annapolis, MD: Naval Institute, 2005.

Jenkins, Expeditions = John S. Jenkins, *United States Exploring Expeditions: Voyage of the U. S. Exploring Squadron, Commanded by Captain Charles Wilkes, of the United States Navy, in 1838, 1839, 1840, 1841, and 1842, together with Explorations and Discoveries Made by Admiral d'Urville, Captain Ross, and Other Navigators and Travellers; and an Account of the Expedition to the Dead Sea, under Lieutenant Lynch*, Auburn: James M. Alden, 1850.

Jochmus, Krieg = August von Jochmus, *Der syrische Krieg und der Verfall des Osmanen-Reiches seit 1840. Aktenmässig dargestellt in officiellen, geheimen und vertraulichen Berichten und Urkunden...*, Frankfurt a.M.: Carl Jugel, 1856.

Jochmus, Notes = August Jochmus, 'Notes on a journey into the Balkan, or Mount Hœmus, in 1847', *JRGS*, 24 (1854), pp. 36-85.

Jones, Baghdad = James Felix Jones, *Memoirs of Baghdad, Kurdistan and Turkish Arabia, 1857* (Selections from the Records of the Bombay Government, 43, new ser.), [Slough]: Archive Edition, 1998 (1st. ed. 1857).

Jones, Journal = Felix Jones, 'Journal of a steam-trip to the north of Baghdad...', Jones, Baghdad, pp. 1-32.

Jones, Surveys = Yolande Jones, 'British military surveys of Palestine and Syria 1840-1841', *The Cartographic Journal*, 10/1 (1973), pp. 29-41.

Jones and Grissom, Chesney = Dorsey D. Jones and J.W. Grissom, 'Francis Rawdon Chesney: A reappraisal of his work on the Euphrates route', *The Historian*, 11/2 (2007), pp. 185–203.

Kark, Consuls = Ruth Kark, *American Consuls in the Holy Land 1832–1914*, Jerusalem: Magnes, and Detroit: Wayne State University Press, 1994.

Kark, Jaffa = Ruth Kark, *Jaffa – a City in Evolution, 1799–1917*, Jerusalem: Yad Izhak Ben-Zvi, 1990.

Karmon, Jacotin = Yehuda Karmon, 'An analysis of Jacotin's map of Palestine', *IEJ*, 10/3 (1960), pp. 155–73, 244–53.

Kawerau, Amerika = Peter Kawerau, *Amerika und die orientalischen Kirchen: Ursprung und Anfang der amerikanischen Mission unter den Nationalkirchen Westasiens* (Arbeiten zur Kirchengeschichte, 31), Berlin: Walter de Gruyter, 1958.

Kedem, Eschatoloogy = Menachem Kedem, 'Mid-nineteenth century Anglican eschatology on the redemption of Israel', *Cathedra*, 19 (April 1981), pp. 55–72 [Heb.].

Kelly, Britain = John Barrett Kelly, *Britain and the Persian Gulf 1795–1880*, Oxford: Clarendon Press, 1968.

Kelly, Mehemet 'Ali = John Barrett Kelly, 'Mehemet 'Ali's expedition to the Persian Gulf 1837–1840', *MES*, 2 (July 1965), pp. 350–81, 3 (October 1965), pp. 31–65.

Kelly, Syria = Walter Keating Kelly, *Syria and the Holy Land: Their Scenery and Their People*, I-II, London: Chapman and Hall, 1846.

Kiepert, Map 1842 = Heinrich Kiepert, *Karte von Palästina nach den neuesten Quellen, vorzüglich nach den Robinson'schen Untersuchungen*, ed. Carl Ritter, Berlin: Reimer, 1842.

Kiepert, Note = Heinrich Kiepert, 'Note über die Construction der Karte zu Consul Wetzstein's Reise', *ZAE*, N.F. 7 (1859), pp. 204–8.

Kinnear, Cairo = John Gardiner Kinnear, *Cairo, Petra and Damascus, in 1839: With Remarks on the Government of Mehemet Ali, and on the Present Prospects of Syria*, London: John Murray, 1841.

Kirwan, Notes = Charles J. Kirwan, *Notes on the Dispatch of Troops by Sea*, Calcutta: Thacker, Spink and Co., 1859.

Klaproth, Analysis = Martin Heinrich Klaproth, 'Chemical analysis of the water of the Dead Sea', *Annals of Philosophy*, 7 (1813), pp. 36–9.

Klaproth, Untersuchungen = Martin Heinrich Klaproth, 'Chemische Untersuchungen des Wassers vom todten Meere', *Der Gesellschaft Naturforschender Freunde zu Berlin Magazin*, 3 (1809), pp. 139–43.

Klein, Evidence = Cippora Klein, 'Morphological evidence of lake level changes, western shore of the Dead Sea', *Israel Journal of Earth-Sciences*, 31 (1982), pp. 67–94.

Klein, Fluctuations = Cippora Klein, 'Fluctuations of the Level of the Dead Sea and Climatic Fluctuations in Eretz-Israel During Historical Periods', Ph.D. Thesis, The Hebrew University, Jerusalem 1986 [Heb.].

Klein, Fluctuations of the Level = Cippora Klein, *On the Fluctuations of the Level of the Dead Sea since the Beginning of the 19th Century* (Hydrological Paper, 7), Jerusalem 1965[2].

Klein-Franke, Jemen = Aviva Klein-Franke, 'J. Wolff and H. Stern: Missionaries in Jemen', Starkey, Interpreting, pp. 81–95.

Kochav, Movement = Sara Kochav, 'The Evangelical movement in England and the restoration of the Jews to Eretz Israel', *Cathedra*, 62 (December 1991), pp. 18–36 [Heb.].

Koerner, Purposes = Lisbet Koerner, 'Purposes of Linnaean travel: a preliminary research report', Miller and Reill, Visions, pp. 117–52.

Koner, Antheil = Wilhelm Koner, 'Der Antheil der Deutschen an der Entdeckung und Erforschung Afrika's', *ZGEB*, 8 (1873), pp. 386–432.

Kreiger, Waters = Barbara Kreiger, *Living Waters: Myth, History and Politics of the Dead Sea*, New York: Continuum, 1988.

Kruse, Seetzen = Friedrich Kruse et al. (eds.), *Ulrich Jasper Seetzen's Reisen durch Syrien, Palästina, Phönicien, die Transjordan-Länder, Arabia Petraea und Unter-Aegypten*, I–III, Berlin: G. Reimer, 1854.

Kurz and Linant de Bellefonds = Marcel Kurz and Pascale Linant de Bellefonds, 'Linant de Bellefonds: Travels in Egypt, Sudan and Arabia Petraea', Starkey, Travellers, pp. 61–9.

Kutluoğlu, Question = Muhammed H. Kutluoğlu, *The Egyptian Question (1831–1841): The Expansionist Policy of Mehmed Ali Paşa in Syria and Asia Minor and the Reaction of the Sublime Porte* (Middle Eastern and Balkan Studies Series, 2), Istanbul: Eren, 1998.

Laborde, Journey = Leon de Laborde, *Journey through Arabia Petraea, to Mount Sinai and the Excavated City of Petra, the Edom of the Prophecies*, London: J. Murray, 1836.

Lamartine, Pilgrimage = Alphonse de Lamartine, *A Pilgrimage to the Holy Land*, Delmar NY: Scholars' Facsimiles & Reprints, 1978 (repr. of Philadelphia, 1838).

Lambert, Battlefleet = Andrew Lambert, *The Last Sailing Battlefleet: Maintaining Naval Mastery 1815–1850*, London: Conway, 1991.

Lambert, Battleships = Andrew Lambert, *Battleships in Transition: The Creation of the Steam Battlefleet 1815–1860*, London: Conway Maritime Press, 1984.

Lambert, Canon = Andrew Lambert, '"Within cannon shot of deep water": The Syrian campaign of 1840', Peter Hore (ed.), *Seapower Ashore: 200 Years of Royal Navy Operations on Land*, London: Chatham, 2000, pp. 79–95.

Lambert, Crimean = Andrew D. Lambert, *The Crimean War: British Grand Strategy, 1853–56* (War, armed forces, and society), Manchester and New York: Manchester University Press, 1990.

Lambert, Franklin = Andrew Lambert, *Franklin: Tragic Hero of Polar Navigation*, London: Faber and Faber, 2009.

Lambert, Last Sailing = Andrew Lambert, *The Last Sailing Battlefleet: Maintaining Naval Mastery 1815–1850*, London: Conway, 1991.

Landy, Beaufort = Sheila Landy, 'Sir Francis Beaufort, 1774–1857', John Wilson Foster and Helena C.G. Chesney (eds.), *Nature in Ireland: A Scientific and Cultural History*, Dublin: Lilliput, 1997, pp. 327–31.

Lardner, Steam = Dionysius Lardner, *Steam Communication with India by the Red Sea: Advocated in a Letter to the Right Honourable Lord Viscount Melbourne, Illustrated by Plans of the Route, and Charts of the Principle Stations*, London: Allen & Hatchard and Son, 1837.

Laurens, Expedition = Henry Laurens, *L'Expédition d'Égypte 1798–1801* (Bonaparte et l'Islam, le choc de cultures), Paris: Colin, 1989.

Lennon, Orientalism = Joseph Lennon, *Irish Orientalism: A Literary and Intellectual History*, Syracuse, NY: Syracuse University Press, 2004.

Lester, Geographies = Alan Lester, 'Historical geographies of imperialism', Brian Graham and Catherine Nash (eds.), *Modern Historical Geographies*, Harlow, Essex: Longman, 2000, pp. 100–20.

Letronne, Communication = Antoine-Jean Letronne, 'Sur la prétendu communication de la Mer Morte et de la Mer Rouge', *JS*, 3. sér. 3 (1838), pp. 495–500.

Letronne, Différence = Antoine-Jean Letronne, 'Sur la différence du niveau entre la Mer Morte et de la Mer Rouge', *JS*, 2. sér. 2 (1817), pp. 244–50.

Letronne, Séparation = Antoine-Jean Letronne, 'Sur la séparation primitive des bassins de la Mer Morte et de la Mer Rouge', idem, *Mélanges d'Erudition et de Critique Historique*, Paris: E. Ducrocq, 1860, pp. 54–155.

Letronne, Séparation 1 = Antoine-Jean Letronne, 'Sur la séparation primitive des bassins de la Mer Morte et de la Mer Rouge', *NAVSG*, 13 (1839), pp. 257–309 (Appendix: Sur la différence du niveau entre la Mer Rouge et la Méditerranée, pp. 309–17).

Letronne, Suez = Antoine-Jean Letronne, 'L'Isthme de Suez: le canal de junction des deux mers', *RDM*, 27 (1841), pp. 215–35.

Lettrone, Trennung = Antoine-Jean Letronne, 'Ueber die ursprüngliche Trennung der Becken des Todten und des Rothen Meeres', *AEVS*, 1 (1842), pp. 201–49, pl. II.

Lieber, Purchase = Sherman Lieber, 'The purchase of the land for "Christ Church" by John Nicolayson', *Cathedra*, 38 (1985), pp. 201–3 [Heb.].

Life of Chesney = [Jane O'Donnell and Louisa Chesney], *The Life of the Late General F. R. Chesney, Colonel Commandant Royal Artillery...*, ed. Stanley Lane-Poole, London and Sydney: Eden, Remington & Co., 1893².

Linant de Bellefonds, Cairo = Pascale Linant de Bellefonds, 'From Cairo to Petra: Léon de Laborde and L.M.A. Linant de Bellefonds, 1828', Starkey, Unfolding, pp. 193–208.

Lindenau, Seetzen = Bernhard von Lindenau, 'Über bey diesem Heft befindliche Karte von Palästina', *MCEHK*, 22 (1810), pp. 542–51.

Lindsay, East = 'Lord Lindsay's letters from the East', *DUM*, 12 (1838), pp. 568–92.

Lindsay, Letters = Alexander William Crawford, Lord Lindsay, *Letters on Egypt, Edom, and the Holy Land*, I-II, London: Colburn, 1858.

Livingstone, Science = David N. Livingstone, 'Science and religion: foreword to the historical geography of an encounter', *JRGS*, 20/4 (1994), pp. 367–83.

Livingstone, Tradition = David N. Livingstone, *The Geographical Tradition: Episodes in the History of a Contested Enterprise*, Oxford UK and Cambridge USA: Blackwell, 1993.

Longrigg, Iraq = Stephen Hemsley Longrigg, *Four Centuries of Modern Iraq*, Oxford: Clarendon Press, 1925.

Lord, England = Walter Frewen Lord, *England and France in the Mediterranean 1660–1830*, London: Sampson Low, Marston and Co., 1901 [new ed.: Port Washington, NY: Kennikat, 1970].

Lorimer, Gazeteer = James Gordon Lorimer, *Gazeteer of the Persian Gulf, 'Oman, and Central Arabia*, I: *Historical*, Part I, Calcutta: Superintendent Government Printing, 1915.

Low, Afghan War = Charles Rathbone Low, *The Afghan War, 1838–1842: From the Journal and Correspondence of the Late Major-General Augustus Abbott*, London: Richard Bentley and Son, 1879.

Lvov, Syria = Petr Lvov, 'Сирия, Ливан и Палестина в описаниях российских путешественников, консульских и военных обзорах первой половины

XIX века', М., 1991 ['Syria, Lebanon & Palestine in Russian travel, consular and military descriptions of the first half of XIX c.', ed. I.M. Smilanskaya, Moscow 1991].

Lynch, Journal = 'Major Lynch's journal of a residence among the Ghilzies 1839–40', *DUM*, 24 (1844), pp. 326–52, 479–504, 576–94.

Lynch, Memoir = Henry Blosse Lynch, 'Memoir, in three parts, of the River Euphrates', *TBGS*, 6 (1841–44), pp. 169–86.

Lynch, Mesopotamia = Thomas Kerr Lynch, *Across Mesopotamia to India, by the Euphrates Valley*, London: Waterlow & Sons, 1879.

Lynch, Narrative = William Francis Lynch, *Narrative of the United States' Expedition to the River Jordan and the Dead Sea*, Philadelphia: Lee and Blanchard, 1849.

Lynch, Navigation = Thomas Kerr Lynch, *The Navigation of the Euphrates and Tigris and the Political Rights of England Thereon, with an Account of Personal Travels, and Oriental Notices from Arab Authors*, London: Strangeways and Sons, 1884.

Lynch, Note = Henry Blosse Lynch, 'Note accompanying a survey of the Tigris between Ctesiphon and Mósul', *JRGS*, 9 (1839), pp. 441–2.

Lynch, Record = Elizabeth C. Lynch, *Lynch Record, Containing Biographical Sketches of Men of the Name Lynce, 16th to 20th Century, together with Information Regarding the Origin of the Name and Topographical Poems Showing the Territories Possessed by Some Branches of the Lynch Family*, New York: William J. Hirten, 1925.

Lynch, Report = William Francis Lynch, *Official Report of the United States' Expedition to Explore the Dead Sea and the River Jordan*, Baltimore: John Murphy, 1852.

Lynch, Visit = Thomas Kerr Lynch, *A Visit to the Suez Canal*, London: Day and Son, 1866.

Macalister, Excavation = Robert A.S. Macalister, *A Century of Excavation in Palestine*, London: Religious Tract Society, 1925.

Macalister, Gleanings = Robert A.S. Macalister, 'Gleanings from the minute-books of the Jerusalem Literary Society', *PEFQS*, 40 (1908), pp. 52–60, 116–25; 41 (1909), pp. 42–9, 258–65.

Macalister, Masterman = Robert A.S. Macalister, 'E. W. G. Mastermann', *PEQ*, 75 (1943), pp. 70–3.

Macalister, Observations = Robert A.S. Macalister, 'Observations of Dead Sea levels', *PEFQS*, 33 (1901), pp. 4–5.

Mackay, Agents = David Mackay, 'Agents of empire: the Banksian collectors and evaluation of new lands', Miller and Reill, Visions, pp. 38–45.

Madden, Travels = Richard Robert Madden, *Travels in Turkey, Egypt, Nubia and Palestine in the Years 1824–7*, I–II, London: Colburn, 1829.

Mahlmann, Russegger = Wilhelm Mahlmann, 'Dass von dem K. K. Vicedirector der Berg- und Salinen-Direction von Tirol und Vorarlberg Hrn. Russegger Bemerkungen über dessen meteorologische Hauptdurchnitte und die barometrische Höhenbestimmmung des Todten Meeres, datirt Hall in Tirol, am 4. September 1845...', *MVGEB*, N.F. 3 (1846), pp. 163–7.

Makdisi, Artillery = Ussama Makdisi, *Artillery of Heaven: American Missionaries and the Failed Conversion of the Middle East* (The United States in the World), Ithaca and London: Cornell University Press, 2008.

Manley and Rée, Salt = Deborah Manley and Peta Rée, *Henry Salt: Artist, Traveller, Diplomat, Egyptologist*, London: Libri, 2001.

Mansel, Grand Tour = Philip Mansel, 'The grand tour in the Ottoman Empire, 1699–1826', Starkey, Unfolding, pp. 41–64.

Map of Syria = *Map of Syria, Constructed from the Surveys and Sketches of the Officers in that Country in 1840 1841, by Major R. Rochfort Scott, R. Staff-Corps, under Whose General Direction the Work was Undertaken, Major F. H. Robe, 87th Fusileers and R. Wilbraham, 7th Fusileers, and Lieut. J. F. A. Symonds, R. Engineers*, London, 1846.

Markham, Persia = Clements R. Markham, *A General Sketch of the History of Persia*, London: Longmans, Green, and Co., 1874 (rep. Nendeln, Liechtenstein: Kraus, 1977).

Marlowe, Relations = John Marlowe, *Anglo-Egyptian Relations 1800–1956*, London: Frank Cass, 1954.

Marlowe, Suez = John Marlowe, *The Making of the Suez Canal*, London: The Cresset Press, 1964.

Marriott, Question = John Arthur Ransome Marriott, *The Eastern Question: An Historical Study in European Diplomacy*, Oxford: Clarendon, 1969 (1st ed. 1917).

Marriott, Relations = John Arthur Ransome Marriott, *Anglo-Russian Relations 1689–1943*, London: Methuen, 1944[2].

Marshall-Cornwall, Soldiers = James Marshall-Cornwall, 'Three soldier-geographers', *GJ*, 131/3 (Sept. 1965), pp. 357–65.

Masterman, Explorations = Ernest W.G. Masterman, 'Explorations in the Dead Sea Valley', *BW*, New Series, 25 (1905), pp. 407–21.

Masterman, Explorers = Ernest W.G. Masterman, 'Three early explorers in the Dead Sea Valley: Costigan – Molyneux – Lynch', *PEFQS*, 43 (1911), pp. 12–19.

Masterman, History = Ernest W.G. Masterman, 'The physical history of the Dead Sea Valley', *BW*, New Series, 25 (January-June 1905), pp. 249–57.

Masterman, Observations = 'Observations of the Dead Sea levels', 'Dead Sea observations', *PEFQS*, 34 (1902), pp. 155–60, 299, 406–7; 35 (1903), pp. 177–8; 36 (1904), pp. 83–5, 163–7, 280–1; 37 (1905), pp. 158–9; 38 (1906), pp. 69, 232–4; 39 (1907), pp. 302–4; 40 (1908), pp. 160–1; 41 (1909), pp. 68–70; 42 (1910), pp. 290–1; 43 (1911), pp. 59–61, 158–61; 44 (1912), p. 213; 45 (1913), pp. 42–5, 197.

Masterman, Summary = Ernest W.G. Masterman, 'Summary of the observations on the rise and fall of the level of the Dead Sea, 1900–1913', *PEFQS*, 45 (1913), pp. 192–7.

Matuszewicz, Notice = W. Matuszewicz, *Notice et plan sur le siege de Saint-Jean-d'Acre*, Paris: Maulde et Renou, 1840.

Maundrell, Journey = Henry Maundrell, *Journey from Aleppo to Jerusalem at Easter 1697*, Oxford: Printed at the Theater, 1714.

McLaren, India = Martha McLaren, *British India & British Scotland, 1780–1830: Career Building, Empire Building, & a Scottish School of Thought on Indian Governance*, Akron, OH: The University of Akron Press, 2001.

Melvin, Galway = Patrick Melvin, 'The Galway tribes as landowners and gentry', Gerard Moran and Raymond Gillespie (eds.), *Galway History and Society: Interdisciplinary Essays on the History of an Irish County*, Dublin: Geography Publications, 1996, pp. 319–74.

Michaud, Crusades = Joseph Fr. Michaud, *The History of the Crusades*, trsl. W. Robson, I-III, New York: AMS, 1973.

Middleton, Administration = Charles Roland Middleton, *The Administration of British Foreign Policy 1782–1846*, Durham, NC: Duke University Press, 1977.

Mignolo, Renaissance = Walter D. Mignolo, *The Darker Side of the Renaissance: Literacy, Territoriality, and Colonization,* Ann Arbor: The University of Michigan Press, 1995.

Mill, RGS = Hugh Robert Mill, *The Record of the Royal Geographical Society 1830–1930,* London: The Royal Geographical Society, 1930.

Miller, Banks = David Philip Miller, 'Joseph Banks, empire, and center of calculation in late Hanoverian London', Miller and Reill, Visions, pp. 21–37.

Miller and Reill, Visions = David Philip Miller and Peter Hanns Reill (eds.), *Visions of Empire: Voyages, Botany, and Representations of Nature,* Cambridge: Cambridge University Press, 1996.

MKL = Meyers Konversations-Lexikon. *Eine Encylopädie des allgemeinen Wissens,* I-XVII, Leipzig: Verlag des Bibliographisches Instituts, 1889–90.

Molyneaux, Expedition = Thomas Howard Molyneux, 'Expedition to the Jordan and the Dead Sea', *JRGS,* 18 (1848), pp. 104–30.

Montague, Narrative = Edward Montague, *Narrative of the Late Expedition to the Dead Sea, from a Diary by One of the Party,* Philadelphia: Carey and Hart, 1849.

Moore, Confessions = George Moore, *Confessions of a Young Man,* London: Swan Sonnenschein, Lowry & Co., 1888.

Moore, Earthquake = J.H. [George Henry?] Moore, 'On the earthquake in Syria in January 1837', *Proceedings of the Geological Society, London,* 2 (1838), pp. 540–1.

Moore, Gentleman = Maurice G. Moore, *An Irish Gentleman George Henry Moore: His Travel, His Racing, His Politics,* London: T. Werner Laurie, 1913.

Moore, G.H. Moore = Maurice Moore, 'George Henry Moore', *The Irish Monthly,* 45 (1917), pp. 18–32 [also, with minor changes: *The Irish Review,* 4 (1914), pp. 34–5, 93–107].

Moore, Kerith = George Moore, *The Brook Kerith: a Syrian Story,* London: W. Heinemann, 1937.

Morris, Admiralty = Roger Morris, '200 Years of Admiralty charts and surveys', *The Mariner's Mirror,* 82 (1996), pp. 420–35.

Moscrop, Measuring = John James Moscrop, *Measuring Jerusalem: The Palestine Exploration Fund and British Interests in the Holy Land,* London and New York: Leicester University Press, 2000.

Murchinson, Address 1845 = Roderick Ian Murchinson, 'Address to the Royal Geographical Society of London: Delivered at the anniversary meeting on the 26th May, 1845', *JRGS,* 15 (1845), pp. xli-cxi.

Napier, Reminiscences = Edward Delaval Hungerford Elers Napier, *Reminiscences of Syria and the Holy Land,* I-II, London: Parry, Blenkarn and Co., 1847.

Naumann, Queen = Ursula Naumann, *Euphrat Queen: Eine Expedition ins Paradies,* München: Beck, 2006.

Napoleon, Guerre d'Orient = Napoleon, *Guerre d'Orient: Campagnes d'Égypte et de Syrie, 1798–1799: Mémoires pour servir à l'histoire de Napoléon,* ed. Henri-Gratien Bertrand, I-II+Atlas, Paris: Imprimeurs unis, 1847.

NBG = Johann C.F. Hoefer(ed.), *Nouvelle Biographie Génerale depuis les temps les plus reculés,* I-XLVI, Paris: Firmin Didot, 1852–85.

Nir, Beginnings = Yeshayahu Nir, 'The beginnings of photography in the Holy Land', *Cathedra,* 38 (1985), pp. 67–80 [Heb.].

Nissenbaum, Analyses = Arie Nissenbaum, 'Chemical analyses of Dead Sea water in the 18th century', *Journal of Chemical Education,* 63 (1986), pp. 297–9.

Nissenbaum, Chemical = Arie Nissenbaum, 'Chemical analyses of Dead Sea and Jordan River water, 1778–1830', *Israel Journal of Chemistry*, 8 (1970), pp. 281–7.

Nissenbaum, Studies = Arie Nissenbaum, 'Studies in the Geochemistry of the Jordan River – Dead Sea System', Ph.D. thesis, University of California, 1969.

Nostitz, Travels = Pauline Countess Nostitz (Former Madame Helfer), *Travels of Doctor and Madame Helfer in Syria, Mesopotamia, Burmah and Other Lands*, trsl. Mrs. George Sturge, I-II, London: Richard Bentley & Son, 1878.

Notes Mer Morte = 'Notes sur la Mer Morte et sur quelques positions en Syrie', *NAVSG*, 18 (1838), pp. 116–17.

O'Byrne = William Richard O'Byrne, *A Naval Biographical Dictionary: Comprising the Life and Service of Every Living Officer in Her Majesty's Navy,...*, I-II, Polstead: J. B. Hayward, 1990 (1st ed. London: J. Murray, 1849).

Olberg, Geschichte = Ernst von Olberg, *Geschichte des Krieges zwischen Mehemed Ali und der ottomanischen Pforte in Syrien und Klein-Asien in den Jahren 1831 bis 1833*, Berlin: Ferdinand Dümmler, 1837.

ODNB = *Oxford Dictionary of National Biography*, Oxford: Oxford University Press, 2004 [http://www.oxforddnb.com/view/article/.....] = H.C.G. Matthew and Brian Harrison (eds.), *Oxford Dictionary of National Biography*, I-LX, Oxford: OUP, 2004.

On the Dead Sea = 'On the Dead Sea and some positions in Syria', *JRGS*, 7 (1837), p. 456.

Oren, Power = Michael B. Oren, *Power, Faith, and Fantasy: America in the Middle East, 1776 to the Present*, New York and London: W.W. Norton, 2007.

Ormsby, Narrative = Henry Alexander Ormsby, 'Narrative of a journey across the Syrian Desert', *TBGS*, 2 (1838–9), pp. 18–33.

Outram, Politics = Dorinda Outram, 'Politics and vocation: French science, 1793–1830', *The British Journal for the History of Science*, 13 (1980), pp. 27–43.

Paxton, Letters = John D. Paxton, *Letters from Palestine Written during a Residence There in the Years 1836, 7, and 8*, London: Charles Tilt, 1839.

Paxton, Memoir = [John D. Paxton], *A Memoir of J. D. Paxton D.D., Late of Princeton, Indiana*, Philadelphia: J.B. Lippincott, 1870.

Perrier, La Syrie = Ferdinand Perrier, *La Syrie sous le gouvernement de Méhémet-Ali jusqu'en 1840*, Paris: Arthus Bertrand, 1842.

Perry, Experiments = Charles Perry, 'Experiments, by way of analysis, upon the water of the Dead Sea; upon the hot spring near Tiberiades; and upon the Hammam Pharoan water', *Philosophical Transactions of the Royal Society*, 17/III, vol. XIII (1742), pp. 48–51.

Perry and Lev, Medicine = Yaron Perry and Efraim Lev, *Modern Medicine in the Holy Land: Pioneering British Medical Services in Late Ottoman Palestine*, London and New York: IB Tauris Academic Studies, 2007.

Petermann, Aufnahmen = [August Petermann], 'Die neuen Englischen Aufnahmen in Syrien u. Palästine: Aufforderung an die Freunde der Geographie des Heil. Landes', *PM*, 6 (1860), pp. 480–1.

Petermann, Jordan = August Petermann, 'On the fall of the Jordan, and of the principal rivers in the United Kingdom', *JRGS*, 18 (1848), pp. 89–104.

Petermann, Wildenbruch = 'Notes on the physical geography of Palestine, extracted from the letters of Colonel Von Wildenbruch, late Prussian consul-general in Syria, addressed to A. Petermann...', *JRGS*, 20 (1850), pp. 227–35.

Pfullmann, Entdeckerlexikon = Uwe Pfullmann, *Durch Wüste und Steppe: Entdecker-lexikon arabische Halbinsel*, Berlin: Trafo, 2001.

Platt, Cinderella = Desmond Christopher Martin Platt, *The Cinderella Service: British Consuls since 1825*, Hamden, CT: Archon Books, 1971.

Platt, Finance = Desmond Christopher Martin Platt, *Finance, Trade, and Politics in British Foreign Policy 1815–1914*, Oxford: Clarendon, 1968.

Pococke, Beschreibung = Richard Pococke, *Beschreibung des Morgenlandes und einiger andern Länder*, trsl. and ed. Johann Friedrich Breyer, I-II, Erlangen: Walther, 1771.

Porter, Giant Cities = Josias Leslie Porter, *The Giant Cities of Bashan and Syria's Holy Places*, London: T. Nelson and Sons, 1891.

Porter, Handbook = Josias Leslie Porter, *A Handbook for Travellers in Syria and Palestine: Including an Account of the Geography, History, Antiquities, and Inhabitants of these Countries...*, London: John Murray, 1858.

Porter, Map = Josias Leslie Porter, *Map of Damascus, Hauran and the Lebanon Mountains*, London: John Murray, 1855.

Porter, Memoir = Josias Leslie Porter, 'Memoir on the map of Damascus, Hauran, and the Lebanon Mountains', *JRGS*, 26 (1856), pp. 43–55.

Presentation Medals = 'Presentation of the gold medals, awarded respectively to Lieut. J. F. A. Symonds, R. E., and to Mr. Edward John Eyre', *JRGS*, 13 (1843), pp. xi-xiv.

Priesdorff, Führertum = Kurt von Priesdorff (ed.), *Soldatisches Führertum*, I-X, Hamburg: Hanseatische Verlag-Anstalt, 1937–42.

Progress 1836-7 = [John Washington], 'Sketch of the progress of geography during the past year, and of the labours of the Geographical Society 1836–7', *JRGS*, 7 (1837), pp. 172–95.

Prokesch-Osten, Mehmed-Ali = Anton Graf von Prokesch-Osten, *Mehmed-Ali, Vize-König von Aegypten: Aus meinem Tagebuche 1826–1841*, Wien: Wilhelm Braumüller, 1877.

Pyenson, Mission = Lewis Pyenson, *Civilizing Mission: Exact Sciences and French Overseas Expansion*, Baltimore and London: John Hopkins University Press, 1993.

Raguse, State = Auguste Frederic Louis Viesse de Marmont, *The Present State of the Turkish Empire*, trsl. and ed. Frederic Smith, London: John Ollivier, 1839.

Raguse, Voyage = Auguste Frederic Louis Viesse de Marmont, *Voyage du Maréchal Duc de Raguse en Hongrie, en Transylvania, dans la Russie méridionale, en Crimée, et sur les bords de la mer d'Azoff, a Constantinople, dans quelques parties de l'Asie-Mineure, en Syrie, en Palestine et en Égypte. 1834–1835*, I-V, Paris, 1837–8.

Rawlinson, Address 1873 = Henry Cresswell Rawlinson, 'Anniversary address', *JRGS*, 43 (1873), pp. clv-ccxxviii.

Raz, Dead Sea = Amnon Raz, *Sefer Yam Hamelach* [The Book of the Dead Sea], Regional Council Tamar: Nature Reserves Authority, 1993 [Heb.].

Reed, Cabinet = Charles A. Reed (ed.), *The Cabinet of Irish Literature: Selections from the Works of the Chief Poets, Orators and Prose Writers of Ireland*, IV, ed. T.P. O'Connor, London: Blackie, 1880.

Reinach, Inscriptions = Salmon Reinach, 'Inscriptions inédites d'Asie Mineure et de Syrie: Recueillies par M. le capitaine Callier (1830–1834)', *Revue des Études Grecques*, 3 (1890), pp. 48–85.

Relief Map = *Relievo Map of Palestine or the Holy Land, Illustrating the Sacred Scriptures and the Researches of Modern Travellers, Constructed from Recent Authorities & M.S. Documents in the Office of the Board of Ordnance*, London [1845?].

Report, Secretary = 'Report of the Secretary of the Navy with a report made by Lieutenant W. F. Lynch of an examination of the Dead Sea' (Congress Papers, 30th Congress, 2nd Session, Executive, No. 34).

Reports on the Navigation = 'Reports on the navigation of the Euphrates', *JRGS*, 4 (1834), pp. 374-5.

Richardson, Loss = Henry Richardson, *The Loss of the Tigris: A Poem. In Two Cantons. With Notes. Inscribed to the Commander, Officers, and Men of the Euphrates Expedition*, London: J. Hatchard and Son, 1840.

Ridden, Britishness = Jennifer Ridden, 'Britishness as an imperial and diasporic identity: Irish elite perspectives, c.1820-1870s', Peter Gray (ed.), *Victoria's Ireland? Irishness and Britishness, 1837-1901*, Dublin: Four Courts Press, 2004, pp. 88-105.

Ripon, Surveys = Earl de Grey and Ripon, 'Admiralty surveys', *JRGS*, 30 (1860), pp. cxxviii-cxl.

Ritchie, Admiralty = G. Steve Ritchie, *The Admiralty Chart: British Naval Hydrography in the Nineteenth Century*, London, Sydney and Toronto: Hollis & Carter, 1967.

Ritter, Comparative = Carl Ritter, *The Comparative Geography of Palestine and the Sinaitic Peninsula*, trsl. William L. Gage, I-IV, New York: T. & T. Clark, 1866 (repr. by Greenwood, 1968).

Ritter, Entdeckungen = Carl Ritter, 'Neue Entdeckungen über die Jordan-Quelle von Major Robe, und über einzelne Punkte von Palästina durch Wolcott, nach Mittheilungen von Herrn Robinson', *MVGEB*, 5 (1842), pp. 124-7, pl. I.

Ritter, Erdkunde = Carl Ritter, *Die Erdkunde von Asien*, VIII/2: *Die Sinai-Halbinsel, Palästina und Syrien*, II/1: *Palästina und Syrien*, Berlin: G. Reimer, 1850.

Ritter, Gaillardot = Carl Ritter, 'Eine von dem Kön. Preuss. General-Consul Hrn. Major L. von Wildenbruch eingesandte "Carte approximative du Ledja et des contrées environantes, dresée pendant la campagne d'Ibrahim Pacha contre les Druzes par C. Gaillardot. D.M.P. 1838." Handzeichnung. Nebst einem Begleitschreiben, dat Beirut, den 16. August 1845', *MVGEB*, N.F. 3 (1846), pp. 249-52, pl. II.

Ritter, Jordan = Carl Ritter, *Der Jordan und die Beschiffung des Todten Meeres*, Berlin: G. Reimer, 1850.

Ritter, Russegger = Carl Ritter, 'Herrn k.k. Bargrath Russegger eingesandte Hauptdurchnitte seiner in den Jahren 1836, 1837, 1838 und 1839 während seiner Reisen in Syrien, Ägypten, Nubien, Ost-Sudan und dem peträischen Arabien über Luftdruck, Lufttemperatur und Luftfeuchtigkeit an den Orten, wo längere Zeit hindurch beobachtet werden konnte, ausgeführten Beobachtungen', *MVGEB*, N.F. 2 (1845), p. 199, pl. A., B.

Ritter, Wetzstein = Carl Ritter, 'Zwei Entdeckungsreisen in die Ostjordanische Städtewüste durch Konsul Wetzstein und Cyril Graham', *ZAE*, N.F. 5 (1858), pp. 339-49.

Ritter, Wildenbruch = Carl Ritter, 'Des kön. Preuss. General-Consuls und Majors Hrn. L. v. Wildenbruch Profilzeichnungen nach barometrischen Nivellements in Syrien', *MVGEB*, N.F. 3 (1846), pp. 270-2, pl. III.

Roberts, Egypt = David Roberts, *Egypt and Nubia*, I-III, London: Moon, 1846-9.

Robertson, Empire = Edward Stanley Robertson, 'The Empire, and Ireland's place in it', *DUM*, 1 (1878), pp. 461–7.

Robinson, Bemerkungen = Edward Robinson, 'Bemerkungen über Herrn v. Bertou's Bericht von seiner Reise durch Wady el-'Arabah vom todten Meere nach 'Akabah im Jahre 1838', *MVGEB*, 1 (1839), pp. 192–203.

Robinson, Dead Sea = Edward Robinson, 'Depression of the Dead Sea and the Jordan Valley', *BS*, 5 (1848), pp. 397–409, I, Supplement, pp. 128–30.

Robinson, Depression = Edward Robinson, 'Depression of the Dead Sea, etc.', BS, 1 (1843), pp. 15–17.

Robinson, Depression etc. = Edward Robinson, 'Depression of the Dead Sea, etc.', BS, 1 (1843), p. 556.

Robinson, Extracts = Edward Robinson, 'Extracts from a journal of travels in Palestine, &c., in 1838; undertaken for the illustration of Biblical geography, by the Rev. E. Robinson and the Rev. E. Smith', *JRGS*, 9 (1839), pp. 295–308.

Robinson, Journal = Edward Robinson, *Biblical Researches in Palestine and the Adjacent Regions: A Journal of Travels in the Years 1838 & 1852*, ed. William G. Dever, Jerusalem: Universitas Booksellers, 1970 (repr. of Boston, 1856).

Robinson, Nachschrift = Edward Robinson, 'Nachschrift zu den Bemerkungen über Herrn v. Bertou's Bericht von seiner Reise durch Wady el-'Arabah vom todten Meere nach 'Akabah', *MVGEB*, 2 (1840), pp. 20–1.

Robinson, On the Depression = Edward Robinson, 'On the depression of the Dead Sea and the Jordan Valley', *JRGS*, 18 (1848), pp. 104–30.

Robinson, Researches = Edward Robinson and Eli Smith, *Biblical Researches in Palestine, Mount Sinai and Arabia Petræa: A Journal of Travels in the Year 1838*, I–III, London: J. Murray, 1841 [American edition: Edward Robinson and Eli Smith, *Palestine, Mount Sinai and Arabia Petræa: A Journal of Travels in the Year 1838*, I–II, Boston: Crocker & Brewster, 1841].

Robinson, Researches Palestine = Edward Robinson, 'Researches in Palestine', *BS*, 1 (1843), pp. 9–88.

Robinson, Syria = George Robinson, *Three Years in the East: Being the Substance of a Journal Written during a Tour and Residence in Greece, Egypt, Palestine, Syria, and Turkey, in 1829–1830, 1831, and 1832*, London: Henry Colburn, and Paris: A. and G. Galignani, 1837.

Robinson, Travels = George Robinson, *Travels in Palestine and Syria*, I–II, London: Henry Colburn, 1837.

Rochfort Scott, Rambles = Charles Rochfort Scott, *Rambles in Egypt and Candia, with Details of the Military Power and Resources of Those Countries, and Observations on the Government, Policy, and Commercial System of Mohammed Ali*, London: Henry Colburn, 1837.

Röhricht, Bibliotheca = Reinhold Röhricht, *Bibliotheca geographica Palaestinae: Chronologisches Verzeichnis der von 333 bis 1878 verfassten Literatur über das heilige Land*, ed. David H.K. Amiran, Jerusalem: The Universitas Booksellers, 1963 (1st ed. Berlin 1890).

Rook, Lynch = Robert E. Rook, *The 150th Anniversary of the United States' Expedition to Explore the Dead Sea and the River Jordan*, Amman: American Center for Oriental Research, 1998.

Roth, Harris = [Johannes Rudolf Roth], 'Nachricht über eine Reise nach Schoa, auf welcher er als Naturforscher den brittischen Capitäin (jetzt Major) Harris im Jahre 1841 und 1842 begleitet hatte', *GABA*, 18 (1844), pp. 12–15, 17–22, 25–31.

Rüppell, Carte = Edward W.P.S. Rüppell, 'Carte du Golfe d'Akaba dans la Mer Rouge, levee en Juillet 1822, par M. Edouard Rüppell', *MCEHK*, 8/IV (1823), pp. 581–91.

Rüppell, Itinéraire = Franz von Zach, 'Itinéraire de M. Édouard Rüppell...', *MCEHK*, 8/IV (1823), pp. 469–76.

Rüppell, Observations = Franz von Zach, 'Nouvelle edition corrigée de la reduction de toutes les observations faites en 1822 en Egypte par M. Edouard Rüppell', *MCEHK*, 8/IV (1823), pp. 332–5.

Russegger, Brief = Joseph Russegger, '[Briefe]', *NJMGGP*, 1839, pp. 305–9.

Russegger, Depression = Joseph Russegger, 'Ueber die Depression des todten Meers und des ganzen Jordan-Thals, vom See Tiberia bis zum Waddi el Chor', *APC*, 53 (1841), pp. 179–94.

Russegger, Lettres = Joseph Russegger, 'Lettres sur la Judée', *Bulletin de la Société Géologique de France*, 11 (1839–1840), pp. 15–19.

Russegger, Libanon = Joseph Russegger, 'Ueber den Libanon', *NJMGGP*, 1837, pp. 169–70.

Russegger, Reisen = Joseph Russegger, *Reisen in Europa, Asien und Afrika*, I: *Reise in Griechenland, Unteregypten, im nördlichen Syrien und südöstlichen Kleinasien*, II, Stuttgart: E. Schweizerbart, 1843.

Russegger, Reisen 1 = 'J. Russegger', *Ausserordentliche BAZ*, 26.9.1838, pp. 2029–30.

Russegger, Übersicht = Joseph Russegger, 'Chronologische Übersicht meiner Reisen in den Jahren 1835 bis 1840', *MVGEB*, 2/3 (1840), pp. 61–73.

Russegger in Palästina = 'J. Rußegger in Palästina', *BAZ*, 20.2.1839, pp. 381–2; 21.2.1839, pp. 389–90; 22.2.1839, pp. 397–8; 23.2.1839, pp. 406–7.

Rustum, Notes = Asad J. Rustum, *Notes on Akka and Its Defences under Ibrahim Pasha*, [Beirut: The American University, 1926].

Said, Orientalism = Edward W. Said, *Orientalism*, London and Henley: Kegan Paul, 1978.

Saint Marc, Marmont = Pierre Saint Marc, *Le Maréchal Marmont, Duc de Raguse 1774–1852*, Paris: Arthéme Fayard, 1957.

Sainty, Admiralty = John Christopher Sainty (ed.), *Admiralty Officials 1660–1870* (Office-Holders in Modern Britain, IV), London: Altone, 1975.

Saul and Thobie, Militaires = Samir Saul and Jacques Thobie, 'Les militaries français en Égypte des années 1820 aux années 1860', Daniel Panzac and André Raymond (eds.), *La France & l'Égypte à l'époque des vice-rois 1805–1882* (Cahiers des Annales islamologiques, 22), Cairo: Institut français d'archéologie orientale, 2002, pp. 171–224.

Saulcy, Esquisse = Louis Felicien J.C. de Saulcy, *Esquisse du littoral de la Mer Morte et de la Moabitide d'aprés la carte inédite, levée en 1851*, Paris 1852.

Saulcy, Narrative = Louis Felicien J.C. de Saulcy, *Narrative of a Journey Round the Dead Sea and in the Bible Lands in 1850 and 1851: Including an Account of the Discovery of the Sites of Sodom and Gomorrah*, ed. E. de Warren, I-II, London: R. Bentley, 1854.

Schäbler, Seetzen = Birgit Schäbler, 'Ulrich Jasper Seetzen (1767–1811), Jeveraner Patriot, aufgeklärter Kosmopolit und Orientreisender', *Ulrich Jasper Seetzen (1767–1811) Leben und Werk: Die arabischen Länder und die Nahostforschung im napoleonischen Zeitalter* (Vorträge des Kolloquiums vom 23. und 24. September

1994, Veröffentlichungen der Forschungs- und Landesbibliothek Gotha, 33), Gotha: Forschungs- und Landesbibliothek, 1995, pp. 113–34.

Schäfer, Pruner = Anton Schäfer, 'Leben und Wirken des Arztes Franz Pruner-Bey', *Janus*, 35 (1931), pp. 249–77, 297–311, 335–43, 360–75; 36 (1932), pp. 59–70, 114–27.

Schienerl, Seetzen = Jutta Schienerl, *Der Weg in den Orient: Der Forscher Ulrich Jasper Seetzen: Von Jever in den Jemen (1802–1811)*, Oldenburg: Isensee, 2000.

Schubert, Erdl = Gotthilf Heinrich von Schubert, 'Denkrede auf Dr. Michael Pius Erdl, gewesenen ordentlichen Professor for vergleichenden Anatomie und Physiologie, Adjuncten der anatomischen Sammlung des Staates zu München', *GABA*, 27 (1848), pp. 889–900.

Schubert, Fündlinge = Gotthilf Heinrich von Schubert, 'Über die organischen Fündlinge des todten Meeres', *GABA*, 11 (1840), pp. 354–64.

Schubert, Meer = Gotthilf Heinrich von Schubert, 'Das todte Meer', *BAZ*, 25.4.1838, p. 873.

Schubert, Reise = Gotthilf Heinrich von Schubert, *Reise in das Morgenland in den Jahren 1836 und 1837*, I-III, Erlangen: Palm & Enke, 1839.

Schubert, Results = 'Die Wissenschaftliche Resultate aus v. Schuberts Reise', *BAZ*, 24.3.1838, pp. 629–30.

Schur, Acre = Nathan Schur, *A History of Acre*, Tel Aviv: Dvir, 1990 [Heb.].

Schur, Dead Sea = Nathan Schur, 'Dead Sea region study in the nineteenth century', Mordechai Na'or (ed.), *The Dead Sea and the Judean Desert 1900–1967: Sources, Summaries, Stories and Material* (Idan, 14), Jerusalem: Yad Yizhak Ben-Zvi, 1990, pp. 2–15 [Heb.].

Schur, Travellers = Nathan Schur, *The Book of Travellers to the Holy Land: The 19th Century*, Jerusalem: Keter, 1988 [Heb.].

Schwake, Krankenhauswesens = Norbert Schwake, *Die Entwicklung des Kranken-hauswesens der Stadt Jerusalem vom beginn des 19. Jahrhunderts bis zum beginn des 20. Jahrhunderts*, I-II, Herzogenrath: Mulken-Altrogge, 1983.

Searight, British = Sara Searight, *The British in the Middle East*, London and The Hague: East-West Publications, and Cairo: Livres de France, 1979.

Searight, Charting = Sara Searight, 'The charting of the Red Sea', *History Today*, 53/3 (March 2003), pp. 40–7.

Seché, Entstehung = Carl Seché, *Das Tote Meer und die Hypothesen seiner Entstehung*, Düsseldorf: A. Bagel, 1891.

Seetzen, Map = *Charte von Palästina reducirt aus den von dem Herrn D. Seetzen an Ort und Stelle entworfenen Handzeichnungen*, Gotha 1810.

Select Committee = 'Report from the Select Committee of the House of Commons, on steam navigation to India; with the minutes of evidence, appendix, and index, 1834', *ER*, 60 (July 1834–January 1835), pp. 445–82.

Shamir, Egyptian Rule = Shimon Shamir, 'Egyptian Rule (1832–1840) and the beginning of the modern period in the history of Palestine', Amnon Cohen and Gabriel Baer (eds.), *Egypt and Palestine: A Millennium of Association (1868–1948)*, Jerusalem: Ben-Zvi Institute for the Study of Jewish Communities in the East, 1984, pp. 214–31.

Shanks, Anti-Slavery = Caroline L. Shanks, 'The biblical anti-slavery argument of the decade 1830–1840', *The Journal of Negro History*, 16/2 (1931), pp. 132–57.

Sharp, Symonds = James A. Sharp (ed.), *Memoirs of the Life and Services of Rear-Admiral*

Sir William Symonds, Kt, C.B., F.R.S., Surveyor of the Navy from 1832 to 1847, London: Longman, Brown, Green, Longmans, & Roberts, 1858.

Shaw, Travels = Thomas Shaw, *Travels, or Observations Relating to Several Parts of Barbary and the Levant*, London: A. Millar and W. Sandby, 1757.

Shehade, Gaillardo = Nadim Shehade, 'Charles Gaillardot', *Archaeology and History in Lebanon*, 12 (Autumn 2000), pp. 35–41.

Silberman, Digging = Neil Asher Silberman, *Digging for God and Country: Exploration, Archeology, and the Secret Struggle for the Holy Land 1799–1917*, New York: Knopf, 1982.

Simon, Tribes = Barbara Anne Simon, *The Ten Tribes of Israel Historically Identified with the Aborigines of the Western Hemisphere*, London: Thames Ditton, 1836.

Smith and Hitchcock, Robinson = Henry Boynton Smith and Rosewell D. Hitchcock, *The Life, Writings and Character of Edward Robinson*, New York: Arno Press, 1977 (1st ed. New York: Anson D.F. Randolph, 1863).

Solé, L'Égypte = Robert Solé, *L'Égypte Passion Française*, Paris: Éditions du Seuil, 1997.

Sparrow, Secret Service = Elizabeth Sparrow, *Secret Service: British Agents in France 1792–1815*, Woodbridge: The Boydell Press, 2004.

Stafford, Murchinson = Robert A. Stafford, *Scientist of Empire: Sir Roderick Murchinson, Scientific Exploration and Victorian Imperialism*, Cambridge etc.: Cambridge University Press, 1989.

Starkey, Interpreting = Paul and Janet Starkey (eds.), *Interpreting the Orient: Travellers in Egypt and the Near East*, Reading: Ithaca, 2001.

Starkey, Travellers = Janet and Paul Starkey (eds.), *Travellers in Egypt*, London-New York: I.B. Tauris, 1998.

Starkey, Unfolding = Paul and Janet Starkey (eds.), *Unfolding the Orient: Travellers in Egypt and the Near East*, Reading: Ithaca, 2001.

Stebbing, Christians = Henry Stebbing, *The Christians in Palestine, or: Scenes of Sacred History, Historical and Descriptive*, London: G. Virtue, [1847].

Stephens, Incidents = John Lloyd Stephens, *Incidents of a Travel in Egypt, Arabia Petraea and the Holy Land, by an American*, I-II, New York: Derby & Jackson, 1858 (1st ed. Harper & Bros., 1837).

Stoneman, Land = Richard Stoneman, *Land of Lost Gods: The Search for Classical Greece*, Norman: University of Oklahoma Press, 1987

Sutton, Lords = John Sutton, *Lords of the East: The East India Company and Its Ships*, London: Conway Maritime Press, 1981.

Sykes, Thermometers = William Henry Sykes, 'On the use of common thermometers to determine heights', *JRGS*, 8 (1838), pp. 435–42.

Thomas, Treaties = R. Huges Thomas, *Treaties, Agreements, and Engagements, between the Honorable East India Company and the Native Princes, Chiefs, and States, in Western India; the Red Sea; the Persian Gulf; &c. Also between Her Britannic Majesty's Government and Persia, Portugal, and Turkey*, Bombay: Bombay Education Society, 1851.

Thomson, Account = William Thomas Thomson, 'An account of a line of levels, carried across northern Syria, from the Meditterranean Sea to the Euphrates...', *Proceedings of the Royal Society, London* 4 (1838), pp. 57–8.

Tobler, Bibliographia = Titus Tobler, *Bibliographia geographica Palaestinae: Zunächst kritische Uebersicht gedruckter und ungedruckter Beschreibungen der Reisen ins heilige Land*, Leipzig: S. Hirzel, 1867.

Tobler, Planography = Titus Tobler, *Planography of Jerusalem. Memoir to Accompany the New Ground-Plan of the City of Jerusalem and the Environs, Constructed Anew by C. W. M. Van de Velde after the Plans of the Engineers Aldrich and Symonds, and of Dr. Tobler*, Gotha: Justus Perthes, and London: Williams & Norgate, 1858.

Tobler, Topography = Titus Tobler, *Zwei Bücher Topographie von Jerusalem und seinen Umgebungen*, I-II, Berlin: Reimer, 1853–4.

Train for Cairo = 'Nachricht von dem Entwurf einer Eisenbahn von Cairo nach dem rothen Meere, zur Verbindung desselben mit dem Mittelmeere', *Journal für die Baukunst*, 2 (1845), pp. 190–200, pl. VII.

Tresse, Installation = René Tresse, 'L'installation du premier consul d'Angleterre a Damas (1830–1834)', *Revue d'histoire des colonies*, 24 (1936), pp. 359–80.

Tuchman, Bible = Barbara W. Tuchman, *Bible and Sword: How the British Came to Palestine*, London: Macmillan, 1984.

Tuchman, March = Barbara W. Tuchman, *The March of Folly: From Troy to Vietnam*, London: Abascus, 1985.

Underhill, Levels = Harold W. Underhill, 'Dead Sea levels and the P.E.F. mark', *PEQ*, 99 (1967), pp. 46–9.

Urquhart, Lebanon = David Urquhart, *The Lebanon (Mount Souria): A History and a Diary*, I-II, London: Thomas Cautley Newby, 1860.

Urquhart, Russia = David Urquhart, *How Russia Tries to Get into Her Hands the Supply of Corn of the Whole of Europe: The English Turkish Treaty of 1838* (Selections from Progress of Russia, in the West, North, and South), London: Robert Hardwicke, 1859.

Urquhart, Russian Progress = David Urquart, *Progress of Russia in the West, North and South*, London: Trübner, 1853.

Urquhart, Transactions = David Urquhart, *Diplomatic Transactions in Central Asia from 1834 to 1839*, London: Thomas Bretelli, 1841.

Van de Velde, Map = Carel Willem Meredith van de Velde, *Map of the Holy Land 1:315,000*, Gotha: Justus Perthes, 1858.

Van de Velde, Map of Jerusalem = Carel Willem Meredith van de Velde, *Plan de Jérusalem; construit d'après les relevés du Lt. Symonds R.E. anglais en Mars 1841 et du Dr. T. Tobler en 1845 et 1846*, Grave F. Delamare, [Paris]: Lemercier, [1858].

Van de Velde, Memoir = Carel Willem Meredith van de Velde, *Memoir to Accompany the Map of the Holy Land*, Gotha: Justus Perthes, 1858.

Van de Velde, Narrative = Carel Willem Meredith van de Velde, *Narrative of a Journey through Syria and Palestine in 1851 and 1852*, I-II, Edinburgh and London: William Blackwood, 1854.

Vardi, Height = Joseph Vardi, 'How was the height of the lowest place in the world established?', Mordechai Na'or (ed.), *The Dead Sea and the Judean Desert* [Idan, 14], Jerusalem: Yad Yizhak Ben-Zvi, 1990, pp. 23–8 [Heb.].

Vardi, Review = Joseph Vardi, 'Historical review' (trsl. Ithamar Perath), Varda Arad and Michael Beyth, *Mediterranean - Dead Sea Project: Bibliography*, Jerusalem 1990, pp. 33–50.

Vaux, Fouilles = Roland de Vaux, 'Fouilles de Feshkha', *Revue Biblique*, 66 (1959), pp. 225–55.

Vaux, Qumran = Roland de Vaux, 'Qumran, Chirbet - Ein Feshkhah', Ephraim Stern (ed.), *The New Encyclopedia of Archaeological Excavations in the Holy Land*, Jerusalem 1992, pp. 1357–64 [Heb.].

Vereté, Consulate = Meir Vereté, 'Why was a British consulate established in Jerusalem?', *EHR*, 85 (1970), pp. 316–45.

Vereté, Palmerston = Meir Vereté, 'Palmerston and the Levant crisis, 1832', *JMH*, 24 (March – December 1952), pp. 143–51.

Vereté, Restoration = Meir Vereté, 'The restoration of the Jews in English Protestant thought 1790–1840', *MES*, 8/1 (1972), pp. 3–50.

Vilnai, Costigan = Ze'ev Vilnai, 'Costigan and his tombstone', *Teva Va'aretz*, 12/6 (1971), pp. 293–95 [Heb.].

Vilnai, Dead Sea = Ze'ev Vilnai, *The Dead Sea and Its Israeli Shore*, Jerusalem: Regional Council Tamar, 1964 [Heb.].

Vilnai, Fate = Ze'ev Vilnai, 'Fate of an historical boat', *Ha'aretz*, 18.9.1963 [Heb.].

Volney, Voyage = Constantin François Chasseboeuf de Volney, *Voyage en Syrie et en Egypte pendant les années 1783, 1784 et 1785*, I-II, Paris: Dessene et Voland, 1787.

Vries, Kaart = Dirk de Vries, 'De kaart van Palestina door C.W.M. van de Velde (1858): een 'autoriteitsstuk', *"Capita selecta" uit de geschiedenis van de kartografie* (NVK publikatiereeks, 18), [Utrecht] 1996, pp. 15–26.

Wagner, Roth = Andreas Wagner, 'Denkrede auf Johannes Rudolf Roth', *GABA*, 48 (1859), pp. 25–46.

Wagstaff, Leake = Malcolm Wagstaff, 'Colonel Leake: traveler and scholar', Sara Searight and Malcolm Wagstaff (eds.), *Travellers in the Levant*, Durham: ASTENE, 2001, pp. 3–15.

Wagstaff, Pausanias = J. Malcolm Wagstaff, 'Pausanias and the topographers: The case of Colonel Leake', Susan E. Alcock, John F. Cherry and Jaś Elsner (eds.), *Pausanias: Travel and Memory in Roman Greece*, New York: Oxford University Press, 2001, pp. 190–206.

Wahrman, Gray Hill = Jacob Wahrman, 'Caroline Emily Gray Hill: The orientalist painter from Mount Scopus', *Cathedra*, 112 (2004), pp. 91–112 [Heb.].

Walckenaer, Rapport = Charles-Athanase Walckenaer, 'Rapport verbal de M. le Baron W. fait à l'Académie des Inscriptions et Belles-Lettres dans sa séance du 18 avril 1834 sur le voyage dans l'Arabie Petrée par MM. Léon de Laborde et Linant', *NAVSG*, 62 (1834), pp. 167–96.

Walckenaer, Voyages = Charles-Athanase Walckenaer, 'Sur les voyages récens des Français en Asie-Mineure, en Mesopotamie, en Syrie et en Arabie-Petrée', *NAVSG*, 65 (1835), pp. 287–317.

Washington, Sketch = John Washington, 'Sketch of the progress of geography, and of the labours of the Royal Geographical Society in 1837–8', *JRGS*, 8 (1838), pp. 235–66.

Watson, Fifty Years = Charles M. Watson, *Fifty Years Work in the Holy Land: A Record and a Summary 1865–1915*, London: Committee of the Palestine Exploration Fund, 1915.

Webber Smith, Athos = 'On Mount Athos and its monasteries, with notes on the route from Constantinople to Saloniki, in June, 1836', *JRGS*, 7 (1837), pp. 61–73.

Webber Smith, Map = *Map of the Interior of the Hedjaz, from Surveys by the Officers of Mahommed Ali's Troops Communicated by J. Webber Smith, Esqr. 48th Regt., Engraved and Published, by Jas. Wild, Geographer of the King, Charing Cross Est*, London [1850?] [BL, Maps 49270.(1.)].

Webster, Policy = Charles Webster, *The Foreign Policy of Palmerston 1830–1951: Britain, the Liberal Movement and the Eastern Question*, I-II, London: G. Bell, 1969.

Weeks, Face = Emily M. Weeks, 'About-face: Sir David Wilkie's portrait of "Mehemet Ali"', Starkey, Interpreting, pp. 7–21.

Weishaar, Untersuchung = Joseph Friedrich Weishaar, 'Chemische Untersuchung des Wassers von dem Asphalt-See in Palästina', Ph. D. Dissertation, Tübingen, 1827.

Wellsted, Book = 'Travels in Arabia, 1, In the province of 'Omán; 2, The Peninsula of Sinai; 3, Among the shores of the Red Sea. By Lieutenant Wellsted, Indian Navy, F.R.S.. [...] London. 1837. Murray', JRGS, 7 (1837), pp. 400–4.

Wellsted, Memoir = James Raymond Wellsted, 'Memoir on the island of Socotra', JRGS, 5 (1835), pp. 129–229.

Wellsted, Travels = James Raymond Wellsted, Travels to the City of the Caliphs, along the Shores of the Persian Gulf and the Mediterranean: Including a Voyage to the Coast of Arabia, and a Tour of the Island of Socotra, I-II, London: H. Colburn, 1840.

Wessels, Nationalism = J.A. Wessels, 'Irish nationalism and the Anglo-Irish: Historical and literary parallels to Afrikanerdom', Mary Massoud (ed.), Literary Inter-Relations: Ireland, Egypt, and the Far East (Irish Literary Studies, 47), Gerrards Cross: Colin Smythe, 1996, pp. 244–51.

Werblowsky, Meaning = Raphael Jehuda Zwi Werblowsky, The Meaning of Jerusalem to Jews, Christians and Muslims, Jerusalem: Israel Universities Study Group for Middle Eastern Affairs, 1983.

Weryho, Slowacki = Jan W. Weryho, 'Juliusz Slowacki in Egypt', Starkey, Travellers, pp. 215–21.

Wilde, Narrative = William R. Wilde, Narrative of a Voyage to Madeira, Teneriffe, and along the Shores of the Mediterranean, Including a Visit to Algiers, Egypt, Palestine, Tyre, Rhodes, Telmassus, Cyprus, and Greece: With Observations on the Present State and Prospects of Egypt and Palestine, and on the Climate, Natural History, Antiquities, etc. of the Countries Visited, Dublin: William Curry, Jun., 1844².

Wildenbruch, Profilzeichnungen = Louis v. Wildenbruch, 'Profilzeichnungen nach barometrischen Nivellements in Syrien', MVGEB, N.F. 3 (1846), pp. 270–2, pl. III.

Wilkie, Sketches = Sir David Wilkie's Sketches in Turkey, Syria & Egypt, 1840 & 1841, Drawn on Stone by Joseph Nash, London: Graves & Warmsley, 1843.

Williams, City = George Williams, The Holy City: Historical, Topographical, and Antiquarian Notices of Jerusalem, London: J.W. Parker, 1859².

Williams, Policy = Judith Blow Williams, British Commercial Policy and Trade Expansion 1750–1850, Oxford: Clarendon, 1972.

Wilson, Dead Sea = Charles W. Wilson, 'The Dead Sea', PEFQS, 32 (1908), pp. 365–8.

Wilson, Lands = Charles W. Wilson, The Land of Galilee & the North: Including Samaria, Haifa, and the Esdraelon Valley, Jerusalem: Ariel, 1975 (repr. of Picturesque Palestine, Sinai and Egypt, I-IV, New York i881-3).

Wilson, Surveys = Charles W. Wilson, 'Recent surveys in Sinai and Palestine', JRGS, 43 (1873), pp. 206–39.

Wood, History = Alfred C. Wood, A History of the Levant Company, London: Frank Cass, 1964².

Wright, Notes = John Kirkland Wright, 'Notes on early American geopiety', idem, Human Nature in Geography, Cambridge, MA: Harvard University Press, 1966, pp. 250–85.

Xenophon, Anabasis 1867 = Xenophon, The Anabasis, or, Expedition of Cyrus; and, the Memorabilia of Socrates, trsl. John Selby Watson, geographical commentary by William Ainsworth, London: Bell Daldy, 1867.

Xenophon, Anabasis 2001 = Xenophon, *Anabasis*, trsl. Carleton L. Brownson, rev. John Dillery, Cambridge, MA: Harvard University Press, 2001.

Zimmermann, Analyse = Karl Friedrich Zimmermann, *Geographische Analyse zu dem Versuch einer Construction der Karte von Galiläa... vornämlich herausgegeben nach den Forschungen des verstorbenen Dr. Ernst August Schulz, ehemals königl. Preuss. Consul in Jerusalem*, Berlin: Reimer, 1861.

Zimmermann, Schulz = Karl Friedrich Zimmermann, *Versuch einer Construction der Karte von Galiläa. Nach den Forschungen des verstorbenen Dr. Ernst Gustav Schulz. Königlich Preussische Consul in Jerusalem*, Berlin: Reimer, 1861.

Zimpel, Jerusalem = Charles Friedrich Zimpel, *Neue örtliche topographische Beleuchtung der heiligen Weltstadt Jerusalem, mit besonderer Rücksicht auf die Leidenstage unseres Herrn Jesu Christi und die Identität der heiligen Orte daselbst...*, Stuttgart: E. Schweizerbart, 1853.

Zimpel, Plan = Charles Friedrich Zimpel, *Plan von Jerusalem mit Darstellung aller Wege, welcher unser Herr Jesus Christus während Seiner Leidenstage zurückgelegt und Feststellung aller dadurch heilig gewordenen Orte. Basirt auf den Plan von den englischen Marine Lieutenants Aldrich u. Symonds, den Geschichtsschreiber Flav. Josephus u. A. C. Emmerich*, Stuttgart 1853.

Zvieli, Galili and Rosen, Acre = Dov Zvieli, Ehud Galili and Baruch Rosen, 'The port of Acre and its approaches in modern nautical charts', *Horizons in Geography*, 56 (2003), pp. 62–77 [Heb.].

INTERNET

Jane Lyons, 'From Ireland', www.from-ireland.net/history/offauth/mayo1834.html
'Property owners County Mayo', www.cmcrp.net/Mayo/Landowner1.html
Kevin Coyne, 'The Moores of Moorehall', doon.mayo-ireland.ie/moores.html

Names Index

Browne, George, 3rd Marquess of Sligo 164, 171
Browne, Howe Peter, 2nd Marquess of Sligo 164, 165
Browne, John Thomas, 4th Marquess of Sligo 164
Bruce, Thomas, 7th Earl of Elgin and 11th Earl of Kincardine 29, 30, 94
Buckingham, James Silk 182
Burckhardt, Johann Ludwig 41, 79, 120, 132, 135, 136, 143, 178, 182, 210
Burton, Nathanael 70, 146, 152, 193, 194
Büsching, Anton Friedrich 126, 128
Byron, George Gordon 59

Callier, Camille-Antoine 30–3, 35, 36, 38, 79, 211, 212, 226–8, 264, 269
Campbell, C.D. 83
Campbell, Patrick 87, 89, 199
Canning, Stratford, 1st Viscount Stratford de Redcliffe 8, 9, 20, 42, 51, 61
Carne, John 140, 153, 155, 249
Cassini, Brothers xx
Castlereagh, Viscount see Vane-Stewart
Catherine II the Great 12
Catherwood, Frederick 241
Charlewood, Edward Philips 68, 101
Chateaubriand, François René de 125, 126, 129, 131, 155
Chesney, Emerilda 101
Chesney, Francis Rawdon xiv, xix, 4, 10, 16, 21, 22, 33, 34, 37–9, 41–52, 55, 59, 61, 63, 64, 66, 67, 69, 70, 73, 74, 78, 85, 86, 88, 90, 96, 101, 146, 178, 220, 235–7, 241, 245, 269, 270, 272, 274
Chorinsky, Frederick 43, 48
Christie, Agatha 257
Chryzanowski, Adalbert 85, 86
Cleaveland, Richard Francis 66
Codrington, Edward 113
Codrington, Henry John 113
Colby, Thomas Frederick 78
Conder, Claude Reignier 270
Cooke, Henry 181
Cooper, Anthony Ashley, 7th Earl of Shaftesbury 89
Costello, Con xiv, 144, 152, 153, 273, 274
Costigan (Costigin), Christopher 144,

145, 147, 148, 150–7, 159, 161, 176, 182, 195, 214, 237, 256, 261, 273, 274
Costigan (Costigin), John 144

Daher el-'Umar 26
Dale, John B. 154, 260
Dalrymple, Alexander 28
Dalton, George Edward 150, 152
Dalton, Mrs. (widow) 150
Damiani, Joseph 190
Daud Paşa 82
Dawson, Llewellyn Styles 26
Day, Archibald xxii
Djezzar Paşa, Ahmed el-Djezzar 3, 48, 94
Doergens, Richard 175
Driver, Felix 29, 169, 269
Duhamel, Alexander 54
Dunbar, Gary S. xx
Dundas, Henry, 1st Viscount Melville 94, 97

Eden, George, 1st Earl of Auckland 15
Edgeworth, Maria 144, 167
Edney, Matthew H. xx
Egmond van der Nyenburg, Johan Ägidius van 128, 155
Ehrenberg, Christian Gottfried 129, 130
Elath, Eliahu xiv, xv, 34, 39, 51, 64
Elgin, Lord see Bruce, Thomas
Elizabeth I 16
Ellenborough, Lord see Law, Edward
Elliot, William S.A. (Dervish Ali) 82
Emil-Leopold August, Prince of Saxony-Gotha and Altenburg 139
Emlyn, Miss 193
Emmerich, Anna Catharina 112
Enfantin, Barthélemy Prosper 147
Erdl, Michael Pius 207, 211, 224, 265
Eriksen, Erik Olaf xiv, 144, 154, 256
Estcourt, Caroline B. 69
Estcourt, James Bucknall Bucknall- 6, 63, 66, 69–71, 96, 199
Estcourt, William John Bucknall- 69
Everest, George xx

Fakhreddine II, Emir 40
Farah, Caesar E. 95–7
Farren, John William Perry 48, 70, 86–9, 96, 178, 179, 188, 189, 191, 192, 199, 200
Fessani 190

Muhammed Ali Mîrza 14
Murat, Joachim 93
Muravyev, Nikolay Nikolayevich 53, 54
Murphy, Hastings FitzEdward 77, 78

Napier, Charles 96–8, 100, 101, 115
Napier, Edward Delaval Hungerford
  Elers 115, 242
Napoleon I Bonaparte xxii, 3, 10, 12,
  13, 17, 21, 25, 26, 29, 41, 43, 47, 85,
  93–5, 133, 220, 226, 235, 269
Naumann, Ursula 64, 69
Nicolayson, John 89, 145, 148–50, 153,
  154
Nicolayson, John, daughter 145, 149
Nikolai I 53
Nissenbaum, Arie 130, 131

O'Connell, Daniel 275
Oldfield, Thomas 47, 48, 50, 93
Orloff, Alexey Fyodorovich, Count of 166
Ormsby, Henry Alexander 75, 81, 82
Osman-Nureddin-Bey 5
Otto I 91, 217

Palmerston, Henry John Temple, 3rd
  Viscount 5, 7–10, 15, 42, 51, 59, 75,
  83, 85–91, 95–8, 101, 107, 108, 120
Paul 171
Paul I 12, 13
Paxton, John D. 68, 146, 156, 157, 161
Peacock, Thomas Love 38, 39, 44, 63
Pearce, Robert 201, 202
Perry, Charles 130
Perthes, Justus 135
Petermann, August Heinrich 111, 143,
  231, 239, 246, 250, 251, 255, 265,
  266
Phélippeaux, Louis-Edmond Antoine le
  Picard de 94
Pliny the Elder 131
Pococke, Richard 79, 130
Ponsonby, John 62, 96, 97
Porter, Josias Leslie 125, 152, 175, 179,
  182–5, 275
Poujoulat, Jean Joseph François 31
Pruner, Franz Ignaz 218

Radzivil, Leo 43
Radzivil, Ludwig Nikolaus 43
Raglan, FitzRoy James Somerset, 1st
  Baron 69
Ramsay, William Wardlaw 201

Rassam, Christian Anthony 79, 80
Rawlinson, Henry Cresswell 75
Rayer 236
Reade, William Winwood 169
Relandus, Hadrianus 182
Rennell, James xx
Richard I 'the Lionheart' 187
Ridden, Jennifer 273
Ritter, Carl 32, 110, 111, 122, 135, 155,
  159, 172, 173, 179, 181, 182, 213,
  218–20, 223, 229, 247, 261, 263,
  266, 267
Robe, Frederick Holt 102–4, 110, 111,
  235, 236, 246
Roberts, David 87, 193
Roberts, John 162
Robinson, Edward xiii, 32, 110, 111, 120,
  157, 161, 174, 216, 217, 219–22, 234,
  239, 240, 242, 246, 249, 250, 255,
  265, 267
Robinson, George 34, 38, 48, 50, 146, 178
Rochfort Scott, Charles 52, 53, 102–4,
  109, 235, 236
Roth, Johannes Rudolf 80, 173, 207,
  209, 211
Rouvroy, Claude Henri de, comte de
  Saint-Simon 147
Rüppell, Edward Wilhelm Peter Simon
  136, 137, 241
Russegger, Joseph 122, 132, 217–20, 224,
  241, 242, 250, 258, 264, 265
Russell, James Thomas 114
Ryder, Alfred Phillipps 236

Sabine, Edward 67
Sabkah 202
Sacy, Antoine Isaac Sylvestre de 33
Sáhela Selássie 173
Said, Edward 95
Saint-Simon see Rouvroy, Claude Henri
  de
Saladin 187
Salt, Henry 136
Saulcy, Louis Felicien Caignart de 196,
  198
Schubert, Gotthilf Heinrich von 120,
  122, 132, 172, 173, 176, 195, 207–
  11, 213, 218, 219, 224–6, 241, 246,
  258, 264–6
Schultz, Auguste 100
Schultz, Ernst Gustav 111, 257
Schur, Nathan 132
Scott 47

Places Index